Small Mediums at Large

THE
TRUE TALE
OF A
FAMILY
OF PSYCHICS

Terry Iacuzzo

G. P. PUTNAM'S SONS
NEW YORK

‖P

G. P. PUTNAM'S SONS
Publishers Since 1838
a member of
Penguin Group (USA) Inc.
375 Hudson Street
New York, NY 10014

Library of Congress Cataloging-in-Publication Data

Iacuzzo, Terry.
Small mediums at large : the true tale of a family of psychics /
Terry Iacuzzo.
p.   cm.
ISBN 0-399-15235-0
1. Iacuzzo, Terry.   2. Psychics—United States—Biography.   I. Title.
BF1027.I23A3   2004   2004050352
130'.92—dc22
[B]

Printed in the United States of America
1   3   5   7   9   10   8   6   4   2

This book is printed on acid-free paper. ∞

To my family,

Andy, Mary, Frank and Rosemary

and to Jackie

and Deborah

CONTENTS

Part one • Small   1

Part two • Mediums   121

Part three • At Large   305

PART ONE

·

Small

Chapter One ·

"Keep climbing," I holler down.

"Only two more flights to go! You can do it!"

The stairs are a great help. How can anyone be anxious or afraid if they're exhausted from climbing? Six flights are a humbling experience. Eighty-two black marble steps worn down from over a century of climbers.

Forty-six, forty-seven, forty-eight . . . She drags one foot across the landings. I feel my toes inside my shoe tracing the outline of the hall window, two large panes and the middle lock on the sash. *Seventy-two, seventy-three, seventy-four* . . . Chewing on my pinky fingernail, I bite it off before she turns around the last flight and sees me standing there.

"How do you do this every day? I'm exhausted."

"Hello. I'm Terry. Come on in. Are you okay? Let me take your coat. Sit over here. Catch your breath."

"Hi, I'm Kate and I'm so out of shape."

She's head-to-toe *Vogue* magazine—mid-twenties, small black dress, black leather knee-high boots, clunky silver jewelry—a scent of fresh perfume and a quick smoke from the subway to my building. I look away, preferring to feel her presence rather than let those details influence me.

"Let me get you a glass of water." At the sink, with my back to her, I feel myself separate. It happens so fast, without trying. A part of me steps to the left, a duplicate me that moves as I do. One me converses normally, while the other me takes in the young woman. I start to be her. She has no idea.

"Body builders and dancers come to see me and even they have trouble with the stairs. It's not an easy climb, especially at ten o'clock in the morning. I only recently got a doorbell. For years the clients had to call from the pay phone on the corner, then I'd run down and open the door. Some days I'd climb over sixty flights. That's four thousand nine hundred twenty stairs almost every day. I'm sure I hold the world's record for stair climbing outside a gym."

I've had this conversation thousands of times. I hear myself talking in the room while my interior voice begins sorting out what I'm going to say next. I hand her the glass of water and motion to her to take a seat at the table. She looks the room over. The stove, the refrigerator and the bathtub are just a few steps from the reading table. In a glance I see how pretty she is, raven haired with perfect, clear skin.

"I'm so nervous," she says. "I've been waiting months to see you. All my friends have been here. Everyone's talking about you."

I start seeing flashes of her in the future. She's smiling and walking with a man. They're in Central Park. He kisses her on the cheek . . . I pull back and look away. It's too soon. I don't want to know this yet.

Her big silver bracelet hits the table and she gives a quick apology.

"You're really famous, aren't you," she says, adjusting herself to the chair. "How long have you lived here?"

"Twenty-five years."

"How could that be? How old are you? You look so young and different from what I expected. I thought you'd be an older woman with lots of jewelry and . . ."

"A crystal ball and a black cat? I'll be fifty-five this year, I didn't feel like wearing the gypsy thing today, and my turban's at the dry cleaners."

"You're not fifty-five! That's amazing! You look so young and so . . . normal."

"You mean, paranormal?"

"You're so funny. I feel comfortable with you. I love your apartment, you have such great sunlight. High tin ceilings are so wonderful. Are those oak cabinets original? I love this neighborhood. I come down here a lot. Do you know that psychic who lives near you, Frank Andrews?"

"Yes. I know him."

"I didn't like him. I went to him for a reading last year. He threw me out of his house! He yelled at me, told me I wasn't listening to him, that I was obsessed with my boyfriend and that my boyfriend was just using me. He called me stupid! And said if I didn't change I was going to get cancer! I left there sobbing. I was upset for weeks after that. He's so mean."

"He's a good psychic, pretty direct, he doesn't have much patience."

I didn't tell her that Frank is my brother. I need her to be open and unafraid so I could read her. I handed her my deck of cards. "Now, let's get started. Shuffle. Don't think about anything in particular, just put yourself into the cards by letting your energy flow through your body and into the deck. Let your mind go. Relax. You can't make a mistake. The cards will fall where they're supposed to."

"How do Tarot cards work?"

"Each card is an archetypal picture representing the changes we go through in our lives. The cards tell stories, something like Greek mythology. I've developed my own understanding of what they're saying from years of working with them. I'll try to explain as I go along. When you feel you've shuffled enough then cut the deck into three piles."

I watch her hands shuffling—a flash of a silver ring through a blur of fingers. For a few moments I have a rare feeling, stillness. Then the bones in my face start hurting. Slowly, a sensation of fluids seeps into the sides of my arms and legs, through my skin. My feet are freezing. My neck and head are gripped by pressure. We were just talking and laughing, now suddenly I'm sad. Why?

I look at this woman at my table and I can hardly remember who she is. She's smiling, watching me, eager to hear what I have to say. What's happening here? I recognize the feeling. Abandonment. Someone just walked out of my life without any explanation.

I look around the room trying to reconnect with myself. In the corner, my old stove from the '40s, its clock always says five after four. On the wall, the green shelf where I keep my tea pots. The refrigerator, the bathtub. Something forcefully shoves me up against the tub. I'm startled. An ornate mahogany bed came flying into the room out of nowhere. Kate is standing next to me. I remember her now, she's the client sitting at the table. This must be her bedroom, her bed—perfectly made. I shift into her being so that I can feel her, so I can know why we're here by the bed. What happened to her? I'm her, right now, I'm Kate, but I can also talk to myself. I'm looking down at the bed. I see a magnificent wedding gown and veil carefully laid out in the center of the bed. They're sleeping, preserved in a dream.

I snap back to the table, hearing myself talking. I have to remember the vision and understand what I'm feeling before it leaves me.

"Your heart was shattered. You had a wedding planned for this past summer. He left you, didn't he? And you have no idea why, do you? Is that what happened?" I close my eyes, "Nathan. His name is Nathan."

"Oh my God, how do you know? You can see that? And you got his name!"

Tears run down her cheeks. "I'm sorry. I'm sorry I'm crying."

"Please, that's why you're here. Don't stop. Don't hold back. You're stuck in a painful memory that you keep reliving. You have to let him go. You want to know why and what happened. And you can't move forward. You're still waiting for him to come back. You're still hoping."

I take the cards and lay them out in a horseshoe pattern. "Let me see what's going on here."

Certain cards catch my eye. The King of Swords—a man wearing a red robe over a suit of armor. He holds a long sword up in the air and looks straight at me. He's a man who's strong, determined, sometimes abusive. The Lightning Struck Tower—brick by brick a tower falls to pieces as two people tumble to the ground. Shock of the unexpected. The Death card—the Grim Reaper, a skeleton clutches a sickle, clearing away an already barren landscape. The Hanged Man—a man hanging upside down from a tree. Where do we go from here?

Kate's crying. I get up to get a box of tissues. By the time I return to the table I know the whole story. I just know it, as though I've known her all my life and have been with her every day. I sit back down and see her looking over the cards.

"It looks pretty bad, doesn't it?"

"Now, let me do the reading. I'm the psychic here." I try to make her laugh and feel comfortable with me so she won't bury the feelings. When I'm inside, it's the feelings that will tell me what I need to know. "Your boyfriend was a romantic, telling you all the things you wanted to hear. He went with you all the way through the wedding plans and then he called it off.

"I've got to tell you, he's done this before. Twice! Did you know this? He told you he broke off with his first girlfriend because she was too young and his parents wanted him to marry her. Then he told you the last girlfriend left him just before they were supposed to get married, but that's not the truth. He left her. This man has tremendous problems. If you ask me you're lucky you didn't marry him.

"Now, we can spend the entire day trying to figure out why he did this, but I suggest you move on and don't look back. If you do, you'll become obsessed with him. You'll stay tied to him for years. Five . . . five years to be exact. Do you want that? You have a choice about how to live the next part of your life and I can help you with that. It's up to you. If you want me to look at him more thoroughly I will, but I'm begging you to move on and see what else is out there for you. When you first came in I saw you happy and in love."

"I am. I'm in love with Nathan."

"No, not with him. I saw you with someone else, another man."

"What do you mean you saw me? Where did you see me?"

"I saw you in the future. I say it in the past tense because I already saw it. It's too hard to change the words, it feels unnatural. I can travel very quickly into the future and come back and tell what I saw. I saw you. You were happy. And you have two children. Two girls. One of them is a born comedian. She has a career making people laugh."

Kate jumps up from her seat and stands facing the big mirror over the tub. Looking at herself she says, "Wait a minute! Stop right there! What? You saw my unborn children!"

"Isn't this why you came here? I saw you. You were a mother. You were happy and laughing with your girls. They're really smart and that one little girl has a sarcastic sense of humor."

Kate started laughing. "Everyone in my family has that biting humor."

"Sit down. Let's look at more things. Shuffle again."

"I'm so depressed. I want to marry Nathan. I thought we were soul mates. Don't you see us getting back together? I want him back. Why doesn't he want to be with me? Did he love me? What can I do to get him back? What's going to happen to him?"

"Slow down! Listen, you're lucky he called off the wedding. You would've been miserable with him. I can see his whole life. There never was going to be a marriage between the two of you. He was planning to run away one month after he met you. I could look into the reasons why he behaves this way, but that won't change anything for you. You were just a character in his confusion. His father left the family before he was three. Is that right? His mother was never home. Raised by nannies."

"Yes."

"He's not going to be in your life. I'm sorry, but that's what I see. Let's leave it at that. Nathan will get married, but not until he's in his late fifties, early sixties and not to you. That's a long time from now. You won't know him. He won't be in your life except in a vague memory that you will rewrite to suit whatever suffering you'll need at the time. You can prevent that bit of neurosis right now.

"Wait a minute. I see a boat, a big sail boat. Was that his? You're having a good time, but you're feeling something is wrong. You're not sure you believe him. He's telling you about his previous relationships and how he wasn't really in love before he met you. He's taken so many women on that boat. He told you then he didn't want to have children. I get the picture.

"I want to know," I continue, "what was the first impression you had—the very first feeling, when you met Nathan? Can you remember?"

"Yes, I thought he was charming and handsome and too good to be true. I thought to myself, 'I could never get a guy like that.'"

"You see, you knew right from the beginning. Did you hear what you said? And he told you his history. You knew, you knew the whole story, but you wanted the picture not the story. We know from the beginning, but we let our needs and desires get in the way of seeing the truth. It's so easy to fall under the spell of someone and disregard the warning signs. Believe me, I've done it myself. I know what it's like to fall in love with someone you know isn't good for you—even when you're a psychic."

"Wow, it must be so cool to be you. I wish I could do what you do. It must be so much fun seeing everything about everybody. Is it?"

"To see everything about everybody is to see the horror and pain of everything too and that's not always fun."

"Oh, I never thought about that. Are you psychic all the time?"

"Yes, of course. It's always there in some way or another, but most of the time I can choose to look away if I want to."

"Terry, I've been really thrown by Nathan. I was so depressed I wanted to die. I really thought I was going to marry him. But you know, I think you're right. Deep down, I never really believed it was going to happen. I just couldn't say it out loud. I want to forget about him. I know I'll get over him one day."

"He's already seriously dating the next girl. I saw it. He was holding a woman's hand across a dinner table. I was him and I was saying the same lines I told my last girlfriend."

"What! Who is she? I'll kill her. Is she one of my close friends?"

"Let's not open that door. I could probably tell you, but you know that's just going to hurt you. So this is where we can choose to look away. Besides, that's his life now and it has nothing to do with you. Should we call the new girl and warn her? We gotta laugh about this now."

"Am I ever going to be happy? Will anyone ever love me?"

In her face I could see her as a little girl. She's sitting on a red-and-white striped couch looking out the window. Crying, she's waiting for her father.

"When you were about six or seven your parents divorced. Your father had visiting time with you on weekends and he left you with your aunt. Was that his sister? The couch—it had red-and-white stripes. Candy-cane colors. Big, wide stripes."

"Oh my God, you can see that? That couch! I hate that couch. My father told me to wait there until he got back. My aunt watched television all day long and told me to stop crying. He didn't spend more then twenty minutes with me, if that much."

"He was with his girlfriend. He didn't care about you. He was using you to get control over your mother. At least you have your mother. She's going through a hard time right now. Your mother is sick . . . I see doctors, treatments, and she's divorcing—again. She'll get through this. I can see that. I see her well. In two years everything will be so different for her."

"I'm sending her to you. Would you see my mom?"

"Certainly." I shuffle and pick out nine cards from the deck. I have something to tell her and I use the cards to focus my thoughts, though I don't actually look at them.

"Now listen to me. Next year you're going to be invited to a wedding. A man will be seated next to you, he'll start talking to you about the houses in the neighborhood where the wedding is taking place. Pick three cards from this pile." I ask her to pick cards to keep her relaxed and engaged. I feel myself being pulled back into her past. She wants to know more about Nathan and I want her to hear about her future. I have to battle with her obsession. I have to fight to not look back.

"He's wearing a light gray suit. On his jacket I see a tiny pin of a bird. It's made of diamonds. It's strange that a man would be wearing this piece of jewelry, but he is. You're thinking he's a nice man. You're not thinking in terms of love or even that you would go out with him. This is not anywhere in your mind. I have to tell you something—he's not handsome. He's not ugly, but he's not the kind of man that you usually look for. But this man is splendid! He's kind and generous, many people love him. He lives in Los Angeles. Married before, older than you, extremely successful. And he adores you. You two are going to be madly in love. This is your man for life."

"No! This is so depressing. I'm going to meet an old, ugly man who was married before."

"Now, that's not exactly what I said. When you meet him, he'll ask you to dance with him. Give him a chance. Just say yes. This is the man you'll marry. You're going to be very happy. I promise that. Do you hear me?"

"How do you get all this? Are you ever wrong?"

"Please, just remember what I said and be open. Stop trying to control your life. Let something unexpected happen. Give him a chance. Don't miss this opportunity. Look for the diamond bird. You're one of the lucky ones."

"What about Nathan? Is he going to be happy? Can we be friends?"

"I'm going to kill you! Better yet I'm sending you back to Frank Andrews. He was right, you are obsessed. I can't believe you even want to consider him. No! The answer is no. You can't be friends. And sell that wedding gown! Get it out of the house. One more thing—don't buy the puppy. You travel too much, you're never home. You'll leave the dog alone."

"You got that right. I want a dog. I went into a pet shop, held a puppy, but I put him down. I guess I listened to my instincts that time. Do I have to sit home alone until I meet 'you know who,' whatever his name is. Did you get his name?"

"No, I'm not sure. I would be guessing. It has to come to me, I have to hear it. Everyone wants names! Okay. I have some for you—you'll meet a man called Stewart. He works on Wall Street. You'll be bored. He talks about himself all night and he just wants to sleep with you. And then there's Ramone, Lenny, Mark . . . wow, you sure get around."

"Lenny! Is he coming back? Wall Street, now you're talking. Those are my kind of guys. You know I could get addicted to this. Can I come once a week?"

"No. I'm not a therapist, besides I only allow one reading a year. Two at the most. I don't want you to become dependent on me. You go practice being your own psychic. Start listening to what you feel. Take the time and listen. Make another appointment after you meet the man from the wedding and we'll go from there. But, you probably won't need to. You're going to be happy. How many times do I have to say it? Now, you better get back to work before you get fired."

"You see me getting fired?"

"No, I do not. Relax."

She puts her coat on and says how much the reading has helped her.

"I didn't bring my umbrella. Do you think it's going to rain?"

"I don't do weather. Now, hurry along and take care of yourself."

"What do you mean by that? Oh my, God. Is there something you're not telling me? Just kidding."

"Bye."

I have twenty minutes before the next client arrives. I dump out her glass of water left behind on the table and wash my hands. Eighteen minutes. The phone rings. I screen the call. A woman I read for is leaving a long message.

"Hello, Terry, do I have a story for you. I came to see you over a year ago. You told me something . . . I can't believe how right on you were. I'll leave you my number and you can—"

"Hello, it's me. I'm here. What were you saying?"

"Terry, I can't believed you picked up. I heard you never answer the phone. Thank you. First of all, I have to confess that after I came to see you, I left feeling very disappointed. I thought you were so off and that you didn't tell me anything. I said to myself, 'She's terrible. What are they all talking about? I'm never going to see her again. What a waste of money.' Well, you told me that I was going to meet a man soon, fall in love with him and get married. You couldn't describe him. You didn't know his name. You didn't know what he did for a living. All you said was, 'I see a can of tuna fish.' A can of tuna fish!

"Well, one day at my job I was put on a team with six other people to design a group of buildings for a shopping center. Oh, you probably don't remember, but I'm an architect. Well, the job turned out to be very difficult. We had insane deadlines to meet. We were working late and weekends. One day, this guy on the team asked me if I'd like to come to his apartment to work on the plans. I knew him long enough, he was nice, so I said okay.

"I went to his place. When he opened the door he started apologizing, 'Come on in. Please excuse my empty apartment. I just moved in and I don't have any furniture yet.' I followed him into the kitchen. It had nothing in it but the sink, the stove and some brand-new cabinets.

"We sat down on two wooden stools and he laid the drawings out on the counter. He said to me, 'Are you hungry? I can make us some lunch, but I've got to run downstairs and get some bread. What would you like to drink?' He turns around, reaches into one of the cabinets and takes out the only thing in it—a can of tuna fish—and puts it down right in front of me on the counter. And walks out the door.

"Well, I'm sitting there in this empty apartment. I'm telling you, there was nothing in it but me and this can of tuna fish. Terry, I wasn't thinking that this guy was someone I'd even be friends with! Now, I'm sitting there with the tuna fish thinking, 'This is my husband?' Anyway, I could hardly concentrate when he came back.

"Now, we're dating. And yes, we're in love. So, I have one question for you. Do you think he's the one?"

"I'm not going to answer that."

. . .

Two minutes before the next client. *Sit down and relax will you?* I check the name in my appointment book. Someone new. I sit down, get up. My toes constantly move. One foot then the other foot. I switch back and forth, curl under, stretch out, tap, tap, tap. *Don't look at the ceiling.* If I do, I'll start counting the squares and I won't be able to stop. *Don't look up.* I forgot his name already. *Check it again.* The buzzer always makes me jump. I listen to him climbing.

"Hello. Come in"

"I'm Max. I used to live in this neighborhood when I first moved to New York—around the corner on Mott Street. I had an apartment just like this with the same kind of bathtub in the kitchen."

He's a good-looking man, tall with dark brown hair and smart tortoise-shell glasses. I admire his bright blue shirt and vintage wingtip shoes.

"My father gave them to me. They were his. They're forty years old."

"Have a seat. Would you like some water?"

"No thank you. I'm fine." I hear him say those words just at the moment I feel a snap down my back from the top of my head to my heels. I'm like a pea being popped out of a shell. At the same time I'm still sitting calmly at the table talking about the way the neighborhood has changed. Behind my chair, another part of me, begging me not to do this reading. Stop right now. I can see myself pleading to get out of the room. Now!

I quickly have to determine if I'm in danger. I've just let a man I don't know into my apartment, so is this warning for me or am I picking up something that belongs to him?

"Have you been to psychics before?" I ask him, not knowing why I'm asking that or what I'm even talking about. I need time to figure out what I'm feeling so I start saying anything. I recognize panic, but I decide to stay with it.

"I have seen psychics. Many times."

I want to pluck out his eyes and choke him. I'm furious. I want to kill him. I plot how I could stab him with a knife from the kitchen drawer. Under the table I feel my foot frantically tracing his jacket collar over and over again and then I switch to his glasses.

"I work with the Tarot. It's amazing how much the cards can tell," I calmly say. What am I talking about? *Please don't hurt me.*

"I've been reading the cards since I was twelve." I see myself throwing boiling water in his face.

I'm getting smaller, shrinking into the corner of the room behind my chair. I turn my face to the white wall and try to disappear. My arms are holding on to my little body. I have my chin pressed into my chest.

Please somebody make me invisible.

I am terrified. Watching myself at the table, I look at the clock, I adjust my chair, I'm talking about something.

I didn't do it. I didn't do anything. Please don't hurt me. Please don't do that again.

Shame. I'm so ashamed. I know he can't hear what's going on in my head. I hope my face isn't expressing what I'm feeling. I must have told him to shuffle the cards, his hands are cutting the deck into three piles. I'll focus on the pictures. That might help me. I arrange the cards out on the table, three rows of five. Reading them from right to left I start with the right bottom corner.

"The Queen of Cups and the Queen of Wands, two women. A young man, the Knight of Pentacles. The Moon, Nine Swords, the Emperor, Three Swords, the Devil. Oh, I see," I say out loud, knowing he doesn't know what any of this means. Hearing my own voice listing off the cards embarrasses me. How ridiculous this is. What am I talking about? I watch myself at the table, I don't know what to say next. The cards are meaningless right now. I sit here silent. My heart's racing. I want to die.

I hear him telling me about a psychic he went to see in London. Can he tell something is wrong with me? "Oh, I've heard of her," I say in a weak voice. I've never heard of her. Why did I say that? Where am I?

"*TELL HIM!*" my voice screams out in my head.

"I have to tell you something." The words fly out of me. I wait a few seconds. "We're sitting here talking, but I'm not here. I'm inside of you. I know how you feel—all the time. I know how much pain you're in. There isn't a second in your life you don't feel pain. Several people hurt you terribly. I know you've been abused."

He's shocked to hear me say this. Taking off his glasses he puts his head down on the table and sobs. I don't move. I don't say anything. I gather all the parts of myself as I slowly merge into him. I make myself do this to become him as fully as I can. Locked inside of him I can feel his clothes around my body, his belt around my waist, the edge of his blue shirt touching my neck, his wristwatch, his father's shoes, his skin, his pain.

A door slams shut behind me. Suddenly, I'm in the dark. Something's touching my head. I reach up and feel clothes. I must be in a closet. A man's voice is screaming at me from the other side of the door. I don't know how long I can hold on to this doorknob. My feet grip the floor with all my strength. I'm only seven. My birthday's next month and Mother promised to take me to Philadelphia to see Jenny. I have to live through this.

Open the door, Max, or I'm going to set fire to this closet! I'm going to kill you, Max! Come out here right now!

You can't kill me. I'm already dead. Where's my mommy? Why doesn't she do something? She never does. I hear her climbing the staircase above me. She always goes into her bedroom, where she won't hear anything.

I look at my client's face, "My sweet friend, I know you've been sexually abused many times. I feel what you've been through. Is it all right that I talk about this with you?"

"Yes," he says quietly. Sitting straight up in the chair with his hands folded on the table like a good schoolboy. He keeps his head down. I feel he's thinking I'm going to yell at him.

"What happened to you defines your every moment. I'm so sorry. You remember everything even though you sometimes think it would be better if you could forget what happened. It's much better that you remember. It's what has kept you sane. You would have been more haunted if you had blocked it all out."

"I've been in a lot of therapy. Nothing helps me."

I feel inadequate. I'm not a therapist or a healer. I can't be the loving mother he should have had. I want to take his pain away, but all I can do is see what happened to him. How can that help him? Why is it better that he remembers everything? Why did you tell him that? What do you see in his future? Look at that.

"There are two women. They're taking you into a room with a man on a bed. I smell dirty pajamas and alcohol."

Terry, stop this now. Don't look there. He knows what happened. Don't go inside these people.

"She was your mother's friend. She tells you that you are an adorable boy while she takes your shoes and socks off. She's taking you upstairs to the man. Your mother is with her. They're watching."

How do I tell him I don't see him happy? That there will never be a day when he won't suffer, when he won't relive this. I don't want to believe this. I believe in healing, in change, in therapy. But he's not going to find it. Can't I just make up something good to help him have hope? What's wrong with that? It's not the truth. I hate this.

I don't tell him I'm really scared for him, that I don't see his future, that he won't make it.

"I'm having a hard time reading you. My own feelings are in the way. I'm sorry."

"They all say that."

"Do you want me to try to look at anything else?"

"No, that's okay."

He leaves. I didn't do enough. I'll probably never see him again. I know I won't be able to stop thinking about him for several hours. In the middle of the night I'll wake up thinking about him, what I should have said, what I couldn't see.

It's starting to rain. The window in the kitchen looks out to the back of the neighboring tenement buildings. There are a few bare trees. Three cats huddle together on the fire escape. Down below a man is doing something with the garbage cans. He throws the metal covers to the ground. The crash turns into music in my head. It gets louder and louder. Big kettle drums, frantic violins and trumpets. Cannons exploding! I remember . . . Tchaikovsky's *1812 Overture*.

"Faster, faster, faster, faster, more, more, more," my brother Frankie shouting out directions at me and my sister, Rosemary. He's waving his hands and throwing his head back conducting the air. A twelve-year-old Toscanini. "Let the music inspire you. Feel its power. Make it yours!"

I don't think I can do this. We're lined up in front of the big picture window in our house in Buffalo. I'm between him and Rosemary.

"Concentrate! Use your arms!" Frankie instructs us. "You have the power! Bring on the snow! Concentrate! You're not trying hard enough. Focus! Snow! Snow! Snow!"

I'm only five and not tall enough to see very much, but if I look straight up I can see the powdered-sugar treetops.

Rosemary moves like a bird, has the eyes of a cobra. Her arms are flailing like she's drowning in an invisible sea. Chanting with determination and authority, "Faster! Faster! Faster! More! More! More!"

"Here it comes!" she yells out.

I jump. She scared me. Stop yelling. I plug my ears. The snow is falling harder. Frankie turns up the volume on the stereo. More cannons.

"Look, you can't see across the street anymore! The houses are disappearing. I did that!" Rosemary smiles triumphantly.

I'm afraid I won't be able to see my mother when she walks down the street. What if she can't get back home if we make a blizzard. I'll just watch and pretend I'm doing it.

"Move those arms, Terry. Come on. Don't give up. See snow! Feel snow! Be snow!"

Frankie gave us this challenge. He knows we can make snow, if we want to, if we try hard enough. Rosemary has no doubt. She's two years older then me and has more practice. "This is easy. Nothing to it," she says.

"Nothing to it . . ." I couldn't make snow. Nothing. I could do nothing for that man. I let him walk out the door, I did nothing. He's part of me now. He'll be with me all my life.

. . .

Every night when I was a child I kept myself from falling asleep. Rosemary and I shared a bedroom with twin beds. She was on the right wall, I on the left. I stayed completely still in the dark with my eyes open, practicing being God, being everyone. I let other people's lives take me away.

I'm crying under a tree in the rain, a baby alone. A man struck by lightning, my blood is sizzling. I'm two people holding each other on the beach. I love you. Will you marry me? My God! I've been shot in the back. Listen . . . do you hear? Bagpipes, playing outside my hospital bed, both my legs are broken. I can't bear this pain. I'm a goat tied up in a barn in Spain. The rope is too tight. It burns my neck. My heart stops . . . I float up through the ceiling, through the clouds, the stars . . . I'm sorry I have to tell you this . . . she's gone. Please, pass the corn, honey. This meal is so delicious. Have a nice day at school, kids. The airplane takes off, I wave from the window.

With the covers up to my nose, I held on to Sparky, my stuffed Dalmatian, as we both watched out for the dark. Terrified of my sister's dead body. Rosemary kept herself tightly wrapped in her sheets, a corpse in a shroud in some faraway tomb. I listened for breathing. Nothing, for a long time. I was too scared to get up to check. Then suddenly, heavy breathing getting louder and louder. But not from her mummified bed.

I thought I saw the curtains move. I waited. The breathing was coming from behind the curtains. My heart was about to explode. A rustling, a groan. I watched, preparing to die. *Hail Mary, full of grace.* The curtains slowly separated. Two white-gloved, outstretched arms came straight out into the room, gliding toward my bed. *Who are you?* I whispered inside my head. *What do you want?* The white-covered hands reaching out to strangle me.

Stopping at my bed, the figure didn't answer. I looked straight up toward the ceiling, praying it would go away. Is this a ghost? A dream? The woman in the nightgown and long evening gloves, her hair tangled up with dried herb branches, stood by my pillow, breathing heavier and heavier. She never said a word. She just stared down at me. *Mommy, why are you doing this?* I slammed my eyes shut and wouldn't open them for anything.

In the morning I woke up in a soaking wet bed. The smell of urine permeated the room. I took off my wet pajamas and Rosemary helped me turn the mattress over. We did this most mornings. My sister looked annoyed, but didn't say anything. My mother screamed bloody murder at me for wetting the bed again. She'd make me help her hang the yellow-stained, unwashed sheets on the clothesline for the neighbors to see.

Almost every night until I was fourteen I wet the bed, never knowing when my mother was coming to play silent night visitor. I trained myself to cling to the edge of the mattress where it was dry. I think this is when I started counting and tracing. Obsessive, endless counting and tracing. Counting all kinds of shapes around me; window frames, eyeglasses, backs of chairs, electrical plugs, the pattern on carpets and fabrics, wood grains, letters and words on packages, newspapers and advertisements. Counting, over and over again. Tracing, around and around and around. My foot and toes tracing constantly or my index finger moving along with my mind. It never stops.

Chapter Two ·

I thought the whole world came to a complete standstill in winter. Frankie, Rosemary and I spent long days together inside the house. We'd wake up and it would be snowing, we'd go to bed and it was still snowing. From the window in our living room, we'd watch the parked cars and houses vanish under white mountains. I was never afraid of being buried alive by snow. I wished for it.

My father's whole life was his restaurant. He was always up early in the morning. The glow-in-the-dark clock read 4:20. I'd hear him moving around in the kitchen; running the water, blowing his nose, knocking the dishes and silverware against the metal table, pouring a cup of coffee. He'd turn on the radio to find out how cold it was. *Good Morning, Buffalo! It's twelve below zero! So bundle up!*

Sometimes, I was struck by a smell, an acid-green pungent smell. The first time I smelled it I was scared that something evil was trying to kill my father. I got up, wrapped myself in my blanket and peeked into the kitchen. It was dark except for the high-blue flame from the burner on the gas stove. I watched my father hovering over the stove, his arm and hand in a tight fist. He didn't see me watching him. Back and forth, he guided his forearm over the flame. He did this to both arms and never showed any sign of pain. His face had an almost saintly glow as he held his arm down over the fire. He was burning the hair off his arms. The smell clutched the dark and gagged me. I pinched my nose as hard as I could and ran back to my bed.

I never asked my father why he did this. For me it was just normal, the way my parents did things. Whenever I asked them questions about themselves, they'd look up into space. I'd look up too, to see what they were looking for.

After my father left for work, I'd hear my mother telling Frankie that school was canceled because of the snow and to look after his sisters. My mother worked as a hairdresser at the Up to Date, her cousin Jackie's beauty parlor. Every morning she left the house carrying a small red leather case filled with scissors and combs. As soon as I heard the door close, I'd jump up and run to the window to watch her walk away down the narrow shoveled path till she turned into a small dot and disappeared into the snow.

Then Frankie would take over. We had plenty to eat. Our pantry was filled with supplies from my father's restaurant. Cases of canned food: fruit cocktail, Chef Boyardee ravioli, wax beans, canned corn and miniature boxes of breakfast cereal. We'd turn the pantry into a grocery store, displaying the boxes and cans, taking turns selling and bagging the food, ringing it up on our Tom Thumb cash register.

Frankie was ten in the 1950s when he became our full-time caretaker. Rosemary was five and I was three. He entertained us with spontaneous dramas. "*The Butterfly and the Dragon,* an ancient Chinese fairy tale in three acts!" He'd make a grand announcement as he entered our bedroom, banging the bottom of a hatbox with a giant metal spoon from my father's restaurant. Frankie transformed his hands into elaborate shadow puppets while Rosemary and I stayed tucked in our beds to keep warm. He'd run between the twin beds and jump on top of them, an exuberant, tireless actor. We laughed like a wild ocean.

One morning, after my parents left, Frankie guided us through the house with our eyes closed. "Now girls, place the palms of your hands over your eyes. And no peeking!" He pulled us by our shoulders one at a time to the side door. Lowering his voice, he said, "Now, it's going to feel very cold, but you'll never forget what you're about to see. Don't open your eyes until I tell you to."

He opened the door with one quick swoop and a blast of frigid air hit us smack in the face.

Frankie shouted out, "Now open your eyes! May I present *The Miracle of the Magic Colored Snow!* Ouuuuoooo."

Outside on the landing was a case of soda pop that had been left out by mistake. In the freezing cold the carbonation made the bottles explode and all the pop ran out leaving a rainbow trail in the snow. The lime green, cherry and pineapple soda made a magic-colored staircase. We believed in Frankie's extraordinary powers.

Frankie was our real mother. He taught us how to make our beds, how to clean the bathtub after using it, how to match up the buttons with the holes when getting dressed, how to open a can of soup. He was confident and funny, constantly moving with the grace of a dancer. He acted out entire operas for us as we sat mesmerized on two overturned milk crates. He gave us lessons in Egyptian hieroglyphics, read poetry and created original full-length puppet shows in a theater he built in our cellar.

Rosemary and Frank looked like brother and sister, two Sicilian gypsies with chestnut hair and dark wild eyes. I had blond hair and a light complexion and looked more like my father. I watched my brother's and sister's every move, wanting to be like them. I was the baby, their little doll, who wouldn't talk.

Rosemary touched everything. She couldn't keep from picking things up and holding them. Objects told her things. She heard intricate stories in her head when she held a ring, a bracelet, a figurine. Any kind of object would speak to her, but personal ones or sentimental heirlooms were best.

"The lady was very sad. After her husband died, she never went out of the house. She wouldn't get out of bed and was always crying. She had a cat that stayed with her on the bed till she died. Her husband gave her this for her birthday." Rosemary said in a low soft voice, as she cradled a ceramic music box with a yellow bird on top in the next-door neighbor's house. I had no idea who she was talking about, but I was fascinated, wanting to hear everything.

Sometimes at other people's houses, Rosemary would pick up a framed photograph of a person she didn't know and tell everyone detailed information she got from looking at the picture. "This man was so mean, he hurt people." With two hands she held up the picture of a smiling man with his arm around a child. "He killed a man! He ran him over with his car and left him on the road. He never told anyone." I'd listen spellbound, but it often upset the people we were visiting. They'd abruptly pull the pictures away from her.

Frankie had visions and dreams that he remembered in detail. One time before I was born, he had a dream that particularly disturbed him. He was with my parents and Rosemary, then still a baby, on one of their regular Sunday outings to Niagara Falls. In the dream, a man with bushy eyebrows wearing a navy blue coat and black hat approached my mother.

"Mrs. . . . Mrs. may I hold your baby?" the man said.

My mother, without hesitation handed the baby to the man. He held baby Rosemary in his arms, talking sweetly to her. He smiled at my mother, then suddenly turned and threw the baby over the Falls. My mother was startled upon hearing this, but listened intently to Frankie as he told his dream, asking him to repeat the details.

The following Sunday the family visited Niagara Falls. It was a cool autumn day. Everyone stood at the railing admiring the beauty of the Falls when out of the crowd a man with bushy eyebrows wearing a navy blue coat and black hat approached my mother.

"Mrs. . . . Mrs. may I hold your baby?"

My mother started screaming, "You bastard! Get the hell away from me!"

The man ran away. She was very shaken and went right over to Frankie.

"You see how important dreams are," she said. "They tell you things."

. . .

Rosemary and Frank were comfortable with the way they saw and dreamt things. Every morning they woke up dying to tell each other the elaborate details of their dreams, each more fantastical than the other's.

Rosemary related hers over a bowl of cereal. "I had a dream last night. You better listen to this. A bomb was dropped on Buffalo. There was so much destruction. Buildings were on fire, people were screaming and running around in shock. I survived, but there were dead bodies everywhere. People started getting up and following me. They knew I knew what to do. I knew where to go. Everyone was dazed. We kept walking. We walked through a blizzard of black snow. We walked all the way to Canada until we were safe. Everyone was crying and carrying whatever belongings they could. I was the one who led them across the Peace Bridge. I was the only one who could see in the dark."

Frankie launched right into his dream. "Last night I woke up with my heart in my throat. I was standing on Niagara Street with a group of people. We were watching a parade. All of a sudden, a big man with matted hair and a straggly beard pushed his way through the crowd and started shooting. He had a rifle in one hand and a pistol in the other. He looked wild—out of his mind. He was screaming something in another language. Then all of a sudden, more men appeared on the roofs of the buildings and started shooting at the crowd. People were running and screaming. I fell to the ground. I was shot in the leg. The street was covered in blood! It was so real. Look at me, I'm shaking just thinking about it."

Rosemary had more to say. "Well, after I went back to sleep I had another dream where I was flying. Well, it wasn't really a dream, I was really flying. I could see the city below me and I was . . ."

"I do that all the time. I'm somewhere new every night," Frankie said.

"What did you dream, Terry? Did you dream about something?" Rosemary asked.

"Stop biting your lips, Terry. Sit up. Don't hide you hands behind your back. Aren't you going talk to us? Say something!"

"Leave her alone, Frankie. You know she doesn't talk. She has dreams. Every night. But she's not ready to tell us yet. Right, Terry? What? Yes . . . oh, okay. I see . . . I know . . ." Rosemary said, reading my mind. ". . . you were flying too . . . over a castle . . . you were . . . uh-huh . . . I see . . . What? Oh . . . Okay. She'll tell us when she's ready."

I sat there frozen and scared, chewing my lips, not really sure what Rosemary was seeing inside my head. I wanted my mother. Was she ever coming home?

"Terry, don't you like your cereal? Do you want toast? Do you want pancakes? Oh you don't? Uh, what was that? What did you say? I can't hear you. Is anybody in there? Did you say something?"

"Stop that, Frankie! She's not going to talk! Leave her alone, you jerk!"

Rosemary then started inspecting the air around my head. "What's that? Don't move. Right above your head. One . . . two . . . three little lights. A red one, right near your ear. A purple one . . . there it goes, the blue one . . . keeps going on and off. Ummm. Did you hear that? What's that humming sound? Shuuu. What was that?"

"Are you seeing those lights again, Rosemary?" Frankie asked.

I don't know if they really saw these things or dreamt these things, but I believed them. And they absolutely believed that these experiences had great significance. I wanted to see that way too. I wanted to be part of them and be accepted by them in their mysterious world, but mostly I wanted to know why. Why were they seeing these things? What did those dreams really mean? Why my family?

I didn't speak until I was six. I didn't dream because I hardly slept. The snow was a comfort to me at night. The bright whiteness from the outside came in through the window, helping me to see the dangers lurking around me and hiding behind the curtains. I started thinking, if I practiced Frankie's technique on how to make the snow fall harder, if I could do it, if I could really make it snow, then maybe I would have power to change things. Then maybe I could understand things. And maybe I could dream.

· Chapter Three ·

Public School #3 on the corner of Seventh Street and Porter Avenue was two blocks from our house. Frankie was in the eighth grade and Rosemary in the second when they brought me to my first day of kindergarten. They took me to the door and Frankie said, "This is your school. We're right upstairs. You can talk to us right here." He pointed to his forehead. "You don't have any choice, you got to go," and they went to their classrooms. I turned to stone.

"One, two, three, four, five, six, seven, eight, nine, ten, nine, eight, seven, six, five, four, three, two, one . . ." I counted the tiles on the floor, my toes inside my shoes perfectly tracing each and every box. I traced the doorways and counted all the chairs. I went round and round the clock tracing each Roman numeral.

I could hear muffled sounds of children laughing. I could see they were children. We were the same size, but they looked like silly babies. Who were these people? Why did I have to be here? I didn't move an inch from the place my brother and sister left me.

A plump lady with white hair knelt down and started saying something to me, but I couldn't take my eyes off the floor. Then I saw my mother's hand. Her knuckles wrapped around my tiny arm. And in a blur of sidewalk, trees and crunchy leaves, I was dragged down the street and brought home. My mother yelling all the way. "Why can't you act normal?" She had to leave the beauty parlor in the middle of a perm and she was furious. I sat on my bed for the rest of the day.

The next morning, Frank and Rosemary brought me back to school. I remember so clearly the moment I understood how to act normal. I went over to a corner of the room. There was a bowl of wooden beads and some string among the children's toys and games. I took the bowl and started stringing them together. One purple, one green, one purple, one green, one, two, three, four . . .

I stayed by myself every day stringing beads, refusing to play games with the other children, until one day the teacher announced a new game, Hide the Key. We'd close our eyes and she'd hide the key to the classroom somewhere in the room. I pressed my hands tightly over my eyes so that not one bit of light could come through. Immediately, in my mind, I saw the teacher putting the key inside a flowerpot. A feeling of power came over me and I started feeling happy. When I opened my eyes I knew where the key was. I went right to it, pulled it out of the flowerpot, yelled out, "I found it!" and handed it to the teacher. She was amazed and also delighted that I took part in the game. Then she hid it again in a different place, and I did the same thing. Some of the children seemed stunned and others upset because they wanted to find it. The teacher gave me a lot of praise and I loved that. I was starting to feel more confident. I talked and I liked it.

The third time she hid the key, I took my time, pretending I didn't know where it was before I revealed the secret hiding place. I heard a loud moan from the children because I had found it again. I liked the feeling I had making them upset. When she hid it again and I found it, someone said I must have been peeking. That upset me because it wasn't true. But maybe I was peeking in a different way. The next time we played Hide the Key I pretended to look around the room under chairs and between books, knowing all along I knew where the key really was, but I let the others find it—sometimes. When the game went on too long and nobody could find it, I'd notice the teacher looking at me as though she was giving me permission to go and "find" it.

Most of the hours at school where excruciating for me. I'd constantly check the clock. I didn't want to be with those kids. I kept trying to send my mind upstairs to Frankie and Rosemary, begging them to come and get me and take me out of there. I could see Rosemary in my visions, upstairs reading a book, or Frankie standing at the blackboard. That made me feel a little better.

I was always nervous and refused to take the daily nap. I would not lie down on the floor and close my eyes. I just wouldn't do it. The teacher allowed me to sit on my little mat while the other kids fell fast asleep. I'd watch her at her desk reading a book or writing something down and I ached to sit next to her and be near her. She was so kind and patient with me. I stayed on the mat, counting and biting my fingernails and lips.

School #3 was the place I learned to read and write. "See Sally jump. Jump, jump, jump." I believed she was suffering as I was because she was so jumpy. And memorizing—times tables—2x2x3x2x5x7 and history facts—much too hard for me. Numbers triggered off more numbers and history made me float away and daydream. My mind could not retain that kind of information. When I tried to read a book, after the first sentence, I'd start making up my own story based on my visions.

I was always worried about big things, like the end of the world. My recurring dream was the sun, the moon, and the earth colliding into one another and exploding. I had dreams about entire cities on fire, cars blowing up and fireballs falling to earth. Dreams about people running and screaming, carrying their belongings, trying to hide. Dreams about soldiers marching through our house, yelling at us to get out.

I was so nervous all the time that I'd wet my pants. Sitting at my desk pretending to be reading, I'd feel the hot liquid running down my legs and into my socks. I knew the whole room could hear the pee dripping on the floor. I could feel all eyes were on me.

I began to miniaturize myself. The side pocket on the dress of the little girl in front of me was folded open. I stared at the flower print, moved through the weave of cotton threads that made the flower, slipped between the creases that lay warm against her hip and curled up inside. I stayed there until I felt safe enough to come out. Sometimes the teacher left me there. When I emerged, all the desks were empty.

At home I would practice, imagining myself getting smaller and smaller. I'd walk through the velvet fringe at the bottom of our couch and crawl inside the tiniest piece of dust under there, shrinking until I became invisible. Curled up inside the dust I'd discover an entire universe, a world of particles filled with galaxies beyond anything I knew I'd ever be taught in school. I understood that in these particles was power. I started imagining beyond myself and the world I was living in.

One day our teacher brought the class into the school auditorium to hear a lecture from a man who came from Washington to teach us how to protect ourselves when the atomic bomb hit Buffalo. He handed out illustrated pamphlets and encouraged us to convince our parents to build fallout shelters in our basements. "There is nothing to be afraid of," he said. I was excited about the bomb. I tried to imagine how I could harness that kind of power inside myself.

"If you're in the classroom when the bomb hits, place your crossed arms over your head, do a deep knee bend and curl up into a ball under your desk." Duck and cover. "Stay there until your teacher tells you it's safe to come out." Washington was confirming my dream.

We had to practice air raid drills that came unexpectedly in the middle of a class. When the siren went off, our teacher, Miss Cirincione, who incidentally was a survivor of the sinking of the luxury liner *Andrea Doria,* jumped up and began the pantomime hand-waving instructions over the deafening alarm. See us jump. Jump, jump, jump. We lined up cross-legged against the wall with our heads in our laps. I was scared, but secretly wished it would happen. After a long period of time, the siren stopped. All I could hear was my own breathing.

Keeping my head down, I heard the other kids running out of their classrooms and joining us in the huddle. Miss Cirincione paced back and forth in front of us, her high-heeled shoes counting out the footsteps to our doom. We didn't dare move. This could be the day.

Then I heard someone yelling, "This is really stupid! You idiots! What are we doing this for? It's not going to happen for another ninety-two years! And when it does, all of you will already be dead!"

Very carefully, I lifted my head and took a peek. I knew that voice. Rosemary was being dragged to the principal's office.

• • •

Because we were Catholics and we went to public school, we were sent to Monday afternoon catechism class at Holy Cross Church. NUNS! Sister Mary Joseph, Sister Teresa Marie, Sister Mary Holy Water, Sister Twelve-Inch Ruler, Sister Run Like Hell! Those Mondays were a challenge, just to stay alive.

"Who made YOU?!"

"God made YOU!"

"Why did God make YOU?"

"Do you know what Monsignor calls you, children?"

"Noooo, Sister."

"He calls you PROTESTANTS!" The old red-faced nun marched back and forth in front of our desks while slapping her palms full force with a ruler.

"Do you know why he calls you PROTESTANTS?"

"Noooo, Sister."

"Because your mothers and fathers do not send you to Catholic school! Jesus is not happy about this! Today, Monsignor Gambino is coming to speak to you about your parents, and he is very angry!"

Trembling, I focused on the painting of Jesus above the blackboard— blood dripping from the crown of thorns, dragging His cross, as He fell for the first time. Twenty-seven thorns pierced His forehead.

"Did you children bring your MONEY for the pagan babies in Africa? Do you know what INDULGENCES are?"

"Noooo, Sister."

"If we can baptize one pagan baby, you will be rewarded with indulgences. The more money you give, the less time you will spend in PURGATORY, you little sinners! Now sit up! Monsignor is coming!" We wiggled in our seats. I had to pee in the worst way.

In came the giant bat. The evil Italian Monsignor Gambino, straight from the old country and stinking of garlic. He had white bushy eyebrows and thin red lips that sliced across his powder-white skin. I never looked into his eyes.

He slammed the door behind him and with one hand grabbed for Vincent Martucci. "What school do you go to?!"

"School Three, Monsignor," poor little Vinny said, dangling from the arm of Satan.

"Do you know your mama and your papa will go to Hell for that?" he shouted in his broken English, as he threw little Vinny back into his seat.

"What is your name?" he asked a shy little girl with blond hair.

"Tammy," she barely said.

"Tammy? What kind of name is this? This is not a Catholic name!" He slapped her across the face, and she burst into tears, as Sister Twelve-Inch Ruler dragged her out of the classroom so Monsignor would not be distracted by her crying.

Thank God I am Teresa Anna Isabella Iacuzzo! Italian and Catholic! And then he spotted Rosemary sitting way in the back of the room, giving him the *malocchio*. Her cold stone face and eyes staring right at him, right into the gates of hell.

Monsignor Gambino kicked the desks out of his way trampling over the children to get to Rosemary. We held on to our desks in terror. He seemed to float above the floor in his long black dress as he brushed passed us. Rosemary didn't wait. She jumped right up from her seat to confront him.

"Yeah, what do you want?" She spit out those words, before he said what he wanted. I was shaking and squeezing my legs together.

"You are a PROTESTANT! And you are going to Hell! Your mother is no good because you go to public school!" he screamed at her, his temples twitching and his eyes ready to burst out of his skull. And then he took his two big clenched fists and boxed Rosemary's ears full force.

"You BASTARD! You! SUMMA NA BITCH! You're going to Hell before I do!" Rosemary screamed right into his face, ran out of the room and straight home. I wanted to follow her, but I couldn't move.

"In the name of the Father, the Son and the Holy Ghost" he blessed us, the red-faced devil, as he left the room kissing his rosary.

When Rosemary got home she told my mother what had happened and my mother went on the warpath straight to the church rectory, to give him hell. She grabbed Rosemary by the arm and went with her to have it out with the Holy One.

"Monsignor, my daughter Rosemary said there was a problem in class today."

"Mrs. Iacuzzo, why don't you send your children to Catholic school? Do you want them to go to hell?" He tried to hold Rosemary down by her shoulder, but she pulled away.

"I know, Monsignor. I know they should. I'll talk to my husband." Then she started laughing nervously and they left.

What happened to, "Nobody better touch my kids or I'll kill 'em!" Our mother was all talk.

There was so much I liked about the Church: the Latin Mass, the music, and the colors of the stained-glass windows, eating fish on Friday, making up sins in confession, the martyrs, the statue of St. Lucy holding her eyeballs in a dish. And the useful and important Catholic information—"Jesus was the only man who ever lived that was exactly six feet tall." And "Never, never bite into a communion wafer or you'll end up with a mouthful of blood."

As Catholics we had been taught about the three children of Fatima, a boy and two girls, like us, who the Virgin Mary appeared to telling them that catastrophes were coming to threaten the world. We knew about St. Bernadette hearing a voice who told her to get down on her hands and knees and dig up a miracle spring where people would go to be healed. And there was St. Joan, chopping off her hair, clad in armor, leading an entire army into battle. She too was commanded by her visions and voices.

And then there's Christmas. Every Christmas my godparents, Isabelle and Iggy Sorgi, sent me a book about the life of St. Therese, the Little Flower of Jesus, my namesake, and a Scrabble game—without fail, every year, delivered by their oldest son. I'm still not sure of the significance of the two gifts, but I tried for years to decode Therese's life through the little tiles in the bag that came with every Scrabble game. I was looking for a message, a sign from God.

Christmas mornings, Rosemary would demonstrate her X-ray vision by holding her gifts and listening to the packages.

"A Tiny Tears doll!" she said, holding the beautifully wrapped present. "Let's see . . . it's red. I see red, and long ribbons. A dancer . . . red ballet shoes! Terry, you got a Betty Crocker Bake Set."

"Stop it! I don't want to know."

Frank, watching from the corner of the room, laughed at us between reading the liner notes of the Enrico Caruso album he'd gotten for his Christmas gift.

"Now, don't cheat, Rosemary. You'll spoil the fun," he'd say.

One Christmas night I was alone in the house. I knelt down in front of the Christmas tree to peek inside the manger. Joseph, the Virgin Mary, the three wise men—a peaceful scene with animals, shepherds and angels all looking adoringly at the Christ child. All of a sudden, a fury rose within me. Rage overtook me. I walked into the kitchen in a kind of trance. I dragged a heavy tool box from under the sink and went back to the tree. I took the baby Jesus out of the crib and with a ball peen hammer I smashed Him to bits.

I carried the broken pieces of Jesus to my room. Among my collection of blown-glass clowns and toy clowns was a clown bottle wearing red baggy pants and a yellow-and-blue patchwork jacket. I hid Him in there. I never told my family that I murdered the infant, and we spent the next few weeks looking through the house for Him. Rosemary believed it was a miracle, that Jesus went back to heaven.

If you hold the bottle up to the light, you can see its tiny head and broken arms inside. I still have it. The clown's painted white face, red cheeks, thick raised eyebrows and sardonic smile look at me as if to say, "I know what you did."

. . .

When I was a child learning about God and all His wonders, the saints and their miracles, I wondered what my family was, God or the Devil? If we could see through packages, find the hidden key, dream of things before they happened, know about someone from looking at a photograph, know the answers before the questions . . . then who were we?

Our mother believed in supernatural things. Vampires, werewolves and angels were all real. That we had the power to wish for things that would come true. That we had the power to strike someone dead just by pointing our finger at them. So we'd better think about this, and think about it for a very long time, before we cursed or wished for anything. She believed that she was a truly good person, but when she was angry even her look could kill. She told us never to tell anyone about our gifts because they would think we were crazy. That's all she said.

My family also had a strange physical condition—simultaneous nose bleeding. At the same time on the same day, our noses would bleed, not just a few drops, but gushing blood. It would happen to each of us, mostly when we were not near each other, but sometimes we would all wake up in the morning with nose bleeds.

"A hell of a thing happened today, Mary," my father would say. "My nose just wouldn't stop bleeding. I got blood all over my shirt."

"What time was that, Andy?"

"Around three."

"No kidding! That was the exact time my nose was bleeding."

When Frank got home from school he'd say, "Just as I was leaving I had this terrible nose bleed." School let out at three. Rosemary too, at the same time.

If I was bored in school and wanted to go outside, I'd think about the blood and my nose would start to bleed. At first, I liked the attention. The teacher would run around grabbing towels to put under my nose. Class came to a halt for the bleeding and everyone would look at me. Often I was sent to the school nurse. Sometimes I'd be sent home when the front of my dress got too covered with blood.

For years I wondered if it might be a stigmata, a miraculous sign resembling the wounds Jesus suffered on the cross. But then the bleeding wouldn't stop. I got very angry with it. We never went to the doctor to find out why this was happening. Andy and Mary didn't go to doctors and rarely took us to one.

The nose bleeding started in the late '50s. Rosemary's stopped when she started high school, but for the rest of us it continued. I eventually went to a doctor to have the veins in my nose seared, but it took until I was in my forties before it stopped altogether.

· Chapter Four ·

People constantly appeared at our house unannounced to talk to my mother when they knew she wasn't at the beauty parlor. The aluminum coffee percolator was always on, the kitchen filled with cigarette smoke and plates of Italian cookies. The neighbors, mostly housewives, came almost every afternoon. First-generation families from the old country—Palame, La Rocco, Favatta, Zendano, Della Neve, Monaco, Bonvissuto, Sciortino, Bagarozzi, Zaccagnino.

"Mary, Rosario hasn't been home for two days. I'm so worried something's happened to him," Mrs. Gandolfo said, lighting a Pall Mall.

My mother was at her best in these moments. Her face glazed over as she slowly stood up from the table. She took her time. A room full of people waited silently to hear what she'd say. She lit a cigarette. She smoked Kents.

"Ah, Lina, that miserable bastard husband of yours! He's with that *puttana* on Chippewa Street. He'll be back. Wednesday. He'll come home crying and all lovey-dovey and he'll want to fool around with you. Then he's gonna go right back to her. That bastard! This'll go on for eight months. Back and forth from you to that hoo'er. Whata ya gonna do? You'll see. What do you give a shit about him for?"

My mother said this as though she had the inside information on him, as though she knew. But she didn't know anything for a fact. This is what came to her in that moment.

"Mary, do you think Chuckie and Beanso are up to something? They've been spending a lot of time with that Salvatore Rizzo from the Projects. I'm not sure this is so good, Mary. They could get in trouble. You heard about him and the stolen cars. Salvatore was in jail, Mary. What am I gonna do? Jesus, I'm so worried," said Josephine, our neighbor who lived in the corner house. She was at our house pretty much every day.

"Forget that. It's not that. He's no good, that Sal, but they're just talking, Jo. They think they're Mr. Big Shots. Don't worry about it. That Sal! The pig is going back to jail this summer for passing bad checks. In June, early July. You'll see! He'll be outta the neighborhood," my mother said, as she opened another tupperware box of Italian cookies. "Those husbands of yours! They'll drive you crazy."

They'd keep my mother at the kitchen table for hours. Coffee, cookies and lots of smoking. Their kids running in and out checking to see if their mothers were there. My mother cursing and getting louder with each question.

"Mary, Mary, when is Jimmy gonna give me a ring? You know about these things. When Mary? He loves me, Mary. Please, Mary, when?" begged Connie, Mrs. Sacco's teenage daughter.

"Never! You're stupid. When you gonna learn? He's using you. Why you wanna do that? You wait it's gonna be a sorry Christmas, Connie. You'll see. I have a hunch. I'll be right, you'll see. You're gonna cry Connie, if you keep waiting for him."

I could tell when my mother was annoyed. She'd pinch her lips under her teeth and blow the smoke out with much more force. Connie fussed with her makeup and curlers waiting for another opportunity to ask my mother the same question. Connie had to know.

"What do you mean, Mary? Tell me more! The ring, Mary, I want the ring!"

"Stupido! Go home, Connie! Go next door to your own house. Go clean the house!"

It wasn't only women who came either. When the men came, Rosemary took great pleasure in making them feel uncomfortable. She'd stare at them as hard as she could. Then she'd whisper, "Go ahead, drink the coffee. Go on, drink it. You know you want it. Go ahead, let me see you drink it." She'd watch them take a sip and then shout out, "I've poisoned it!"

She liked to believe she was Lucrezia Borgia. She wore a blue scarab ring that opened up where she kept her imaginary poison. My mother would get so mad at her, she'd start yelling at the top of her lungs.

"Don't listen to her! It's not true, the coffee's good! You kids! Get the hell out of here! Go hang the clothes on the line! Go do something! Go play on the Thruway!"

In the backyard we'd try to copy our mother. Frankie was thirteen then, Rosemary was eight and I was six. We'd pretend to be busy raking the grass or playing a game as we'd look from time to time toward the screen door from a distance in the yard. My mother and the men having intense conversations, their faces held close as they whispered. She paced around the kitchen looking worried. Smoke swarmed above their heads.

Frankie, Rosemary and I huddled together concentrating on what was happening. We wanted to know what the adults were talking about. My brother and sister were much better at this than I was. I was still learning, following along. They'd both get that look that my mother had when she was seeing the future; as though they were trying to hear the words of someone talking from several rooms away.

Frankie's eyebrows would be raised up high on his face when he was getting information. He'd start giggling.

"Well, girls, ah, it's like this. You see, that man with the mustache? He works with Uncle Sandy, and ah, let me see . . . Oh, okay . . . Oh, it's not very interesting." He'd stand there "listening," not letting us in on what he was getting.

"Frankie! Oh, come on! Tell us! Is she having a baby again?" Rosemary was frustrated that she couldn't get any information yet. She held her temples with two fingers pressed tightly to her head and focused into the kitchen with her eyes closed. "Oh rats! They're speaking Italian!"

"Oh, no!" Frankie said.

"What? What are you getting? Don't hold out on me now, buster. Besides, I want to see if I'm getting the same thing you are. You go first," Rosemary said, challenging Frankie.

"There's a man. He showed up in a big car, a Cadillac—I think he's a priest. I can see a white collar . . . and he has . . . a gun . . . and he's walking . . ." Frankie was starting to tell us what he was getting when Rosemary interrupted,

"I saw the gun!" She was so excited, "I swear! I swear! I saw the gun too! He had it in his jacket, like this." She put her hand to her side. "Yes, he's a priest all right! What about Uncle Russell? What's he saying? Is he asking her for money again?"

"This time it's serious, girls. There could be a lot of trouble," Frankie said.

"Oh, geez Frankie! Can't you hear? What's wrong with you? Uncle Russell is lying to mother. I can hear the entire conversation in my head and he's full of baloney. Mother will find out soon enough. She knows he's lying now, but it's her brother. She's going along with it and she'll give him what he wants. Stupid fool!" Rosemary said.

.　.　.

My mother always came alive around other people, but around us she was silent. After everyone left the kitchen she'd sit on our front porch with her arms folded for long periods of time and stare into space not saying a word. I tried to feel what she was feeling. Nothing, I could feel nothing.

When I was young I'd try to get her attention by pulling on her housecoat. She never responded. I'd keep yanking her housecoat. After several tries, she'd snap at me and push me away. "You summa na bitch. Get the hell out of here!"

I wouldn't go away. I tried again, but she yelled louder. "Look at me you little piss pot! You see my teeth? No, you don't. That's because I lost them all when I had you. You took everything I had left away from me."

I remember watching Rosemary screaming and holding her breath trying to get my mother's attention, but she didn't respond to her either. Except once.

"Please, Mommy I don't want to wear this dress to school," Rosemary said.

"Oh you don't, do you?" My mother lunged toward her and with her two hands reached under the collar and ripped the dress off Rosemary and tore it into shreds. Rosemary stood glaring at my mother sitting at the kitchen table staring into a cup of coffee.

"What are you looking at?" Mother said. "I oughta get out of this chair and kill you myself."

I was always so determined to get my mother to come out of her trance and pay attention to me that one time I was not going to stop tugging at her dress for anything. She was drinking a cup of coffee when I started pulling and pushing her—suddenly she threw the coffee in my face. It was warm, thank God. She was furious and screamed, "Get away from me you little pest!"

When I was ten, I overheard her tell the neighbor that she wanted to have an abortion when she found out she was pregnant with me, but my father said absolutely, "No!" I asked Rosemary what that meant and she explained it to me. I was heartbroken.

* * *

I really don't know very much about my mother—the facts I mean. She was called Little Mary because she was so tiny. She was part of a large Sicilian family, the Mongiovis. *Mangia ovi* means "eat eggs." Her parents were from from Campobello di Licata. Baldassare and Guiseppa came through Ellis Island in 1907 and moved to an area of Buffalo called Dante Place. My mother pronounced it Danny Place. It was rough and wild, right on the Niagara River. There were blocks of overcrowded, rundown tenement buildings with small airless rooms packed with immigrants. Police corruption and the new young Italian gangs ruled the neighborhood. There were constant knife fights breaking out in the taverns. It was not unusual to find a dead body floating facedown in the canal. When my mother was around seven years old she and her cousin, Jackie, used to sing and dance on the docks for the sailors who threw pennies to them from the ships. On the outer edge of Dante Place was a huge garbage dump where the children rummaged to find useful things. Little Mary spotted a brand-new shoe in the heap. It just happened to have a leg attached to it.

In the early 1900s, when streams of immigrants were coming to America, lots of Sicilians went to Buffalo. The great waterways, flour and steel mills provided work opportunities. My grandfather was a carpenter who worked for the railroad. Each morning after he had his breakfast of milk and bread, the nine children shared whatever scraps he left behind among themselves. When he came home from work he'd put his lunch box on the table and the children fought over what was left in the box. One day they opened the box and found a wounded bird. My grandfather had rescued it and brought it home to mend its broken wing. He let them keep the bird as a pet and they sacrificed their bits of bread for him. Most days the eleven family members and Jimmy the Crow shared a meal of pasta fagioli, bread and an apple around a potbellied stove.

My grandmother, a gentle, loving woman, had no power over my grandfather's temper and strict hand. He wanted to protect his children from the influence of the new America. Silent films were an enticing new invention when my mother was a kid and my grandfather forbade his children to go. When they did and got caught he would tie them tightly to the bedpost and leave them there for the afternoon as punishment. The girls were not allowed to cut their hair. When they did they carried their braids in their purses and reattached them before they got home.

Calogero (Charlie), Guiseppe (Joe), Carmelo (Carmen), Rosario (Russell), Calogera (Clara), Ignazio (Iggy), Crocifissa (Coreen) and Santo (Sandy) were my mother's brothers and sisters. Before my mother was born, my grandparents had a baby girl named Maria. When she was two years old, they bought her a pair of patent leather shoes. While playing outside, she scraped and dirtied the shoes. My grandmother was furious. "You'll never wear those shoes again!" she shouted at the little girl. Within the next few days the baby got sick and died. Nine months later my mother was born. They named her Maria too. All the girls in the family, including the baby that died, were born in April.

My mother was in her early twenties when her mother died from grief worrying over her sons while they were away during World War II. Being the oldest of the girls, her brothers and sisters looked to her as mother. She was there for them for whatever they needed, never saying no and never asking them for anything.

Ever since my mother was twelve years old she has gone for help to only one friend, whom she acquired by buying a raffle ticket for a nickel. Her name was drawn from a box and she won the prize: a Sacred Heart of Jesus statue three feet high, His index finger pointing to His bloody heart. She kept that prize with her and talked to Him every day of her life. A thousand times we heard how she won the statue. Her eyes glowed as she retold the story of the miracle where the statue came to life and told her He'd be there for her, no matter what happened. He was so much a part of our life I sometimes wondered if He was my other brother.

He stood on a pedestal in the dining room looking down at us, blood dripping from His temples and palms. His eyes followed me as I walked past Him terrified, but with a raised fist. "Just go ahead and try something. I'll knock you down!" I tested my courage by challenging that piece of plaster.

My mother hated my father's family. It all started on her wedding day. As a crowd gathered to catch a glimpse of the newlyweds coming out of the church, a little girl yelled out, "Quick! Hurry! Come and see the bride!"

"Who the hell wants to see the bride?" my father's sister Angie said loudly, so that my mother could hear.

This story was combined with another, in which my father's sister said to my mother, "Ya know, Mary, by rights, Andy should've married Mamie's sister."

My mother yelled back, "Who? That whore! Go to hell! Everybody had her on the pool table! You know why her eyes are so dark? Because she's full of shit! Up to her eyeballs!"

My mother loved an audience. We kids all knew each and every story and could tell them ourselves with the same Italian-American inflection and hand gestures she used. We took turns standing behind her back and moving our mouths word for word as she told her stories. We'd listen as though it was the first time we ever heard them, saying things like, "Oh, really! Wow, she said that?" We'd always start laughing and she'd turn around and yell, "You summa na bitch and bastards!"

She never went to church except for weddings and funerals. We were convenient Catholics. Although raised in the Church, my father wasn't a believer. But he told us we should go to church anyway, just in case it was true. "You never know," he said. My parents always had a look of being removed from the world, in deep thought, longing to be somewhere else. When I was young I thought maybe they were mystics or saints. That they had come from some faraway place to teach me something important. I kept watching and waiting, trying to figure out who they were.

Like all good Italian Catholic girls, I went through a nun phase. Mine lasted about a week. It was the candles and medals, rosaries and relics that I really liked. We had our share of holy statues and religious paraphernalia that we played with. We'd dress up the Sacred Heart of Jesus statue in my mother's clothes. Our little Infant of Prague had a few changeable fancy capes. There were lots of statues—St. Teresas, a couple of St. Francis, St. Anthonys and too many Virgin Marys to count. Frankie had a brown leather box in his dresser drawer for his collection of holy medals, rosaries and scapulars. The most precious treasure in it was wrapped in silver paper, it was a relic—a tiny piece of a dress once worn by St. Therese, the Little Flower.

The best piece of Catholicism in the house was our Last Rites Crucifix. It hung on the wall over Mary and Andy's bed. The top of the cross slid to one side and contained holy water, white candles and a rosary. It was part of our favorite game, EXORCISM. We'd each take turns at being possessed by the Devil. Rosemary would run around the dining room table throwing her arms up in the air screaming in a mad frenzy until we'd wrestle her to the bed to perform the ritual. Frankie could cross his eyes while drooling and rolling his head around. He was so good, I really believed he was possessed. When I used up all the holy water on him, I ran to the sink and blessed a bucket myself and drenched him.

We kept a devil statue locked up in a birdcage downstairs in the cellar. I believed that devil knew every time we were upstairs playing our game and I'm sure he felt real terror whenever we slid open the wooden crucifix. Three exorcists in one house is something to be afraid of, really afraid.

The mothers in the neighborhood would bring their sick children to our house. They'd trust my mother before they'd ever go to a doctor. A loud knock at the side door and a crying child would be carried into our kitchen. Mary would look the child over and she'd know right away if the job called for bigger guns.

"Quick! Go and get Nonna!" she'd yell out to one of us kids.

We'd run down the street as fast as we could to find Nonna. Everyone called her Nonna, but she was nobody's grandma that I knew. Nonna was a very tiny woman in her late nineties. I was afraid of her, yet I wanted to be her. She was frail, but she had power. She spoke not a word of English, dressed only in black, a kerchief always covered her head.

I remember one time when they brought a young boy to our house. He was struggling to break loose from two women who carried him in. One held him up from under his arms, the other grabbed his feet as he kicked and screamed in terror as if they were trying to kill him. They held him down on our kitchen table while everyone waited for Nonna to arrive.

Saying the rosary all the way, it took her twenty minutes to walk half a block. I think she was no more than three feet tall, all hunched over. When she entered the house everyone went silent. She had her rosary beads tightly wrapped around one hand and her holy water in the other. The child immediately became quiet when Nonna touched his head. Praying in Italian, she threw the holy water on the child and into the room on the people watching. Then she asked for a raw egg. Someone ran to the refrigerator and brought out a dozen. She picked one from the carton and cupped it in her hands. She moved her outstretched arms over the boy's entire body, swaying back and forth. Praying and crying, she asked everyone to pray with her. All eyes were on the egg. Some women were weeping and others fell to their knees making the sign of the cross over and over again. Then Nonna stood quietly for a moment and looked up to the ceiling praying to God. When she was ready, she took the egg and broke it open into a bowl. CRACK!! The sound shook the room. Nonna handed the bowl to the boy's mother, who broke down sobbing.

"*Dio mio! Dio mio!* Mother of God!"

The bowl was passed around the room. The egg yolk was completely black. Nonna and Jesus had removed the illness from the boy. The mother carried the boy, who was sound asleep, back to her house. My mother put the coffeepot on and Nonna was taken back home. No one said any more about it.

The next day I saw the boy riding his bicycle down the street.

· Chapter Five ·

My mother was obsessed with our ears. She had to get the wax out. She'd yank us under a lamp shade and scrape our eardrums clean with a bobbie pin. Her mother taught her an ear cleaning method that was used in Sicily. Using a jumbo knitting needle as a mold, she'd wrap gauze dipped in hot paraffin wax to make a long tube. Placing one end of the tube at the opening of the ear, she'd light the other end until a large flame sent smoke down into the ear and somehow withdrew the wax from the blocked ear. Then the bobbie pin and a splash of hydrogen peroxide to complete the procedure. Our neighbors lined up to get their ears cleaned. People swore it cured them of ear maladies no doctor could fix.

When I was ten my hair started turning brown. My mother decided I should be blond again. She wanted me to have clean ears and blond hair. She told me that if anyone asked why my hair was blond, I should tell them that I was in a play. My mother perfected all the latest bleaching procedures she learned at her cousin Jackie's beauty parlor by practicing on me. Throughout grammar school I was platinum, ash, champagne, corn silk, streaked, high-lighted, frosted. I was in a lot of plays.

· · ·

One Sunday afternoon, Aunt Anna, my Uncle Charlie's Polish wife, herself a Lana Turner blond, came to pick up my mother and me in her big white Cadillac to take us to Jackie's apartment. I sat in the back listening to beauty shop gossip and the latest on Cousin Jackie.

Everyone talked about Jackie in whispers, calling her "Black Jackie" behind her back. I never knew what color her hair really was. It was always different. Jackie kept going off to Mexico with some boyfriend and coming back with a carful of stuff. It was after one of those trips that we went to visit her.

Jackie opened her apartment door with a grand flair. Her short cropped hair was hot-poker-white. She was all made up in green eye shadow and bright red lips—squeezed into a halter top and black Capri pants. *Mama mia!*

"Come on in gals. You're looking pretty good today," Jackie said, as she squeezed my face and smiled.

"How's by you, Jackie?" Aunt Anna said.

"Now, isn't it about time for a drink? Rum and Coke, ladies? How 'bout you, baby? Can she have a little rum, Mary?"

My mother didn't answer. She just snarled.

Cardboard boxes and half-opened wooden crates were all over the place. The room was a Tijuana market crammed with pinatas of donkeys and clowns, piles of embroidered clothes, copper pots and straw hats. Black Jackie handed me a lemonade. She picked up a Mexican ukulele and started strumming and dancing around the room. I couldn't take my eyes off of her. She was liquid fire.

"Jambalaya, catfish pie and Billy gumbo. 'Cause tonight I'm gonna see my caro mio . . ."

"Jackie! Jackie! Shut up! Where are the birds? We came here to see the birds, Jackie," Aunt Anna interrupted.

I could have listened to her sing all day.

She put down the ukulele and brought us to her bedroom, slowly opening the door. The bed was covered with piles of clothes. And more boxes and crates everywhere. Surrounding her bed and on top of the boxes and her dresser were about twenty small birdcages balancing on top of each other. Each cage had two birds crowded inside. Beautiful birds. Sad birds. Jet black sleek satin wings with a purple shine in just the right light. Their beaks were yellow and they had pale orange skin flaps on either side of their head. She told us they were mynah birds and explained how to feed them.

"Whatever you do," Jackie said, "don't whistle, because once they learn that then they'll never learn to talk."

My mother and Aunt Anna each chose a bird. They handed Jackie an envelope of money and we said good-bye. Before I turned away, Jackie bent down and checked my roots, pinched my cheek and winked. I tired to memorize the scent of her perfume. She whispered something to me in Italian and closed the door. All the way home in the car with the bird on my lap I tried to figure out the meaning of the secret message she whispered only to me. And I dreamt of a day I could drive to Mexico with Black Jackie, just the two of us.

. . .

Our bird stayed in the cage in the dining room. We stared at it and it stared into space. It was clearly my mother's bird. She called it Andy. We called it Satan. My sister, brother and I lined up in front of the cage taking turns saying, "Hello, hello, hello, hello." Forever. Remembering not to whistle.

My mother brought home a larger cage, an instructional book and a record: *The Parakeet Training Record.*

"Your parakeet can teach itself to talk!" Thank God. I had no voice left.

"Hell-o bay-bee! Hell-o bay-bee! Want a kiss? Want a kiss? Hap-py day, sweetheart. Hap-py day, sweet-heart." Over and over again we played that record. Nothing happened. We gave up and my mother started yelling at it.

This time the bird talked back: "What'sa matter wit you, stupid? Go to hell, you summa na bitch," in the exact voice of my mother.

. . .

My mother was a collector of knickknacks, thousands of them, displayed on every available surface in the house. Her tea-cup collection from our frequent trips to Niagara Falls was displayed in the living room in an enormous gold shadow box. One special Chinese cup fascinated me. It was black and gold with a fire-spitting dragon around the bowl. When you held it up to the light, at the bottom of the cup, you saw a voluptuous naked lady sitting on a rock. I looked at her whenever I was alone in the house.

My mother loved all this stuff, but she never cleaned the house. She didn't think about those kinds of things. Rosemary and I took it upon ourselves to dust, vacuum and keep things in order. And if we didn't do it, it didn't get done. It was a lot of pressure on Rosemary. She really wanted everything clean and didn't want to be embarrassed when her friends came over. I didn't care much either way, but I helped her.

We did our own laundry too. The bathtub would get filled with the family's dirty clothes. In order to use it we had to keep up with the washing. We had to stand on milk crates to reach the clotheslines in the cellar and in the backyard.

We lived in the lower flat of our fourteen-room house and rented out the upstairs. For a few years a large family of ten lived above us in the upstairs flat. One of their sons, Raymond, kept trying to persuade us to play strip poker. His Uncle Hank, who lived with the family, set up an elaborate model train system in the attic with an entire village with houses and lakes, miniature people and farm animals. He even made a sky with clouds and flying airplanes. Raymond was always trying to get us to take off our blouses right there by the Lionel.

Behind our house on Niagara Street was a police station and bowling ball factory. Many of the houses on our street had small rear cottages in their backyards that at one time were probably for servants. My mother rented our cottage to a succession of people who lived back there for only one or two years. I loved the little cottage. It was a dollhouse, its own little world. I longed to move into it and live apart from my family.

· · ·

On summer days and Saturdays, Rosemary and I spent a lot of time on the porch watching the comings and goings of Seventh Street with our friends, Lucy and Carol Ann. Frank would be off riding his Schwinn bicycle with the boys. Three mornings a week a large open truck filled with fresh fruits and vegetables came to the block. The truck stopped in the middle of the street and an old man stood among his produce ringing a loud brass school bell. Mothers screaming and screen doors slamming, baskets and paper bags flying, everything got dropped to go buying. The old man's wife sat up front polishing apples. We'd often catch her blowing her nose on the same handkerchief she used to shine the apples with.

"*Fagioli! Watermelon! Gaguzza! Melanzana!*" the old man sang, accompanied by the ringing of his bell.

Across the street, and two houses over, lived Mr. "Stingy" Millay. In the garage in his backyard he kept a piece of a dream. On the days we knew he was letting the dream out, we'd all squeeze together on my mother's gliding porch set. Pushing the squeaky couch back and forth, waiting forever for him.

Then it would happen—the sound of ball bearings rolling up the garage door. Mr. "Stingy" Millay backed up very slowly out of his driveway. Then out it came, on the back of a small truck . . . there they were . . . four child-size ponies: white ivory, shiny red, jet black, and emerald green. Their heads throwing back their wild flowing manes. Majestic gold bridles with real leather straps to hold on to. The saddles painted with ivy, stars and roses. It was our very own merry-go-round and it lived on our block. The hurdy-gurdy music hypnotized us and we went flying off our porches for a ride. "Stingy" never smiled and gave very short rides so we had a secret agreement, never get on too soon . . . wait . . . stall. This way we could keep it out as long as we could. A nickel a ride. *Take me away from here. Take me far away.*

· · ·

Rosemary had our mother's gaze, that distant look. I'd watch her sometimes dancing alone to ballet music in the living room. She'd get lost in the twirling and be unaware that anyone else was in the room. Once I saw her stop in the middle of her dance and cat walk over to an open box of chocolates. She took a bite out of the bottom of a piece and replaced it in its little brown paper cup. She'd then go back to twirling and suddenly stop and speak. While she was talking, her face looked like she was watching the entire universe unfolding before her. Whatever she saw or was listening to, or getting directions from, she'd report what she heard to the room. I happened to be listening.

"They're not going to bury people in cemeteries in the future. It will be forbidden. The bodies will be too contaminated, they'll poison the earth. Everyone will be cremated." She'd twirl a little bit more and continue. "Everyone will be driving a bubble car. Accidents will be a thing of the past. Cars will just bounce off each other." More twirling. "A wall of water will roll out of the sky and cover most of the East Coast." Spinning. Stop. "Marriage licenses will have to be renewed every five years. Couples will have to go before a review board." Twirling. "People will carry telephones in their pockets." She would do this for about an hour, then walk away not saying any more about it.

· · ·

Frankie, Rosemary and I were entrepreneurs. We conducted seances in our cellar for the neighborhood kids. We charged two cents per ghost session. Rosemary collected the money. When the kids arrived, one at a time, we made them crawl into a large empty soap powder barrel from my father's restaurant. We banged on the outside of the barrel as we rolled it through the cellar making howling banshee screams for a gruesome effect. At the end of the ride, the dizzy child was seated at the table with the other waiting guests. We had painted over the cellar windows so it was pitch-black in the middle of the day, except for a small red lightbulb that hung over the seance table.

We had placed Chianti-bottle candleholders throughout the cellar. Frankie lit them after everyone was seated. The candles illuminated several rubber dolls' heads hanging from the ceiling, their mouths and necks painted with dripping blood. There were other dolls wrapped like mummies. Our devil in the birdcage, along with Frankie's two pet toads, Frankenstein and Einstein, were also part of our horror chamber experience. On the stone cellar wall, a pair of white stuffed gloves held an ax covered in blood. A scratchy record of "The Funeral March" played on a small record player.

Frankie, dressed in a black Japanese robe and a turban decorated with our mother's jewelry, told the kids what to do. "Everyone hold hands around the table. Be very still and wait for the voice to speak." No one moved. "Do you hear that? Listen! I believe we have a visitor!" He said, quivering, in his best theatrical Bela Lugosi voice, as he dangled a rubber shrunken head on the end of a stick. "It seems to be a woman from the other side. Hello, are you there? Hello? Speak to us, my dear departed soul. Give us a message. Please, speak to us today. We so need your guidance and we ask you to speak. Please. Say something. Please, say something!"

I was hiding in the upstairs closet. In the closet was a laundry chute, a box with a lid for throwing clothes down to the cellar. I had been listening to the screaming children, waiting up there patiently for my cue, holding the vacuum cleaner hose tightly to my mouth while the other end dangled down into the chute.

I said in a faint voice through the hose, "I am here, dear children, I am hererererer . . ."

"What was that? Did you hear that? Shhhhhh, be quiet," Frankie said.

I then put on my quavering, unearthly voice. "Is . . . Dominic . . . thererere?" "Dominic . . . Dommmmm, Dommmn, Dommmminiccccc." My voice trailing off into the hose.

"Yeah, I'm here. What do you want?" he answered back in a cocky voice. I wasn't so sure he believed I was a spirit, but I kept going anyway.

"Do not . . . disrespect the dead. . . . You are not dooooooing very well in schoooooool and I am not haaaaaappy."

"Who's that? Who's talkin' to me? What's your name? Who the hell are you?" Dominic asked.

"I'm your grandmother!" I shouted, trying to hold back my laughter.

Dominic hollered back, "My grandmother has some good pair of lungs—she's shopping in Tonawanda today!" All the kids laughed and so did I.

Rosemary never liked when we played seance. She wanted to do it for real. She took her conversations with the dead seriously, insisting everyone sit longer while she gave them real messages from the dead.

"Sit still and be quiet! I know someone's here." She closed her eyes and concentrated. "Yes, yes. I'll tell them." Rosemary said, listening to the spirits. This made the kids feel uneasy and one by one they started leaving the cellar.

Rosemary yelled at them, "Joey! Your Uncle Mario knows you stole his stamp collection! He wanted your cousin Pauly to have it. He says give it back to him or you're gonna have big trouble!

"Lucy! Lucy, you better listen to this! Your grandfather is telling me you're too young to be kissing that boy you've been meeting in the park after school. You better stop and stop it now! Your grandfather is really angry! Carol Ann, your Aunt Millie says stop cheating in school. And do your own homework!"

They were way out of the house running down the street and Rosemary would still keep going, shouting messages at them from the cellar window.

· Chapter Six ·

I was born on October 31, Halloween. 1948. I believed I was born on that day for some special reason, that I had secret power because of it. Every year I'd have a costume party where all the neighborhood kids came dressed in homemade costumes. Before they arrived, Rosemary and I tried to envision what everybody would be dressed as and what gifts they'd be bringing me. Rosemary was really good at this and I was desperate to be too. I wanted so much to impress her.

On my tenth birthday our mother made our costumes out of some old heavy curtains she found in the back of the closet. In a tiara and fairy princess dress I closed my eyes and told Rosemary what I saw. "Mary Paula is wearing an old man's hat . . . I see a jacket with patches and straw . . . a scarecrow! She's holding a stuffed Scottie dog."

Rosemary, the Queen of the Gypsies in a white brocade dress and mother's costume jewelry, said, "Mary Jane is a ghost. I see a white bed sheet over her head with two holes cut out for eyes. I don't know if I should tell you . . . she's not carrying a present. She forgot it. It's on her bed where she left it. She's going to keep it for herself. She didn't really forget it. She planned this from the beginning . . . two days ago."

"What! Send her a message with your mind. Tell her that's not right."

"Now, go back to concentrating, Terry. Forget about it."

I closed my eyes and put my mind back on the front door. "I see Carmen and Joey coming up the steps. They're dressed as policemen and they each have a book for me."

"I think you got that wrong. You're not trying hard enough, Terry. You're just guessing. You'll see. You're close, but not exactly right."

The time arrived. "Trick or treat! Money or eats!" The little goblins came in: Snow White, a nun, beggars and pirates, a Chinaman and my favorite cousins, Carol and Nancy, dressed as gypsies. I knew they'd be gypsies, but I didn't say it, phooey.

Then in comes Carmen and Joey. "See what I mean? They're burglars, not policemen. You got the story, not the picture. There's a difference."

I got the Scottie dog right and I have to confess I knew about the Elvis pencil case that Lucy was giving me because Carol Ann leaked it out and told me in the backyard the day before.

After the birthday cake and opening the gifts, Rosemary brought out her Ouija board. Frankie had given it to her as a present for her tenth birthday. Most of the kids left when the board came out—they were afraid of it from past parties. They knew Rosemary could contact the spirits on her Ouija board like she was dialing a telephone.

"Ouija, Ouija is anyone here tonight? Do you have something to tell us?" Rosemary asked the board.

"What's taking so long?" Snow White said.

"Shhhh. Show some respect. It takes time. Concentrate!"

The scarecrow, the skeleton, the fairy princess, two beggars, Snow White and the Queen of the Gypsies sat in a circle and waited for an answer. Our cuckoo clock struck ten and the skeleton screamed.

"Shhhh! You kids are impossible. Now shut up!"

Cuckoo, cuckoo, cuckoo . . .

Rosemary's small hands delicately touched the planchette as it glided slowly across the board. She whispered the letters, "S-T-R-E-G-A."

Trembling, one of the kids said, "I'm scared. What does that mean?"

"Witch! *Strega* means witch. It's Italian!" Rosemary snapped. "Stupido," she mumbled. "I'm sure it's a good witch. Now concentrate."

"Ask it who I'm going to marry," Lucy said, all excited. "Hurry up!"

"You can't rush the board. Shut up. Write everything down. Every letter."

"J-A-C-K."

"Jack? That's not Italian. I don't know any Jack," Lucy said, confused.

"It's in the future, Lucy. What's wrong with you?" Rosemary was getting annoyed with us.

"When am I going to die?" Beans yelled out.

"Don't ever ask that!" Rosemary warned. "This is serious."

"T-I-M-E-T-U-R-N-S-T-H-E-W-H-E-E-L."

"What does that mean?"

Carmen grabbed the board. "Let me do it. Give it to me!" He placed his hands on the triangle planchette and it began to move wildly around the board. Lucy spelled out the letters. ". . . a man, murdered, this house, pushed, stairs, death."

Carmen's eyeballs rolled back in his head and he started screaming as he fell backward and fainted. The kids ran out of the house, some laughing, some screaming. Rosemary picked up her beloved board and hugged it, and then threw a glass of cider at Carmen's face. It ran all down his eyeglasses.

When he came to, we had to walk him home because he was so terrified. I was scared to walk alone with Rosemary. I was never sure if she was a witch or not. I loved having a big sister and I wanted to be close to her, but she kept me at a distance. She was secretive and fiercely guarded her mysterious knowledge.

When other girls were reading *Little Women* or Nancy Drew stories, Rosemary was checking out books from the library on witchcraft and magic. She said those books only confirmed what she already knew. Rosemary told us she was a witch in another life. She wrote her name backward in her school books and threatened her friends with spells when she got mad at them. I was petrified when she'd stare at me. If we were fighting, she'd grab hold of my arm and dig her fingernails into me until she drew blood. I'd try not to show any pain and stare right back at her, but she always won and I'd break down crying.

On days when we weren't being little mystics we played with dolls and board games. Like most kids we had bicycles, noisy metal roller skates, jump ropes, hula hoops and paddle balls. Rosemary was fun to play dolls with. The dolls had full lives, family histories and complicated love troubles.

"Tanya's parents were divorced when she was six," Rosemary told us, as she brushed the hair on a chubby rubber doll. "Her father was Russian and he was seeing another lady. And when her mother found out she got really mad and cut up all of his clothes. Then she kicked him out of the house. That's why Tanya needs so much love. She'll never get married. But she's going to have a baby. A boy.

"This doll is Babette, Babette the thief. She likes to go out in her red velvet coat with the white fur collar. It makes her feel rich. She takes money from her boss's bank account. She's sad all the time. The money never makes her happy."

Looking back, I think she was hearing the stories of the manufacturer of the dolls or the factory workers who handled them. We'll never know. Rosemary had my mother's confidence about the information she got. They both just said it, right on the spot. They both had no doubt and no worry about anyone's reaction.

I remember one Thanksgiving when my mother's side of the family had gathered at our house for the big feast. A loud knock at the side door and Rosemary jumped up from the table and followed my mother. It was Rosemary's job to take the coats. She'd collect the coats and hats and bring them to the bedroom, place them on the bed, then go back to the table and wait for more guests. She seemed to like doing this. Everyone was seated and ready to eat dinner, but Uncle Joe hadn't come yet. Where's Joe? We waited and waited, but the smell of the turkey pushed fourteen hungry people to all agree, "Let's eat!" We had the turkey, and we waited. The trimmings, the salad, and still no Joe. Nobody knew where he was. We kept going to the window to look for his car. Finally, we went on to the pumpkin pie and coffee. As the roasted chestnuts were going around the table, we heard a loud knock at the door. My mother jumped up from the table with Rosemary right behind her. My mother was furious when she opened the door. A cold blast of November air followed Joe into the sitting room.

"Well, Joe, where the hell have you been!" my mother said.

"Happy Thanksgiving to you too, Mary," he said, removing his scarf and handing it to Rosemary. "I had to go to the factory, something came up." He placed his overcoat on Rosemary's outstretched arms.

"Oh no, Uncle Joe, you weren't at the factory. You were at Aunt Anna's," Rosemary said, as she held the coat that told her everything.

"All right, Rosemary, go put the coat on the bed now."

Joe was mortified. He stood there fumbling and hesitated before coming to the table.

Later that night my mother asked for details. "Rosemary, what did you see when you were holding Uncle Joe's coat?"

"Mommy, Uncle Joe and Aunt Anna were kissing."

Rosemary confirmed what my mother had sensed, but hadn't wanted to admit all along. Uncle Joe was having an affair with his brother's wife.

"Thank you Rosemary, now go in the kitchen and help wash the dishes."

Chapter Seven ·

Sunday was the day we got to be a family. My father liked to go places and do things. Sometimes my mother went and sometimes we went alone with Andy. Crystal Beach Amusement Park in Canada was a short afternoon drive from our house. We went there to swim at the beach and go on the rides on the midway. Frankie and I went for the games of chance. He liked to knock down the wooden milk bottles with the baseballs and shoot the BB guns. I liked the roulette wheel. Rosemary was always looking for a fortune-teller.

"I see a long life. You'll travel many miles from home. You will acquire many riches," the gypsy told Rosemary as she held her hand inside the musty tent.

"Ah, come off it! You could do better than that. Do you know how to read palms or don't you?"

"Can you do any better?" the gypsy snapped.

"Give me your hand. Come on. Let me see it." Twelve-year-old Rosemary took the challenge. She could hold a person's hand and get information from touching them, as well as see things in the lines of the palm.

"You got trouble here. Your husband is looking for you. How should I put this? I see blood—lots of blood. You better be careful. He's mad and he knows about the money." The gypsy was shaking.

"Rosemary let's go now. Don't upset the lady," my father said.

Andy got a big kick out of us at Crystal Beach. At the roulette wheel I liked to shout out a number before it stopped. Quite often, I'd pick the winner.

"Place your bets ladies and gentlemen. No more bets."

The wheel would spin and I'd yell out, "Number five!" The wheel stopped. Sure enough, I swear, it's the truth . . . number five. I'd do it again. Another number . . . I hit it.

Sometimes a crowd would gather to watch. "Do it again, little girl." People would place their bets on the number I called. They'd cheer and want me to keep going. My father would hurry me away.

My favorite game was the bobbing and floating ducks. As the plastic ducks bobbed around in a large pool of water, you got to pick one duck. If you picked the duck with the hidden star you won a prize. I always knew which duck had the star. I'd watch them float by me and I'd feel my arm being drawn to the star. My father never let me do it too many times. "That's enough," he'd say. "Let the other kids win."

Most of all, the Sunday place where I was the happiest as a child was Niagara Falls. "Two adults and three children please. Round trip. Niagara Falls." I couldn't wait to hear my father say those words.

Niagara would keep on falling all week just waiting for us to arrive. We'd board the bus with detailed instructions from my father on what to say if we were going to visit the Canadian side of the Falls and had to go through customs.

"Now, what do you tell the man when he asks, 'Where were you born?'" he'd say, testing us every single trip.

"Cuba!" Rosemary shouted.

"Buffalo!" I said, telling the truth.

Frankie was thirteen, too old to be quizzed on what he would say. My mother sat alone looking out the window.

"Now, you know if the customs officer wants to pull you off the bus and ask you questions we could get stuck sitting there all day. So you know where you were born and you have nothing to declare? Right!" Andy instructed.

"Yeah," we three said for the hundredth time as the bus drove out of Buffalo through an abandoned Main Street, past the red brick factories and faded painted wooden houses that lined the streets one after another with the weight of a colorless sky pressing down on everything.

As soon as we got to Niagara Falls we headed straight to the same diner, ordering the same lunch every time: five open-faced roast beef sandwiches with gravy, French fries with vinegar, and four loganberry drinks. My mother had coffee, half and half.

My family walked much too slowly for me. I had to get to my Falls, I had to get there fast. From a distance I heard the water crashing on the rocks below, a thunderous, enormous sound calling me. To me the mist enveloping the sky above the Falls was a giant ghost. I ran and ran to her until the heavy iron railing stopped me. Grabbing on with all my strength, I hoisted myself at full force up to my waist and dangled over the railing with my last breath. Sometimes I'd hear people gasp, fearing I was going to jump over. I'd let go and fly, balancing by my waist as I looked down into the rushing water below. I was flying! What a thrill! There she was! Waiting for me!

My father got very nervous, but he couldn't stop me from doing it. He loved Niagara Falls as much as I did. He'd tell us stories about the Iroquois Indians who lived around the Falls. How the Indian Chief sacrificed his favorite daughter to the Falls. Lining us up along the railing, he'd tell us to focus our attention straight into Horseshoe Falls.

"Look through the mist, do you see behind the Falls? Are you looking? Do you see the people? Tell me what you see. Do you see the entrance, right there in the middle? That's the gateway to the next world! There are people who live behind the Falls. Can you see them?" He kept looking at the Falls with such love and excitement, as though he were viewing it for the first time.

Niagara Falls was my real mother. I wanted to live with her, sleep next to her. Here, I felt thrilled to be alive. I'd become very upset seeing other people look at her. I wanted everybody to go home. I wanted to be alone with her.

The *Maid of the Mist* was my favorite part. Andy and I would usually go on the boat alone. Rosemary was afraid of the water and would stay with my mother and wait for us. Frank had been on it enough times and preferred to look at the formal gardens.

Before you board, they give you a raincoat. Most of the people on the boat are tourists, first timers who don't know what to expect. Me, I knew the best spot to stand.

The boat pulls out slowly and travels through the choppy water past the American Falls, a serene yet powerful cascade of water. You think, "Oh, this is nice." Then the boat moves along toward the right and the water starts to get more turbulent and you grab hold of the railing so you don't fall on the slippery deck. Water sprays in your face as the boat moves forward. You're starting to get pretty wet. And now, you're going straight into her heart! The boat is a bathtub toy, helpless next to her power. You stand there either in utter fear, utter joy or complete surrender. You're inside Horseshoe Falls. You look around, and all you see is water. She holds you there—and she owns you. The power of the water, the sounds and the spray on your face leave you speechless, breathless. It seems like an eternity that you are facing her. I just smile and open my entire being. I never want to be anywhere else. I want to die there. Right there on the boat.

I'd often lag behind at the end and beg the captain to let me stay on for another ride. Sometimes he said yes, if it wasn't a busy day. For me, leaving the boat was like walking away from a love I'd never see again.

"Well, come on kids, let's get a souvenir," my father would say, trying to comfort me. Rosemary wanted a flying saucer hat. Frank picked out a black velvet painted pillow depicting *The Illumination of the Falls at Night*. I chose a snow globe with Niagara Falls safely held inside. My mother got a pack of cigarettes. Andy wanted a hot dog. We got the bus back to Buffalo. I shook the snow the whole ride home.

Chapter Eight

Mary and Andy were some pair. She was a Sparkling Sherry out-of-the-bottle redhead, tiny, with a good figure. He was a lookalike of the actor George Raft. They met in 1939 when they were asked to be the best man and maid of honor at their friends' wedding. He knew the groom, she knew the bride. My father liked to tell the story of how he would try to kiss my mother before they were married, but she wouldn't do it. He said kiss, but I knew what he meant.

"I'm not some cheap Lover's Lane floozy," she'd say.

They both told this story, I guess to teach us some lesson about honor and virginity. Well, they told me and Rosemary. I doubt they felt Frank needed to hear it.

Engaged for a year, they got married in June and honeymooned at Coney Island. When they checked into the hotel, my father signed the guest book and the desk clerk handed him the key.

"Your room is upstairs to the right, Mr. Pinto."

My mother grabbed the guest book and read the entry. Anthony Pinto.

"Andrew! Who the hell is Anthony Pinto?"

"Mary, you should never sign your real name to anything, just in case someone is looking for you." She gave him a smack and they went upstairs.

Big Red and Toots had a way of talking to each other, a knowing without saying. She thought she was controlling him and he'd just laugh at her. She'd get angry when he wouldn't answer anything. He'd look straight ahead in his best Mount Rushmore face and ignore her. Mary smoked her cigarettes one after another. Andy hated it. "Look at her! That's disgusting," he'd say to us.

"Ah, shut up and mind you own business! I don't inhale. You bastard."

She'd just start laughing and puff away and he'd laugh too.

Every morning Andy ate salad for breakfast. Mary had her Stella D'Oro cookies, a cigarette and coffee—half and half. Half coffee, half milk. Andy told us that he was a true American Indian from the Wop-a-Ho tribe. I believed it for a long time until I found out what "wop" meant—without papers, for the wave of Italian immigrants who came to America in the early 1900s.

Andy and Mary kept a small silver gun hidden in their top drawer. They called it Little Willie. Little Willie had a real presence in our house. Between the Sacred Heart of Jesus and Little Willie we felt pretty safe. To make sure that Little Willie was in good working order, once a year Andy and Mary would go "down the cellar" and test him. They'd aim the little pistol into an old stuffed chair and fire. I could imagine Big Red holding her ears closed while Andy played big-time mobster. Or was it the other way around? Whenever a stranger came to the door, my mother would shout out, "Quick, Andy! Get the gun!" She'd say this even when Andy wasn't home to scare them off. No one was getting into Mary's house who wasn't invited.

My father had a lot of charm and a big smile, a Boy's Town Christmas-stamp kind of smile. If you asked him what he did for a living, he'd say he was a "restaurant man." He wore his restaurant apron down to his ankles and always smelled like a fish fry. Sometimes he'd just burst out laughing, never telling us what would set him off. We just laughed along with him, not knowing why.

We used to watch Andy comb his hair, watching himself in the bathroom mirror and making the most peculiar faces. He'd stick out his jaw and puff up his cheeks, squint his eyes, then open them wide.

"Hey kids, come here, watch this." He'd turn to us standing very still with his arms at his side. At first, I didn't know what I was supposed to be seeing.

"Did you see that?"

"No."

"I'll do it again." Andy combed his hair back as we stood there watching him standing stiff as a board and concentrating. It took a few long seconds, and then like Moses at the Red Sea, his hair parted by itself, straight down the middle! "Magic!' he said.

I had no idea how he could do that. I was dazzled.

Andy was our own private circus with stories, tricks and presents. He was always laughing at himself, at what was happening in the world and at my mother. He'd bring home surprises for us just about every night. Not just one, but a whole case of candy bars, or toys someone was selling in the restaurant. He once brought me a banjo. If he brought home a pineapple, it was as if he had found a bag of gold. For our birthdays he'd give us silver dollars for every year of our age.

Once a week, my father would leave us a special surprise. With bags of change from his cash register, he laid out intricate patterns of pennies, dimes, nickels and quarters. Beautiful three-ring circuses of money. Copper and silver coins, all over the top of the kitchen table for my brother, sister and me to find when we woke up. We never asked him if he left the money; like little thieves we just took it. I still believe that money is magic. It just appears and reappears.

One time, he called us on the telephone from the restaurant. He was so excited, "Now, you kids be on the porch and wait for me. I'll be home in fifteen minutes. I have a surprise for you, I'm bringing home a big, ripe, juicy melon!" A melon?

Well, we all went out on the porch to wait for this melon Andy was all excited about. Big deal, right? So here comes Andy, walking really fast down the street. He flies up the front stairs, two at a time, takes a grand bow and removes his hat. Yikes! He had shaved all his hair off and was bald! This was our melon? We didn't think it was funny, but it was very funny watching Mary have a big fit and chase him around the house. She was furious.

Andy did things his way, no matter how my mother would explain it to him. She was capable of doing everything for the house—plumbing, gardening, painting, cooking and fixing. One time, she was painting the dining room and she asked Andy to help her with the ceiling. He said, "Nothing to it. Sure, give me the brush." She wanted to go out to the backyard for a smoke. When Mary returned, we heard a loud scream, she was horrified to find that Andy got up on the ladder and painted his name in big bold letters on the ceiling. A–N–D–Y. She never asked him to help her again.

One bitter cold, dead of winter day, we watched Andy from the window. He was outside in his shirtsleeves making snowballs with his bare hands and piling them up on a large restaurant tray. We held the door open for him as he struggled with the tray back into the house. He took the snowballs to the refrigerator freezer.

"Daddy what are you doing with those snowballs in the house?" we asked, knowing his answer was probably going to be something strange.

"When my birthday comes on June the two, I'm going to throw the snowballs at a wall." His birthday was July 19. He liked to say June the two.

My father was a kind and gentle man, for a tough Sicilian. He was expelled from school in the fifth grade for punching a teacher and he never went back. He said the teacher was Irish and hated Sicilians. But I never heard my father raise his voice, never saw him angry. Once in a while, he'd go out in the backyard, pour lighter fluid over the ants and set them on fire.

Andy knew things without reading about them. He knew what was going to happen to the world in the future. During a Sunday dinner, out of the blue, he'd just blurt out a piece of information.

"America was settled by the Mongolians. They walked for thousands of miles across the ice. It took them years to get here. They're the original American Indians. One day, the colored people and the Chinese will intermarry. They'll make the new breed of Indians, then they'll take this country back right out from under us." He said this, certain that he knew it was true.

"You'll see. They'll take all the money away from us one state at a time. They're gonna have a lot of fun doing it. Yes sir, they'll have a lot of fun. No one will even notice until it's too late," my father said, howling with laughter as he told us this. "The Indians are gonna win it all back in a poker game. Ha! You'll see. They'll run this country again."

"Oh Toots, shut up!"

"Your mother, the War Department."

"*Va Fungule!*" Mother said.

. . .

Iacuzzo, in American, is pronounced, I-cue-zoh. In Italian it's EE-yah-cootz-oh. The *Iacu* means we're from the ancient tribe of Jacob and the *zzo* means little. Iacuzzo means "little Jacob." My father was the oldest of eight Iacuzzo brothers and sisters: Andrea (Andy), Paolo, (Paul), Salvatrice (Sally), Santo (Bill), Maria (Marie), Angeline (Angie), Rosa (Rose) and Joseph (Joe). They all looked up to Andy and he did everything for them.

His father, Francesco, was born in Termini, on the sea not far from Palermo. He left there in 1907 when he was thirty and came to America, landing at Ellis Island, and immediately went to Brooklyn to stay with relatives who came before him. Three years later, his wife, Rosa, and her infant son, my father, boarded the ship *Duca Degli Abbruzzi* and joined him. The trip took two months over a rough sea. After a few months in Brooklyn they moved to Buffalo, a booming city where many other Sicilians were already living. Francesco came to America with enough money to buy a building and open a grocery store.

My father had only three jobs in his life. During the First World War, when he was eight, he delivered telegrams for Western Union. He'd knock on the door with his pile of telegrams and ask to speak to the missus of the house. He always met with a strange response. People would start screaming or fainting. Some would chase him down the street cursing or threatening to kill him. Confused by this, one day he sat down on the curb, opened the telegrams and started reading them. In big bold letters:

"I'M SORRY, MRS. BAILEY, BUT YOUR BELOVED SON HAS BEEN KILLED IN ACTION."
"WE REGRET TO INFORM YOU MRS. PORTOFINO, YOUR HUSBAND IS DEAD."
"IT IS WITH MUCH REGRET THAT WE MUST TELL YOU . . ."

Andy read enough. He threw the rest of the telegrams in the garbage and went home.

In his teens it was a factory job. The machine he was working on was near a large open window with a spectacular view of the Niagara River. One hot summer day, he looked out at that beautiful river and thought, "What am I doing here?" And he walked out the door and went swimming.

The next day when Andy returned to work the boss asked him why he left. He told the boss, "I was supposed to be in here when I could be swimming? Look at that! Isn't she beauty-full?" he said, pointing to the river.

"Andy, you like it out there? Then go out and stay out!"

He then took another job in a factory that manufactured colored cellophane. His job was to sort out the different color lots, but Andy was color-blind and got fired for mixing up the greens and the roses. I can testify to his eye weakness. One day in the early '60s he called from the restaurant all excited to tell us about the new mint-green Studebaker Lark he'd bought. He wanted us to wait out on the front porch to see him drive down the street. We were all anxiously waiting when Andy pulled up and the car was the color of a Nova Scotia salmon.

This was Andy's last job. After that he went to work in my grandfather's grocery store, which later became my father's restaurant, the Terrace Bar and Grill. The restaurant was near the courthouse and a short walk from the Memorial Auditorium where they held sports events, concerts, the Friday night fights, the policeman's ball, the rodeo, the Ice Capades. Elvis Presley performed there in 1957.

It was the last stop just before the entrance to the New York State Thruway heading out of Buffalo, so it attracted a lot of truck drivers, drifters and the odd lot from the auditorium. People with names like Yonkers, Lefty and Welfare Sadie, as well as the police commissioner and men out on parole all went there for a beer and something to eat.

The restaurant was cavernous. It was a long walk from the front door, through the center tables, past the red leather booths along both sides of the wall to the long counter where you'd place your order. The room, cooled by ceiling fans with greasy wooden blades, was always packed. Sometimes in summer or on snow days when I didn't have school, I'd get up early in the morning to go to the restaurant with my father. My brother and sister rarely went. I loved going to the restaurant. I could eat as many doughnuts as I wanted from the fresh delivery. The French crullers were my favorite, then the Boston cream. I'd eat them all. Andy didn't mind.

With my little hands, I'd help my father peel potatoes, remove leaves from the cabbages, crack open eggs and set up the coffee cups. The huge refrigerators were like another country. They were packed tightly with cold cuts, cheeses and meats and pop. I couldn't wait till someone ordered a pop. It was my job to get the bottle, yank the cap off with one upward pull on the bottle opener and hand it to the customer. Golden Vernor's Ginger Ale, lemon green Squirt, Orange Crush, Queen-O Wild Cherry, Burgundy Grape, Dad's Root Beer and plenty of Coca Cola.

Never knowing who I'd meet on any given day, I loved getting lost in the menagerie of customers. My father would crouch down to my size and point: "See that guy over there. He's the fire eater from Ringling Brothers Circus. That one over there, with the curly blond hair is Gorgeous George, the star of the wrestling matches. See that pretty lady over there, in the back booth by the window? She always eats alone. Her name is Virginia Ding Dong Belle. She's a stripper at the Palace Burlesk. Those cowboys back there are from Oklahoma. They're in town with the rodeo. Look Terry! Look who's coming in the door. The midget wrestlers."

Andy would hand me a sandwich plate, I'd bring it over to the customers. Most often I'd get a shiny new dime for my tip. My father cooked, served the food, cleaned the tables, washed the dishes and worked the cash register—all by himself. He had an amazing ability to memorize orders from a roomful of people shouting at him all at once.

I don't know where my father learned to cook. I think he just made it up in the beginning. "Sure, I'll make that for you."

There was no Italian cooking in his restaurant. It was an American diner, a greasy fries, sandwiches, soup, steaks and chops kinda place. All dinners were $1. Stuffed peppers, really thick soup, fried chicken, meat loaf and gravy, beef stew, the Friday fish fry, ham, steaks, fresh turkey and any kind of sandwich you'd want. For dessert, ice cream and homemade pies. And the ever-flowing coffee.

"Andy, that turkey was the best I ever ate in my life! Could I have some more?" a customer would say. Without hesitation, he piled more on the dish, with no extra charge. He was always feeding the drifters and "bums" as we called them in those days, people who lived under the bridge nearby. He didn't want anyone to be hungry.

My mother liked to tell a story over and over again: "The only time I ever saw your father get angry was when a man came in for a handout and asked for something to eat. Andy gave him a bologna sandwich. The man said, 'What's this? I don't want this. I want ham.' Your father grabbed him by the collar and threw him out. That ungrateful summa na bitch!"

My father kept the restaurant open only for breakfast and lunch. But he'd stay there way into the night unless my mother insisted he come home early, which rarely happened. He liked to hang around there, maybe talk to the men. He didn't have much interest in sports, but he could always pick a winner. And he knew the score before the game was even played.

"Andy?" Someone would ask. "Got any tips? The World Series starts tomorrow. Dodgers? Yankees? Who's it gonna be?"

Andy would roll his eyeballs up at the ceiling. He'd point his index finger upward like some kind of lightning rod: "Yankees 5. Dodgers 2," he'd say, without hesitation—right off the top of his head.

"Andy, what's the Kentucky Derby horse? To win? You've never been wrong, not once. You're always on the money and mine's on you."

"Andy, how many rounds? Will Rocky go down? Marciano? Patterson? Sugar Ray?"

"Twelve! Out cold," Andy said, confidently. He knew, he just knew, like he could tune into some cosmic radio station and get the results before the game. He *never* got it wrong.

"Andy, I put two hundred on Diamond Judy last week. Sure enough, doubled my money! You were right! Damn, how do you do it, Andy? What about Spring Fever in the fifth? Tick Tock to show? Spanish Pedro at the Downs? Andy, what do you see? Come on, tell us how you do it. Who do you know at the track?"

My father just laughed. He'd didn't know how he did it. Didn't have those kinds of discussions. He never bet on his own predictions and he never wanted any money for them either. It amused him, that's all. The bar would be packed with men watching the Saturday night fights or the baseball games on the fuzzy black-and-white television, but my father never joined them. He sat by himself at a table behind the counter, listening to the shouting coming through the archway, enjoying his Pepsi with milk. "Better spend your money on a T-bone steak," he'd say.

.   .   .

My Uncle Bill, my father's brother, lived upstairs above the place with Aunt Betty. He took half of the space and turned it into a bar you entered through an archway from the restaurant. On days when I felt really brave, I'd sneak through the archway into the bar to play some songs on the Wurlitzer juke-box. My favorite—Hank Williams, "I'm So Lonesome I Could Cry."

The bar was always crowded by the middle of the afternoon. I had to sit out of sight on cases of beer stored under the bar. I'd listen to the men talking and arguing, and the monstrous sound of hawking up phlegm. Above the bar the whole wall was painted with different sports events. A baseball player ready to strike, a football player leaping in the air to catch a pass and my favorite, the jockey, hunched over clutching the reins, nose to the finish line. Sometimes, Uncle Bill would let me collect the empty beer bottles and glasses from the tables. I liked being out there with the people and making more tips.

Once in a while, my uncle would say, "Get back in the restaurant, quick!" A cop or the police chief was coming into the bar. I'd run off as fast as I could, ducking into the ladies' room on the way out, winking at the black silhouette of a lady's profile painted on the door. There was only one toilet and a rusty sink in the little stinky room. Overhead a dim bare lightbulb. The tobacco-brown walls held a retractable linen towel roll with blotted lipstick kisses all over it. There was a hole in the wall near the toilet. My Aunt Betty claimed that men used it to spy on women using the room. She was always warning me to stuff the hole with toilet paper, but I never did. The hole worked both ways.

I liked hanging out back behind the restaurant where the stray cats and dogs looked for scraps. I'd sneak some food, feed them and go sit inside an old broken-down car parked next to the rooming house Uncle Bill owned. He'd rent day rooms to transients and hourly lovers. Occasionally a drunken man would stagger in with a teenage girl.

Sitting in the old clunkers pretending to be driving far away from Buffalo, I'd look up at the rooming house windows trying to catch a glimpse. In the windows I'd see an old man in his underwear sitting on the edge of the bed, another man shaving at the sink, a woman and a young boy dancing, another woman drinking whiskey from a bottle. Sometimes I'd doze off in the car and be awakened by the strong scent of coffee from McCullagh Coffee Company next door. Everyday they roasted their beans and the whole neighborhood smelled the waves of coffee.

. . .

I remember one night staying at the restaurant with my father later than usual. The place pretty much emptied out by the late afternoon, but this particular night, a lot of the men came back to the restaurant bringing other men with them. They moved the tables and chairs around and ordered drinks from the bar. The place got smokier and more crowded. I could hear parts of conversations over the music coming from the bar.

"I don't believe this. Really? One time at McClousky's he brought three. How often does he come here? You sure he's going to come tonight?"

Someone pulled the plug from the jukebox and the whole room stopped talking. The man appeared at the door.

"I told you he'd be here," I heard one man say.

A huge dark-skinned man with a gray beard stood for a moment at the door. He looked around the entire room before he took a step. I climbed on top of some cases of canned food so I could get a better look. The man had on a wrinkled white suit and his head was wrapped in a rose-colored turban. He was carrying what I thought at first was a sack of potatoes. I realized it was a little girl. I could see her underpants beneath her hanging dress.

"Who's that? What's going on, Daddy?"

"That's Mr. Moon. Get down off the boxes. Stay here."

I couldn't stop looking at the little girl. She had an old woman's face, but a little girl's body. A face like a funny doll . . . folded eyes, a wrapped, flat face. She was wearing a faded blue cotton dress and white socks with red Mary Jane shoes.

Mr. Moon stood her up on a table in the center of the circle so that all the men could get a look at her. She didn't move. With her head lowered, her stringy dirty hair covered most of her face, her lifeless arms just dangled by her sides. She started chewing her fingernails and so did I.

The men stared at her. Some wiped their foreheads with their handkerchiefs. My father wouldn't let go of my hand. We stayed behind the counter. Then the men started shouting out numbers and the little girl started trembling. She was really scared. They were bidding on her. The man was selling her.

Mr. Moon pointed to a truck driver and said, "She's yours! Come over here and get her." The truck driver took the little girl off the table and carried her out the door.

Some men left right away. Some went into the bar. My father started clearing the tables and closing up for the night. I went into the telephone booth and closed the door. I sat there under the warm light with the telephone, dropping my dimes into the slot and listening to the little bells as the coins fell down. When my father was done he came to get me and we went home on the bus.

Hear the lonesome whippoorwill. He sounds too blue to fly. The midnight train . . .

Chapter Nine

The speckled upright piano was center stage between the two bedroom doors where we made our entrances into our family theater, the sitting room. Whether it was "Sunrise Sunset," "How Much Is That Doggie in the Window" or "Come Back to Sorrento," my mother played every song with a sassy honky-tonk style; something you might hear coming out of a striptease joint. When she was a young girl she sat down at a piano and just started playing. Music was part of her life with her family. Her oldest brother, Charlie, had been a professional accordion player on the radio.

When we wanted to take lessons, she always agreed and my father combed the pawn shops to buy us instruments. They never got angry if we got bored with them even after one week. Like all good Italian boys, Frankie took lessons on the accordion. I tried myself on a half size, but was always terrified of getting my young developing bosoms squeezed between the bellows. I switched to a banjo, then a clarinet, and then a guitar. Rosemary *eeeked* away over the strings of a violin, her birdlike fingering pretending to play. My mother just played louder along with us.

She was somebody else when we were all performing. Smiling and winking at us, hollering out to the neighbors to come watch us sing and dance.

"Frankie, do *The King and I! The King and I!* Terry, sing like Judy Garland.

Do the 'The Trolley Song' for Mrs. Palame. Rosemary, Terry, do that dance to the Yma Sumac record. C'mon, you know the one I mean."

In the mid '50s, theater and dance came into our lives. Our dance teacher, Miss Norma made us disciplined and focused and we started to get strong and gain control of our bodies. Rosemary loved ballet, content to be dancing in her own world in a room filled with ballerinas. I discovered something that changed my life—tap dancing. The numbers in my head had a place to go. Ripping up the floor like a wild maniac, moving my feet and counting out steps to my heart's content.

We took several classes a week and had professional quality dance recitals. My mother sewed all the costumes for the school, enjoying her newfound status as a designer. Regular written progress reports were given out by Miss Norma.

"Terry is a fine student and should definitely consider a career in the theater. At times she is a little spunky and forgets that the teacher is her superior, but she will outgrow this. I feel all other activity should be secondary if she wants to enter the theater world and become an entertainer, as it is very demanding. However, she has the stamina and desire."

"Rosemary should reconsider her direction. She does not take to being corrected and is difficult and spiteful. Perhaps another career would be more suitable for her."

"Frank is excellent in all things and has a future as a major star in show business."

Frank studied acting at the Studio Theatre School. Saturday nights at our house were often filled with dancers and actors. They'd push back the dining room table and rock and roll all night long. My sister and I would jitterbug too. Honky Tonk Mary was in the kitchen making Sicilian pizzas while some of the performers could be found hovering around her telling their troubles and listening to her advice.

I'd see Rosemary on the couch, holding the hand of one of the actors, reading his palm, telling him about his future in show business or that the ghost of Sarah Bernhardt was standing behind him, just a little bit over to the right.

The actors talked to me like I was one of them. "Terry, you must get Frank to take you to see *The Cherry Orchard* this season." "Have you read any Arthur Miller? I think you would find him interesting." "You should call yourself Teresa. It's much more dramatic." "They're casting *The Miracle Worker* for next season. You should audition. You'd make a great Helen." The room was buzzing with theater talk and Fats Domino.

Broadway actress and dancer, that's what I wanted to be. Auditions were starting for the role of Baby June in Studio Theatre's production of *Gypsy*. I desperately had to have it. Instead, I got the part of the back end of the cow.

Fantasy Island was a brand new amusement park halfway between Buffalo and Niagara Falls on Grand Island. It was designed to be a mini-Disneyland with theme rides and actors. Miss Norma took full advantage of the opportunities there for us. Frank and I auditioned with a clown act that Frank created for us. Frank was the mime. I did all the talking in the act. He was Kim and I was Kimbo. He was influenced by his admiration for Marcel Marceau and I by Giulietta Masina in the movie *La Strada*. I copied her clown face, a pale white face, sweet red lips, a red dot on the tip of my nose and two black teardrops. We were hired and they gave us our own building shaped like a birthday cake. We brought the house down for the five- to eight-year-olds.

After a few seasons, the park added a Western town. Frank was promoted to Cactus Pete, the cowboy clown who couldn't shoot straight, and I got fired. I was too young to be a cancan dancer or saloon girl. I went home, put my makeup box under the bed and stayed in my bedroom and cried. I was eleven years old and out of a job.

It was early October 1959 and Frankie said he was leaving. He wanted to study acting and pantomime in New York City. He was nineteen and he was ready to go. I couldn't believe it. What about me? You're just going to leave me here in Buffalo? He took out the suitcase, the one covered with decals from his trips to Albuquerque, Montreal, Niagara Falls . . . He packed up and left. Just like that, in such a hurry. He didn't even discuss it with me. He just left.

I was alone in the house most of the time. Rosemary was thirteen and she wanted to be with her own friends. With Frankie gone, she could have her own room. She took his and she didn't want her baby sister hanging around.

I didn't go out of the house very much. I wandered around, going from room to room, sitting in the closets and looking through drawers. One day, I went through Frankie's desk, looking at the things he left behind; playbills, concert programs, old photographs. I had just unrolled the photograph of his eighth-grade graduating class trying to find an image of him, when I heard a knock at the door.

I peeked through the curtains to see who was there. It was Uncle Russell. "Hello, is your mother home? Are you by yourself?"

I was. He came in and walked through the house like he was looking for something. He went into every room, all the way to the kitchen to see if anyone was in the house. I watched him, wondering why he was doing that. He came back to the living room and closed the drapes. He came right up to me and pulled me toward him. His black hair and bushy eyebrows engulfed my vision. He began kissing my face and lips and said something in Italian in my ear. I didn't understand him. I didn't say anything. I froze.

He pulled up my small white blouse and his fingers found my breast. He licked my face and neck while he unfastened my shorts. He was so much bigger than me and my face pressed hard against his stomach and I couldn't breathe. He smelled of Pall Malls and aftershave. Mumbling in Italian the entire time, he walked me to the couch, placed me down and got on top of me. I said nothing.

This was my uncle, the man my sister and cousins teased and danced with at parties. My mother hemmed his pants and ironed his shirts. He came to our house every week and told his troubles to my mother and she consoled him time after time. This was my uncle who lived in our cottage for a while, and every day my mother fed him. My father gave him money and never complained when my mother would drop everything for him. This was my uncle and he was inside of me.

I remember what I was wearing: blue-and-white check Bermuda shorts, a white blouse and sandals. I remember a huge bouquet of dried silver pennies in a vase on the coffee table, a thousand eyes watching me. I remember him asking me what time my mother comes home and that he'd come back tomorrow, and don't tell her that he was here today. I remember I said nothing. The screen door slammed shut and he left.

I sat on the couch. Then I went to the kitchen to get one of my father's butcher knives. I sat back down on the couch waiting for my mother to come home. I didn't know what I was going to do with the knife. I wanted my mother to see me with the knife. I wanted her to notice—something was wrong.

She came into the house. "What are you doing?"

"Uncle Russell hurt me." I cried when I said it. I was surprised that I could cry. She seemed to know exactly what I meant. I could tell by the look on her face that she believed me.

"Just don't tell your father! He'll kill him and your father will go to jail!" She took the knife away from me and put it back in the kitchen drawer. That was it. Nothing more was said to me.

I went to my room. It felt like the world stopped.

Later that night, I overheard my mother on the telephone screaming at my uncle about what he did to me, but nothing seemed to change after that. He still came over some Sundays and sat at the table with my mother and father and had coffee and cake like nothing had happened. My father never knew. I know he would have killed him, at least I hoped he would have.

When my uncle visited I'd leave the house and wander around Buffalo. I'd get on a downtown bus and ride to the end of the line and back. I often wondered why the bus driver didn't ask where such a young girl was going all alone. No one ever asked me. Sometimes I'd buy a child's ticket to a movie and take a seat alone, placing my sweater or jacket on the seat next to me pretending that I was with someone. Wishing someone was sitting next to me, I made up a mother in my mind and we went to the movies together. She was tall and had blond hair and blue eyes with beautiful soft hands. She had to bend down to kiss me on the cheek. I'd talk to her about everything and she'd protect me. She'd be there when I was dying.

· Chapter Ten ·

Frankie changed his name to Frank Andrews, Andrew being his middle name after our father. He shared a small apartment on the Upper West Side of New York with an opera singer he knew from Buffalo and studied acting and mime while supporting himself as a tour guide at the Museum of Natural History. His letters were filled with his adventures—going to private parties at the Cloisters, seeing Boris Karloff walking in Central Park, hearing Judy Garland perform at Carnegie Hall. It sounded so exciting! And made me jealous. But in every letter, without exception, he asked, "When are you coming to visit?"

His new friend, Jay, made him aware of how extraordinary his psychic gifts were, the things we all took for granted. He urged Frank to develop these natural gifts, to study and use his talents to support himself.

Jay sent Frank to an English psychic named Rolla Nordic, who gave classes in the Tarot. She read his cards and told him he had a great future as a psychic. He immediately enrolled in her class.

Reading the Tarot came easily to him. Already believing that his visions and dreams gave him insight into future events, using the cards along with his visions opened up a way for him to begin seeing for others. The Tarot was like reading a script of someone's life. He practiced on his friends, who were astonished at what he could tell them. He was starting to see that he had power.

Rosemary and I were always excited when his letters came, addressed to us in thick black ink with an Egyptian Ankh drawn next to our names. Sometimes he'd draw a circle with a star in the middle with some ancient symbols around the circle, or he might just write the word *Venus* next to his name. It was so mysterious. We'd try to decode it with one of Rosemary's occult books.

He wrote to us about the Tarot, palmistry and metaphysics, about how he was developing a following, as friends told other friends of the accuracy of his predictions. His world was opening up.

I met the real Auntie Mame, and my friend Jay and I are making money renovating Judy Holliday's old apartment in this amazing building called the Dakota. The apartment belongs to the producer of Barbra Streisand's television specials. I saw Maria Callas in concert. She was sensational! I've been attending a lecture series with an Indian mystic named Krishnamurti. My life has changed. I am deep into the study of magic. Save your money, it will set you free.

I'll see you next month. I'm coming home for a week. Oh, did I tell you I'm living with Jay? We're renting a loft on Canal Street on the edge of Chinatown. You'll like him. He's a Taurus and a sculptor and he's from Georgia. His manners are impeccable and he's very intelligent. Not like me.

Love, Frank.

"IMPECCABLE,": *1. faultless; irreproachable: impeccable manners 2. not liable to sin; exempt from the possibility of doing wrong.*

I crossed out the boxes on my calendar. The day came, finally. Frankie got out of a taxi with one out-of-control white poodle puppy who practically pulled him to the ground. Rosemary and I ran up to him and jumped up and down with the puppy. We were delirious with surprise. My mother's face was not pleased. I knew she was already planning to get rid of the puppy. She looked like a butcher sharpening two knives across each other ready to slaughter. She thought Frank meant a *stuffed* poodle dog.

His name was Dante Roterr, named after Dante Place where my mother grew up. I thought, more like Dante's Inferno, after the hell this dog could cause.

"It's also *Ro* for Rosemary and *terr* for Terry," Frank said.

Rosemary pointed out the similarity to Tarot. "It's sounds like *Terr Ro.* Like the Tarot cards."

"Wow, I didn't even think of that," Frank said.

"Can we keep him, Mom? Can we? Please." What choice did she have? She never said no to Frankie. He was our dog, we were already in love and we were keeping him. Frankie failed to mention that this little puppy was a standard poodle, which meant a big one! And he wasn't fixed and constantly tried to hump us.

Frankie looked different. His hair was long and he wore a big silver ring on his finger that an artist he knew made for him. His leather sandals were custom-made on Bleecker Street in Greenwich Village. But more than that, he had a new kind of confidence when he spoke. The flat "a" from his Buffalo accent was gone, completely vanished.

Later that evening Frank waited until he and I were alone. Rosemary was out with friends and my parents were sitting outside on the front porch. He wanted to show me something. Clearing off the dining room table, he took away the Lazy Susan and the lace tablecloth. He sat for a few moments and looked at me very seriously, as though he was about to tell me where he hid the gold.

"I want to tell you about something remarkable. I'm going to show you the door to internal mystery. There are places inside of you that you can go to see the entire universe. If you have the key, you can unlock the passageway to know everything about anything. I have the key, and I have one for you.

"But remember, you can use this for good, or for evil. That is up to you. Whatever you choose will come back to you many times over. This is very serious. It can lead you to heaven—or hell.

"The first thing a student of the occult learns is silence. Some people won't believe you, some may laugh—leave them, they're hopeless. This is not a game, and don't ever use this to impress people. *Tarot* means path. It is the beginning of the way."

I watched as he slowly unwrapped a small package covered in silk. He peeled away the dark purple scarf as though he was freeing a baby bird he had been caring for. The first thing I saw was the brown, green and black plaid on the back of the cards. I've always been haunted by plaid. Even as a child, a plaid blanket or furniture covering would give me a strange feeling all over, a kind of homesickness. I had to have plaid saddle shoes, plaid book bag, skirts and pajamas. It was my second skin. The plaid on the back of this small deck of cards seemed familiar.

"The Tarot dates back to the fifteenth century. The oldest deck was found in Italy; it's a mystery where they first came from. Some people think India or Egypt and that the gypsies carried them throughout Europe."

Frank told me what to do. "Now shuffle the cards, but not like you would a regular deck. Like this, through your hands. You don't want to bend them. Let go of your mind. When you feel ready, cut the deck into three piles with your left hand. And now, put them back together into one pile."

Let go of your mind? What does that mean? I just shuffled and hoped for the best. I hoped I picked the right cards.

With one grand sweep of his hand, he fanned them out facedown across the table into a wide horseshoe. "Now pick with your left hand. One by one, until I tell you when to stop. Pick with the opposite hand of the one you use all the time. That's because it opens the subconscious mind—the place of truth of who we are. If you were left-handed you'd pick with the right." He turned each card over and gave them a title.

"The Queen of Wands, the Lightning Struck Tower, the King of Swords, the Nine of Swords, the Four of Swords and the Death card! This is so intense for a first reading."

"What does it mean?"

I could tell from the pictures it looked pretty much like how I felt. A king swinging a big sword, a man falling off what looked liked the leaning tower of Pisa as it was being struck by lightning, and *the Grim Reaper*—these were the cards I picked? That skeleton was telling me something.

"What happened? Something happened that made you very depressed."

Could he know what happened to me from those cards?

"Pick a few more cards and hand them to me." He turned them over.

"The Fool. Three of Cups. Seven of Swords. Two of Cups. Strength. The Star. Ace of Wands. Seven of Pentacles. Six of Wands."

Some of the cards looked alike to me. I thought I should just listen, although I wanted to know what everything meant. He looked them over and told me what he saw.

"You're just beginning an amazing journey that will go on for your entire life. You'll take lots of risks because you want to know everything. People will think they know you, but you have secrets. You'll always be wanting your freedom. You're going to write. You're going to leave Buffalo."

"Where is the Buffalo card?" I said. *Leave Buffalo? You don't need a deck of cards to know that.*

I wanted to know more, hear more about myself. He picked up the cards from the table and wrapped them back up.

"Here, this is for you." He handed me the deck and a signed copy of Rolla Nordic's book, *The Tarot Shows the Path*. "To Terry, with best wishes. Blessings, Rolla. 1961."

This little book—only 127 pages long and holding the answers to everything. The story of everyone! The library of the unknown! It's mine—and Frankie gave it to me.

I was thrilled to have something from his new life, but I felt that he was also saying, "Here kid, you're on your own. This will get you through."

I held the cards; this was something I could share with him from far away. The cards could be our private telephone line, like two tin cans and a piece of string. They reminded me of the holy cards of the saints we got at church, but these held meanings only we could know. I had a lot to learn and a lot to teach myself. He left me with that.

Frankie stayed in Buffalo a few days. He visited the neighbors and some old friends came by, but I could see how different he was from them. They still seemed like teenage boys on their bicycles, but Frankie had been somewhere else and he had met people who had told him to question Buffalo and Seventh Street, our world. I watched him comb his hair in the mirror as he took a much longer look than usual. He didn't say too much to me after that. I had a book and a deck of cards. Frank Andrews went back to New York City.

*   *   *

During this time I had a recurring dream where I flew, without a plane, over the Atlantic Ocean to London. I could feel the wind on my face and over my body as I held tightly to my deck of cards in one hand and steered myself with my free hand. Flying above the choppy water I could see London Bridge and the city lights. At Buckingham Palace I flew in through a window that was always left open for me. Waiting in the drawing room was Queen Elizabeth. I read her cards and advised her on her family and the affairs of the empire. She told me her worries and I predicted several events for her. I made this trip numerous times and each time I went back she'd tell me how much of what I told her had come to pass. She always said how happy she was to have me as her personal advisor and confidante.

To this day, I remember watching her hands; first pouring me a cup of tea from a silver tea service, then shuffling the cards. After every reading I went to the window, stepped up to the ledge, leapt and flew home. I felt that if I ever met the queen in real life she'd say she remembered me.

.   .   .

With eighth-grade graduation it was finally time to leave Public School #3. My class assembled in the auditorium for the ceremonies. Having been elected the vice president of the class, I gave the welcoming address. In those days girls weren't allowed to be presidents, only vice presidents, secretaries or treasurers. I'd come a long way from the kindergarten room where I couldn't talk.

A committee of students wrote the class prophecy. Mine said, "Teresa Iacuzzo will become a fortune-teller and live in Chinatown in New York City."

It was all over, no more grammar school. I'd be leaving the neighborhood and following Rosemary on to Bishop O'Hern High School, a Catholic school for girls with uniforms and *nuns!* I was just marking time until I moved to Greenwich Village, so I didn't care what high school I was going to. For me, Bishop O'Hern was as good as any.

I said good-bye to my friends and walked home from school down Seventh Street for the last time. I sat on the porch steps in my pink chiffon dress and sling-back heels worrying about my future.

Andy came over and sat next to me. "Do you wanna go to Ted's for a hot dog?"

"Sure, why not. Can I drive?" My graduation party was a foot-long with mustard.

The summer seemed endless. Andy still liked to go to Niagara Falls on Sunday, but I was the only one who wanted to go with him. We'd drive there and do the usual roast beef lunch and look at the Falls. We didn't talk to each other very much and I could feel he missed the old days. My mother had a job at Chef's Restaurant making salads. She said the customers could tell when the lettuce was cut with a knife and not torn by hand. They'd complain if it wasn't done right. On weekends she brought home pounds of garlic and sat in front of the television, hand peeling each clove. She did this on her own time and for no money. This was her excuse for not joining us at the Falls. She had to peel the garlic.

Rosemary was always busy with her girlfriends, shopping, going to the beach, talking on the phone about boys and the latest *Seventeen* magazine. Overnight she seemed to change, wanting to be accepted, to be normal. Rosemary was still Rosemary, she just hid her powers, storing it up I'm sure, for some classmate who might cross her in the future.

She hated the way I dressed. I wore my brother's left-behind shirts and cowboy boots, a belt that spelled *Niagara Falls* in Indian beads and an embroidered Mexican blue felt jacket that Aunt Coreen sent from Albuquerque. And sunglasses day and night. Sometimes, Rosemary would invite me to the beach with her friends, but I hated the beach except in the fall or winter. Besides she'd get embarrassed when I'd wear a heavy wool sweater and black mittens in July. I wanted to be covered at all times.

Rosemary was thin and stylish and had lots of boyfriends. Polite boys with blond hair and blue eyes, collegiate boys in Madras jackets and Princeton haircuts. Saturday nights they went to basketball games and drove their father's cars. But one of her boyfriends was different from the others. Neal Elliott, a loner, a James Dean type, with dark auburn hair. He came to our house on a motorcycle and while he waited on the porch for Rosemary to get ready he'd talk to me.

"Neal, that's a witch's pentagram around your neck, isn't it?"

He said it was the Star of David and he belonged to a temple where he was studying the Kabbala. I was so intrigued. Rosemary told me later that he was Jewish. I'd never met a Jewish person before.

Neal had been to New York a few times and had the same dream I did, to live there. He asked me if I'd ever been to this jazz club or that music place. I hadn't been anywhere like that, but I wanted to go. He was really interested in who I was and talked to me like I was onto something he wanted to know about, not the other way around. He said he liked my mind and called me an "original weird-o." I took that as a great compliment.

I spent most of that summer alone, down in the cellar among the junk, boxes of theater costumes, old clothes and what was left of our Horror Chamber. I dressed up in crazy getups and played 45s on the small tabletop record player, dancing by myself around the old furniture while the dolls hung on ropes from the ceiling.

I played the talking parakeet record over and over again, *"Hap-py day, sweet-heart. Hap-py day, sweet-heart. Want a kiss? Want a kiss?"*

· Chapter Eleven ·

The St. Joseph nuns covered their heads with a long black veil over a square crown of starched white linen that squeezed in their foreheads and half of their cheeks. This and the big white bib on their chests made their faces look like they were popping out of a dinner plate. Some nuns were loving, some should've been arrested. This school was the perfect place for me—one part horror chamber, one part Catholicism.

The night before the first day of school, I unwrapped the uniform that I would wear every day for the next four years: a white short-sleeved shirt under a navy blue jumper, knee socks and penny loafers. That was it. No jewelry, no hair ornaments, no perfume. We were allowed a navy blue cardigan sweater for those cold Buffalo winters and one long-sleeved blouse to be worn when a priest was visiting the school to spare him from seeing our arms.

September 1962 and all its radiant autumn around my feet, burgundy, coral, cantaloupe and rust with the promise of a new adventure. I could be anonymous in this navy blue sea of teenage girls. In the courtyard of my new school I walked over to the statue of the Virgin Mary standing in the middle of a few rose bushes. I asked her to get me through this and promised I'd try not to be too bad, if I could help it.

I was desperate for a glimpse into my future. Most nights, I sat on my bed, trying to teach myself the Tarot from the book Frank gave me. I got confused with all the different meanings of the cards and my interpretations were always bleak. I picked the swords and the scary looking cards over and over again, the man hanging upside down, the Death card. It was frustrating, but I kept trying to make sense of it.

I'd search the advertisements on the backs of science fiction comic books and movie star magazines for a fortune-teller, an oracle, a reader and advisor and I'd send them my questions along with two dollars. "Will I move to New York City? What will I be doing with my life? Will I fall in love?" I had to know. After weeks of waiting for a reply, a letter would come from some exotic place like Wichita Falls, San Bernardino or Saskatoon—from Madame Tatiana, Master Omar or Mrs. Ruthie. It rambled on about marriage and children and yes, of course—I'd be moving—someday, sometime, somehow with someone. "Just have to have patience and wait."

The early '60s were the Camelot years and Jackie Kennedy made my life hell. Rosemary copied her style and decided it was time for me to be a girl. My mother was always pointing out how beautifully dressed Rosemary was and how her figure, perfect and tiny, was just like hers when she was her age. She bought me the Playtex Living Girdle. Believe me, there was nothing living about it—the boa constrictor of all girdles.

"To build a wardrobe, you must shop for just one item a week. This way you won't feel overwhelmed by so many choices. Look at these magazines and decide what you want to look like," Rosemary advised me.

Only reincarnation could make me look like those models. I was just under five feet and had full breasts and chubby thighs. I stuffed myself into the girdle, put on a navy blue and lime green paisley dress and high heels, and took myself to the Bishop Fallon High School dance on Friday night. Fallon, the boys school across the street from our school, held mixers in their gym, closely monitored by the nuns and priests from the schools. If you were dancing too close, one of the Catholic police would come over and whisper in your ear, "Make room for the Holy Ghost," and gently separate you.

There were a few times I'd get asked to dance by a polite young man, but I was stiff and couldn't make light conversation, so usually after one dance they'd say thank you and walk away. I sat in the bleachers listening to the music and then I'd start reading the crowd. Who was going to ask who to dance? What were they going to do after high school? Would any of them find true happiness? This got me through many awkward nights.

Then one day everything changed. I was a sophomore in high school.

November 22, 1963. Sister Agnes Clare, our principal, interrupted our afternoon world economics class. Over the loudspeaker, holding back tears, she told us that President Kennedy had been shot and killed in Dallas, Texas. The things that mattered didn't seem that important anymore.

We were all in shock. Nobody said a word. We ran home to our televisions to see what happened. A feeling of anticipation came over me. I paced the floor and traced the square of the television screen over and over again. I couldn't sit still and I had an overwhelming feeling that something wasn't finished, that something else was going to happen.

I was scared. I felt our country was in serious danger, I had a sense of something dark looming. Glued to the television, I watched as the FBI was removing the assassin from the building in handcuffs. A crowd of people were standing around watching when suddenly this man, Lee Harvey Oswald, was shot right in front of my eyes. "I knew it! I knew it! I knew it!"

In this moment something started to unlock in my brain. A way of seeing. No, recognizing how I *already* was seeing. I made the connection in that single moment. A murder, an altering of a life miles away, this real-life event as it was happening on a black-and-white television screen, showed me how my brain and my body worked. It gave me a way into my own visions. If I could pay attention to the specific feeling inside of me and move that feeling into a vision, then call up a small screen in my mind—I could watch the future. It was at this moment that I understood the power of my ability to direct myself to a specific place in time. There were no limits.

The combined events of the shock, the sadness and my vision all happening at the same time opened me up to a place beyond my own pain. I could see and feel together, in a way I hadn't known before. I understood that if I could lower my resistance and move out of the way, I could get in!

Now, I needed to practice. I needed to work on people and try to feel and see their future life. I had to get clearer images and more details. I brought the Tarot to school and started reading my friends. The church calls fortune-teller's cards the Devil's Bible. The nuns had no idea I was reading it every day in school. I became counselor and good listener to the girls, the keeper of their secrets, but mostly their hope for the future that a boyfriend and husband was on the way.

The shuffling took place in the back of the locker room.

"Now make three piles . . ." I had one of the girls keep a lookout by the door, listening for any unexpected nuns.

We gathered around in a huddle. I kept my voice low as I read each girl one at a time.

"You're going to get a call from a guy you met a few months ago. You don't know that he's been thinking of you. I see you dancing with him. He's from a rich family . . . Williamsville, I think. His father is a doctor. I see blond hair . . . blue eyes. I see a red MG, cool car. He's going to call you and ask for a date. I know this will make you happy at first, but . . . I'm sorry to tell you this, but . . . before the prom . . . he'll break up with you. What I think you should do . . . don't go out with him! I see you crying. This is bad, really bad. I see you hurt. Stay away from him. He plays games with girls.

"Your boyfriend is looking at rings . . . for another girl. Break up with him now! This weekend, dump him. Just don't tell him I told you. I don't want to get in the middle of this. I'll read your future after him in a few weeks, once you get over this. I've a strong feeling you're going to be in love with someone new before the summer starts. Don't worry. Try not to suffer so much over the jerk, promise?

"Girls, could we have some privacy? I need to say something I don't want to say in front of all of you. Will everyone just stand back for a couple minutes? I don't know how to tell you this and I promise I won't tell a soul—you have a pregnancy in your cards. I can't really tell if it happened yet or not, but be careful. I hope I'm not telling you this too late.

"Shuffle and cut the deck. Let me see what this says . . . Wow! You have amazing cards! Are you lucky. You've hit the jackpot. You're going to college . . . and you're going to be a mother . . . and you're going to move away from here."

"That's pretty cool. How do you do that?" A voice called out to me from the crowd. It was one of the girls I'd seen in some of my classes but had never talked to. She was tall, thin, with long straight hair and root-beer brown eyes.

"What are you in for?" she said.

"Desertion. I fled my childhood."

"My name's Virginia. Call me Ginny."

"Teresa. Terry. Do you want to hang out?"

We threw our books into our lockers and ran out of there. "Follow me," I said, "I know a great place. Nobody knows you there. You can sit all day and they'll never ask you to leave."

We walked for blocks down Main Street, past the vacant automobile showrooms, empty storefronts and pawn shops until we got to my hiding place, the Greyhound Bus Station. We took a table in the corner of the coffee shop and ordered French fries with vinegar and two cherry phosphates. You never saw the same people twice there. Everyone was either leaving or meeting someone getting off the bus. A room filled with people constantly looking at the clock or checking their watches. They all seemed anxious; I felt right at home. You got five songs for a quarter on the jukebox—the Beach Boys, the Beatles, the Supremes, James Brown.

The bus station became our hangout. Almost every day after school we talked there for hours, about everything. We were both from immigrant families who were never around, never asked us what we were doing.

I hate Algebra, I'll never use it a goddamn day in my life. Have you heard of Edgar Cayce, the Sleeping Prophet? Have you read Franny and Zooey? *My family's from Poland. Mine, Sicily. Let's go to the cemetery and take pictures in front of the mausoleums. Astral projection—that's when you leave your body and fly away to other places. Wanna share French fries? My brother is a psychic in New York City. Is he married? There's a new Bergman film playing. Wanna go? I don't think I believe in Jesus. Do you believe in life after death? Do you have a boyfriend?*

We changed our names. She was Holly Golightly and I was Ambrosia Melon. We'd make up stories about Golightly and Melon. Golightly had a rich Aunt Catherine who was always asking her to move to England and Melon was always worried she would. Melon was going to write poetry, live on a houseboat and never stop traveling. Meantime, I was filling school notebooks from cover to cover with the months of the year. Writing with my left hand using a thick black fountain pen, pretending I was taking notes. January, February, March, April, May . . . over and over again.

In my junior year I was elected class president. Even though I was the most popular girl at school, considered a free thinker, a wise person, and very funny—I felt dead. Everywhere I looked, in peoples faces, in most children, I saw pain. And I could see it on my own face, but I couldn't feel it. In the cellar I'd prick my arms with straight pins, trying to feel.

Buffalo was dead, a town of day after day gray. It was hard to believe there'd ever be a way out of the bleakness of those days. I started going to the park to wait for strangers, just to see what would happen. I told no one about this. If a man came and sat next to me on the bench and asked me to go with him, I'd willingly follow him back to his house. This was dangerous. I wanted it to be. He'd go to kiss me and struggle with me. I'd have to fight to get out.

To be killed . . . brutally murdered . . . floating facedown in the river . . .

found dead on the side of the road . . . that's what I wanted. So nobody would know who I was when they found me, I cut all the labels out of my clothes and never carried identification.

Looking for another life, I stood in the dark behind the huge trees on the front lawns of massive Victorian houses and peeked into windows. I'd watch a woman sitting on a couch reading a book to a child. Floating my being through the window into the child, I struggled to feel myself held by the mother. I wanted so badly to feel that kind of love.

In another house, kids in an upstairs bedroom jumping up and down on the bed. Laughing and falling down. I'd try to feel the fun; push my body to let go and laugh. I tried to imagine that feeling, tried to remember. I must have felt that once.

I watched another woman setting a table for dinner. If only I could be part of a family like that. Looking in, I went from room to room. *Pace the floor. Stir the soup. Why hasn't he called? Pour myself a drink. Go to bed. Stop fighting. Finish your meal, sweetie. Give me a hug. Turn out the light. Please, sing that song to me again. Get out of the way! Do we have to keep fighting like this? Come to bed. Good night, my angel.* Moving from house to house, hiding in the dark, trying so hard to feel, to belong. I was a pair of eyes looking out from a body cast.

Chapter Twelve

The World's Fair of 1964 was held in New York City and Frank invited the entire family to come to stay with him that August. Andy didn't want to leave the restaurant or the French poodle. Rosemary wanted to stay home with her friends. I wanted to go alone, but Frank insisted my mother come to the fair, see where he was living and meet his new friends. My mother and I took the Greyhound bus together. We hardly said a word to each other. I had become very formal, very polite with her.

"Yes, Mother. No Mother. Do you need anything? Are you comfortable, Mother?"

Frank met us at Port Authority Bus Station and we took a taxi downtown to Canal Street. We zoomed through the streets. There were so many different kinds of people. Who were they? How did they get here? I could be one of them. I could get lost in these streets and disappear. I was dying to explore it alone. I couldn't believe I was here with my mother.

Canal Street was crammed with factories and junk dealers selling bolts and screws, fans, tools and secondhand office furniture, scales, electrical gadgets, rubber and plastic gizmos, plumbing parts and military surplus. Blocks and blocks of vendors on the sidewalks in front of every building. I loved the busyness of it. Frank's loft was on one of these blocks, next door to the Three Roses Tavern.

Frank unlocked the door to his building and let us into a small dark hall. The street sounds faded as he bolted the door behind us. Directly facing us was a long steep flight of stairs, the whole thing tilting to the right. It was hot and smelled like musty machine oil. I held my suitcase in my arms and started up. My mother mumbled all the way up as Frank coached her telling her she must lose some weight. She laughed and cursed on every landing. We could hardly breathe when we reached the top.

"Welcome to Canal Street. They say if you can't find it on Canal Street, you can't find it anywhere in the world." A tall thin man with a high forehead and light brown wiry hair extended his hand to welcome us. His long fingers and strong handshake told me he was in charge here.

"This is Jay. We call him Mr. Maxwell," Frank said.

So this was a loft. I was always too embarrassed to admit I didn't know what one was until now. A big white open room with high tin ceilings, an old comfortable couch, shelves filled with art books and a potbellied stove. Jay's marble and wood sculptures were everywhere. A real artist's loft.

Frank took a huge bowl out of the refrigerator and served us our lunch in blue-and-white marbleized tin bowls.

"Gazpacho!" Frank announced.

This is soup? Cold soup? Andy would be horrified. It was delicious.

Frank ground his own beans with an antique grinder to make our mother her coffee. A recording of a woman singing opera filled the room.

"The subway is the only way to get around. It takes just twenty-seven minutes to get from here to the natural history museum on Eightieth Street."

Not listening to Frank, my mother started in on the news from Buffalo. "Did I tell you? Connie met a guy from Lackawanna. He's nice looking too. She finally got her ring. He's divorced, with three kids already. What's she want with him? I heard he's a two-timer. Something's wrong with her."

Then Frank said, "Jay studied with the man who sculpted the Alice in Wonderland statue in Central Park. He takes very few students, but he knew Jay was exceptional. Do you hear that noise? The woman living upstairs is a crazy maniac—completely out of her mind. She stomps around above our heads in her motorcycle boots and it drives Jay mad. He fights with her all the time."

Mother went on. "Your father told Aunt Betty to get the hell out of the restaurant once and for all. He had enough of her. He told her where to go.

Your father never gets mad, but when he does, you better watch out. Get me some more coffee, Frankie. Don't you guys use sugar around here?"

They went from subject to subject without stopping for air and never responding to what the other said.

"Franklin Pangborn, will you be so kind to serve me a bit more of that fabulous gazpacho?" Jay said, speaking very slowly, enunciating each word.

Franklin Pangborn?

"Mary, do you make pasta limone? It's an exquisite dish from Northern Italy. A very delicate taste."

"What the hell is that? You mean spaghetti with lemon? Who the hell ever heard of putting lemon on spaghetti? Never heard of such a thing, Jaaaay!"

Uh-oh.

Jay ate lunch with us and then went to the back of the loft to work in his studio. Frank whispered to us, "I should tell you . . . Jay used to speak with a heavy Southern accent, but he went to Berlitz and within ten days he got rid of it. He's so disciplined. I'm here because I was hired by a very rich woman who is Jay's patroness. She was so worried about him because he doesn't stop to eat when he's working. I have to tell him when to go to bed, when to go out for a walk, when to eat. You know, he's going to be a famous artist. He wouldn't survive without me."

I asked where the bathroom was. Frank came with me to show me how to flush the toilet with the pull chain from an oak box near the ceiling. I closed the door and looked out the window at the roofs of the factories below. There was a big piece of candy with a bite taken out of it painted on the side of the building across the street. Luscious red juice dripped down over the letters— Cella's Chocolate Covered Cherries. I started thinking—if I couldn't find myself on Canal Street, I couldn't find myself anywhere in the world.

That week Frank ran us all around New York. We spent two days seeing the World's Fair. He took us to the Spanish furniture shop on Christopher Street where he and Jay worked making faux antique tables for the owner and sometimes selling for him. We went to restaurants, Central Park, the Cloisters, Chinatown, Macy's and Gimbles. I had my first chocolate egg cream at Dave's luncheonette on Canal Street.

I was desperate to be on my own, but my mother did not let me leave her side. Jay made dinner, some evenings their friends joined us. They were people who had moved to New York from all over the country to study acting or painting. I listened to their stories and watched how they moved around the loft, but something didn't seem real to me. Maybe because my mother was there, everyone seemed too polite. Everyone seemed to be acting or hiding something. I wanted some time alone with Frank, but he had us on a tight schedule, every moment planned.

I couldn't figure out Mr. Maxwell at all. People seemed nervous around him. He sat at the head of the table and they waited on him. At dinner, while Frank was talking a mile a minute to mother, and mother racing even faster, Jay turned to me and asked me the oddest questions.

"Now tell me Terry, are you saving your money? When you sleep—do you have your head pointed north? Do you like boys or girls?"

Jay explained to me how to handle myself if I ever got into a situation where an argument was about to erupt.

"Terry, always keep yourself composed, stand perfectly still, smile and remember to be Switzerland. Be Switzerland. Remain neutral, don't take sides and you'll go through life without one bit of difficulty."

He finished his dinner, excused himself, went into his studio and closed the door. A few minutes later, he wanted Frank. He called from behind the door several times, then Frank jumped up and hurried to him. I could feel the tension coming through the door. My mother sat with her arms folded looking annoyed, not saying a word. We just sat there waiting. I moved some bread crumbs into a square pattern on the table with my index finger.

After a while Frank came back, cleaned up the kitchen and put my mother and me in his bedroom. He then went to share Jay's bed in his room. I had to sleep with my mother. I stayed close to the edge of the bed and tried to block out her nonstop talking.

"Frankie knows so many nice people. He's going to take me tomorrow to meet an actress he knows on a soap opera. What's it called? Come on you remember which one. What the hell is it? Oh well . . . Frankie's giving me an opal ring. He's having it made for me by that jeweler he knows. Did you see those silver lamps in the Spanish store, the ones hanging from the ceiling? Frankie said I'm getting a set sent home for the parlor. All his friends love me. I had them all laughing."

I said nothing. She stayed awake half the night reading a Harold Robbins novel, never asking if the light bothered me.

After seven days in New York we went home. We took the daytime bus and I couldn't sleep. All the way home she talked about Frank. I sat there catatonic.

Chapter Thirteen

Every day I dreamt about going back to New York. The following summer I did, this time by myself. My mother didn't object. Frank would take care of me. It was 1965, Frank and Jay were living in a six-flight walkup studio apartment.

I took a taxi from the bus terminal. I loved telling the driver, "Perry Street. Greenwich Village, please." I rang the bell, and Frank ran down to help me with my suitcase. He was happy to see me. I was feeling so many things all at once. I wanted to hug him, but I couldn't do it. In our family, we don't touch.

Climbing the stairs up to his apartment, I wondered who lived behind each door. A strong smell of incense filled the third-floor hall. It was so quiet. We didn't see anyone, but I could hear music playing softly from behind one of the doors.

Jay was sleeping on the bed in an alcove and didn't wake up when we entered, or he was pretending to be asleep. Frank, not whispering, introduced me to the four tiny dogs.

"These are the Papillons. *Papillon* means 'butterfly' in French. This is our first dog, Wings, Golden Wings of Elbenard. Isn't she a beauty? This one is Peter de Gebelin, we got him from a breeder when he was eight. He was champion at Westminster in 1955. Lilibet, she's the crazy one, named after

Queen Elizabeth. That's the queen's nickname. She couldn't pronounce 'Elizabeth' when she was a little girl. She called herself 'Lilibet.' And this is Sunday Punch, we call him Punin. He weighs only two and a half pounds. He's eleven. Not too bad for an old dog. Peter and Wings are Lilibet's parents. I want to get more dogs. I love having them."

"Chili and rice!" Frank announced, holding up two cans in the air. "Armor Star, it's the best brand you can buy. Other days, we have rice and chili. Or chili and rice and cheese, or rice and beans and chili. Or cheese and rice and beans or cheese and rice and chili without beans. On extravagant days we chop up an onion and some ground beef with it. Now that's a real treat. But today is really special because you're here. We have . . . sour cream!

"We're saving our money to buy real estate. If you don't buy a house, then you'll spend all your money on rent and you'll just be a slave to the landlord. Are you hungry? I hope you like chili."

"I'm starving. I'll eat anything." I was so hungry, the Papillons were starting to look good.

Frank handed me a large bowl of chili. I remembered the same blue-and-white tin plates from Canal Street. Jay got up to join us. "How was your journey on the bus to Emerald City, my dear?" he said, wiping his eyes with the palms of his long-fingered hands.

I felt uncomfortable near Jay. He towered over me and I had to stand back to look up at him so my neck wouldn't hurt. I looked down at his feet. He was wearing yellow Moroccan slippers with pointy toes that curled up.

"The bus ride was long and boring, but I'm here."

"What are your plans, while you're in New York?" Jay asked. "We want to invite you on Sunday to see a performance of our dear friend, Paul Swan. Paul has his own dance company, choreographs all his own work at his own theater. He makes all these fantastic, very elaborate costumes. He's an original, a true artist. You will love him. You must come with us."

"Sunday?" I said. "You mean tomorrow?"

"Sunday? Is that tomorrow? Oh, time is such a mystery. One day into the next, and then you're gone. Whenever you go to open a window, you should put one foot in front of the other, keeping your mind focused on every step. Approach the window with gentle anticipation and raise the glass very, very slowly with both hands, as slowly as you possibly can. Never, never exert force. Breathe through your nose and take your time with everything you do. This is how you will live to be one hundred."

Yes, Jay.

I didn't want to go to a dance recital on my first day in New York, but I was their guest and I wanted Jay to like me. Frank said he would take me out for a walk around the neighborhood after lunch. I put my suitcase on the cot they'd set up for me near the window next to the fireplace.

The Village was like a friendly hometown neighborhood. People stopped and asked about the dogs and Jay, whom they always referred to as Mr. Maxwell. They had long conversations with great details about their problems. Frank knew so many people here. When they walked away he'd fill me in on the story.

"Oh, he just got out of the mental hospital for having a nervous breakdown after his girlfriend had an abortion without telling him. He thinks he's a writer, but he's just stoned all the time. He asked me to read his cards once, but he never showed up for the reading. He doesn't want to know the truth. He's a mess."

A man with long red hair walking an Afghan dog stopped us. "Oh, Frank, I'm so glad I ran into you, I met this new girl. Do you have any feelings about her? Is there anything you see I should know? Does she know how I feel about her? Frank, what can you tell me? I have to know. I have to be careful. Remember what happened when the last one left me. Frank?"

Frank didn't stop for him, we kept right on walking, "It's nice to see you, take care. Bye."

Frank leaned over and whispered to me, "You have to protect yourself from some of these people or they'll destroy you. You can't help everybody. You can't answer every question they have wherever they want it. Be polite and tell them you're busy. Sooner or later something or someone else will get their attention."

We turned onto Hudson Street, a wide street filled with secondhand furniture stores selling oak tables and chairs and stained-glass windows that were lined up on the sidewalks in front of the shops. I never saw so many antique shops before. There were cafes with outdoor tables where people sat all day, grocery stores with wicker baskets filled with fruit and vegetables and fresh breads without paper wrapped around them. We didn't have anything like this in Buffalo. We shopped at the A&P and Tops, big supermarkets. Frank showed me the White Horse Tavern, where Dylan Thomas and the Beat poets hung out. Hudson Street was exciting and alive.

"That old lady in that ratty fur coat coming toward us is out of her mind.

Don't stop if she starts talking to you. She owns an antique shop on Bleecker Street and if you let her, she'll go on all day about her aches and pains. Cross the street when you see her coming. Hello, how are you today, Miss Browning?"

"Oh Frank dear, please tell Mr. Maxwell to come see me today. I have some very rare Royal Crown Derby plates and tea cups I want him to see. They just came in and they'll be gone quickly. Tell him he better come soon."

"Did I tell you about the woman I read for the other day?" he said to me. "Listen to this, it's so amazing. It was the first time we met. The minute she walked in, I was overwhelmed by the sadness I felt in her, even though she acted cheerful. Before she sat down, I said to her, 'There's a woman with long curly hair that walked in with you. I can see her standing right next to you. I see her—she's engulfed in flames. She says her name is Emily.'

"The woman burst into tears. She told me that her sister was just killed in a fire. I saw her face. She was looking right at me, smiling, and she wanted me to tell her sister that she was at peace."

Frank pointed to the places he shopped and the buildings where famous writers and actors lived.

"See that Japanese girl coming toward us . . . she pretends she's an actress. Her boyfriend is a big official at City Hall. He's married," Frank whispered. "She does nothing but sit in her apartment all day and wait, just to see him for a few hours a couple times a week. I read for her three times. She always picks the same cards, the Tower and the Devil. And almost every other card is a sword. The Devil is almost always an indication of a liar or someone who's obsessed or controlled by something. She just won't give him up. She suffering, but she'll never change. She's a masochist."

What's a masochist? I really didn't want to know.

We hurried along. Everyone seemed to love Frank. They'd sparkle when they saw him coming. He was gracious even when he didn't stop to talk.

A scruffy, short, bearded man walking a sheep dog passed us. He said a quiet hello, keeping his head bent low as he walked along. He was wearing a raggedy straw hat, love beads and jeans.

"Hello," Frank said, as the man passed without making eye contact. "Watch him, watch what he does. See how he keeps looking around to see if anyone's following him? He's an undercover cop involved in something serious, but he won't say what. The hippie clothes are a disguise. He's always checking under his car for bombs. We talk, once in a while. I told him I'm a psychic and he asked me if he'll be killed. I said he wouldn't, but it might get close. He told me his real name. He's Italian. Keeps to himself, seems lonely, doesn't have any friends. I told him, 'One day, they'll make a movie about you.'"

In the morning, Jay and Frank took me to Sutter's Bakery a couple of blocks from their house. We got fresh croissants and brioches. And cappuccino, a little dream in a cup, which—so hard to imagine now—I'd never even heard of. Up until then my breakfast had been a miniature box of cereal. Then we headed uptown to the recital.

"Now you mustn't laugh," Jay instructed me as we stood outside the building where Paul Swan's studio was. "Whatever you do, don't laugh. He is very serious about his art. He lives to dance."

Paul Swan was no swan. He was an old man of about eighty-five with crusty, dirty feet and his scalp was blackened to hide his baldness. His hands had brown makeup between his fingers to make them look longer. He pranced out from behind a bed sheet strung up on a clothesline in his studio costumed in strips of chiffon held together with large safety pins that he made no effort to conceal . . . or anything else beneath his makeshift toga. Shuffling his feet from one side of the floor to the other, he threw his arms up in the air in a dramatic pose, then he'd scurry to the other side of the room and do the same thing to the other wall. He'd stand still in each pose for several minutes, focusing into space.

Covering the walls were photographs and paintings of a young handsome Rudolph Valentino look-alike, which I assumed was our Swan. Many were large nude portraits of a young man in his prime. I looked around at the five other people in the audience and noticed that Frank was having a hard time staying awake, while Jay was enchanted by every move the dying swan made. *What was my brother doing here?*

Jay leaned into me and whispered, "His flautist is a student from the Juilliard School of Music."

The music had nothing to do with the dance. If a flute could sound like a jackhammer, that was what this music sounded like. The Swan seemed irritated and kept looking at his accompanist with disapproving eyes.

"All I can hear is that goddamn music! I can't concentrate on what I'm doing!" he yelled in anguish at the student. No one moved a muscle, except Frank, who suddenly woke up.

A skinny man wearing glasses and a spiky flaxen wig stood in the back of the room laughing.

"Did you get that? That was sooo . . . great," he droned to the man next to him, who was filming everything with a movie camera.

"Thank you, Mr. Swan. You're fabulous. Thank you. Isn't he fabulous?" He said, as he headed for the door.

The dancer was furious and refused to continue. Jay and Frank jumped up and started to applaud wildly. "Bravo! Bravo!" The dancer quickly forgot about the rude interruption and the flute player, and took a long, grand bow. I joined in the clapping, happy it was over, after more than three hours.

We left the studio and walked down Broadway toward home. The New York City air and traffic noise were heavenly. Jay told me that Paul Swan danced with Isadora Duncan, the mother of modern dance. I knew who she was from my dancing school days and had something to talk to Jay about.

"Who was that guy with the movie camera? How disrespectful. How could he laugh at Paul? He's a genius, a brilliant artist! The end of an era!" Frank said, dramatically, imitating the Swan's dance movements on the street.

"Now, Frank, have some respect. Don't make fun of Paul. He's very courageous and he's keeping an art form alive. That man with the camera was Andy Warhol; he calls himself a painter and a filmmaker. He always has a group of people around him. They have these parties that go on for days. I don't get what all the fuss is about," Jay said. "Warhol is rude and arrogant."

I was exhausted running along to keep pace with Mr. Maxwell's long stride, but I was too shy to say slow down. Frank and Jay looked very funny together. Jay, at six-feet-four, towered over Frank's five-foot-five.

"Now, come along, Franklin Pangborn. We've got to get downtown to take the dogs out. What did you think of the recital, Terry?" Jay asked.

"Ummm, it was interesting, Jay. How old is Mr. Swan? Did he really know Isadora Duncan?"

That night I was unable to sleep. The cot was only about twelve feet from the bed Frank and Jay were sleeping in and I could hear them both snoring. I stayed awake watching the people in the building across the street. A woman in a slip paced the floor, she'd stop to cool herself in front of an electric fan, her hair blowing back off her shoulders. In another window, a man slept on a couch with a cat in his arms. All night I made up stories about these people and stayed awake listening to the sounds of talking and laughing coming from the street below.

Suddenly in the darkness I heard someone at the door. The locks were turning and I could hear keys jingling, then the light from the hall sliced into the dark apartment. A man stood in the center of the room three feet from my bed.

"Norvin! Is that you?" Frank called out.

"Did I wake you? I'm sorry. Go back to sleep."

"Norvin, it's three-thirty in the morning. You went to get a quart of milk. Where have you been?"

"I got the milk," he said, opening the small refrigerator, blinding me with light while he put the milk away.

"Norvin, that was three weeks ago! Were you with Jason again?"

"Frank, shush, go back to sleep."

"Norvin, my sister's here. I'm sure you're scaring her half to death. She's sleeping in your bed."

A red-whiskered man sat right down on my bed, "Why hello, miss. I'm Norvin. I'm pleased to meet you; I've heard so much about you," he said in a slow Texas drawl. He shook my hand and held it for a while, looking right at me—a beautiful smile—soft, gentle hands. His eyes were the same color as his freckles. I wasn't scared. I was wide awake and curious. How come he had keys to the apartment? Who was he?

"Well, if you don't mind, I'll just curl up on the floor right here in my sleeping bag or I'll go if you want me to."

"Norvin, don't go. Stay, we haven't seen you in so long and if you go, it might be weeks before you come back. I want to hear what you've been up to," Frank whispered loudly from the alcove.

"Go to sleep, Norvin!" Jay shouted.

I watched this beautiful stranger unfold his sleeping bag and fall so quickly to sleep. He seemed familiar to me. I was feeling something I'd never felt before or at least ever said before, that maybe I knew him from another life. I tried to imagine where. I had a sense that we would be lifelong friends.

I must have finally fallen asleep. The next thing I heard was the cranking of the coffee grinder. I got up and took my clothes to the bathroom to get dressed. I listened from behind the door to Norvin telling a story.

"So then this guy comes running into Jason's apartment with a Puerto Rican drag queen in hot pursuit. My lord was she carrying on, yelling, 'I'll kill you, I'll cut you up!' She was waving a butcher knife in one hand; with the other hand she was grabbing and trying to strangle a parrot. The parrot was clutching onto her wig for dear life and looked like it was thinking of flying off with it. The drag queen was trying to get the parrot to let go of the wig without knocking it off her head . . . well, of course she didn't want her boyfriend to see her without the wig, even when she was trying to kill him! She kept tripping over her dress and falling on the floor. The whole time, the bird was screeching, 'Alice! Alice! Alice!' The drag queen was waving that knife and screaming. 'I'll kill you, you motherfucker!'"

"Shuuuu Norvin! My sister!"

I came out from the bathroom, "Don't stop. What happened? Did she kill him? Was there lots of blood? Finish the story, please."

"Norvin, watch out for my sister. She's a Scorpio! She loves this kind of thing. Why don't you take her around today and show her the city. Do you want to go, Terry?"

"Yes, I'd love to," I said, thrilled to hang out with Norvin. This was a guy I could talk to.

· Chapter Fourteen ·

Norvin was a slow walker and so was I. He'd even stop in the middle of the sidewalk when he was engaged in a story that needed a bit of acting. His eyes were always fixed on me, like I was the only one in the world at that moment. We'd walk a few blocks and he'd say, "Oh, come on, let's go in here." We'd go into an antique shop or a thrift shop, and he'd try on a hat like Napoleon wore or he'd show me a dress he had seen last week that he thought would suit me. "Look at these old surgical tools. Imagine getting your leg cut off with this!" he'd say, flying around the shop, waving a hacksaw above his head.

Norvin seemed to have been through every shop in the Village. He laughed and talked to everyone as though he had known them all his life. He was having so much fun and he didn't want to miss anything. Time didn't matter.

I was pretty shy around Frank and Jay, but Norvin asked my thoughts on everything. I felt like I could say anything to him about myself, my brother or even about him.

"Norvin, may I ask you something?"

"Anything you want to know, dear. Ask me anything. There's nothing you can't know."

"Why does Jay call Frank Franklin Pangborn? What does that mean? Franklin Pangborn? Who is that?"

"Franklin Pangborn was an actor in the movies of the thirties and forties. He always played a sissy. He wore big round glasses and his hair was slicked down. He'd go around with his pinky in the air saying, 'Tinky-winky,' or something like that. You know what a sissy is, don't you?"

"Yes, but Frank isn't a sissy."

"No, it's affectionate for Jay to call him that. It's quite sweet really."

"So Norvin, tell me the truth. Are they, you know . . . boyfriends?"

"Yes, they love each other very much. But I think Frank still needs to find himself. He needs so much more, and Jay controls his life, but Frank needs that too. Your brother is just a little kid. Jay is grooming him for the outside world. Frank would be lost without him. Jay is devoted to him. If it wasn't for Jay, your brother would be living in a roominghouse eating corn flakes out of the box.

"Come on, follow me!" Norvin said. "First, let's get an Orange Julius and a hot dog. I'm starving."

We crossed over Avenue of the Americas and walked up Eighth Street past the record shops and used bookstores.

"The drink of the gods!" Norvin said, his red beard and mustache glistening with white foam. Orange Julius was a secret formula, a delicious orange frothy drink.

I followed him as we backtracked across Eighth Street, where we stopped in front of a building that looked like a small castle, the Jefferson Market Court House. Next to it stood a massive black brick building surrounded by a high iron fence. It looked like an old dungeon and seemed to swallow up the entire block. We stood on the sidewalk with about a dozen other people all looking up.

I listened to a voice shouting down from a small window, "Mommy! Mommy! Get me out of here! I can't take it anymore! They're beating me in here, every day! Mommy! Jesus Christ! I can't take it! Look at my eye. I can't see!"

A woman yelled from another window. "When I catch you, Rosalie. I'm gonna kill you! How could you put me in this place?"

"Come up here little white girl! I wanna show you my big black ass!"

Norvin was laughing when he said, "The Women's House of Detention.

I've been told this place is worse than hell itself. It's the mother of all jails. They got everyone all mixed up together. The blacks, the Puerto Ricans, the lesbians. Once in a while they toss a transvestite in by mistake, so they got some poor sucker who has to feel around to check for balls. Don't ever get yourself in there. A pretty little thing like you—they'll kill you. If that happens, get yourself some big butch bull dyke to take care of you."

From above, a woman starting yelling and waving her arms through the bars. "What you looking at down there? Fuck you, motherfucker. This ain't no zoo. I'm gonna kill you when I get out of here!"

Norvin told me, "Last week I saw a rich blond lady brought in here. She was cursing and spitting at the cops. Must've been a shoplifter or maybe she got caught kissing her black boyfriend. They'll arrest you for anything these days. They're just pigs getting off on it. Some of our friends were arrested last year for cruising in the subway toilets. A cop comes in and makes a pass at you and the next thing you know you're handcuffed and thrown in jail. They all got off though without having to do any time. Some crazy old queen we know who used to be a minister years ago put on his collar, grabbed a Bible and went to court pleading for mercy. The minister told the judge he'd help the boys change their ways and they let them go. The cops do that all the time to queers. Sometimes they make you suck them off and then they arrest you."

A sad voice from behind me called up to a woman in the prison. "Linda! I miss you, baby! You faithful? Don't you go with nobody in there! I love you!"

I looked at the young woman standing next to me. She had a boy's haircut and wore blue jeans, a white undershirt and heavy black boots, much too hot for summer. She was yelling up to another woman in the prison. In anguish she tried to reach her hand from her place on the ground. They were both crying. I swallowed hard and kept staring up. She covered her face in a handkerchief and sobbed.

"C'mon on, sugar, let's go to Central Park," Norvin grabbed my hand and we flew down the stairs at Sheridan Square into the subway just as the train was approaching. I knew why I loved this city. Wherever I walked there was always a train beneath my feet. A train could always make me feel better. The train that took my family to Rochester to see the lilacs in spring, the trains my father took us to watch at the Buffalo station, the train under the Christmas tree. Nobody can find me on a train. And that sound, counting each passing rail through cities where nobody knows who I am—as I'm carried by an engine that nothing can stop, with a whistle that says, "Get out of my way!"

Central Park was green and cool, children playing by the lake with toy sailboats, people relaxing on the lawn, taking in the sun. I followed Norvin past the Alice in Wonderland statue, through the mall of elm trees, around the Bethesda angel fountain, across a white porcelainlike bridge, up a hill past dark boulders to a thick wooded area called the Ramble.

"Now be quiet and follow me. Just walk along and don't stare, act like you always come here. Pretend you're a bird watcher looking for a yellow-bellied sapsucker." He laughed.

I saw some men standing alone, like Greek statues in a museum waiting to be admired. Among the bushes and shrubs were handsome young men, older men and men not so handsome. There must've been at least fifty of them slipping in and out of the woods. I didn't look up at the trees and pretend to be bird watching. I wanted to see everything. I felt a little uneasy in this forest of men, but I trusted Norvin. And it was a bright sunny afternoon.

"This is a hot pickup spot. If we're lucky we'll catch a glimpse of . . . Quick, look over there." He pointed to a small clearing. An attractive dark-haired man in a business suit was leaning against a tree. When I looked down, I could see his penis sticking straight out from his neatly pressed trousers. He stood there casually, relaxed in his own world. I was startled and very embarrassed.

Norvin whispered to me, "He's waiting for some guy to come over and suck him off. It'll happen. He's probably married. I'm sure his wife is over by the lake right now with the kids. That type is always in here. "

I was sixteen and I looked like twelve. I wondered what the men thought about me being in there. I caught the eye of one man who quickly turned away, but most of them didn't notice me. I wasn't what they were looking for. Three young men disappeared into the bushes. Two others on a bench were kissing, not caring who was watching. A man and a woman pushing a baby carriage strolled into the Ramble and quickly turned around to leave when they saw two men with their arms around each other. The birds went on chirping, the squirrels chased each other up the trees.

"How ya doing, sugar, seen enough?" Norvin seemed to find the whole thing delightful, as if he'd just shown me the pandas at the children's zoo.

"Isn't this dangerous, Norvin? Where're the cops?"

"Oh, they come around. Sometimes they have a big roundup. But some of the cops are nice and tell you to move along. Most of them don't want to go to court with this, they're too embarrassed. Do you want to go back downtown? Let's walk."

Norvin told me all about his family in Texas. How his parents abandoned the family and he, being the oldest, stayed and raised his three sisters until the last one graduated from high school. When he knew they could take care of themselves he took off and went hitchhiking all over Europe. He had just come back a few months before I met him.

In 1962 Norvin met Jay, who introduced him to Frank one day at Le Figaro Cafe on Bleecker Street. It was a rare day out for Frank, who, Norvin told me, was like a prisoner then, working day and night renovating the loft on Canal Street where they lived. Norvin said he felt that he and Frank were like brothers from the moment they met. Frank and Jay sort of adopted Norvin. He came and went as he pleased, sometimes disappearing for days or weeks. This infuriated Jay because he worried, but Frank loved it because Norvin always came back with a new adventure story.

We were walking along and I just blurted out, "Norvin? What's it like when two men have sex together?" He told me, without any shame or hesitation. I could have been asking if he liked ice cream or if it gets hot in Texas.

"Well, it's the same as when straight people have sex except you have two dicks instead of one. Hasn't anyone explained anything to you before? What else do you want to know, sugar? Ask me anything."

"What's a blow job like?"

"Here, take your thumb and put it in your mouth, like this, and move it in and out with your lips wrapped around it. That's what it feels like."

I did what he said, but I didn't think it was any big deal. There must be more to it than that.

I asked him everything about men with men, and I made him describe all the positions, how it was for him, how he knew what to do and was he ever in love. This was so much better than Bishop O'Hern's marriage class, where the nuns explained sex to us by passing around a plastic model, "The Visible Woman," pointing to the parts of the body that were reserved for our future husbands.

* * *

The day passed into night so quickly. Norvin grabbed my hand, cars and trucks racing past us, we ran recklessly across the West Side Highway to the river just below Christopher Street. Several empty trucks were parked side by side with their back doors open, men going in and out of the cavernous holes. It was dark, just a thin slice of moon in the sky. I didn't want to be there. It was getting to be too much for me, but I didn't want to say anything to Norvin. I was hoping we'd leave soon.

We watched the men look around, then hoist each other up into the trucks. Norvin explained to me what was going on.

"There're probably about fifteen or so men in there right now having sex. Nobody forces anyone to do anything they don't want to. Some guys go in just to watch. On a hot summer Saturday night there might be thirty to forty guys crammed inside. It's wild. The danger is, you could get caught—but that's part of the thrill. They take turns watching for the cops. The cops know what's going on here. I've seen them go inside the trucks and stay there for a while—in full uniform too."

We walked a few blocks down the highway to an abandoned shipping dock. At one time ocean liners anchored here. Most of the windows had been knocked out and seagulls made nests in the rafters. The foundation had huge holes where I could see the water below. I could hear the pier creaking as it moved with the current. I didn't realize there were people in there until a tanker passed and abruptly illuminated it all.

Men were everywhere, up in the broken window frames, in the rafters, sitting on piles of wood. Worrying about falling through the holes in the floor or being arrested, I started to panic. There were two men having sex a few feet from me, one man was on his knees in front of the other.

Back in a corner, I could see a faint outline of a man bent over an oil drum, his pants were on the ground around his ankles. I moved away toward the door as a group of men started pulling each others' clothes off. Norvin took my hand and led me out of there.

The next thing I knew, I was following Norvin into a bar across the street from my brother's apartment. It was dark except for a few red lights and the glimmer from the jukebox playing country & western music. Painted on the window: INTERNATIONAL STUD. Norvin explained that it was an S&M bar.

"Sadomasochism. I'll tell you about that later."

The place was packed with men, wall-to-wall black leather and sweat. Norvin led me through the crowd to a small room in the back. It was smoky and I couldn't breathe. At four-feet-eleven, my nose was level to the men's armpits, and those hairy trees were very ripe. I caught a glimpse of a man—naked except for his boots. He was blindfolded and tied to a chair. Suddenly a man started yelling, "Hey you, little girl! Who brought you in here? You gotta go!"

I guess it was the owner or the bartender who wanted me out of there and out right now. I wanted to stay and see what was going to happen, but Norvin grabbed me and we went across the street to the apartment.

Out of breath from climbing the stairs, Norvin and I fell into the room, sweaty, thirsty and smelling like New York City's docks and bars. Frank and Jay asked about our day, "Did you have a good time? What have you two been up to?"

I went to the bathroom and heard Norvin say, "Oh, the Jackson Pollock show at the Whitney was amazing. Let's see . . . we went to Central Park, had blintzes in the East Village, went to the top of the Empire State Building, Times Square, the Statue of Liberty. I'm exhausted. We've been all over the city."

That night, before I fell asleep, I wondered how I could go back to Buffalo, put on my school uniform, sit at my desk and be who I used to be before I came here. In the morning, I told Frank I wanted to go for a walk by myself. He agreed I should explore the Village on my own.

"Make sure you come back by five. I want to take you to meet Rolla."

I was looking forward to meeting Rolla. She had autographed her book for me. The book I'd been using to teach myself the Tarot. Frank told me that she was a real English witch.

. . .

Alone for the first time in New York, I felt free. I wondered about how I fit into what I had seen the night before. I sat on a bench in Washington Square Park, watching people and thinking about how everybody has a story. And everybody makes that story whatever they want it to be. We're all going to die one day and be replaced by somebody else. Me too. One day, I won't exist anymore. All the years I'd longed for that because I was so unhappy, now I wanted to make an adventure of my life, I wanted to find my own way. I could do that here.

. . .

That evening, Frank, Jay, Norvin and I went uptown to West Seventy-second Street to Rolla's for dinner. I could smell roast turkey from outside her apartment door. I'd never had roast turkey in the summer.

I couldn't tell how old Rolla was; her white hair was pulled back in a bun and she had a sly, sweet smile and soft glowing skin. Her piercing blue eyes looked right through you. What could she see about me? I was dying to know. I tried to keep my thoughts clear. I was nervous and immediately started counting.

Rolla reached out and took my hand and held it for a while. I felt calm and welcomed. "My dear, how delightful to finally meet you. Having an adventure in the city, are we?"

I pulled my hand back. Could she know about last night? Could she really read my mind? Does she know what I'm thinking right now?

Rolla was exactly what I imagined a real witch would be like, a good witch, that is. She was plump and kind and spoke with an English accent. She had two Persian cats that took turns sitting on her lap and staring at us. Her apartment had lots of fresh flowers, a big fluffy sofa and English antiques. She told us a story about her father.

"When he was a young man, he taught himself magic from books he found in the attic of an old church. A new moon ritual required a piece of pure silver. To make sure of its success, he took every piece of silver from the house: the candelabras, the tea service, forks, knives, spoons, even my grandmother's silver comb and hair brush. He wrapped up everything in a tablecloth. At midnight he went to the edge of a cliff and pleaded to the moon to grant his wish. And with one grand swoop, he shook the bundle out and all the silver went tumbling down the rocks to the sea.

"The next morning, my grandfather asked him if he had taken the silver. He said he had, but he didn't dare say why. He was beaten, called a thief and banished from the house. My father, distraught, set off into the woods. He had been walking for hours and was cold. Suddenly, out of the pitch dark, two enormous white horses appeared pulling a carriage. The door opened, a man inside the coach said to him, 'So there you are. I heard you calling me. I've been looking for you. Get in!' You see, the moon granted his wish. He had asked for a teacher of magic, that man in the coach was the High Priest of Abingdon coven."

Norvin started laughing uncontrollably. He laughed so hard he slid off the couch. I don't think he believed Rolla's story. Rolla jumped up, sending the cat flying off her lap, and stomped off into the kitchen.

I was thrilled to be there listening to these stories. I didn't care whether they were real or not. Jay told us that he was being pursued to join a coven of witches formed by a zodiac circle. They needed a Taurus, which he was. They felt he had just the right power to complete the group, but he declined.

Frank told Norvin to behave himself and go help Rolla in the kitchen. When Rolla bent down to take the turkey out of the oven, Norvin leaned over her and said in a loud witch's cackle, "Would you like to see my oven little girl?"

Rolla was so mad, she bumped her head on the stove when she stood up, which made Norvin laugh ever harder.

"Get out of my house, you devil!"

"I'd be delighted, you crazy old coot." And he walked out the door.

We went on with the meal as if nothing had happened. At the end of dinner, Rolla closed her eyes for a few minutes. I thought she fell asleep, "I wish I had some chocolates," she said as she opened her eyes.

Ten minutes later her doorbell rang. She answered. Standing in the doorway was a man in a delivery uniform. She signed and came back to the table carrying a box.

"Oh look! A candygram from dear Madeline. How thoughtful of her. Here Frank, pass it around, would you dear?"

How did she do that?

We each took a piece of candy as Rolla told a story about Madeline, another witch, living in England.

Chapter Fifteen

My school days were finally over in June 1966. I finished my exams without putting much effort into them, and graduated—barely. I tore my school uniform to shreds, said good-bye to the nuns and my friends and never looked back. Truthfully, I was really scared, I didn't know what I was going to do next.

After sitting on the porch all summer waiting for something to happen, I came to the realization that I had to get a job. I needed money to get to New York. I fantasized about being a newspaper reporter, but I didn't have any skills or confidence. Choices were scarce: the Trico windshield wiper factory, supermarket checkout, department store sales clerk. Hens & Kelly department store was hiring. The woman who interviewed me liked me. She said she had the perfect job for me—selling gift certificates. I sat at a little desk in front of a row of elevators. Even though I wasn't the information booth, shopper after shopper stopped to ask me what floor was such and such on.

"Miss, what floor—sheets and towels? Bras and girdles? Honey, where's the furniture? Ladies' room please, where's the ladies' room?" All day, people would shout questions at me. A woman approached me and before she said a word, I shouted at her, "Third floor, ladies' dresses, in the back!" I tried it again on a man, "Toys on two!" I said with great self assurance. He was dumbfounded.

Sometimes I'd get angry because they'd think it was no big deal, I was supposed to know exactly what they wanted and what floor they were going to. But often enough I'd hear, "How did you know what I was going to ask you? What made you say that? How did you know that's what I was looking for?"

I hardly sold a gift certificate. Instead, I told them the perfect gift to buy. I got very skilled at predicting their needs. And doing this helped me keep my mind away from the torture of counting the ping, ping, pings of the opening and closing elevator doors. By then it was the holiday season and shoppers arrived in droves. Everyone was in a hurry, screaming questions at me all at the same time. My eyes and mind blurred, moving quickly from one shopper to another. Between the elevator pings, the bombardment of questions and the repetitive Christmas music, sensory overload jostled my brain into immediate focus. I could go straight into the mind of each person.

"You'll find your husband's robe on the fourth floor. And don't ask me how I know." Santa's Workshop? *Deck the halls with boughs of* . . . "You were going for the casserole dish weren't you? You won't find it in this store." . . . *Maids a milking* . . . "She doesn't want another robe. Perfume, get her perfume. That's what she really wants." Gift wrapping? *You better not pout* . . . "He has enough sweaters—hated the purple one you got him last year." Where are scarves? Men's gloves? "Your sizes are all wrong, you didn't bother to ask." How did you know that? *Five golden rings!* "Don't tell me . . . you really do want a gift certificate."

I went to the personnel office begging for a different job. The only opening they had was for a file clerk. They sent me to a tiny room with no windows and five older women typing customers' bills on huge, noisy machines. My job was to collect the charge slips from the pneumatic tubes that came up from the selling floors and file them in the appropriate alphabetized accounts. Tedious and boring, but I had a job, and a goal. I was making $1.15 an hour.

One day, instead of just filing the sales slips away, I started reading the accounts. There were heart-wrenching letters in the files explaining why the monthly bill hadn't been paid. "Please Sir, I'm sorry I'm unable to make a payment. My husband walked out on us, ran off with my neighbor's daughter. I have no money, the baby is sick and I'm pregnant again."

Nobody checked these files and I was the last one to read the bills. I felt sorry for these people, I ripped up the charge slips and threw them away. There were so many hard-luck stories, my heart broke every time I read one. I had to do something to help. Slip after slip went into the trash. This was long before computers; everything was handwritten on a piece of paper. A few times a customer called the store questioning why their new refrigerator or bedroom set didn't appear on the bill. Was there some mistake? I'd send them a corrected bill.

I worked there for almost two years and saved every paycheck, following Jay Maxwell's advice that money would set me free. I think I helped a little to set Hens & Kelly free too—they sold the store a few years after I left.

In 1967, the Summer of Love, Golightly and I were still friends after high school and we wanted to be part of the hippie scene we were hearing about. There were two bars right next to each other on Franklin Street, Laughlin's and the Tudor Lounge. They were always filled with a mix of bohemians, college students, political radicals, bikers, artists, hippies and drunks.

Laughlin's and the Tudor were walking distance from my job at the department store and I went almost every night and on weekends. Even though it was a bar, I didn't really drink a lot there. I went to be with people I could talk to. If someone looked interesting or maybe even looked like a person I'd never speak to, then that would be the person I'd want to meet. I began to question and think, to voice opinions, learning about a bigger world than the one I knew.

Almost every night, and often until closing time at four in the morning, we sat and talked—about the horrors of the Vietnam War, foreign films, poetry, the difference between love and relationship, while the jukebox played. Jefferson Airplane, the Beatles, Janis Joplin, Bob Dylan, the Doors, the Grateful Dead, Jimi Hendrix, soul music.

It was hard to talk to Rosemary, we were living such different lives. She was getting serious with Bob, a boyfriend who surprised her with a diamond engagement ring hidden inside a bag of peanuts. Rosemary and her friends were all planning weddings: the dress, the cake, the honeymoon. When she asked me to be the maid of honor at her wedding, I recoiled like Dracula being forced into the sunlight. High school ruined my belief in the Church. Too many restrictions, judgments, guilt and sins. I swore I'd never set foot inside it again.

One Saturday night at the Tudor, I was sitting with some people, when in walked someone I recognized from a long time ago. Handsome, confident and walking right up to me—my sister's ex-boyfriend, Neal Elliott.

"I always thought about you, wondering how you were. How's your sister?"

"Getting married!" I said, overenthusiastically.

He pulled up a chair and we talked all night. The last time I saw Neal I was a young girl standing on the porch watching my sister ride off with him on his motorcycle. Now he was telling me he had a three-year-old son and was married to the woman he'd had the baby with, but they no longer lived together.

Unlike other guys I'd met, Neal didn't just talk about himself. He wanted to know what I was thinking, what my interests were. He was fascinated by everything I said: my visions, what I thought was going to happen in the world, why I liked the things I liked, what I wanted to do with my life. I told him everything. We stayed in the bar until closing time, went to a diner for breakfast and then he drove me home.

I didn't dare tell Rosemary I was interested in her ex-boyfriend. Especially this one, the wild one, who was still married. I'm sure she knew, or at least that I was up to something. You can't hide much in my family, but I learned early on I could take part of the real story and mix it up with something else, confusing the issue a little bit so if they picked up something psychically I could say they were sort of on the right track. Or if I had to, I'd convince them into believing that it was something they were seeing that was going to happen in the future. They'd be happy with that.

I couldn't wait to tell Golightly about my night with Neal. I called her and told her to meet me at the Balcony, another secret spot. In a downtown department store called AM&A's, there was a small balcony above the main floor where you could sit, rest and watch customers shop. She met me there that afternoon. Although I'd been up all night, I wasn't the least bit tired. I was too excited.

"Golightly, guess who I was out with all night?" I told her everything. "We talked about New York. He was just there a few weeks ago. Neal is the coolest. You know, he wants to . . ." As I was talking I saw a woman slip a bottle of perfume into her coat pocket.

"There's something I have to tell you, Melon. I met someone. I really like him—a lot. I'm getting married. In August."

I heard exactly what she said. And then I couldn't hear anything. I could see her mouth moving. Her face changing in slow motion. I slipped into a dark hole—then it all started going so fast. I crashed into a black wall. The sound of her voice bounced against the wall and reverberated inside me.

"We'll be moving to an air force base as soon as he gets transferred."

From the hole I riveted my eyes only on the shoplifter. "What did you say?" I said with my voice. *Why are you stealing the perfume? You know you have cancer and you're not going to do anything about it. Why?* "You're getting married to who? How come I never heard of him?" *I'm sorry, I'm really sorry your mother was killed in that accident. You're not thinking clearly. It's only been two months.* "What do you mean he's in the air force?" *She's leaving the store. Don't leave yet! I think I can help you.* "You're marrying someone in the military?"

"He's a great guy. I didn't know how to tell you. I knew you'd be upset."

I was frantic to find someone else in the store to focus on. But I was so confused, I couldn't get inside anyone. I tried, but no one would let me in. I started to panic, and I could hear my voice say, "What about New York? I thought we were going to move to New York together. I can't believe this. I got to go. I got to go home."

I ran down the stairs to the main floor and pushed my way through the shoppers. I ran down the street looking for the shoplifter, trying to block out what I was hearing. First Rosemary and now Golightly.

.   .   .

That weekend I met Neal and he asked me if I was ready to change my life forever. "Are you kidding? Just tell me what I have to do. I'm ready." He picked me up and we drove to an old Victorian house to meet a friend of his. On the couch in the living room he showed me a little orange pill.

"This is LSD, acid—Orange Sunshine. Do you want to do it? It's going to last about twelve hours, maybe more, but the most important thing is to try to remember you're on a drug, and it will eventually wear off. No matter how much you might think that it's your mind, remember, it will wear off."

I didn't even think about it. I just popped it in. Nothing seemed to happen for a long time. I could hear music . . . way in the back of my head. I heard every single word, every note. Then the singing voice separated from the music. I was amazed to see the voice floating in the air by itself. It bounced off the walls and appeared right in front of my face. I was singing along, reading the words in the air when suddenly the flowers on the couch swallowed me up.

Ooooo, this is nice . . . I'm falling backward . . . deeper . . . . so soft, oooo. These are all feathers. Oh, that's my arm reaching up . . . my finger tracing this giant spiral of silver wire. Round and round in big circles. Oh! I'm inside the couch! Get me out of here! Wheeeee . . . . I bounce right up. I'm back. Wait a minute. That's a lion, isn't it?

Right there . . . in that doorway. Be quiet. I think he's coming over here. Oh boy. Are you going to jump up? Here then, sit next to me. Let me pet you. How come you're so tiny?

The lion was telling me about a secret cave in the middle of my palm. All I had to do was follow the life line to the mound of Venus . . .

"Hello, hello, Terry, are you all right? Are you with us? Are you ready to go?" Neal came to get me and we left.

The car turned into the Wild Mouse ride from the amusement park. I gripped the dashboard as we bounced along on the rubber track. Driving on the Skyway through the blood-orange clouds of the Lackawanna Steel Mill, its fiery black smoke stacks against a lemon Jell-O sky; an Arabian cartoon landscape. I was flying! And I couldn't stop laughing. When I moved my hands, waves of rainbows poured from my fingers and bubbles popped out of my mouth when I spoke. Buffalo is really beautiful on acid.

Black turbulent water, I'm coming in. I want to be a river. No you don't. Just stand here and look at the stars. There's the constellation of the Taj Mahal. Look over there at that magnificent bird. It just tumbled . . . into a fiery tree . . . and did you see that? The tree's a butterfly. Who's that woman? I recognize that face. She's walking across the sky with the butterfly. Ah, the moon just took her away. Big Dipper, scoop me up and pour me into this beautiful river. Please, pick me up and take me. What's that I see out there? Look at that! Way out in the distance. See that? A giant paw . . . coming up out of the water . . . and now the other one. Oh my . . . it's the lion . . . out there swimming.

And then it started to wear off when the sun was rising. Neal drove me home. I tiptoed into my little girl bedroom and crawled into my twin bed. All around the room the eyes of my clown collection were watching me. My eyes were bulging out of my head and my heart was beating like I'd run around the block twenty times. I couldn't sleep. I couldn't even close my eyes.

A short while later, my mother came into my room and asked me where I'd been all night. She'd never before asked me when I was out late or didn't come home. She knew.

"Nowhere special, Mother. Just hanging out."

· Chapter Sixteen ·

In August 1968, Golightly got married. She wanted me to be in the bridal party, but I couldn't do it. She wasn't only getting married, she was leaving Buffalo right after the wedding. I sat in the last pew of the church by myself, crying like I was attending a funeral.

Rosemary and Bob set their date in early September, just one month after Golightly's wedding. I had this dreadful fear of being left behind with my parents for the rest of my life. My mother was still working at Chef's Restaurant making salads and peeling garlic. My father had lost his restaurant about six months before when the city decided they wanted to demolish the entire area to expand the New York State Thruway. He drove by every day to look at the empty lot, now a field of weeds and wildflowers. My father became the short-order cook in a new place my Uncle Bill opened on Niagara Street, The Roman Inn, a little dive on the corner with a clam stand out in front on the sidewalk. I learned how to swallow oysters there.

The time was just right for a family wedding. Maybe it would cheer us all up. And Frankie was coming home. I agreed to be Rosemary's maid of honor. I promised to behave in church, but under no circumstances would I agree to receive Holy Communion at the wedding Mass.

"Oh, come on, Terry, grow up," Rosemary said.

A couple of weeks before Bob and Rosemary got married they had to consult with the parish priest at Holy Cross Church about the sanctity of marriage and the holy vows. It was a formality that all young Catholic couples went through before the wedding to make sure they were ready for the lifetime commitment.

At the end of the sessions, the priest asked Bob and Rosemary to sign a paper stating that they understood the seriousness of the vows they were about to take. Bob signed it without reading it. Rosemary sat down and read every single word.

When she was finished, she said, "Bob, I'm not signing this."

"What? Why not, Rosemary?"

"I don't want to say."

"Rosemary. Sign the paper!"

"No! It says here in this paragraph that I must denounce the occult and all fortune-tellers. I can't do that. I'm not going to sign this. I can't sign this. I will not sign this! So, I guess we can't get married."

"Rosemary, just sign the paper," Bob said, through his teeth.

"No!"

The priest asked her why she wouldn't sign the paper. She told him straight out that she believed that some people could see the future and that there was a lot to learn from other philosophies besides Catholicism. She didn't want to elaborate about herself or her family right there in the rectory.

The priest got quiet for a moment and Rosemary prepared herself for a lecture and a big fight.

"I want to show you something," the priest said, taking a sheet of paper out from under his desk blotter. "Here, look at this." He handed her the paper. "I went to an astrologer not too long ago; this is my horoscope. Can you tell me, Rosemary, what do you think of my chart?"

She looked over the chart and told him what she thought. They talked about metaphysics, astrology and why the church has a problem with it. Bob was a little uncomfortable, but if it got Rosemary to sign the paper, he didn't care.

After all that, Rosemary still wouldn't sign the paper. The priest said, "Don't worry about it. You can get married anyway." He gave her seven Mercury dimes to carry with her on the wedding day and a warm hug goodbye. They looked at each other acknowledging some part of themselves they knew they shared. This was going to be their secret.

The day before the wedding, Rosemary kept to herself. She wasn't talking very much and snapped at everyone who asked her what was wrong.

"What the hell's wrong with you, Rosemary? You got that puss on all day?"

"Shut up, Mother! Leave me the hell alone. Don't ask me anything!" Rosemary slammed the door to her room.

"Who wants to go to Ted's for a foot long?" my father said, trying to find a solution.

I asked Frank, "What do you think is wrong with her? Do you think she had a premonition and she doesn't want to say?"

"I have no idea."

"What do you mean, you don't know? We're all psychic in this family. How come we don't know?"

"You know Rosemary can tune us all out if she wants to. She can put up a block that no one can penetrate. How do you think she does that?"

"I wish I knew. I wish I knew what was upsetting her."

"I'm sure Mother knows."

              · · ·

Frank had come home the day before and was trying to warm things up around the house with his stories from New York City. He and Jay had bought a house in Little Italy and were renovating it while they still lived in the studio apartment on Perry Street. He showed us photographs.

"Frank, started any fires lately?" I said.

"Cut it out. What did I know? I never owned a house before. How was I supposed to know you have to check the fireplace to see if it's usable before you make a fire. You should've seen that fire I had going. It was fantastic! So, I almost burned the house down. But it's looking good now. We work on it whenever we can. Norvin is camping out on the first floor to keep an eye on it. We plan to rent it until we can afford to live there. If you come, you can live on the top floor."

"Frank, there are six papillons in this picture. Don't you have enough dogs?" I said.

I looked up and saw Rosemary crying and banging her fists on the dining room table.

"What's the matter with you? What the hell are you doing?" Mother said.

"Rosemary, are you all right? Why don't you tell us what's wrong?" Frank tried to comfort her.

"I don't want to get married. I'm not going to do it. I'm not going through with this."

"Hooray!" I yelled out, thrilled there wasn't going to be a wedding.

Mother started yelling, "What the hell are you talking about? Everyone will be there tomorrow. What's everyone gonna say if you don't show up? I'm sorry! You just forget about it! Stop crying! You're gonna go whether you like it or not!"

"Get Bob on the phone and talk to him about it," Frank said.

"I can't talk to him. I can't tell him I don't want to get married."

"You have to. Should I call him and tell him to come over?" Frank said.

"Stay out of it, Frankie!" Mother screamed. "Don't you dare call Bob! We're going to Holy Cross Church and she's getting married!"

"Drop dead! Leave me alone!" Rosemary slammed her door . . . again. She called Bob on the phone and he came right over.

"Why are you doing this, Rosemary? Talk to me. Why did you change your mind? If you don't want to marry me, well fine, just tell me what you want. If you want me to go, I'll go and I'll never see you again."

Rosemary screamed back, "I don't want to marry you. That's all!"

"I'll be at the church tomorrow. If you don't come . . ." He walked out the door and out of the house.

I came out of my room. Mother was standing, staring out the living room window. Andy was sitting outside on the porch.

Rosemary's crystal-beaded wedding dress hung on the front of the china cabinet like an old ghost from one of our childhood seances. Frank and I looked at each other. Without saying, we both knew in that moment that we were different—and more alike than ever. We went out to sit with Andy and talked about the neighborhood, how things were changing. Mother sat alone smoking at the kitchen table. Rosemary wouldn't come out of her room.

In the morning we weren't sure whether there was going to be a wedding or not. I woke up to Andy's pink plastic radio on the kitchen table yelling "This is WKBW Buffalo, New York radio! Home of the Bills! Good morning, sunshine!"

Hey Jude don't be afraid. Take a sad song and make it better . . .

Mother put on her pale champagne silk dress and matching shoes. She had her hair freshly dyed for the wedding, "Stigmata Red." She was striking and powerful all dressed up—the mother of the bride. Andy was so handsome in his classic black tuxedo. My mother made him soak in the bathtub the night before so he wouldn't smell like a fish fry at his daughter's wedding. Frank adjusted his father's bow tie. We all got ready, just like nothing had happened the night before.

"Andy, can you still part your hair without touching your head?" Frankie asked him.

"You remember that?" Andy laughed.

We could hear Rosemary talking on the phone to one of her girlfriends. We didn't dare ask what she wanted to do. We just waited to see if she was going to come out of her room.

Mother asked sweetly, "Frankie, zip up my dress for me, will you please?"

I came out of my room and stood in front of the piano, knowing exactly how a parakeet perched on a swing in a cage feels. Swimming-pool blue from head to toe, pill box hat, veil and gloves. I'd rather die than be seen like this. It was only a dress, but it had such power over me. I wore my cowboy boots under my gown hoping nobody would notice.

"You summa na bitch! You're not wearing those boots! Take them off right now! What's wrong with her? She's crazy! *Ubatz!*" my mother screamed.

I changed the cowboy into a fairy princess and wore the high-heeled blue shoes. Rosemary finally emerged, wearing her glorious wedding gown, fragile and luminous.

"Rosemary, you look beautiful," Frank said. "Are you sure you want to do this? Are you sure you want to get married? If you want to go to New York and think about this, there's time to postpone everything, if you're not ready. You can stay with Jay and me till you're really sure you want to marry Bob. I can go to the church and tell everyone that there's been a slight change in the program. We can still have the party. What do you want to do?"

"Rosemary, just go to the airport in your dress. Get on a plane and go to New York. You've got some money in the bank. You can get a job there. This is your chance!" I was trying to be helpful and hoping for the excitement. I thought it would be so cool if she didn't show up for her wedding. What a drama for Buffalo!

Mother started screaming, "The hell with all of you! She has to go! Everybody's in the church already! What the hell is wrong with all of you? ROSEMARY!"

Rosemary didn't say anything. She carried her veil in one arm and walked out of the house. We all followed her into the limousine that was waiting for us in front of our house. It drove down Seventh Street and around the corner, then four blocks to the church. We could have walked.

"I'm getting married in the morning." I think Frank sang the entire score of *My Fair Lady* on that short ride to Holy Cross Church. The photographer was waiting; he lined the five of us up on the church steps for a picture. Andy and Mary were happy. Frank, the tallest in our family at five-foot-five, had long sideburns and looked dashing in his black silk suit. Rosemary smiled, and I stood there thinking how selfish I'd been not trying to help her figure out what she wanted to do.

I was the first to walk down the aisle, followed by the other blue parakeets. I could see Bob standing at the altar, smiling, looking greatly relieved that Rosemary had arrived. Bob was handsome and solid. He looked like a young Michael Caine in a spy thriller with his blond hair and black horned-rimmed glasses. German-Austrian-American, loyal, kind and straightforward, an only child, Bob went to church every Sunday and worked hard as an accountant. He was in love with Rosemary and he was about to be joined in holy matrimony to the Iacuzzos, all of us, a family of mediums, for the rest of his life.

It was the usual Catholic ceremony complete with the Mass. When the priest came to give me Holy Communion, Rosemary snapped, "No, she doesn't want it!" And he passed me by, like I wanted. When the vows were read, we all held our breath waiting for Rosemary to say, "I do."

Leaving the altar, I followed behind the newlyweds with the best man on my arm and accidentally stepped on Rosemary's long trailing veil. It made her head jerk back and she turned around, giving me a dirty look. Rice and rose petals, photos and tears. The cars drove off to the wedding hall for a party.

We danced to rock and roll, the hokey pokey and the tarantella, ate prime rib and wedding cake. I caught the bouquet and quickly gave it away to my cousin Charles. Everyone was asking Frankie about New York like it was as exotic as Tasmania. It's only five hundred miles from Buffalo.

All the Mongiovis, Bob's parents and some of the Iacuzzos, the few my mother liked, were there. And all the Italians from Seventh Street, asking, "Is

Bob Italian?" The bride and groom posed for photographs, collected wedding envelopes, then left for their Miami honeymoon.

. . .

I spent most weekends with Neal tripping on acid. We'd drive around Buffalo going nowhere, listening to music. My mind was a transistor radio attached to a kaleidoscope. I was living an endless technicolor dream. I don't know how I ever got to work on Mondays. The keypunchers at the office were starting to be concerned about me. I had big dark circles under my eyes and I came in late almost every morning.

One gray, cold November day while sitting in the car waiting for Neal, I spotted two men sitting in a car across the street. Neal had gone to buy some acid. When he came out of the house, one of the men in the car pulled out a camera and started taking pictures of us. We drove out of there in a hurry. They didn't follow us, but this made us very uneasy. We knew we had to get out of Buffalo. That night we decided to move to New York together.

I told my mother and father it was time for me to go, just to see if I liked it and I was sure I'd be back, not to worry.

"Did you call Frankie and tell him you're coming?" my mother said.

"Yeah, uh-huh," I mumbled.

"I bought the Gremlin for you. Why do you want to go there for?" Andy asked. "What are you going to do in New York?"

They didn't say much more than that. I was terrified to leave Buffalo. Maybe I was just pretending about moving to New York. I was almost hoping that my mother and father would object more, be angry about my leaving. Maybe they'd try to talk me out of going. They said nothing.

I quit the job without any notice. I had saved two thousand dollars for this day, hoping I could live on that for a long time. I hid the money in my boots and looked around my room for what I could carry away with me.

I packed a suitcase of clothes, a Mexican straw shopping bag with my favorite record albums and a round tapestry hatbox filled with a thousand tabs of acid. The taxi came to take me to the airport. I waved out the window to Andy and Mary and they waved good-bye back to me. My entire life clutched in my throat. They looked like two little children left in the house all day not knowing if their parents were ever coming home. We had changed places in that moment and my heart ached for them. I knew what they were feeling. I had stood at that window for twenty years.

Neal met me at the airport. We boarded the plane to New York. I sat in the middle between Neal and a woman in a smart suit who was going to the city on business. She stared out the window for most of the flight.

"You know, New York is the only place in the world where there is no sky," she said as she leaned into my shoulder.

"Here, take this," I said, as I handed her a little purple pill.

PART TWO

·

Mediums

Chapter One

November 12, 1968. The day I arrived in New York City. I had just turned twenty. Neal and I moved into an apartment in Crown Heights, Brooklyn. It belonged to some friend he knew in Buffalo. As soon as we got there he told me to call him Harris from now on. He wouldn't explain why. He didn't want to talk much about anything and he always seemed to be thinking about something he didn't want to discuss. In bed we'd start to make love, but then he'd stop. He said he felt like he was raping me, that I showed no feeling. I didn't. I followed him without question, doing everything he wanted to do, going where he wanted to go. I was numb. I didn't know what I was doing in Brooklyn or who I was or where Neal fit into my life. I just knew I'd left Buffalo and here I was.

Neal seemed shallow and fake. How come I didn't notice this in Buffalo? He wore the hippest clothes, he knew all the latest music, he said he wanted to be somebody, but he was all pretend. He stopped wearing his gold star that I thought was so mystical. I started to wonder if he really was Jewish. He never mentioned it again.

Neal and I were walking around Brooklyn when he started talking about astrology and dreams and even the Tarot—things I was interested in. He was repeating back to me exactly what I'd said the day before as though they were his own ideas. It was somewhere on the Promenade in Brooklyn Heights that

I looked over to the skyline of Manhattan; it was so close I could almost touch it. I decided then that I didn't want to be with Neal. We'd lasted all of six days.

I called my brother from a pay phone and asked him if I could live with him. Frank sounded happy to hear from me. "We wondered where you were and when you were going to show up. How long have you been here? Why didn't you call us?"

"Did Mother call and ask about me?" I asked.

"No, she didn't."

"Are you sure? She hasn't even called to ask if you heard from me?"

"No. What are you doing in Brooklyn? Listen, Jay and I discussed it; you can stay on the third floor of Mulberry Street. We'll talk about it when you get here. When are you coming?"

"I'll be there in an hour."

I grabbed my stuff and half of the supply of acid and left without telling Neal, who was out on one of his mysterious walks I couldn't know about. I asked someone where the subway was and got out of Brooklyn as fast as I could. The only thing on my mind was why my mother never called to see if I got to New York all right. I'm her daughter, I picked up and left without explanation, she didn't even react, never said a word. Never called to ask what happened to me. Nor had my father for that matter.

I met Frank on Perry Street and we walked across Bleecker through the Village to Little Italy. Frank carried the tapestry hatbox, unaware of its contents. He told me that he and Jay were working at a market research company and that he was doing lots of readings on the weekends. He didn't ask me anything about Brooklyn. I was relieved. I wanted to forget Neal as fast as I could.

When we reached Mulberry Street Frank started whispering, "Now, don't look . . . don't turn your head until I tell you. Not yet! Don't turn around."

I had no idea what he was talking about.

"Okay. Look now . . . across the street. Do you see the storefront window where the old men are playing cards? That's the Ravenite Social Club. It's the headquarters for the Gambino family. You know, the Mafia. Don't stare. Keep walking. If you ever have to walk by the place, just keep your eyes straight ahead. C'mon let's go in the house."

Frank and Jay always referred to the house as Mulberry Street. It was built in 1825, right across the street from St. Patrick's Old Cathedral and graveyard surrounded by a red brick wall fifteen feet high and a city-block long. The wall sagged and waved from over one hundred years of standing there. Their house used to belong to the church and had been the home to the parish's nuns. What else would I be moving into but an old convent?

Frank and Jay offered me the third floor rent free in exchange for helping out with the renovation. The house had electricity and running water and not much else. There still was a faint smell of smoke and charcoal from the fire that Frank had started.

"This house is haunted," Frank said. "I'm telling you now so you won't think you're imagining things or going crazy. I'm not kidding; we've heard babies crying in the walls. I've also seen a figure of a woman in a long dress and bonnet floating up and down the staircase. She's probably one of the nuns. You'll hear her walking the halls at night. I saw her full face once, right up close. Other people that came here told us they've seen her too, mostly on the first floor. Also, the lights don't always work. We haven't finished the wiring yet. You have to play with the switches and eventually you'll get it to work. One other thing—your stuff might get moved around by the ghosts, but don't worry, they don't steal. I think *we're* probably disturbing *them*. Welcome to Mulberry Street!"

The third floor would be my new home. There was a mint green sink lying on its side on the floor in the large empty kitchen, and no stove or refrigerator. There were holes in the walls where I could see into the next room. The walls with their broken plaster and paint looked like bizarre maps. And large chunks of the ceiling were missing.

The sun poured into the front room through two large windows that directly faced the enormous stained-glass window of the church. Patches of faded blue and silver wallpaper were peeling away. Some of it had already been removed. The razor blades and shavings were swept neatly into a corner. The floors were bare and worn down. A marble fireplace had a decorative covering; a little child, its small hands holding its chin up.

In the corner on the floor, a twin-size mattress covered in stains. A tall lamp with no shade stood in the middle of the room. There was a bathroom with a toilet and a cast-iron tub that worked. I could get water from the tub. A small skylight was in the ceiling above.

"I have to get going. Jay's meeting me in ten minutes in the Village. Norvin might be here later, but you can never be sure. His schedule is unpredictable."

"I'm really looking forward to seeing him again."

"Jay will be here tomorrow sometime in the afternoon to talk to you, so make sure you're here. Here's the keys. You're on your own. Enjoy yourself."

And he left. I listened to the staircase creaking as he walked down. I heard the front door close and I went to the window and watched him latch the iron gate and walk down the street. He turned the corner on Prince Street and was gone.

I locked the door and stood in the middle of the room for a long time in my coat and hat. I was alone in a house with nothing in it. I tried to remember that for so many years I had wished to be here, and now I was.

I looked out the window feeling numb. I was hungry and scared. A man on a roof of a tenement building opened a large cage. Letting out a flock of pigeons, he waved a long pole with a cloth tied like a flag at one end. The pigeons followed his motion and flew around in circles in the gray sky.

It was late November and beginning to get cold. It was starting to get dark and I had nothing to eat. I was afraid to go downstairs and out on the street to get some food. I didn't have a blanket and there were no curtains on the windows. The radiators were ice cold. Shaking, I pulled my arms in tight. The ill-fitting windows were old and rattled violently when the wind blew. My first night alone in New York, in a haunted empty house.

I lay down on the mattress with my clothes and shoes on and covered myself with newspapers I'd found in the kitchen. I remembered the photographs I had in my bag. I took them out and looked at them in the soft light from the street lamp. A snapshot of Mary and Andy pretending to have a snowball fight, pictures of my school friends. I felt I'd never see these people again. Now, nobody even knew where I was, except Frank.

· Chapter Two ·

Even though I grew up in a restaurant, I never learned how to cook. My father could only make food in large quantities. My mother didn't have the patience to teach us. Whenever we were in the kitchen with her she'd get annoyed, so we stayed out. Because she worked, she didn't cook that much at home, we ate canned goods and leftovers that Andy brought home from the restaurant. At least I knew how to use a can opener.

A box of Ritz crackers, two sticks of beef jerky, a can of corn and a carton of orange juice. The Puerto Rican bodega was just down the block from the house. When I got back I could hear the heat banging up through the radiators. Someone must have lit the furnace. I put the orange juice outside on the window ledge to keep cold. Finally, I was able to be in the house without my coat on.

Jay knocked on my door. "How did you enjoy your first night here? I trust you were comfortable. Isn't it a lovely house? It has so much potential." He kept on talking while he walked through the apartment looking into all the rooms. I followed right behind him. He made me so nervous, and I was convinced he came over to tell me he had changed his mind.

"Terry, Frank and I would love you to stay here on Mulberry Street. You can keep an eye on the place. Norvin is on the first floor, but he often disappears for days at a time, and we want someone to be in the house to make sure it's safe."

Jay kept his dapper camel hair coat on and repeatedly twisted his leather gloves while talking over my head, never once looking at me.

"In exchange for staying here, you can do some simple work around the house. I'll show you what to do. We can also work together on weekends."

"Of course, Jay, I'd love to help out," I said, relieved to know he wasn't asking me to leave.

"Now, Terry, I want to discuss something with you," he said as he examined a broken windowsill. "I really don't want to involve you, but your brother and I are extremely worried that we might lose this house if we can't make the payments." He paced the floor in front of me. "I want you to think about what I'm saying before you answer." Stopping perfectly still, he stood and looked right at me. "Do you have any money you can lend us? We'll pay you back with interest and we'd be deeply, deeply grateful."

Without thinking, I said, "Yes, I have two thousand dollars and I'd be happy to lend it to save the house."

"Good! When can I have it?"

"I have it right here." I went to my bag and gave him the money.

It was everything I had in the world.

"Well, I have to get going. Here's the list of the work I want you to do. I also spoke to Frank, and there's an opening at the market research company. You can start on Monday. You can work there part time and then help out here in the house too. Here's a toolbox and some gloves. Just do what you can. I've got to go now. By the way, your friend Neal came by Perry Street looking for you, and I told him you were here. He's very handsome. What's his story?"

I didn't say a word. I felt awful. I was hiding from Neal, and now I had a job that I didn't want and a list of chores I could never finish.

I read the list. Jay wanted me to go into every room of the house and scrape off seventy-five years of wallpaper with a razor blade, strip the paint off all the spindles and banisters, make sure to use the fine brushes for the crevices on the newel post so I get all the paint underneath, remove every nail, screw and tack to prepare the floors for sanding, go over every inch in every room, etc., etc., etc.

I felt like an indentured servant. I ran down the stairs and knocked on the first-floor door.

"Norvin, are you in there? Hello. Hello. Norvin? Norvin?"

I had started back up the stairs when I heard the locks turning.

"There you are!" he said "I didn't want to bother you. Welcome to the house. Do you like it here? Come on in."

Norvin's place was not much different from mine except he had a bit more furniture and some odd collectables from the garbage. There was a big bass drum, an empty birdcage and a copper-colored bicycle in the middle of the room. His rumpled bed was the main feature of the place, along with lots of books and overflowing ashtrays.

"Did I wake you? I'm sorry. I can come back later." I was so relieved to find him home.

"No, I sleep at different times during the day. I don't live by a clock. I heard Jay. Did he give you your list yet?" he said laughing, lighting up a Benson & Hedges. "Don't pay any attention to him. He gets off on playing lord of the manor. I got one of those lists too. It's right here on the bathroom wall. I do what I can around here and the house will get done one way or another. The first trick is to not let Jay get to you, and never show fear. He'll get the work out of you—he talks you into it, and you start believing it's good for you. He's amazing. Jay can work for fifteen hours without a break and he expects us to keep up with him. As Nietzsche says, 'What doesn't kill us, makes us strong.' Are you hungry? Do you want to go to Chinatown for something to eat?"

I got my hat and coat and two hits of acid. I didn't know if Norvin had ever tripped before, but I wanted to trip with him. For me, he was the Fool card in the Tarot come to life. He was free. He lived beyond limitations; a curious and fearless, ageless child, filled with desire for experience and wisdom. For Norvin, the truth changed with every moment. He held on to nothing.

"Norvin, have you ever tripped before? You know, LSD, acid?"

"Why, do you have any?"

I held out my hand. "Windowpane; it's really good," I said, like I was tempting a baby to the ledge of a building.

"Why not? I trust you. Let's do it," he said, opening his mouth.

Windowpane was LSD, absorbed into a quarter-inch square of paper-thin hardened gelatin. I placed the holy wafer on our tongues.

Just three blocks from the house is the Bowery, which continues straight into Chinatown. As we walked along, I couldn't keep from smiling, thinking, *I really live here; this is my neighborhood.* "Is the church wall really that wavy?"

A few blocks on the Bowery I looked down and stopped dead in my tracks.

"Norvin. Do I see what I think I see or am I tripping?"

"You mean, the bloody arm with all that oozing pus sticking out from that filthy carpet?"

"Stop it! Yes, I mean that arm. Thank you."

"That's real, honey, you're in Little Calcutta. Don't worry. He's too drunk to notice you. He's right where he's supposed to be. Just step over him."

I started to wonder if what I was seeing could possibly be uncountable numbers of people lying side by side on the sidewalks. Mostly men, although I did see a few women, huddled in doorways, curled up inside refrigerator boxes and old storage crates, sleeping under bedspreads and rags strung together.

We walked past some men warming their swollen hands over a fire in a garbage can, a broken chair sticking out from the flames. Sparks shot up around their bloody cracked-open faces. Norvin and I talked about the difference between them and us, and who was more free. We didn't know whether to help, ignore or accept the situation.

"Hello, Mr. Norvin, how ya doing?" I was surprised, some of the men seemed to know Norvin. He told me that once in awhile he brings one of them back to the house and gives them a shower and something to eat. He swore me to secrecy. Jay would have a fit.

The Bowery was an endless strip of wholesale restaurant-supply stores and lighting fixture shops. Store after store of industrial-sized pots and pans, stacks of porcelain dinner plates, coffee mugs, stoves, grills, freezers and all sizes of butcher, carving knives and cleavers. On the Bowery, you could buy everything you needed to operate a restaurant. I couldn't stop thinking of Andy.

Just past the kitchen supplies, the lighting stores razzle-dazzled with millions of crystal chandeliers, each one more elaborate than the other. Shivas with thousands of extended arms covered in prisms reflecting the blinding sun. The stores were packed with lamps, whirling ceiling fans, delicate porcelain figurine lamps, Tiffany glass shades and ultramodern chrome and brass fixtures. Las Vegas showgirls glowing and shimmying all around the room. LSD heaven!

"Let's go in here," Norvin said. We took one step through a door, suddenly the underworld of the Bowery, the snake pit of humanity, dissolved into a diamond palace.

In the store, a young Italian salesman in a pinstriped suit approached us. I was watching my reflection in one tiny crystal, when I noticed it had been duplicated inside every single other crystal tear drop hanging from a six-tiered glass monster in the corner of the room. How did they get my image? Who gave them my photograph?

"Hello. May I help you, sir?"

"My wife and I are looking for a chandelier to hang over our bed. We just got married, so it's got to be perfect, you know. How much is this one?" Norvin said, pointing to a massive gaudy chandelier covered with crystal fruits and vegetables, a colored-glass supermarket of grapes, cherries, tomatoes, bananas and eggplants (it was made in Italy) all strung together with green glass beads.

"What do you think, dear?"

With eyes as big as flying saucers, Norvin was admiring the young man. The salesman politely answered every one of Norvin's questions about the crystal fruit. I was laughing so hard I couldn't stay in the store another minute. I grabbed my husband's hand, yanked him out the door and we ran along the Bowery.

We tumbled down the stairs into a basement Chinese restaurant on Doyers Street. I could never eat on acid, but I loved looking at food. I swear I saw a seahorse in my soup. I followed the Chinese army up a mountain in my moo goo gai pan until Norvin plopped a large helping of rice on my plate and all the soldiers turned into cherry blossoms.

I reached over, took Norvin's soup bowl and began looking into it.

"What are you doing?"

"I'm reading your fortune."

"What does it say? Can you really read soup or do you make it up?"

"I can read anything. I tune in to the patterns in the bowl and say what I see. It's like reading a tea cup. Do you want to know what it says in your bowl, Norvin?"

Holding his bowl in my hands, I turned it around three times and from side to side to study it. It was only a bowl of soup, but to me it was Norvin's universe.

"Let me show you. See right here, under that noodle, there's a slice of pepper next to three tiny fish bones—this pattern tells me something about your future. It says you're going to have a son . . . and grandchildren. And not with *me!* I'm serious. I can see children in your soup."

"I believe you. What else is in there?"

"You're going to go back to Texas. You're never coming back. Well, you might visit once, but you won't live here anymore. Probably because of the children. That's going to be a big sacrifice for you, but I don't think you have a choice. See that piece of chicken clinging to the bottom of the bowl? That's your big heart telling you what you have to do."

He picked up the bowl and drank the rest of the soup.

"Oh my God, you just ate your grandchildren!"

"What's it say in your bowl, Terry?"

"I never read for myself. I don't want to know. Who would want to know their future? I'm just kidding. I love readings, I'd love to have one. But it's not easy to read for myself. I'm too critical. I get in my own way of seeing myself."

"Doesn't Frank read for you?"

"He's read my cards a few times. He told me that Rosemary and I would be killed in an airplane crash together. I don't believe that. But it scared me, I'll never fly in a plane with her. I think he was just trying to kill us off. Sibling rivalry.

"You have to be very careful who you let read for you. Once you're told something by someone, they have power over you. That information stays with you your whole life. It gets encoded in your mind and it can haunt you. You'll wait for it to happen. You'll look for it in your life. I used to think about this when I read for my friends in school. I could see how much power I had. They'd keep asking me what I knew about them and their boyfriends. Now, I go wherever they go because I've handed them the map. And I have to live with this."

"Wow, you are so wise, an old soul."

"Oh, come off it. I just think about these things all the time."

Norvin paid the bill and we left.

"Don't forget your fortune cookie, Norvin."

"I don't need it. I am the cookie."

Walking through Chinatown, I thought I was in another country. It was effortless to slip into another place and time. I just let go. Here in old China, through the doorways and winding streets, I looked at people and instantly seemed to know everything about them. Every person I made eye contact with took me along with them. I followed a Chinese man with a long braid and black silk pajamas into a back alley and up some stairs to a crowded opium den. I leaned against the wall in a dark room watching the amber glow from the opium pipes, as the half-dead stretched out on small cots. I could see their souls hovering a few feet from their bodies as they drew in the smoke from their long pipes.

There was a funeral for an old woman in the third-floor apartment of a tenement building on Pell Street. Her body laid out on the couch. On the wall above her head were photographs of her ancestors who went before her. I touched her hand and she opened her eyes. "Come with me," she said.

Three Chinese prostitutes in tight silk dresses stood in a doorway, one of them petting the embroidered dragon on her shiny black dress; inviting Norvin to come join them. We walked out of Chinatown down Mulberry Street watching China transform into Italy.

When we got to our house Neal was waiting for me. I grabbed Norvin's hand. I'd been dreading this.

"Hi. How are you?" I said nervously.

"Do you know him?" Norvin asked.

"This is Neal, my friend from Buffalo."

"Are you tripping? You look a little out of it."

Norvin opened the door to the house and we all stood in the hall for a few minutes.

"Are you okay, sugar?" Norvin asked.

"Yes, it's all right. We'll go upstairs."

"Call me if you need anything and I'll come right up. Good night."

"Thank you for a great day, Norvin."

We hugged. I didn't want to leave him. Neal followed me to the third floor.

"Look, if you don't want to know me, that's cool. I don't care about the acid. You can have it. Do you want more? I can get whatever you want. I'd like to see you some time. We could go to the Fillmore East and hear some music. Janis Joplin is coming next week. You love her. We gotta see her. I heard about a festival they're putting together next summer. Three days of some great bands—Dead, Jefferson Airplane, Janis, Jimi. It's happening up-state, in Woodstock."

"I want to go to that. Get us tickets. I'd like to do these things with you, but I'm going to live here by myself."

"Do you want to go out now? Get a drink or something?"

"No, I'm tired and I've been out all day."

"I feel like you don't want to know me," Neal said.

"That's not true. I'll go to the Fillmore with you on the weekend, okay?"

"Yeah, I get it," Neal said and he left.

I was far from tired. The speed in the acid was keeping me awake. I laid down on my mattress in the dark until I knew Neal was way out of the neighborhood. I felt bad about how I was acting toward him, but I just wanted him to go away. I don't know how long I had been lying there when I heard the door slowly open to my apartment. I was certain I'd locked it when Neal left, but I could hear it creaking open. I didn't move.

Step . . . silence . . . step . . . standing in the doorway . . . looking right at me and not moving . . . a tiny woman in a coat and hat with soft cloth bags in each hand by her sides. She said nothing . . . I was paralyzed with fear.

For what seemed like an eternity, she just stood there in the doorway . . . and then walked very slowly toward me. I couldn't scream. I couldn't move. She stood about a foot away from me. I could smell her musty clothes and see the wrinkles on her hands. I was afraid to look up to see her face. What did she want? Who was she?

She started opening the bags and placing things on my bed. I didn't look, but I could feel her covering me with something as I lay there helpless. One by one, carefully, she emptied the contents of the bag. I could feel something hard and dry touching my skin. Something . . . fur! I looked up and saw my entire bed covered . . . with dead cats. I was being crushed and I couldn't breathe. If I didn't get up, I knew I was going to die. I ran into the closet and pulled the door shut behind me. It was silent. I knew I had to face what was out there. When I got the courage to open the door, I slowly stepped out into the room. There was no one there. There were no cats on the bed. The door was still locked.

Chapter Three

Monday morning, Grudin/Appell Market Research Company, Madison Avenue. I had to do it or I wouldn't eat. I was on time, 8:30 in the morning, wearing my pomegranate red Spanish boots, Navy-issue bell bottoms and an embroidered velvet gypsy vest. I'd braided my hair with ribbons and flowers in two rolled loops on the sides of my head.

The boss called me into his office. Frank was all Brooks Brothers—brown tweed three-piece suit, a red carnation in his lapel and perfectly polished brown wing-tipped shoes.

"Good morning, Miss Iacuzzo," he said, his hands tucked snugly into his little vest pockets. "You'll be starting today on a cherry pie study we're conducting all over the country. What we're looking for are the results from schoolchildren ages five through nine who prefer an all-natural ingredient pie over a totally synthetic one. You'll read the answers to those piles of questionnaires and code them in preparation for keypunching. Sit over there at the table next to that young lady and she will explain *coding* to you and show you what to do. Her name is Dana. Don't bother me with anything. I'm sure Dana will have the answers for everything you don't understand. I don't allow any talking in this office except about work. Have a good day, Miss Iacuzzo." Mr. Andrews, the boss, handed me a red pencil.

The room was filled with out-of-work actors, presentable hippies, artists, bored housewives and transient New Yorkers. Everyone said, "Yes, sir, Mr. Andrews," and "No sir, Mr. Andrews." He paced the floor like a strict schoolteacher. When someone laughed under their breath, he'd playfully whack them on the shoulder with his ruler. It made the whole room laugh even louder.

Frank stopped at the desk of a lovely young woman: "You didn't go home last night, Miss Graham. You can't expect to do a good job here if you don't get enough sleep." She lowered her head pretending to be embarrassed. He paused and looked straight at her. After concentrating for a few seconds with his arms folded, Frank said, "They're calling you for that play you auditioned for last week. You got the part. You'll know by tomorrow afternoon."

"Oh, Mr. Andrews. Thank you! Thank you! You're seeing that? They liked me? Will I get along with the director? Is the play going to have a long run?" Miss Graham held on to his sleeve, thrilled at what he was predicting for her.

"That's enough! Get back to work!" Frank said, pushing her away and dusting off his suit jacket, pretending to be the mean boss.

Frank seemed to love all the attention. I don't think he actually did any work other than to keep the employees producing. I watched him walk over to a young man with long hair sitting in the corner. "Give me your palm." Frank held the young man's hand and started to read him. "You were taken away from your parents when you were quite young, Mr. Bradley. Ummm, lots of lovers, though. Watch your lungs. Prone to bronchitis."

Dana leaned over and whispered to me, "Frank gives us psychic messages when we're good. We all wait for him to choose us. It's a gift if he picks you. What's it like to be his sister?"

I didn't answer.

I tried to pay attention to Dana as she started explaining to me the principles of coding, but I was caught up in watching Frank talking quietly to the young man as he got up and followed Frank into his office. He closed the door.

Dana was a petite hippie in a long flowered skirt, Mexican peasant blouse and Earth shoes. She spoke softly to me from behind her granny glasses and waist-length hair that covered most of her face.

"This is column A. Here are all the responses having to do with taste: one, 'it tastes sweet'; two, 'not sweet enough'; three, 'it's too sweet'; four, 'it tastes sour'; five, 'it tastes fake'; and so on down the list. Column B is about packaging. Column C is about price. If they say any of these answers, you mark the number that corresponds with the response next to the box at the end of the sentence. Use your red pencil. If a respondent says, 'I don't know' or has no answer, you make an x for don't know or a y for no answer and remember to always loop your y's. The key punchers get angry if they can't read your writing."

"This is stupid," I said.

"I know, but it's easy and everyone here is really nice. We all hate it, but we need the money. Frank said we all lived together in a past life. We were peasants in the seventeenth century, picking grapes in France. He was our king, of course," Dana said.

"Of course," I said and we laughed.

"Here, these are your piles." She pointed to five stacks of one hundred three-page questionnaires that had to be completed by noon.

The kids hated the all-pure ingredient, natural cherry pie. They said it had no flavor and tasted fake. The completely artificial pie was the favorite. The client, who was promoting the all-natural pie, wanted the end results to be in favor of their product so they could sell it as "Preferred by Children All over America" in their advertising. They would have been very upset to find out that their pie was a failure. We were told by the client's project director to switch the answers from one to the other to make it seem that the kids preferred the natural pie over the artificial. We had to keep the client happy; they'd invested a lot of money in this study.

Market research coding was tedious and boring. I went in the mornings and worked on the house in the afternoons. I found out more than I wanted to know about toothpaste, razor blades, frozen sausage, sanitary napkins and dog food.

The job kept me from going completely crazy from loneliness and gave my life some structure and a paycheck. I'd work at the office and go back to Mulberry Street to work some more. I'd eat a sandwich or a bowl of cereal for dinner. Norvin had given me an overstuffed orange chair he'd found on the street. It didn't have a cushion. I sank in that chair many nights alone in the dark.

After I had been working at the company for a couple of months, Dana invited me to her apartment for dinner. I burst into tears at the offer. She was my first friend in New York besides Norvin, who I didn't see that much except in the house when we were pulling nails out of the floorboards or scraping wallpaper together.

One Friday night I took the subway to Dana's place on East Ninety-second off Second Avenue. She buzzed me in and I climbed the stairs to her apartment. It took her forever to unlock the many locks on the door. One had a metal pole bolted into the floor and braced against the door that made it impossible to push the door open from the outside. As she opened the door, I could hear the pole dragging across the door. She said it was a police lock.

Candlelit and ripe with patchouli oil, Dana's was instant India. Pink Floyd was playing on a small record player. As I followed her to the living room, I felt I was being watched. Was anyone else in the apartment? I could feel someone take my hand and guide me in, but no one was there. We walked through her railroad apartment, one room following another through beaded curtains to her living room and sat on an Oriental carpet. Along one wall an altar crammed with pictures of saints, mystics and deities. Sai Baba, St. Therese, Ganesha, Joan of Arc, St. Francis of Assisi, Saint Germain, Jesus, Maharishi Mahesh Yogi, the Virgin Mary. Even Geronimo was up there on the altar. Dana had all her bases covered.

"Do you trip?" she said, getting right to the point. "I have some Purple Owsley. It's beautiful and clear and I'd like to share it with you."

I took off my shoes as she placed two tiny purple pills on a silver tray, one for me and one for her. She poured tea from her grandmother's silver teapot, we swallowed the acid while we talked about cats. Dana had nine. They all settled in around us, curled in our laps, above our heads, watching from the bed. She told me each one's name and I got them all confused. She then lit a small brass pipe of hashish. The walls began to undulate.

Dana started telling me, "I've seen miracles. There are saints among us who live ordinary lives and have given up their place in heaven to be here on earth to help us and teach us how to live. I have a teacher, Hilda Kirkbright. She's a healer. I've seen her perform miracles many times. I don't do anything without talking to Hilda. She's with me always and I can talk to her constantly," Dana said, as she pointed to the middle of her forehead. "Hilda is a living saint. I'll take you to meet her. She told me last year that I was going to meet you. She said we were nuns in the same convent in the Middle Ages in France and that you and I have work to do together in this life. Do you have a guru? Who are you following? Who is your teacher?"

"I don't follow anyone. I don't believe in living saints. I believe we all have power and we can all make things happen. Everything we need to know is already inside of us."

Dana stood up and held out her hand to me. "Come, I want to show you something, follow me."

Get up? My legs had turned into jelly, I didn't think I could move. Holding Dana's hand, I slowly tiptoed down the hall, followed by a procession of cats. I could hear the sound of water bubbling. The room was lit by the light of an aquarium that stood in the middle of the room. She approached the tank like a monk entering a holy cave.

Dana spoke softly through the glass. "Hello, fine sir. Please forgive us for interrupting you. I want you to meet my new friend, Teresa Isabella. We were nuns together in a past life. Is it all right that we're here? Can we talk to you?"

I couldn't see who she was talking to. I stared into the water, all I could see was green water plants moving with the air bubbles. There was a small pile of rocks in the corner of the tank, but I couldn't see anything else. Then to my amazement, from behind the rocks out walked a little tiny man in a frog suit. I think it was probably some rare form of frog that walked upright, but this thing was incredible. It had little hands with fingers and its eyes looked right up at me. It moved slowly through the tank and kept pointing at me.

In a quiet, gentle, sweet voice, Dana talked to the frog for quite a long time and then she looked at me. "He is one of my teachers, Rama Maya. He just told me, 'Terry could teach you things about the universe.' He said you came from a faraway planet to the modern world and you have information about how to transform our lives. Will you be my teacher?"

"I'll be your friend. And I'll tell you what I know. We can talk until the sun comes up and we can have a good time. And you can tell me what you know. I bet I can learn a lot from you too. Let's go in the other room. Do you have a Tarot deck? I'll read your cards."

I didn't feel comfortable being thought of as a teacher of the universe. What did that mean anyway? What did I know? I was just appointed Head Mystic Time Traveler—by a frog. Maybe he knew something about me that I didn't. I thought he'd probably been underwater too long.

I read Dana's cards all night long. She had a Rider-Waite Tarot deck. Different from mine, the Rider-Waite deck has pictorial images on every card. My deck, the Swiss deck, only has pictures on the twenty-two Major Arcana. *Arcana* means a hidden thing, a profound secret. The fifty-six Minor Arcana depict cups, swords, wands and pentacles, which in a regular fifty-two card playing deck would be hearts (cups), spades (swords), clubs (wands), diamonds (pentacles), from one to ten. All decks have court cards, Queens, Kings, and Pages, (the Jacks). But the Tarot kept the Knights.

I asked Dana to shuffle the cards and then place them in front of her. I fanned them out in a huge semicircle around her and then asked her to pick one card and hand it to me. As I turned it over, the ink that formed the image on the card leapt off the paper and sprang into life right in front of me. Standing there . . . a fully realized, living breathing Tarot card.

At the window with his back to us was a tall man with very broad shoulders wearing a long brown cape and crimson hat. He looked like a nobleman from the Renaissance. I was speechless and I waited a few moments to see what would happen. He hardly moved, but stared out the window for a long time. In one hand he held a staff that was almost as tall as he was. I noticed the staff had tiny green buds growing out of it. Another staff just like it was planted firmly into the floor. He stood between the two staffs. Slowly he turned and looked right at me and said. "What would you say of me? What will you tell her of why I've come?"

In one outstretched hand the man held a globe of the world. I stood up to look at the sphere. I poked my finger into the water of the brilliant blue oceans. I touched the continents of Africa, Australia, South America—I could see tiny lights on the part of the earth where it was nighttime.

"Dana, look! This is the Two of Wands! He's offering you the world! He wants you to know that this world belongs to you. Hold out your hands!" I took the small globe of the world from the nobleman and offered it to Dana. "Go wherever you like on it. Take the adventure, it's yours. I'm handing you a dream!" I repeated the words he said to me. Dana sat on the bed watching me, but she wouldn't take the world. I held it in my hands and watched my own reflection on the curve of the world become the map of the earth. As the world turned into a bubble, the nobleman looked into my eyes with love and said, "The frog was right."

I could feel and see a silver fluid seeping through my brain, the acid had taken full effect. "Dana, pick another card." She didn't say anything. She just watched me flying around the room excited.

She handed me a another Tarot card and as I looked at it I heard heavy breathing in the back of my head and three loud knocks on the floor. I jumped out of my skin and spun around to face the strong presence behind me.

A knight in full armor! All right—a white horse in the apartment. I'll be all right. Take it easy. Just tell the horse to stop banging his hoof on the floor.

"Drink from the cup of love," the knight said. "First drink for yourself and then pass it along to others. This cup will never empty. You must have courage to drink from it. You must have courage to love. The courage to feel."

I took the cup and gulped it right down.

Dana had gotten onto her bed and covered herself with a quilt. "Dana, this is the Knight of Cups. Have a drink. It's delicious! I've never tasted anything like this before. Come on, Dana, drink this!" She turned away.

I had a long conversation with the knight about love. Was there love in this world for everyone? How is it possible to love yourself then? How could you love without ego? Isn't love selfish? I need more experience. This would take years to understand. We argued and laughed and I got on the horse and rode through the apartment drinking the sweet almond liquid from his gold chalice.

"Dana, there is no reason to be unhappy! Let go! Get on the horse with us," I called out, waving to her from the saddle.

Dana had already pulled another card and handed it to me. I got down from the horse and looked at the card. It was the Nine of Swords. A woman wrapped in a quilt sits up in a bed holding her head in her hands. She has just awakened from a nightmare and sits on the bed in terrible anguish. Above her head, nine very sharp swords hang on the wall.

"This is me. Look. I am the Nine of Swords," Dana whispered, as she held up the card to show me. She was frightened and crying. I'd not seen her like this before. I wanted to help her and tell her what to do. I wanted to be able to understand why she was suffering. I wanted to take her suffering and hold it inside me so I could carry it for her. I stayed with her and absorbed the pain she was feeling. It hurt so terribly.

I sat on the floor next to her bed and held her hand trying to comfort her. I had been so completely absorbed and excited by the Tarot that I didn't see her hiding in the bed. The cards pulled me with such a force, I felt insatiable. I wanted to ask them everything. The Tarot was my living library. With help from the cards, I could read my own book about who I am. I could read for others and help them figure out why and where they might have gotten lost. The Tarot showed me how I could become a mirror. If I looked through it, I could see others through myself. Mirror into mirror into mirror. We could change the direction of our lives by reading the details of where we've been.

The shuffling helps us let go of control. Pick the cards, follow the pictures. Read the story and have the courage to change. The possibilities are endless! It all seemed so easy for me, so clear. But life isn't always like that.

"Look Dana, we're in the sky! Come on, let's get away from here." The room was the basket of a hot air balloon. When I leaned over, just a little bit, I could see the whole world below. The walls of the building had fallen away and we were floating in space far away from New York City. Far away from pain. Far away from thinking. We held on to the basket and sailed through the stars as the cool breeze of the night blew around us.

Dana seemed to let go for a moment. She laughed at my delight with the world. I could play with the room around us, make the cards come to life, dance and sing, tell stories of my childhood.

We got together every weekend for almost two months, tripping from Friday night till Sunday, traveling wherever the cards took us. During that time the Tarot burned into my soul. Reading about my life or Dana's for hours on end, I formed a personal relationship with each card as it came to life for me.

Ever since, I've seen the living Tarot wherever I go.

    . . .

Dana kept insisting that I go with her to meet her teacher, Hilda. I agreed to go one time and see who this woman was. We went uptown to a church where she held her weekly meetings. It was filled with people eagerly awaiting Hilda's appearance. I found a seat while Dana went around greeting her friends. A woman dressed in an Indian silk sari came out from a side entrance and stood before us. Hilda was a middle-aged American woman. She looked just like a Catholic holy card, head tilted, eyes to the clouds. She spoke to us like she was putting a baby to sleep. The audience was entranced.

She told us about the power of God and that we had to practice being God in everything we did. We were divine and we could also make miracles happen. Okay, I got that. What are we doing here? There was something about spiritual teachers, gurus and holy people I just didn't trust. It bothered me that I was such a nonbeliever. I wanted to feel the power of healing, the presence of Jesus, the miracle of Divine transformation, the enlightenment of the Buddha, but I didn't—and I wouldn't pretend. I saw them as people like me, like all of us. I didn't feel anything special in the presence of spiritual people and I wanted to know why.

I looked around the room, everyone had a dazed look in their eyes. Dana was crying, moved to tears by everything that Hilda said. Hilda's words were comforting. She talked about Jesus and quoted various Indian teachers. Dana told me that I could have private time with Hilda and she would guide me on my path in life. She'd explain how my present life experience was based on other lives I'd lived before. Dana didn't make a move without her. I knew I could never give that much power over to anyone.

At the end of the meditation, Dana introduced me to Hilda.

"Hello, have I met you before?" Hilda said as she took my hand. There was something so familiar in her touch. I remembered the feeling. Was it her hand that guided me down the hall through Dana's apartment? I felt a sense of peace and calmness come over me.

"How is your sweet frog, Dana?" Hilda looked at me and winked.

. . .

Dana and I talked all night about spirituality and the meaning of the journey of life. She was convinced that most of her problems where carried over from the lives she had lived before. Terrified of entering a building alone, she had to have someone meet her in front of the building or she wouldn't go in. Hilda told Dana that in a past life she was attacked and beaten very badly, left for dead until someone found her dying inside a stable. She said this explained why Dana couldn't enter a doorway without feeling overwhelming fear. She had to face this fear from that other life or she'd carry it into the next one. Dana was struggling with this. She was also getting a lot of attention with it, setting up schedules with friends to escort her wherever she went.

The next weekend Dana and I got together, and she talked constantly about Hilda. It reminded me so much of my mother when she too talked about Frank over and over as if there was no one else alive on earth. Dana was very excited that I had met Hilda. She wanted me to go to see her alone and explore why I was so skeptical about everyone on Dana's altar. I was resistant. I didn't feel Hilda would have that answer for me.

Dana and I tripped on acid a few more times and I was starting to feel that I was finished with those weekends, that it was time for me to do something else. I could see that Dana wouldn't let go of her problems and she was becoming very dependent on me. I listened to her endlessly and tried to console her. I read her cards and tried to find solutions and explanations for her life. She was starting to hint at the fact that maybe I too was a living saint. This annoyed me. I was no saint. I just wanted a friend.

One of my last nights at Dana's apartment I started playing with the radio. I moved the dial from song to song, station to station. A man's voice came over the airways:

"An announcement today from the Vatican—St. Brigit, St. Lucy, St. Ursula, St. Philomena, and many other popular saints, including the patron saint of travelers, St. Christopher, have all been decanonized for lack of proof of their existence," a spokesman for the Catholic church stated. After much consideration, there is not enough historical evidence that these saints ever existed. Many of these saints' stories were based on legends and pagan mythology. They have all been dropped from the Roman calendar and are no longer recognized by the Roman Catholic Church."

"*What!*" I screamed. Dana thought that I was going crazy. I couldn't stop laughing. I must have rolled around the floor for twenty minutes. I couldn't explain to her why I was laughing so hard. We were in two different places and I knew then it was time to move on. We argued over what we believed to be true. I thought she was naive. Dana said I was irreverent. She was very serious about all things spiritual and I found it interesting and sometimes hilarious. St. Christopher could no longer protect me on any future trips! The Vatican took away his power. So much for sainthood. I went back downtown to Mulberry Street.

Jay was starting to get upset with me because I wasn't keeping up with my part of the bargain—work in exchange for free rent. He approached me when I got home.

"Terry, where have you been these weekends? I've got to finish the second floor. We're renting it the first of the month. Go upstairs and work with Norvin on the bedroom. He's painting today. You said you'd help."

"Norvin, what should I do? Is Jay really mad I haven't been around?"

"Oh don't even think about it. The house is getting done. He put an ad in the *Times* to rent the second floor. What have you been doing out there in playland? Grab a brush and paint those baseboards."

I told Norvin everything about my weekends with Dana and my confusion about believing in the things I saw outside of myself.

"Norvin, I have to ask you a serious question. Have you been listening to the radio today or yesterday? Did you hear anything peculiar about the Catholic church and what happened to the saints?"

"You mean, how they all got kicked out because there's no proof they ever existed?"

"Oh, Hail Mary! It really is true, thank God."

"Those crazy Catholics. Who would believe anything they say?"

"Norvin, why aren't you using a roller to paint with? It would be much faster."

"Jay doesn't allow us to use rollers. He wants everything done with a brush by hand."

"Yes, boss. What past life are we paying for this time? How come we're always the servants? Something's wrong with this theory," I said.

"Hey, sugar, do you want to go to Boston some weekend and get an astrology reading with somebody really good? I heard about this woman, Isabel Hickey; she's supposed to be the best. She's written several books. They call her the Mother of Astrology. I'll call and we can go for a weekend. Do you want to?"

"How 'bout this weekend? Why wait? I'm ready. Where will we stay? What are you going to tell Jay?" I said.

"We can stay at the Y. It's cheap. What time were you born? We have to give her the exact time so she can draw up our charts before we get there. Shuuu, here comes Jay. Get to work."

.   .   .

Boston in 1969 was not a place that welcomed hippies. It was winter, I was wearing my mother's 1940s raccoon jacket with its big padded shoulders. On top of my head, a wild coypu fur hat that resembled human hair. It bristled straight up in the front and its long ear flaps, when tied up, looked the way some men comb their hair over to cover their baldness. Norvin's huge white Swiss Army coat with a curly sheep lining made him look like the Abominable Snowman. I could never understand why the Bostonians were so threatened by his black-and-green polka-dotted clogs. But the sight of six-foot-something Norvin with his long red hair and beard, blue jeans and those clogs, and me with that dead animal on my head seemed to frighten people.

We arrived early for our appointment with Isabel Hickey, so we wandered around Boston and came upon an open-air market. We were excited about having an astrology reading, being in Boston, being alive. Everything fascinated us.

In the market, Norvin became inspired by a cartful of bright red apples. He was amused by the methodical way the apples were stacked, he acted like he'd never seen red before. When he put out his hand to choose one, an angry burly man jumped out from behind the stand and screamed in his face, "Those apples are not for sale, to you!"

"I beg your pardon? Excuse me sir? What did you say?" Norvin said.

Several men came out from around the market and told us to get out, go away, right now! We couldn't believe it. What did we do? I took Norvin's arm and said, "Let's just walk out of here nice and slowly." He asked them to please explain why we couldn't buy an apple from them. The men tightened around us. They offered no explanation. I was watching this scene thinking I was in a dream or in the Tarot's Seven of Swords. We were being misunderstood as a threat as they were threatening us. My mind was racing and I was afraid for our lives. Thinking about the Tarot kept me calm.

Some of the men with taped up baseball bats gathered around us hitting them in the palms of their hands. They just didn't want us there and Norvin realized they weren't open to discussing this. We held each other's hand and walked out of the market, followed all the way out by the mob calling us queers and threatening our lives.

Norvin sat on a bench and cried. I was angry and hurt. We walked through the pristine tree-lined streets to find Isabel Hickey's house, hoping that our readings would take our minds off what had just happened.

Norvin went first, and she said it was fine if we listened to each other's readings. Miss Hickey read enthusiastically. She went over every aspect of our charts and gave us detailed information on our personalities, our relationship to our family members and what we wanted to know most of all, what was going to happen in the future.

She told Norvin that he would go back to the place where he was born and stay there most of his life. I said to myself, I told him that! From the soup bowl. She described Norvin's personality to perfection. She could see his quirky playfulness, his desire for family and his conflict between freedom and loyalty. She strongly encouraged him to write, sculpt, paint—not just live out his art, but to put it into some kind of form. Norvin was delighted with his reading.

Then it was my turn. Miss Hickey looked at me for a long time before she spoke. She had a kind, sweet face and a motherly nature.

"Terry, thousands and thousands of people are waiting for you to tell them what to do."

I heard what she said and I thought for a moment about what this might mean. I could go into the travel business or maybe become a traffic cop.

"Your chart is powerful! I haven't seen one like this in many years. You have phenomenal psychic ability. People will listen to you and follow what you say. You have the sun and moon in Scorpio and Jupiter on the ascendant, square to Venus in Virgo. That gives you the ability to have great compassion for people and a keen sense of the details of the human psyche. Your innate knowledge of esoteric matters is extraordinary! Your ability to articulate the most abstract information in plain language will be so helpful to people."

What does all this mean? The moon conjunct with what? In the first house of who? I was too shy to ask her what it meant and I was so caught up in her excitement of who she said I was that I didn't want to interrupt her or appear naive.

"I strongly suggest you study astrology or numerology, Kabbala, all of it. Make it your life's work. People are waiting for you. Here's a copy of my book; take it and read it and think about what I'm telling you. I've never seen a chart like yours. You've got talent, insight and compassion. I think I said that enough times."

I was overwhelmed, but I did feel somewhere inside me that I knew what she was talking about, especially coming from my family. There was one thing I knew, I could never be a professional psychic. Frank's the only one in the family that can do that. I couldn't take that away from him. I could never tell him what she told me. It's all right if I read the cards for myself or for my friends, but I'm afraid he would be furious if I got any attention for it.

Before we left, Miss Hickey looked over my chart one last time and then paused for a moment and said, "There's one more thing I need to tell you. If you ever go to Europe, you will be raped. It's here in your chart. Saturn and Mars crossing your house of . . ."

I couldn't even pay attention to what she said about the technical reason for the horrifying news. All I heard was that I was going to be raped! I couldn't believe what I was hearing. I went into a kind of shock. I remember not saying anything, not asking her, Where? When? What year? What country? Can I avoid this?

I looked at Norvin and he was shaking her hand good-bye. He helped me with my coat and then we were on the street. I was stunned. We walked aimlessly for several blocks talking about our readings.

"Norvin what am I supposed to do? Did you hear what she said?"

"Listen honey, don't worry about that now. There's nothing you can do about it now. Maybe it means something else. Maybe she got the interpretation wrong. Maybe she was just jealous of you. She gave you this glowing reading and then she took it all away. You're the next generation of psychic mystics. Maybe she's afraid you'll replace her. And if it is true, what she said, then there's nothing you can do about it except be careful or just don't go to Europe."

"Thanks a lot. How can I not think about this? It will be in my mind forever. I just can't erase what just happened. I have to live with this."

"You're going to have to learn that if you go to psychics, you're not always going to hear what you want to hear. It's not always going to be a happy story. Now, are you going to give all your power over to that reading? Are you going to let it crush you?"

"I have so much think about."

I just wanted to go home. We left on the bus and Norvin tried to cheer me up by telling me funny stories about Texas, but I felt like I had made a terrible mistake having that reading. She tattooed my mind with an image I could never remove.

⋅ ⋅ ⋅

Jay called Norvin and me to a meeting on the second floor of Mulberry Street. We stood at attention and listened to our orders.

"We have three weeks to finish the halls and the second floor. We've rented the second floor to a couple, Mr. and Mrs. Michael Deming. They're sophisticated and hardworking. He owns a framing business on Broadway and Houston. They love the house and are moving in on the first of the month. You are never to show them the first or third floor. I don't want them to know that the rest of the house is unfinished. Don't get involved with them. They are the tenants and want to be left alone. They like this neighborhood because it's quiet. Norvin, promise me you'll stay out of their way. Terry, I'll tell Frank that you need time off from coding so you can work all day in the house. I want you both to start today. We have to get their floor finished."

Jay left. He expected nothing less than perfection from us.

"Well, I guess from now on the Bowery boys will have to get showers somewhere else," Norvin said. "I'm hungry! Let's go to Puglia's."

I was always ready to go out to eat. There's only so much cereal and beef jerky you can take in one lifetime. Puglia's was an Italian restaurant on Hester and Mulberry, a few blocks from our house. The seating was family-style, picnic tables with red-checked tablecloths and everyone crushed together. Nasty-tasting red wine was served in small glasses. We were certain it was made in a bathtub in the basement. The garlic bread was so pungent you'd reek for days from every pore of your body. A robust redhead with excessive red lipstick and blue eye shadow painted up to her eyebrows sang heartbreaking Italian songs, accompanied by a skinny old man on an electric guitar.

Norvin sat across from me with some English tourists and three young Italian-American couples from New Jersey. The music was getting louder, the garlic bread stronger and the wine never stopped. Everyone was shouting over the music and I couldn't hear what anyone was saying. I looked intensely at every person in the restaurant. Maybe it was the wine, or exhaustion from the trip to Boston, I didn't know why, but I felt I had to know all these people in the deepest possible way. I stared right through them and forced myself in. I felt like a lost spirit trying desperately to enter a body, any body. I went around the room hearing everybody's thoughts. I looked at every face and became them. My whole body was feeling what they were feeling: confusions, frustrations, longings and disappointments, humor and fears.

Joey, please just say you love me. I'll do anything for you. You're my whole world and I'll die if I can't marry you, a young woman said to herself.

I want to move here. I can get an apartment in this neighborhood. I could waitress. This is so cool. I was the girl in the corner.

You bastard, you cheap bastard. I hate you! I need the money and I'll kill you! I swear I will, came from the mind of the middle-aged man in the gray suit. His face looked like he was bored, but inside he was screaming.

Who's going to pay this bill? I haven't got any dough. Oh, God I don't want to keep this baby. I gotta tell him tonight. I'm still hungry. O sole mio. I miss Lisa. I've got to call her. Why did we break up? I don't have enough money to get home. I'm too fat. Why is he paying so much attention to her? I hate my hair. O sole mio. He hates me. This is great! I'm falling asleep. This is so great! I want to go home. If my father knew I was here he'd kill me. Why am I saying this food is great? The lasagne tastes like rubber.

"Terry! Terry! Hey girl, are you all right? Hey, hey." I felt Norvin pulling at my sleeve and calling me. "Let's go home. I've had enough. Have you?"

Mulberry Street was spinning and my legs could barely hold me up. I couldn't stop seeing the carnival faces from the restaurant. Norvin tried talking to me on the way home, but I couldn't hear what he was saying. I was inside a tunnel, slipping away.

I fell onto my bed with my clothes on and passed out until morning. I woke up horrified to find the pillowcase covered in vomit and blood. I had thrown up in my sleep and my nose had bled. I could have choked to death. I washed up and went downstairs to work on the second floor. Norvin was on the ladder painting the ceiling.

"Good Morning, sugar. How ya feeling? Good news! We have the day off tomorrow."

"I'm okay. Do you have any coffee? Why do we have off?"

"Frank is giving a lecture on palmistry at the Temple of the New Dawn. Are you going to go?"

"I didn't know anything about it. He didn't tell me he was lecturing. How come he didn't invite me? Do you think he doesn't want me there?"

"Just come. He probably forgot or he thinks he told you. He'd be thrilled if you were there. You're his sister. Of course he wants you there."

Chapter Four ·

The Temple of the New Dawn was a spiritual center on West Seventy-second Street run by two elderly women, Nesta Kerin Crain and Doris Herzog, who devoted their entire lives to the study of metaphysics. Nesta was a psychic, a trance medium and card reader who could channel the dead, speaking in different voices and in several languages. Born in England in the early 1890s, she was nearly eighty when I met her. At that point she was no longer doing private readings, only lectures, but once in a while one of the voices would slip out of her during a normal conversation.

Nesta was four-feet-ten-inches tall and strong as a diamond. As a child actress in London in 1904, she was cast as the original Tiger Lily in the first theater production of James M. Barrie's *Peter Pan*. She still had the program. Czar Nicholas II of Russia was so taken by her after he saw her perform he asked her what he could give her in return. She said she wanted one of his sleigh bells. The heavy black iron bell was a gift she treasured all her life.

In the 1920s Nesta, traveling alone, went to the Orient instead of doing the expected European grand tour. During her journey she collected a huge number of gongs, bells and singing bowls from Japan, China, Tibet, Nepal, India, Burma and Malaysia. She collected everything else too: Buddhas, embroidered Chinese robes, paintings, bronze elephants, incense burners, carpets, books, carved furniture and many, many other objets d'art.

Her partner, Doris, was born in Memphis, Tennessee. Ten years younger than Nesta, she liked to think that she had lived a past life in the Memphis of ancient Egypt and came back to life in this new Memphis. She was raised in an upper-class Southern home, played tennis and went to debutante balls. She studied journalism in college, became a newspaper reporter for William Randolph Hearst in Hollywood, then published detective stories. MGM paid Doris $50 for the right to use one of her book titles for a film, *Some Like It Hot*.

Doris, a woman of strong character and honesty with snow-white hair and bright blue eyes, stood straight up at six feet tall. A tattered copy of Madame Blavatsky's *Secret Doctrine* was never far out of reach. She read it over and over again, incorporating Blavatsky's teachings into her lectures on magic, occult philosophy, ancient Egypt, Tibetan and Indian metaphysics, UFOs and conspiracy theories. Doris kept files on everything and everybody from newspaper and magazine clippings. Her friends and correspondents at one time or another included Harry Houdini, T. E. Lawrence (of Arabia), Amelia Earhart, Nikola Tesla, Vladimir Nabokov and many movie stars— Norma Shearer, Joan Crawford, Mary Pickford, Douglas Fairbanks, Marion Davies, Charlie Chaplin . . .

She was a frequent guest at San Simeon, the Hearst castle in California, until she was blackballed in the 1930s by Mr. Hearst for refusing to publish an exposé on Clark Gable. Hearst had heard rumors that Gable was fooling around with young gay men and he wanted Doris to investigate the story. She confided in her friend Louella Parsons and told her of her dilemma. After telling Doris to stick to her convictions, Louella betrayed her by going to Hearst and telling him that she would do the story. That was the end of Doris's career in Hollywood.

Doris tried desperately to get another job, but every newspaper in the country turned her down. Hearst ruined her career. Desperate and penniless, she came back East to New York. Someone told her that her luck might change if she went to see Nesta Kerin Crain for a psychic reading. Nesta loved to tell the story that Doris's cards were so terrible and her future so grim that she felt sorry for her and asked her to move in with her. I think they fell in love the day they met and never spent a night apart. Doris was waited on and worshiped as the fine Southern Lady of Nesta's heart.

Frank was the darling of the Temple of the New Dawn. He was being groomed as their successor. He was a handsome twenty-seven-year-old with a sparkle and enthusiasm for new ideas about mysticism, and he was devoted to Nesta and Doris. They looked to Frank as their own Jiddu Krishnamurti—much like the Theosophists, who adopted Krishnamurti in 1911 and brought him from India to London to be the new spiritual leader of their group, the Order of the Star of the East. Frank was Nesta and Doris's hope for the future.

The Temple was one large room with a raised platform that displayed an altar with Buddhas and flowers and candles. Doris came out first to welcome the faithful followers, about forty of them. She was dressed in one of the Chinese robes, a turquoise silk, embroidered with large red flowers. The sleeves of the robe were much too long for her and covered the tips of her fingers. Her small velvet Chinese hat had long green tassels that hung on either side of her head.

"Welcome to the Temple of the New Dawn!" Doris said, striking a huge circular shiny brass gong that made the entire room vibrate for several minutes.

"Just a few announcements before I introduce you to this afternoon's speaker. In two weeks we will have our traditional Wesak ceremony commemorating the Buddha's birth. Following on the same program, our dear Nesta will be harmonizing on the gongs with the vibration from the Wesak ceremony. You won't want to miss this, folks. Then the following week I will give a lecture on *Documented Stories of the Strange and the Unknown*. You won't believe your ears. Make sure to be here.

"Tonight we are honored to hear a fascinating lecture from an inspired psychic and palmist, whom we are extremely fortunate to have discovered. His lecture is titled *Divination: The Art of the Ancients Revealed through the Hands* . . . Here he is . . . our very own . . . Frank Andrews!" and she struck another *gong!*

Norvin and I sat in the back of the room, which was filled mainly with elderly women and a few nice-looking young men. Jay was there too, sitting at a card table at the door, collecting the donations in a small wooden box.

They had dressed Frank up in a black satin robe trimmed with a gold collar and cuffs. He spoke to us for about thirty minutes on the lines and mounds in the palm of the hand and drew diagrams on a blackboard. Frank was so at ease speaking to the audience. He knew his subject well, was witty, charming and patient with all the questions, "What do you see in my hand, Mr. Andrews?" "Will I ever make any money?" "When will I meet my one true love?" "How long will I live?" He instructed the audience to relax and raise both hands up so that he could examine how they held their fingers together. I knew what he was looking for because he had asked me to do the same thing once. I held up my hands with my fingers spread wide apart.

"Oh, I see my sister is in the audience. She knows that a widely spread open hand represents a person who is free." He laughed at my demonstration of playfulness. When he mentioned that I was in the audience, the whole room turned around to see who I was, and I turned around with them pretending that I too was just another audience member looking for Frank Andrews's sister. Norvin thought that was hilarious. I loved making both of them laugh.

Frank ended his lecture and then introduced Nesta to the audience.

"Now close your eyes and look! Our beloved, magical Nesta Kerin Crain . . . performing for you this afternoon . . . *Thunderstorm over the Himalayas!*

The audience broke into applause and Nesta appeared on the stage wearing an ice-blue Chinese robe with matching skirt and little red slippers. She looked like a tiny dancing doll let out of a music box. Her elaborate headdress with tassels, red-and-green pompoms and gold braiding had flowers woven through it. She stood in front of two tiers of hanging gongs and banged on those gongs with soft covered hammers till the whole building shook. Waves of electrical current passed through my entire body. She hit those gongs like a wizard controlling the weather. And with my eyes closed, I could see thunderstorms of the Himalayas had come to New York City.

I sat in the audience wondering where I belonged in this world of metaphysics. The ancients were dead. Their wisdom no longer seemed relevant to the complexities of the modern world. I wanted to free myself from somebody else's version of history, the laws of science, the rules of religion and spiritual dogma. I was more interested in exploring the ancient lost city inside myself, a place I was certain had answers for me. I believed that the truth was really simple, uncomplicated and could be found only in the heart.

. . .

Norvin and I worked on Mulberry Street every day to get the house finished in time for the new tenants. I spent hours stripping the newel post at the foot of the staircase. Its twists and turns of carved wood were caked with one hundred and forty-four years of enamel, stain, dirt and story. I thought about everyone before me who came in contact with the post. Who were they and how did they get here? What brought them to this house? How is it we all came to stand in this same spot at different times in our history? After all those hours and layers, I felt I could breathe again when I finally saw the oak.

I touched and wondered about every grain and knot of wood in the floorboards, every brush stroke on the walls, every nail, scratch and scar from its life as a house. Tenderly, I absorbed every inch of the house as if my life depended on it, as if I'd never see it again.

Mulberry Street was Norvin's and my home. I didn't want anyone else moving in. Our days of living alone in the house and doing what we wanted were over. Jay insisted we stay out of sight, locked in on our floors and invisible around the new tenants. We took down our clotheslines in the living room. No more roller skating in the house, no more loud music, tap dancing or bringing the homeless inside for a shower and a meal. Who were these Demings and how were they going to fit into our world? In one week we would find out.

When we finished the work, Norvin and I dropped acid and stayed inside the house on the second floor, which was now pristine, almost holy. Norvin acted out one of his dreams. I got fixated on a windup clock on the window ledge, one of the few things inside the apartment besides a broom and dustpan. I couldn't take my eyes off the clock. Forward or backward? Are the hands moving? Was time just a series of numbers balancing on the end of a stick? If I set the clock ahead would I miss the thoughts I'm about to have in the last lost hour? It was raining outside. The clock and the rain were perfectly synchronized.

From out of the air small children starting appearing everywhere in the room. One, two, three, four . . . they kept coming, one after another, from the center of the room, out of nowhere. Some were crying, curled up and shivering against the wall. Others ran back and forth, up and down the walls and across the ceiling. They all seemed lost and confused. Most of them were quiet except for the crybabies, who were starting to irritate me. Seventy-two, seventy-three, seventy-four. The rain, the clock, the children's cries, all keeping time.

Now older people carrying ladders and rolls of paper came through the hole in the air where the children had come out from. They set up their ladders and started wallpapering over the white walls we'd just finished painting. *Wait just a minute, please!* I got up and went over to look at the pattern on the wallpaper. It was fantastic! Intricate cutouts, black silhouettes of my childhood moving across the wall. There were my mother and father leaning against the railing at Niagara Falls. They turned and waved at me from the wallpaper. Mrs. Murphy, my sophomore English teacher, was there, in the classroom, holding a book above her head, smiling and pointing at the book and then to me. High school in the courtyard. A trail of Halloween goblins going door to door. Dante, our French poodle, running around the tulip tree in front of the cottage in our backyard. There was Rosemary, laughing, flying through the house on a broomstick. And Frank, chasing her with a butterfly net.

It made me sad. I told Norvin I wanted to go to my apartment and be alone. He was ready to go outside anyway and walk around the city. We said good-bye and I went upstairs. I stood on the spot where I first stood when I came to the house almost a year before, remembering those days. When I touched my arms and felt my skin it started to crack and fall off my body. On the floor, peelings of my skin mounted up around me. Time was falling off my body.

In the bathroom mirror I stared at my image. All I could remember were my eyes. Deep in the brown and black of the center of my eye, I fell backward into a tunnel. My face changed rapidly through centuries and lifetimes. A man, a woman, a baby, an animal, an insect, a poppy. One split second I was an Indian, a monk, a wolf, Chinese, caveman, African, Victorian, pilgrim, Eskimo, deformed, beautiful, a face after a face, changing and changing, folding into itself. I ran forward and backward through time.

Then all the skin on my face turned to liquid, dripped down and swirled around the sink, disappearing into the drain. I looked up into the mirror and saw my skeleton. Through the holes where my eyes once were, I went down deeper into myself—all the way back to silence. I drifted and drifted until I was gone. I was no one.

The next thing I remember, I woke up freezing on the bed. My body was shaking. I jerked violently. Something very heavy was on the end of the bed. I looked up and saw a thin, naked young man with black curly hair curled up on the foot of the bed. The soles of our feet were pressed together. He was trying to push his way into my body through my feet. I kicked as hard as I could to get him off of me. I was terrified. I knew he wanted to embody me. He would kill me. I fell into darkness.

At six o'clock in the morning I was shocked awake by the church bells from across the street. I had vomited in my sleep again and my nose had bled quite severely. The sheets and pillowcase were covered. I smelled awful. I couldn't go on like this. I had to stop taking acid. I was so thin. When I looked at myself in the mirror, I could see that I had ruptured the blood vessels in my eyes and face. I was sick and depressed.

"Norvin, are you up?" I knocked quietly on his door. I didn't want to be alone.

He opened the door, happy and awake, thrilled to be alive. "I had an incredible night. I went to Central Park—the stars were like jewels. I met some people from Brazil. We went dancing. I had this dream. It was so wild. Then I was . . ." I listened and forgot for a while what I had just been through.

"Norvin, in a few months it's going to be 1970. Doesn't that sound weird, 1970? I can hardly say it. I'm so depressed. I'm so old. I don't understand anything."

"Ya know sugar, one day you're just going to laugh at all this. I promise you that. It's all just going to fall away. Life is to be hopped on and off, just like that. We don't stay here too long. It's going to go by so fast. Life and death—it's all the same thing. When I die and they ask you, 'What was the cause of death?' Tell them, 'Life!' Now, just go and enjoy yourself and don't be too serious about anything. Let go! Just let go and live! Do whatever you want to do in your life. There's nothing you have to be, and nothing you have to figure out. It all just is. Just is." He hugged me and then offered me a doughnut.

Chapter Five

Rosemary and Bob seemed to be settling into married life. They had cock-tails at home after work and went out with their friends on weekends. Bob had a job as an accountant for a men's clothing manufacturer. Rosemary worked at an insurance company. When she applied for the job she wrote down that her hobbies were astrology and witchcraft. She was stunned when they published it in the new employees' brochure.

Frank and Jay had somehow gotten the money together to buy another house, this one in Buffalo, a Victorian with rental space. Jay offered Rose-mary and Bob a deal—low rent in exchange for managing the house and the other tenants. They moved into the third floor and Rosemary got her list of duties from Jay: collect rents, shovel snow, take out the garbage, cut the grass, wash the windows, keep the halls clean and listen to the complaints of the other two tenants.

I went to visit them. It was my first trip back to Buffalo since I left almost a year before. I stepped off the train in my black hooded cape and granny sunglasses. Rosemary was waiting for me at the station. In five minutes, I felt out of place and started questioning why I had come back.

"What a beautiful house this is, Rosemary." The sweeping staircase and stained-glass windows in the entranceway were magnificent.

"It's a lot of work, but we like it here and the neighborhood is great. Do you know they're buying another house? Jay took me over there to see it a couple of weeks ago when he was here. He wants me to help him fix it up. I said I would. I don't know when I can do it, but I want to help. Bob had a fit. Jay is always asking us to do things for him. He asks me to drive him all over Buffalo—he doesn't drive. We don't have any time, but I just can't say no."

We compared notes on the renovation work we were both doing for Jay. I wondered where they got the money to buy another house—and where was the money they owed me? We felt we didn't have a choice. We were helping our brother and were doing what we were told to do.

"How's married life?" I asked, as we entered their third-floor apartment.

"Oh, you know," Rosemary said.

No, I don't know, I thought. I don't have any idea. I didn't really know what to talk to Rosemary about. I was a hippie and she was married and manicured.

Rosemary showed me the apartment. A green silk brocade sectional couch, a French provincial bedroom set, a wrought-iron kitchen table, an antique French telephone.

We talked about their friends, who were also newly married, their plans to buy their own house and if they were ever going to have children. She seemed to be careful with her answers and a bit apprehensive, questioning why I was asking.

"How's your mother and Andy?" I said.

We always referred to our mother as "your mother."

"What do you care!" she snapped back.

"Are we going over to visit them tonight?

"No. We all go to lunch on Sunday. That's what we usually do. You can call them on the phone if you want and let them know you're here."

I was a little nervous to call. I hadn't spoken to them since I left. I never called and they never called.

I dialed their number on the fancy French telephone.

"Hello, it's Terry."

"Oh, Terry, you're at Rosemary's? She told me you were coming. Is Frankie here?"

"How are you, Mother? How's Dad? Can I say hello to him?"

"He doesn't talk on the phone. He's watching TV. How's Frankie?"

"Mother, Rosemary and Bob will pick you up on Sunday, for lunch."

"How's your, brother? What's Frankie been doing?"

"He's fine. We'll see you on Sunday, Mother."

"Okay. That's what they always do. Bye."

"Bye."

"I'm fine too Mother," I murmured to myself as I hung up the phone.

Bob came home from work and I was very happy to have one of those after-work cocktails.

"So Terry, how's Fraaaankie?" Bob said.

"He's good. He's studying palmistry and doing lots of readings at hotsie-totsie parties and he's the boss in a market research company."

"That's nice," Bob said.

"How's work?" I asked.

"Fine."

"How are your parents, Bob?"

"They're good. How's Norvin?"

"He's good." How could I elaborate? I didn't want them to know about my acid trips. "I'd like to go to the flea market tomorrow. Would you like to go, Rosemary?" I said.

"I don't know. What do you want to do, Bob?"

"Whatever you want to do, Rosemary."

"It's up to Terry. She's the one visiting."

After waiting two hours for them to shower and dress, and for Rosemary to make sure that no faucets were dripping and that all doors and windows were locked, we finally got out of the house.

We poked around the endless tables of other people's stuff looking for a treasure at a bargain price. I was excited when I found a Black Watch tartan Scottish tam.

"Oh, if I were you I wouldn't buy that hat," Rosemary said.

"Why not? I love it," I said, admiring myself in the mirror.

"I wouldn't buy it!" she snapped.

"Well, just tell me why. I want to know."

"The woman who owned that hat—well, she just wasn't very happy."

"Tell me everything! I want to know!" I said and tossed her the hat.

She held it close, with her eyes closed. I looked around to see if anyone was watching us. Rosemary was completely absorbed.

"She was a young girl, about sixteen," Rosemary said. "Dark hair, green eyes and so in love. I can feel that. He was her whole life—an older man, she was in love with him. He promised her everything." Rosemary was quiet and she put the hat back on the shelf where I had found it.

"Well? What happened? Don't leave me hanging!"

"I wouldn't buy it, if I were you."

"Rosemary, I'm going to kill you! Tell me what happened to her."

"He didn't come back. That's all I'm going to say."

"What do you mean? What happened to her?"

"She killed herself. Don't ask me how. It doesn't matter. That's enough! I don't want to say anymore. If you want that hat, then buy it, but don't blame me if something goes wrong!"

I wanted that hat and I was willing to take my chances, but I walked away, just in case.

Rosemary went to another table to examine some crystal wine glasses. She looked at them for quite a long time. She'd close her eyes and waited, then put them back on the table. I watched her put the side of a black marble bookend up to her ear. What was she listening to?

Sometimes it was more interesting to watch Rosemary than to ask her about what she was doing. At that time in her life she was secretive and protective about her psychic knowledge. I noticed that she touched very few objects at the flea market and the ones she did touch, she usually bought, after holding them for several minutes.

"Rosemary, I love these amber beads. What do you think? The man who's selling them told me they're from the twenties. Excellent condition. From Russia. And red amber is hard to find."

Rosemary grabbed them out of my hand. "They're plastic and from the fifties!"

"Is that psychic or do you know amber?"

"What difference does it make?" she said. "I saved you a fortune."

Rosemary spotted something and walked quickly to a table in the corner. I followed along behind her to see where she was going in such a hurry.

"I knew it! There it is! It was calling me! How much is it? Fifty dollars? Thirty-five and I'll buy it." She got what she wanted—three iron mermaids standing on their heads, their tails holding up a crystal ball. Rosemary was happy and ready to go home. I didn't dare show her the Scottish kilt pin I bought when she wasn't looking, a grouse foot, very dead, what's there to read?

Sunday came and we drove to Seventh Street to pick up my parents for lunch. My stomach knotted as the car turned onto the block. Andy was already at the window waiting for us to arrive. He watched us get out of the car. I waved to him and he waved and smiled back.

"Hello, Mother. How are you?" I leaned toward her and gave her a frozen kiss as she stood stiff in response.

"Oh hi, Terry. When did you get here?"

Bob started giving orders, "Okay. You ready? Where's Rip? Come on! Come on! Let's go! I'm hungry! Get your coat on, Big Red!"

Rosemary and I stood by the door.

"Oh shut up, you summa na bitch!" My mother was laughing as she yelled at Bob.

"Rip! Get over here, you're taking too long!" Bob called to my father in the living room.

"I'm coming. I'm coming," Andy said, shuffling through the dining room, already in his coat and hat for the last twenty minutes.

"Bob, why do you call him Rip?"

"Because all he does is sleep. Rip Van Winkle."

"Bob, where are we going today?"

"Now, Mary, where do we go every Sunday? You tell me. You should know by now."

"Oh, shut up you wise guy. We don't always go to the same place."

"Yeah, Mary, we're going to the Ritz Buffalo this time for lunch, okay? Now, put your coat on. Do you have to wear that hat?"

"You bastard! *Va caca!* Go to hell! I like my hat. What's it to you, mister? Mind your own business!" Mother said, wrapping her head in a fake fur pillbox hat with a neck scarf attached to it. It looked like it had been sat on many times.

I was in the backseat of Bob's car between Big Red and Rip. I had only been in the house for ten minutes, not even a chance to look around my old room. Rosemary was in the passenger seat saying, "Bob, watch that car. Bob, the light is green. Watch that lady, Bob, she's not looking where she's going. Bob, go faster, turn quickly at the corner, there's going to be a blue station wagon, it's ready to pull out. We can get that space right in front of the restaurant."

"Yes, Rosemary. Okay. Rosemary."

We arrived at the restaurant just as the blue station wagon was pulling out.

The Merry Go Round was a fast food place with bright primary colored walls and paper place mats honoring famous clowns throughout history— Clarabelle, Emmett Kelly, Red Skelton, etc. A little kids' restaurant.

"Bob, what are we doing here?" I whispered.

"They like it. This is where they want to eat. Andy, aren't you going to take your coat off? Mary, take that rat off your head! Right now!"

"Just get me the chicken fingers and my coffee half and half and mind your own business!"

"Mary, when the waitress comes you can tell her yourself what you want. What do I look like, your butler?"

"Terry, how's Frankie? Has he seen, ah . . . what's her name from the soap opera, the actress I met who Frankie took my picture with and we . . ."

"Mother! Tell the waitress what you want!" Rosemary blurted out.

"Gimme the chicken fingers. You know what I like. The ones in the basket. Okay, miss." She leaned over to me and whispered, "I only eat one or two and bring the rest home for the dog; she waits for it. I don't even like them. I have my coffee, that's all I want."

I watched Andy sitting at the head of the table drifting away, lost in his thoughts. I was remembering how the two of us used to go for drives in the Gremlin to Niagara Falls. I missed those days. We never said much to each other. I had no idea what he was thinking, never able to get inside of him, and no courage to ask him about anything. What was I waiting for? I started to tear up, so I turned to my mother.

"Mother, have you seen the house Frank and Jay are buying on Hodge Street?"

"Now how the hell would I see that! Who's gonna take me over there?"

"Just ask Bob and Rosemary, I'm sure they will."

Bob rolled his eyes. I was sure he had enough to do.

Andy suddenly snapped out of his daydream. "That Jay gave me a job. Ha! Yeah, he wants me to take out the barrels at the houses."

Rosemary informed me that "barrels" meant garbage cans.

"Well, is he paying you, Dad?" I stupidly asked.

Andy laughed out loud and mumbled, "Paying me? That's a joke. I do it for Frankie. Besides, it gives me something to do. It's all right."

"What's with this Jay?" Mother said. "He comes around in the morning before I have my teeth in and wants to have coffee with me and asks me if our house still has a mortgage and if I thought of 'refinancing.' What does that mean? What's he asking that for? Who the hell does he think he is, Cowboy Ta Ta?"

"Cowboy Ta Ta! I haven't heard that in years!"

Bob and Rosemary and I just laughed till we cried and Mother said, "What the hell's the matter with all of you? You summa na bitches." And she laughed too.

I could see my parents were still children. All they wanted from life was to laugh, go out for a meal and then go back home to Seventh Street. I had missed these people. They were quirky and funny and I was a lot like them, but I didn't think they had a clue who I really was. The next morning I boarded the train called the *Maple Leaf* and looked out the window for eight hours at the autumn landscape through Western New York—Rochester, Syracuse, Rome, Utica, Schenectady, Albany, Hudson, Poughkeepsie. . . . I knew it would be a long time before I would return.

Chapter Six

He reminded me of an older George Harrison, the youngest, most spiritual Beatle. She was handsome, with a strong face like Anna Magnani, the Italian movie star. Mr. and Mrs. Michael Deming. I was intrigued.

"How do you do? Call me Natalie. And this is Michael."

I was holding on to the oak post at the foot of the stairs when I was briefly introduced to them. Jay gave me a dismissive smile, which I knew meant, "Go back upstairs."

"How do you do, Mrs. Deming? Hello, Mr. Deming."

Sometimes we'd pass each other on the stairs. She'd try to engage me in conversation and I'd walk away quickly. I was curious to get to know her, but this was forbidden by Jay.

I tried to hear or catch a glimpse of them as I passed their door, but we kept different hours and I never heard anything. I often rolled in in the middle of the night. They didn't seem to be around on the weekends.

I'd been spending a lot of time with Arline, a new friend who was also a coder at the market research office. She lived alone, tucked away in the Bronx. I'd often stay at her place when it was too late to go home or I was too stoned to go anywhere.

Arline could put together old hats and scarves and thrift-shop clothes and look spectacular. Antique jewelry, shoes and something like a 1920s jacket with a fox collar would send her into ecstasy. We smoked pot and hashish and spent weekends tripping on psychedelics, going to flea markets or the Fillmore East to hear music. Often we'd just stay inside her place talking—about the office, Frank and Jay, her newest crush or dumping her latest boyfriend. The Bronx seemed so far away from Little Italy, and I loved going there. Arline's apartment was on the ground floor, in the back of a large tenement building. To get there you had to walk down a narrow brick-paved alley between two buildings, then past the garbage cans to a door around the back. Nobody could find me there.

Arline had studied cartography and loved old maps and tales about New York. She told me odd pieces of history, like when the Irish immigrants were on their way to Ellis Island, they were so taken by their first sight of the shimmering green shores along the Hudson River that many of them fell overboard from excitement.

Arline could scare me to death with the details of how fast the coastlines of the continents were changing. She knew how long we had before the melting polar ice cap would drown us all. We didn't want to waste a second, so we spent hours in the house dancing around her living room, reading the Tarot, braiding our hair. It was during that time we discovered the real meaning of life—decorating and redecorating.

. . .

I had just come home from Arline's one afternoon and had hardly taken my coat off when I saw a piece of paper slipping underneath my door. For a moment I wasn't sure if I was hallucinating. I was afraid to bend down and pick it up. The note read, "Come downstairs. The coffee's ready!" It was signed, "The Second Floor."

I didn't know what to do. What about Jay? It's only coffee, friendly neighbors. I got dressed and knocked on their door.

"Well, hello! Do we have cooties or something?" Mrs. Deming said, as she opened the door. "You always seem to be in such a hurry. Don't you like us?" She laughed, but got right to the point.

"Hello, Mr. Deming. How are you?"

He was sitting in a wingback chair smoking a brown Nat Sherman cigarette and reading the *New York Times*. Mr. Deming was an elegant, thin gentleman in his mid-fifties with a brown and gray mustache and light brown eyes. Still holding the newspaper, he peeked up over his bifocals and smiled at me.

"Please, call me Michael."

I didn't feel comfortable calling them by their first names or even being in their apartment, but I was immediately drawn to them.

"Let me show you something funny," Mrs. Deming said, as she took me into their bedroom. Next to their bed was an enormous refrigerator. "Michael gets hungry in the middle of the night. He likes to have food right near him when he wakes up," she laughed. "Actually, we love this apartment, but the kitchen's too damn small. I love to cook, so I need this big monster. So we sleep with a refrigerator. Who cares if people think we're kinky?"

Mrs. Deming seemed alive with laughter and sensuality, thirty-three, smartly dressed, with thick, short, dark brown hair. She questioned everything I said, wanting to know exactly what I meant: "Explain that." Almost immediately she told me that she was seeing a therapist.

The apartment was decorated with antique furniture and paintings, with fresh flowers in every room. She poured me espresso in a tiny porcelain cup. I didn't tell her it was too strong for me. I acted poised and confident, but I was scared to bits.

I didn't want the afternoon to end. They asked me about my brother and Jay, Norvin and the house. At first I was vague, and then I started telling them everything. They told me I should stand up for myself. I needed to talk, but then I started to panic, knowing that I had said too much. I excused myself and said I had to go.

"I love getting to know you," Mrs. Deming said. "Don't be a stranger. Would you like to go shopping next week? I need to get some things at Bloomingdale's. We could go together." She gave me a hug and he waved from the chair.

"I'll let you know. Thanks again. Bye."

I went upstairs and smiled—and freaked! Bloomingdale's? Me? I never knew anyone like them.

I started spending a lot of time with the Demings. When I'd come home and their door was open I'd say hello and they'd invite me in and we'd often eat dinner together. Their cat and dog waited outside my door for me. Mrs. Deming gave me presents and always asked if I was all right. She asked me why I took LSD. I couldn't answer. It started me thinking about the "why" of everything I was doing. She suggested I make an appointment with her therapist. A shrink?

Then they took me to the country for the weekend. I'd never been "in the country" and I was thrilled. Their house was built in the early 1800s, a stone farmhouse filled with art, antiques and big fluffy beds. They owned seven acres in the middle of a working farm in Martins Creek, Pennsylvania. In the front of the house was a cornfield. On one side of the house were rolling hills of alfalfa and in the back, thick woods. Fruit trees, raspberry bushes and wildflowers were all over the property. An unused barn that once housed dairy cows was a place to dream in. The countryside was alive with sweet scents I'd never known before.

The Demings took me to auctions, barn sales and for long drives in their country car, a 1950s Bentley. Mrs. Deming loved cooking with fresh vegetables from the farm stands. We ate on antique plates and full-service silverware, always by candlelight, at their French country table on their delicate chairs. When they finished eating, Mr. and Mrs. Deming turned their forks over with the tines facing down on the plate. I liked that and started doing it too.

After dinner, I'd always wash the dishes. Mr. Deming would often ask me if I'd like to join him outside to look at the stars. Standing there in the alfalfa fields he'd point out the constellations to me. It surprised me how close I felt to him and that I trusted him completely. I loved watching him look up at the sky with his arm pointing in the air.

With the fresh night air and several glasses of wine, we'd all start yawning and go to bed early. Under a down comforter the size of a giant cloud, I'd sleep the best sleep of my whole life. Life with the Demings was a fairy tale. They were like parents to me, teaching me how pleasurable life could be.

When Frank invited me to tea one Sunday and I said I couldn't come because I was going to the country with the Demings, he became furious.

"I'm their landlord! What are you doing with them? Jay is really upset because you haven't been there to work on the house on weekends. He's alone and there's so much to do. How could you leave him like that? *And,* tell your friends, *the Demings,* I wasn't happy with having to fix the glass in the door when Michael got locked out and broke the window!" Frank's face turned blood red.

"Frank, I'm sure he'll pay for it, and if he doesn't, then ask him to."

"That's not the point. He broke my window! They're also late with the rent check. It's already the fifth, and where is it?"

"Frank, call them. They're very nice."

I told the Demings what Frank said and how upset he was. Mrs. Deming said, "Tell your *brother* that Michael had to sweep garbage off the front stairs three times this week. And if he wants the check he can come over and get it!"

I could see what was happening. I felt I was responsible for this tension by spending too much time with them, and telling them how I felt Frank was ignoring me and having me work so hard and how I resented taking orders from Jay. This was turning into a big mess.

I went to see my friend Arline for advice.

"Terry, what are you doing with those people? They are so straight. Frank is furious. He hates them and he's jealous."

"How do you know? Who told you? Did Frank say something to you?"

"Well, while you've been in the country doing your D. H. Lawrence thing—"

"Arline! It's not like that! We are not a ménage à trois. I wish. But we're not!" I said, clarifying the situation. "Now, finish what you were saying."

"Well. You know Raoul, Christina's son? Christina from the office," she said, with a little smile on her face.

"Arline! I know who she is! Where are you going with this? Arline, don't tell me you're sleeping with him. What happened to what's his name? The guy you met at Mamoun's, that souvlaki place on MacDougal Street?"

"You mean the waiter? He didn't last long."

"Raoul, okay he's cute, but does his mother know? You little devil."

"Honey, we are not sleeping. Does he know how to . . ." she said, slowly riding her tongue across her lips.

"Arline! What about Frank? What did he say? Does he know about Raoul?"

"What part?" She burst out laughing.

"Arline!"

"Okay, all right. I'll tell you. Frank told Christina that he's upset that you're never home and that you're talking about him to his tenants. And he told her that you're a drug addict. That's what Raoul told me."

"He's always telling people I'm a drug addict. That's so stupid. And how does he know I'm talking to the tenants?"

"He's psychic! He's your brother."

"Oh shit! Arline, what should I do?"

"Go see Reverend Clifford."

"Who's that?"

"Reverend Clifford Bias. He's supposed to be the best psychic in New York. I've never been, but I've heard he's good. You need some insight from somebody who doesn't know you. Check it out and if you like him, then I'll go."

"Thanks for the advice. I'm sure he knows Frank. Everybody knows Frank."

"Well, don't mention his name. Besides you have different last names. He'll never put it together," Arline assured me.

"I thought you said he was psychic. Holy Mary Mother of God! This is what I need now, a psychic? What good am I? I don't know what to do. Let's get a drink. Remember alcohol?"

"Don't worry, and get out of the middle. Call Clifford," Arline said again.

• • •

I made an appointment. Reverend Clifford told me to come Wednesday afternoon at three to the Ansonia Hotel on Broadway and West Seventy-third Street. The Ansonia was a massive Beaux Arts–style residential hotel built in 1899, with ornate ironwork balconies and fancy French corner towers. The lobby looked like Louis XIV decorated it. During its history, Babe Ruth, Enrico Caruso, Sarah Bernhardt, Florenz Ziegfeld, Toscanini, Stravinsky and many other famous people lived there. Once upon a time it had a Turkish bath, two swimming pools, restaurants and several shops in the lobby, but by the time I got there it was a dump.

"Hello, come in. How do you do?" Reverend Clifford towered over me. When he shook my hand, at my eye level I faced the front of his shabby gray suit dotted with fresh splatters of lunch.

"Have a seat over here." The room was gigantic and probably hadn't been painted since the hotel was built. The furniture either came off the stage of the Metropolitan Opera or was borrowed from the lobby downstairs. He led me to a pair of lumpy stuffed chairs. I sat directly across from him. With his eyes closed, I had a few minutes to look at him while he prepared himself to read me. Tiny beads of sweat started popping up between the few gray strands of hair across the top of his head and on his forehead and upper lip. After a few seconds, he sprang to his feet and started talking up to the ceiling.

"My dear, you have tremendous power!" He said with his eyes still fixed on the ceiling as he waved his hands around my head like he was fluffing up a pillow.

"You must surely know this. Your aura is so bright and fluorescent, with a blue-green variegate complimented by red and orange!"

I looked up to see who he was talking to. The high ceiling looked like it was covered in wedding cake frosting. I heard what he said, but I couldn't take it in.

"Young lady, do you know who you are?"

I started to pay attention.

"Now listen to me very carefully. I have something extremely important to tell you and I'm going to get right to the point. In your most important past life you were a magician. The highest of priestesses. You sat on the throne of power. You and your family were all magicians. And you are back together again. In this life, the power you possess is unlike any that is known here at this time in the world." He bent down and started to whisper to me, "You were involved in rituals and performed ceremonies where you made miraculous things happen.

"Now . . . you must begin to do this work again in this life. Here, write this down—exactly as I tell you. Are you ready? I am going to remind you of a ritual you already know from deep in your soul. It will come back to you as you begin to ignite the process. Do you understand me so far?

"I want you to choose a holy day, a holy day that means something special to you. On that day . . . you will reclaim your wand. Your magic wand! You've been searching for it through many, many incarnations. But now the time is right. This time you must get back the wand!

"There is only one way to do this. You must make it yourself. Now, I want you to do exactly as I say. Are you listening? Go into the woods and take a virgin knife with you. A knife that has never been used. Do you hear me? Find a tree, preferably an ash or a poplar. Trust me—you and the tree will find each other. Choose a branch that has never touched the ground. That's very important, do you understand? It must be as long as your spine and as thick as your thumb." He held up his thumb and slowly moved it toward my face. "You will know exactly what words to say at that time. Believe me, it will all come back to you. These words are emblazoned in your soul. With the wand in both hands make a complete circle . . ." He stood in the center of the room with his arms stretched out in front of him and started spinning around. "Bring it over your head and across the top of your body as you . . ."

He went on at great length telling me how to reclaim my power using the wand. He reassured me that the wand would tell me what to do. My problems would be solved once I had my wand back, he said. I was astonished. This was not what I was expecting to hear.

I felt really silly about asking him how to resolve the situation with Frank after he told me that I was a long-lost high priestess. What if this was the way to solve all my problems? I wasn't ready for this. He told me that I was surrounded by lights, that nothing must ever own me and how I had to flow with everything that came into my life. Nothing would stay that wasn't supposed to be there. He said I would help a lot of people and that good things were going to come to me. I could make magic happen again.

"Now go and do what I told you!"

I paid my twenty-five dollars, shook his hand and left.

Chapter Seven

The wall was building between Frank and me and the Demings. Frank ignored me at the market research office, barely saying hello. Everyone there knew something was going on between us. When he would go out after work with some of the coders, I was never invited. We each told our version of the story to just about everyone in the office. I said he was an egomaniac and a control freak and he told the same people I had drug problems.

It was hard hearing from the other coders about Frank and the things he was doing. They seemed to know more about him than I did. He didn't come in to work one day and I heard some of the girls whispering. I asked what was going on.

"Frank's really upset. He lost one of his dogs."

"What? What happened?"

"Well, I heard he put a spell on a woman he was angry at. He wanted her to fall in love with a man and have the man leave her soon after. It worked. But then, right after that his favorite dog died."

I ran out of the office and sobbed inside the stall of the ladies' room. I couldn't talk to him about it, fearing he'd just yell at me. I couldn't believe he would do such a spell. He knows the consequences of doing harmful magic like that. It always comes back to you. I felt sorry for him.

After several weeks of avoiding Frank at the office and feeling depressed,

Mr. Deming offered me a job working at his framing company. I happily accepted, further infuriating Frank.

I worked with Mr. Deming developing a mail order business for the picture frames. It was a small factory in a loft on Broadway, a few blocks from Mulberry Street. The people working there were like a big family. One day I walked passed Mr. Deming's office and caught a glimpse of him passionately kissing his secretary. With all the trouble I was getting myself into, I knew never to mention this to anyone.

During that time I became even closer to the Demings, spending most of my time with them. They took me with them to the country almost every weekend. She insisted I call her Natalie, but I liked being formal with her. We talked at length about my life, Frank and my family. She made me think about why I was living the way I was. She gave me a big hug and a kiss whenever she saw me and sat close to me on her couch. I wasn't used to this, but it made me feel good, feel loved.

I called Frank and Jay several times to try to see them for dinner or a visit, but they would always say no with some excuse that I knew was being made up on the spot. Most of my communications were with Jay, who always answered the phone. When I'd ask for Frank, Jay would say he wasn't there. Frank refused to speak to me. I'd put the phone down hurt and confused. I was incapable of demanding that he speak to me. I felt terribly guilty.

I went to Frank's lectures where the rooms were packed with people who'd lined up to hear him speak on the Tarot, the Rune Stones, palmistry, numerology, the I Ching, astrology and spirituality. They were drawn to his youth and good looks, his ability to speak naturally with humor and insight. He never used notes. Hardly anyone in those days had the knowledge that Frank had. He told his audience that ancient wisdom was available to all of us and we needed to start using it now. Frank had them spellbound.

He gave spontaneous psychic information and predictions to many people in the audience. Frank was happy to accommodate and they wouldn't let him leave the stage. Some people said they felt healed listening to him, they wanted to touch him. Frank told them that they were probably feeling good from the energy in the room and because of what they were learning. He discouraged them from thinking he had miraculous powers.

Whenever someone in the audience asked him about his childhood he'd briefly mention Buffalo or say he was from Upstate New York. He never mentioned that he had two psychic sisters or that he had any sisters at all. At the end of every lecture, I'd make my way to the stage and stand in line to congratulate him, but his response to me was always cold and distant. He'd say hello like I was a stranger and then move on to the next person.

Norvin and Arline knew how upset I was about Frank. They gave me "this is how families are" kind of advice. Norvin often held my hand through the lectures, knowing I was suffering.

The Demings didn't believe that Frank was psychic. They just assumed he was a con man. Everything about him, right from the beginning, annoyed them. Telling them my personal troubles didn't help.

One day after work, Natalie called me into their apartment.

"I got a call today from your brother. He told me to make sure that I buy the Sunday *New York Times* and carefully read the real estate section. That was it, that was all he said. And he hung up on me when I tried to talk to him."

"The real estate section, what do you think is going on?"

"I have no idea. He's a wacko nut job!" she said.

I felt really terrible and confused and at the same time protective of my brother. It's all right if I call him names, but I don't like to hear it from anyone else. I knew what was coming, but I didn't want to read it in the Sunday paper.

When Sunday came, the Demings and I read the real estate section together. Mr. Deming went over every column looking for evidence of Frank's mysterious message.

"I think I've found it! Listen to this: 'Little Italy. Charming, three-story house in undiscovered neighborhood. For sale by owner. No tenants. Immediate Occupancy. $55,000.' This must be it. Is this their phone number?" Mr. Deming read the number out loud. It was Frank and Jay's. "Does he really think he's going to get fifty-five for this place?"

"Well kids, I guess we're moving!" Natalie let out a hardy laugh.

I was stunned. Where was I going to go? How could he throw us out like this and do it through the newspaper? I had to go upstairs and think.

"I'll see you later. I have to go."

I was in shock and denial. Maybe it was just meant for the Demings. Maybe he doesn't mean me. About an hour later there was a knock on my door. It was Jay.

"Now Terry, I have something to tell you. I just found out that my mother has to move out of her house in Georgia and I've asked her to come live here on Mulberry Street. She's getting older and she needs me to look after her. She'll be living here on the third floor so I have to ask you to find other accommodations."

"When is she coming?"

"In two weeks, on the first of the month."

"Oh no . . . Jay, if I have to move . . . then I'll need my two thousand dollars back that I lent you. You said I'd be paid back whenever I needed the money. I'm going to need it to find another place to live."

"That will not be a problem, Terry. I'll prepare a check for you and I'll leave it under your door."

"No. I'll come to Perry Street later and pick it up."

"No. That will not be possible. Frank and I have guests for dinner. I'll have the check for you and I'll give it to you tomorrow. I promise. I've got to go now. Good-bye and good luck. Things will work out for you."

He left and I knew he was lying. His mother wasn't going to move into my apartment. Why can't he just tell me the truth, that he wants me out of here? I went downstairs to tell the Demings that I had just been kicked out of the house and they said they had just had the same visit from Jay, except he said that he was going to be living on their floor.

A few days passed and I didn't know what I was going to do. Mr. Deming called me into his office.

"Terry, have you thought about where you're going to go?"

"No, I have no idea. I heard about a commune on Staten Island, but I haven't seen it yet."

"You know, Natalie has been wanting to leave New York for quite a while now and she'd love to move permanently to the country house. How would you feel about living there with her? She'd love the company and she really is very fond of you."

He seemed excited with the idea and pleased to be helping me. He pointed out all of the advantages about living in such a beautiful, peaceful place.

"What about my job here?" I loved this job and I didn't think I'd leave New York just yet.

"Why don't you think about it? Talk to Natalie and see what she says. It's really great out there. I only wish I could do it."

Now I was really confused. I was too young to live on a farm. It seemed like a place you'd retire to. What am I going to do there? And what about money? I have to work. I loved being with Natalie, but New York City was my dream. I had nowhere to go and ten days left to figure out what to do. If I didn't go, then I might not see her again. I was starting to panic.

Frank and Jay wanted all of us out. Norvin told me he would only be there for a couple more months and then he was going to Buffalo to work on another house that Frank and Jay were in the process of buying. Norvin told me the truth. Jay's mother wasn't moving into my apartment. He would never bring his mother here. And they weren't selling the house either, it was Jay's way of getting us out. Norvin said he'd decided to go back to Texas after he finished the renovation. His sister had young children and he felt they needed him there. He said he thought it was a good idea for me to go to the country for a while, clear my head. He said he'd come visit me. He promised.

. . .

It was early spring 1970 when we moved to Martins Creek. I set up my room and every day discovered something about the wonders of country life—having lunch outside, dropping seeds into soil, the smell of hay in the barn. I loved it when Natalie hugged me and asked me if I was happy. I said I was, not really knowing exactly what happy felt like.

While driving the car, she'd reach over and touch my knee, holding her hand there for what seemed like eternity. I often had to look away out the window. Her touch made me blush and I didn't know how to respond or what she actually meant by it.

We sat on her bed as she taught me needlepoint. I wrote poetry to her. We did yoga together in front of the fireplace. Often, she'd ask me to rub her shoulders, showing me exactly where to put my hands on the small bones of her neck to relieve her pain. I liked touching her.

I was rebuilding myself from many months of self neglect and taking drugs. Throughout the day Natalie and I would find ourselves laughing. I watched her when she couldn't see me, from the crack in the barn wall or from the upstairs window. I needed her—and I wanted to kiss her.

I was twenty-two and coming alive sexually. I was confused between my need for mothering and my attraction to Natalie. She'd sometimes call me while she was in the bathroom and I'd answer her through the door. I could hear the water running and she'd shout out that she couldn't hear me and tell me to come in. When I opened the door, I'd find her standing there naked just looking at me. She wanted to know what I was doing. I'd start counting the tiles on the wall.

I had no one to talk to. I didn't know what to do. Afraid of rejection, afraid of being asked to leave my home again, I didn't tell Natalie how I was feeling. I couldn't help feeling like a guest in their house. I'd be alone all week with her until Mr. Deming came on the weekend. Once in a while he didn't come because he had to stay in town. I liked it when he didn't come; I liked my own private world with Natalie, even though I was confused about it.

I hated seeing Natalie change when Michael was around. She was so confident and alive, laughing with me all week, and then when he was there she waited on him, made all the meals and poured him drinks while he read the newspaper. Tense and depressed, she smoked his Nat Shermans and walked by herself in the hills. He constantly criticized her and complained about grocery money she spent, but then he'd drive up in a brand-new Jaguar. Mr. Deming drank more. Mrs. Deming cut her hair shorter.

I felt I shouldn't be there. I didn't know what to do or where to go. And each of them started talking to me about the other. I'd lay in my bed awake in the dark listening to their muffled voices arguing on the other side of the bedroom wall. After the fighting—the springs in the antique bed and the moans of making love. I plugged my ears, crying.

. . .

I sent Frank several letters telling him how I was doing, pretending that I was fine and nothing had happened between us. I'd ask him to return the money I lent him, telling him I needed it to buy a car or I might be enrolling in school. I needed to hear from him; I needed to know that everything was all right with us. Two thousand dollars was a lot of money and I wanted it back. I never got an answer. Silence. After several weeks of waiting, one day a letter finally came.

Dear Terry,

You were a resident on Mulberry Street for twenty months, therefore we have deducted $100.00 for each of those months as payment of rent. We do not owe you any money.

When friends of ours ask us how you are, we tell them that you died. You left with the enemy and we consider you dead. Do not try to contact us.

Sincerely,
Frank Andrews

I ran up into the hills, crying and terrified. I sat down in the middle of a field surrounded by a carpet of purple alfalfa flowers and wept. Looking down where my running had cut so deeply into the field, I followed the trampled path with my eyes from the bottom of the hill back to myself, over and over again. Did Frank hate me that much? Is this a declaration of war? What do I do now?

Then I got angry. I worked hard in that house. Jay promised he'd pay me back. "I'll draw up the check tomorrow." He robbed me! They're buying another house! That money was mine and I needed it. Frank couldn't have written that letter. I'm dead!? I knew how powerful Frank was. I was scared that he would do magic on me. How could I protect myself? I had to do something. I remembered Reverend Clifford Bias's words. I got out of the field and ran to my Catholic missal. I had to find out the next holy day.

I had saved my prayer book from high school and flipped through the pages frantically. I had to find the day. *Saints' Feast Days. April. May. June.*

I read out loud, "St. Anthony of Padua. Feast day: June 13. Patron of the Poor. Finder of lost articles."

Holy Mary Mother of God! I can't believe it! That's tomorrow! St. Anthony will help me find my missing magic wand. This is a miracle! A sign from God!

I ran and found Natalie pulling weeds in the garden. I asked her if she had plans to go into town to do any shopping and she said she did need a few things.

"Can we go now?" I asked urgently.

We got in the car and went to Falk's, a giant supermarket in Easton about thirty miles from our house. Falk's was a store that sold everything from corn flakes to shotguns. I knew I could buy my virgin knife there. In the twenty-minute ride in the car to the store I devised a plan to distract Natalie so that I could go to the hunting and fishing aisle and pick out my knife.

Natalie pushed the shopping cart, filling it with groceries she needed, carefully reading labels, checking her list and writing notes as she moved along. While she was doing that, I secretly filled the basket with items she'd never buy.

"What the hell is this?" she said as she held up a jar of Fluff marshmallow spread. "I didn't buy this. And what are these chocolate-sprinkled doughnuts doing here?" She yanked out the bag of orange candy peanuts, the giant box of Lucky Charms and the jar of pickled pigs' ears.

"Are you crazy? Very funny. Ha. Ha. Now go put this stuff back. Yuk, who would eat this crap?"

I ran around the store with my arms full of these exotic gastric treasures, putting them back where I found them. Some of them didn't make it back. I needed time to pick out the knife. I did have second thoughts about giving up the Lucky Charms.

Exhausted and breathing heavily, I ran up to the man behind the display case selling knives.

"What can I do for you, ma'am? Let me know if I can show you anything. Looking for a Bowie? Is it for huntin', fishin'? Your husband needs a scaler?"

It took me a moment to take this all in. I was in a store that sold food, refrigerators, baby clothes, guns and ammunition. I was talking to a man standing in front of some terrifying-looking shotguns, a case full of revolvers and knives that I'd seen only in Westerns at the Niagara movie theater in Buffalo.

I looked over the display case. I knew it would just jump out at me. It was here. It had to call me.

And then I saw it! A pocket knife with a dark green handle and a four-inch shining blade—my Excalibur.

"Can that knife cut a branch off a tree?" I asked.

"I beg your pardon ma'am? Is that what you need it for? These aren't pruning knives. We have some of those in the gardening department. They'll have what you're looking for. Two aisles over."

"No, I mean is it sharp enough to cut wood?"

"You can do some serious whittlin' with that blade. Yes, you can."

"Yeah, whittlin'. That's what I want it for. I whittle."

"Nice hobby. Passes the time."

"Yes, it does. How much for that knife?"

"That one will cost you six dollars and seventy-nine cents, ma'am."

"I'll take it!"

"Thank you."

I ran back to Natalie, who was in the middle of a discussion with the butcher about how she wanted her porterhouse cut.

"That looks delicious!" I said out of breath.

"I thought I'd cook it with some shallots and baby onions with haricots verts and some roasted potatoes. I also got the shad roe you love."

"I can't wait," I said.

As soon as it got dark, I told Natalie that I was going to go outside to look at the moon. She asked if I minded if she stayed in. She wanted to read.

I was afraid of the woods at night even though I believed the scariest thing in the woods was my own mind. But this night . . . I was exhilarated. I was on a mission.

Praying to St. Anthony to guide me, I walked into the trees to find my magic wand. The crunching leaves under my feet got louder and louder with every step. The sound of my own footsteps frightened me into thinking someone was following me. Do I go this way or that way? Don't think. Pray. I trust. Nothing can harm me. You know why you're here. You know what you have to do.

The half moon gave me enough light to see my way through the trees. Walk. Keep walking. Pray. Have no fear. The house was out of sight and seemed to be very far away. St. Anthony are you with me? St. Anthony, be my guide, lead me to my magic wand. Pray. Walk. Tremble. Pray. *Yea, though I walk through the valley of the shadow of death.*

I heard a rustle. Something moved in the trees above my head. I jumped and looked up as I was walking and crashed hard against a tree! My heart leapt out of my chest, my head was throbbing. I found the tree.

Shaken, I wanted to run. Slow down and breathe. *As thick as my thumb, as long as my spine.* Where are you? Oh, St. Anthony, patron saint of lost objects, help me find my wand.

I circled the tree a couple of times looking straight up the tree trunk, but it was too dark to see the branches. I went around like a buzzard looking for prey. I knew the wand was on that tree. Then light from the moon appeared from behind a cloud. For one quick moment, I saw the branch. It was above my head about a foot higher then my arm could reach.

I fumbled, rushing to get my virgin knife out of my pocket. Please, moonlight stay with me. Don't move the clouds back yet, please. You have power, ask for what you need! Give me that branch! I jumped up as high as I could and with one slash of the knife I cut the branch from the tree. It fell down through the air and I caught it with one hand.

I stood there stunned, with the branch in my hand. I couldn't believe I got it. I put it behind my back to measure that it was as long as my spine.

Now what do I do? I started laughing. This is ridiculous! If anybody knew what I was doing out here! I laughed out loud and forgot about the werewolves and vampires behind the trees waiting to ravish me.

You have power! I know that, and I must take it now! It's only you here, nobody else. Nobody's watching you. Do it! This is real. You must believe. You do believe. Claim what's already yours! You know what to do. Hold the wand and command what's yours. Say the words out loud. You know what they are.

I thought of my mother. Her face came so clearly to me. She believed, without a doubt, that the power inside of her could kill someone if she directed it toward them. Could she hate that much to kill somebody? She knew the secret thoughts of people and she terrified us with that knowing. She believed in things that she didn't understand and was frightened of her own power. I'm the child of a long line of magicians—and so is Frank and so is Rosemary. We are a family with power that must learn how to use it again. Is this evil? Is this testing us? Has Frank done magic on me? Does he really want me dead?

This is when I must let go. I must be my own person and fight for my life. This is the night to believe, to believe without a doubt that I am a priestess. That magic is alive. I held the wand with both hands and twirled around in a circle saying an incantation to the woods, the sky, the waters, the earth. *North, South, East and West, I claim the four directions and call my power into this circle. I am fearless and I cast my wish upon myself. No one can harm me. I go on into my life knowing that I have asked for what is rightfully mine. I accept the responsibilities that come with this act and am honored and humbled to take my place among the highest of magicians. St. Anthony, on this your feast day you've helped me find my lost magic wand and I thank you. May all the saints and angels protect me and send me into the world to do good. I make no deals, no compromises. I only promise to use my power for good. I will just do what I must do. Keep me safe and humble, always. The power is mine and I am grateful for this gift. I accept this branch as the channel to the highest forces to command at will what I need to carry out my life. Thy rod and thy staff they comfort me.*

I bring to life the first and second cards of the Tarot: the Magician and the High Priestess.

I can't tell you what else I did out there that night or what I saw in the visions that materialized before me. The wish I made on the wand is sacred and my secret to the grave. I claimed myself and my own force. I took the power that was rightfully mine. It was time now to go back and let life unfold, trusting I'd know what to do.

That night I knew I had to begin to separate myself from my family. I missed my father. My sister had begun another life with someone outside the family. I wanted to let go of being obsessed with my mother and brother. In my mind, they were one person.

I wanted to know the reasons behind why my family did what they did. I had to know before I could free myself, before I could fully understand who I was. I had to know myself without them before I could have real power.

After several weeks of not having any money, I did what any powerful high priestess with a magic wand would do—I got a job. My choices in the country were limited: supermarket checkout girl, dairy barn cleanup helper, salesperson for Mary Kay cosmetics. Not very promising. I decided to try a factory position not far from our house that said, "no experience necessary." I went for an interview.

They asked me my educational background, explained what the job entailed and hired me on the spot. Could I start the next day? I needed the work and it seemed easy enough.

Natalie drove me to the factory the next morning at seven. She said she'd stop by the local garage and ask if they had an old clunker around the shop that they might want to sell for a couple hundred bucks. She'd lend me the money so I'd have my own transportation. She was not going to chauffeur me to the factory every day. I loved the idea of having my own car.

The factory manufactured ladies' dresses. Simple, cotton, American, "I have no opinion about anything" kind of dresses. Flowers, paisleys, plaids and stripes—one style in every size. My job—put the belts on the dresses, size 16. Loop it through, third hole from the end, buckle and move to the next dress as fast as I could. I stood in one spot all day until the whistle blew for lunch, then again until a ten-minute break and finally, released at four.

Women stood every three feet along the line, belting the other sizes. We were not allowed to talk to one another. At the lunch table I sat alone and no one would talk to me. I tried to start conversations, but they were quickly cut short. I'd see them whispering to each other about me. They couldn't figure out what I was doing there. I picked up bits and pieces of conversation. They were middle-aged, married women with children in school or much older widowed or divorced women. I was so much younger and clearly not from around there. I looked a lot different too. My hair was permed into tight little curls and I wore white face powder and red lipstick.

At the lunch table several ladies read the Bible while they ate their bologna and cheese sandwiches. Their lips would move as they read silently to themselves between the bites. They'd smile at me only when they caught me looking at them.

After lunch and back on the line, whenever one of the "Bible belters" walked by me I'd hear them quoting some scripture. The usual brainwash about the streets paved with gold and Jesus as your personal savior. They'd get right up behind my head and start that damn preaching.

"And He shall send Jesus Christ, which before was preached unto you."

"Get away from me!" I'd smack the air around them the way you'd kill a mosquito when they'd get too close. They made me so angry. They all had that dazed look of being possessed by Jesus. Every day I'd find Jehovah's Witness pamphlets slipped in my locker and inside my box of belts. That gave me the creeps. Once one of them started talking to me. For a brief moment she appeared normal until the conversation slipped into the salvation of my lost soul. I started letting spit drool out of my mouth when they came around preaching. I'm sure they thought I was the Devil.

I'd been working there for almost four months when I got a call from Arline, saying she wanted to come to see me. On Saturday morning I went to the Easton bus station to pick her up. I hardly slept the night before, I was so excited. Arline was coming to Pennsylvania to visit me! I couldn't wait.

I picked her up in my 1959 Buick Le Sabre. When she got off the bus, wearing a buckskin fringe jacket and cowboy boots, I almost crushed her to death with my hug. I'd missed her so much.

"What the hell color is that?" she asked, about my car. "It looks like pumpkin shit!"

"Get in, it's my rocket ship. I got it for a hundred bucks. I'd be lost without this car. I'll show you the countryside. Hang on Calamity Jane!"

We drove around the winding country roads past the farms, blasting the radio, singing and smoking pot. I forgot what it was like to be with someone my own age. I was having so much fun. I felt cool again. We talked about her lineup of boyfriends, my job at the factory, the recent death of Janis Joplin. And had she heard anything about Frank?

"I'm hungry. Where can we eat?"

"Let's go back to the house and grab something from the fridge."

When we walked into the house I was surprised to see that Natalie had the table in the sun room set for lunch with her Limoges china and silver.

"Wow, Terry, this is fancy. Do you always eat like this?"

Natalie appeared out of the kitchen carrying a silver tray with a pitcher of fresh lemonade. I stared at the slices of lemon swirling around in a whirlpool of ice.

"I thought the three of us should get to know each other, but I wasn't expecting the Wild West. Arline, you should sit here. Terry, bring in the rolls.

"So, Arline, Terry tells me that you studied to be a cartographer. Now tell me, what do you think you're going to do with that? I mean can you really make a living drawing maps?"

"Arline's professor called her the Rembrandt of cartographers," I said, passing the asparagus to Arline.

"I'm an artist, Mrs. Deming. Life will show me how to take care of myself."

"Good luck! You're going to need it," Natalie laughed.

Arline flared her nostrils looking straight at Natalie. I crossed my eyes at Arline and stuck out my tongue covered with bread and butter. We both starting giggling. Natalie pushed back her chair and excused herself saying she had errands to do. She left her plate full and walked out.

"What's her problem?" Arline said.

I shrugged my shoulders and we finished lunch. Arline said she wanted to check out the country stores and junk barns so we got back in the car and went looking for bargains. We drove for a long time, Arline was very quiet. She just stared out the window and played with the fringe on her jacket.

"Pull over! Pull the car over! Right now!" Arline demanded.

I turned the steering wheel and slammed the brakes, pulling the car over to an abrupt stop on the side of the road. "What's the matter? What's wrong?"

"I just want to know—what are you doing here? I mean what are you doing with these people in the middle of nowhere? For Chrissake, you're listening to James Taylor! Are you going to spend your life here? What's happened to you? Hendrix is dead! Janis is dead! The Beatles broke up. And you're belting dresses for Jesus! I can't stand it!"

"Arline, I had nowhere to go. What was I supposed to do? Frank threw me out."

"Nowhere to go? What about Marrakesh? San Francisco? You were going to move into that commune in Denver? I thought you had a ticket on a freighter to Portugal?"

"I did. I returned it."

She started in on me, "Listen to me! Will you give up wanting a mother and grow up! You went from Frank and Jay to her. What's the difference be-

tween them? Don't you have your own mind? Get out of here or you're going to die! She'll ruin you. You're not like these people and you'll never be,
thank God! Now listen, I'm moving. I'm leaving New York and I'm going
to Oregon. I've made up my mind. I've been following the teachings of Paul
Twitchell and the Eckankar movement. I've never known freedom like this
before. Eckankar teaches you to think for yourself. It's all about soul travel
and astral projection. You can go anywhere you want inside and outside of
yourself. You know, you do this stuff already. It's everything we talk about.
Eckankar shows you how to break the endless cycle of reincarnation. You
need this. You're headed for a repeated pattern here. Look at what you're doing! It's not good karma. I feel really free for the first time in my life. Come
with me to Oregon. We'll be with people who think like us. Let's go back to
the house and get your stuff. We can drive this pumpkin mobile out West.
You got to get out of here today!"

"I can't. I'm not ready to do that. And you know how I feel about gurus."

"He's not a guru. He's a teacher."

"It's not my thing. I'm not interested and I don't even want to hear about
him. What kind of guru is called Twitchell?"

Arline looked sadly at me, "Take me to the bus station. I want to go
home. I can't stand to see you like this."

"I thought you were going to stay the weekend. Please, don't go yet."

"I have to. I don't want to go back to that house. I don't like that woman.
She's mean, controlling and she's teasing you. Can't you see she has the hots
for you? I saw how she touched your hand when you passed the butter. She's
playing with your head. And she's using you to get attention from her husband. You're her plaything. Face reality!"

"Arline!"

"Take me to the bus."

We sat in my car in the parking lot until the bus came. She was hard on
me. Part of me knew she was right. She was trying to get me to see what I
was doing, but I just couldn't leave. I didn't want to go Oregon. I didn't want
to work in a dress factory. I was in love with Natalie, but I couldn't tell her. I
didn't want Arline to go. I missed New York terribly.

"There's the bus. I gotta go. Think about what I said. I'm going to leave
in a couple of weeks and I want you to come. Do I have to kidnap you? Oh,
I almost forgot—here's a present for you."

Arline took a shoe box–sized present out of her alligator traveling bag and handed it to me. It was wrapped in a worn-out map of the Bronx and tied with an old necktie.

She bent down to give me a hug. Arline was a lot taller than me, and in her cowgirl boots she was a giant.

"Good-bye, kid. I love you. Think hard about what I said. Promise me? You mean a lot to me and I want you to be happy."

"I will. I'll see you again before you know it. I love you too."

I waved good-bye till I couldn't see the bus anymore. I wondered if I ever would see her again. I got in the car and drove home with the present in the front seat where she had sat.

When I got home I unwrapped my gift. Under the lid of the box was a sepia-colored photograph of railroad tracks with a note from Arline on top of some tissue paper inside the box. In her most perfect calligraphy she wrote a line from a Buffalo Springfield song.

"There you stood on the edge of your feather expecting to fly."

. . .

There in the box, I could smell 'em. Arline's special brownies. Arline's hashish brownies—I knew just who to share them with.

I went early Monday morning to the dress factory and placed the box on the center of the table where the ladies always had their morning coffee before they started the day. "Help yourself!" I said. I think they thought I finally had come over to their side. They devoured the whole box of brownies.

Jesus is alive! Hallelujah! I could see it hit them right away. Arline never skimps on the main ingredient. I'm sure those ladies had never known the Holy Spirit until that day. They were being born again and again. They were smiling and belting and singing their Sunday hymns. One woman was dancing in and out of the dresses singing and laughing. One woman walked into the foreman's office, pushed him aside and took the loudspeaker and started reading from her Bible. Everything was delightfully out of control. Those ladies were so stoned. Several of them huddled together laughing and crying and speaking in tongues. "Praise the Lord! Say Amen, Jesus!" I saw a woman on her knees weeping into a bunch of size-12 red-and-white striped seersuckers. I started thinking I better get the hell out of there before anyone caught on. I ran to my car, ripped the Jesus pamphlets off from under the windshield wipers and tore out of the parking lot as fast as I could. Holy shit!

Now what? It was worth whatever happens to me. I don't care! I laughed all the way home. Hallelujah Jesus!

I told Natalie I'd been laid off without warning because the work ran out. After talking about what to do next, she came up with the idea that I should go to the local business school to learn typing and shorthand. I wasn't excited about the idea, but I called the school the next day to find out the class schedule. Then I phoned the factory and told them I couldn't work there anymore because I just got a call and I had to take care of my ailing parents in Nebraska. Nothing was said about the brownies. Maybe I was saved by Jesus after all.

New York City seemed very far from Pennsylvania and Buffalo seemed even farther away. I loved the country, but I wasn't sure what I was doing there. I drove around alone in my car listening to the radio and eating Twinkies. I'd wander in cornfields pretending I was on another planet. Silos became spaceships and dairy cows aliens. The country postal clerk was a spy and waitresses in diners might be the real mother I'd been looking for all my life. I was doing the same thing again. Getting bored with myself.

I was so lonely, and my suppressed feelings for Natalie made me frustrated, confused and angry. I was readjusting my perceptions of the world without acid or marijuana. I think Arline's brownies were my last ticket to the outer spheres. I stayed in my room a lot and counted the days I'd been there. How was I going to get out of here? The same question I'd asked myself for so long in Buffalo.

I hadn't spoken to Rosemary in months. I was too depressed to call. One day I woke up thinking about her. In the car on the way to the store, I couldn't stop thinking about Rosemary. I starting feeling something was wrong. I had to call her as soon as I could. When I walked in the door Natalie told me that Rosemary had called and to call her right away.

"Hello, Rosemary, how are you? Is something wrong?"

"Well no, not exactly."

"Rosemary, what's going on? Just tell me."

She took her time. "Well . . . let's see, I have two things to tell you."

"Yes . . . I'm waiting . . ." She loves suspense. Rosemary always speaks very measured and slowly. It drives me crazy.

"You'll never believe what happened," she started getting excited. "I went to the drugstore in my neighborhood on Saturday to pick up my prescription and it wasn't ready. I was so annoyed. I went home and called them three times to see where it was. Three times! They kept telling me it wasn't ready yet."

"Rosemary, what happened?"

"Wait, I'll get to it. Be patient."

"Well, I started to get this bad feeling that the store wasn't going to be there if I didn't get the prescription on Saturday. It made no sense to me, but I was panicked about getting that prescription on Saturday. The drugstore is open on Sunday and the pharmacist promised me he'd have it ready on Sunday morning."

"And? Hurry up. What happened?"

"I'm telling you! I went there the next day as soon as they opened and asked for my prescription. When the pharmacist handed me the bag a cold chill came over me. I looked at him and felt a terrible feeling. I knew that something was wrong. I felt ill and had to get out of there. I didn't even want to wait for my change. As I turned to leave the store, I was shocked—the room looked empty. The shelves had nothing on them. Everything was gray and black. I felt like I was walking on broken glass. I ran out the door. I ran all the way home with the most dreadful feeling.

"It was about half an hour later that I heard sirens. Fire trucks and an ambulance rushed past my house. I ran out onto the front porch and my neighbor told me that she'd heard that the drugstore had blown up! There was a gas leak and three people were killed! I knew it! I knew it! I knew something was wrong when I was in there."

"Rosemary, did you blow the place up because you were angry?"

"No! I wouldn't do that. Who do you think I am? I see things! I've seen auras since I was a baby. I know when bad things are going to happen. I can see it. A couple of weeks ago I was talking to a woman who lives on my block; we bumped into each other on the street. As we were talking, I could see her whole body turn silver and black right before my eyes. She looked like a negative from a photograph. I was shaken, but I kept on talking to her.

"Later that night, I got a phone call from my friend. She'd heard that the woman I was talking to on the street died from a brain hemorrhage. It happened just a few hours after she left me. She seemed perfectly fine when I started talking to her, but when I saw her aura change I knew that something was wrong. I can tell when someone is sick. I can see when someone is going to die soon. I really can. You know I can do that."

"What does Bob say about all this?"

"He knows. I don't hide who I am with him. Besides, he asks me for psychic advice all the time. He thought I'd change after we got married and was away from the family, but now he's used to it. I'm just sorry I didn't tell that woman to go to the hospital. Maybe I could've done something to save her."

"Don't be so hard on yourself. I don't think you could have prevented what was supposed to happen."

"I'm not so sure. When I want to do something, it usually happens. I make it happen! I use my powers. And nothing can stop me."

"Rosemary, you said you had two things to tell me. What's the other?"

"Oh, I'm going to have a baby. How's the country? What have you been doing lately?"

· Chapter Eight ·

Churchman's Business School in Easton was a small school with a two-year program teaching basic office skills. I enrolled. Even though I had no intention of working in an office. I had to do something and I didn't want another factory job. I applied for a loan and looked for a weekend job. The one I found was on a dairy farm wiping cow's udders before they were hooked up to a milking machine. But after making too many jokes, I was relocated to bottle washing.

I fantasized that Churchman's was a school for spies. Shorthand, the mysterious secret code. I took typing, letter composition and grammar classes. My essay "From Deer Hunting to Road Kill" about all the dead animals I saw in the country was published in the school newspaper. This blew my cover. The students knew I was definitely not one of them.

I was twenty-three, older than most of my classmates. Many of them were learning skills to help manage their family farms. We had to look and act professional, addressing everyone as mister or miss. I owned only one dress, a burnt-orange shift with long sleeves. It was my costume. I wore it every day and thought nothing of it until one of the teachers approached me and asked if I needed clothes. He said his wife and I were about the same size. I felt naked. He could see me.

All the classes took place in one room. At the end of a class each teacher would ring a small bell on the desk to announce that the class was about to change. One teacher always said, "Okay class," as he shook the bell. It drove me mad. I went into the room one day before anyone else was in there and removed the clapper from the bell. When the teacher said, "Okay class," shaking the bell, nothing happened. He shook it harder and harder. The whole class roared, but he didn't think it was funny. I got up from my desk and gave him back the clapper. He replaced it without saying anything to me and shook the bell. "Okay class." Dictation began.

"Hey you! You, from New York." A woman about my age with dark curly hair was trying to get my attention. Although I heard her, I didn't respond right away. I didn't want to know anyone there.

"Hey, New York. I'm talking to you. Hello. Hello."

"Excuse me? Do you mean me?"

"I can tell you're from the big city. What are you doing here? I'm Jessie."

"Hello. I'm Terry. How did you know I'm from New York?"

"Look at these idiots. A bunch of morons and inbreds. You're not like them. I'm from New York too. Howard Beach. I'm just here so I can get a check from the state. I got a kid, Justin. He's four years old and it's just the two of us. You wanna get together after we get out of this hole?"

"Okay. I guess so."

I met her after class and we stood in the parking lot talking about astrology. She told me she knew how to read charts and would like to see mine sometime. I told her I was psychic. She asked me if I wanted to follow her in my car and go to her house. I accepted. She took the country roads at eighty miles an hour.

Jessie lived in one of those suburban towns in New Jersey, over a bridge across the Delaware River, about a twenty-minute drive from the school. A friend of hers who was babysitting her son met us at the door and left as soon as we got there. Jessie showed me around the house.

The living room was crammed with fake Italian provincial furniture, peach brocade couch and matching chairs. On the wall above the couch was a big velvet painting of San Marco Square with a working clock in the tower. Her pearl-white bedroom set had a ruffled skirt around the bed. It all smelled of tea roses. She turned on the stereo and played a stack of 45s, the latest top ten.

I had a bad cold, couldn't stop blowing my nose. She poured me a cup of tea as I took a swig from my cough syrup called Silence Is Golden.

"Oh, even your cough syrup tells me you're Scorpio. They always have secrets. I bet I know what yours is."

I was too scared to ask her what she meant. The cough medicine was making me woozy and I think the tea had brandy in it.

Jessie was leaning against the refrigerator with her arms crossed smoking a cigarette when she asked me, "So, if you're psychic . . . I mean . . . can you see things all the time or do you have to be in some kind of trance or something. Can you look at me right now and know things about me?"

"Yes, if I want to. But I'm not doing that. I can look away. Why are you asking? Do I make you nervous?"

The telephone rang.

"Saved by the bell," Jessie said, "I'll be right back." She went into the other room and I sat at her kitchen table noticing her Hummel statues on the windowsill. She came back a few minutes later.

"How long have you lived here?"

"Too long. Do you know who's buried in the cemetery not far from here? Jayne Mansfield. In Pen Argyl. I can show you, we'll go over there sometime. I'll tell you, I'm not going to end up here like her. Not me, babe."

I wasn't sure I knew what she was talking about.

"I had my son when I was sixteen. I was just a kid, for Chrissake. His father sold ice cream to us little kiddies right in front of our school. One day, he invited me to sit on his lap inside his Good Humor truck. I was so young, what did I know? I used to meet him after school. Nobody knew about it. He taught me a thing or two. I thought it was love. I got pregnant. He split. My parents had a fit. Jesus, it broke their heart. Oh, I love this song. "*Me and Mrs. Jones, we got a thing going on.*" She sang along a little out of key.

"Later, I found out my ice cream man did some time for getting caught with some other underage girl. Ha! So, now I got this kid. Nobody helps me, but I do what I gotta do to survive and get that check. I don't feel guilty. I need it. 'We meet everyday at the same cafe. Me and Mrs. Jones.' Christ, I gotta feed my kid. So, what about you? What the hell are you doing here? Are you hiding from the law or something? C'mon, who did you kill? You can tell me."

"I didn't kill anyone. Really, I swear. I have this brother and . . ."

"So you want to kill your brother."

"Will you let me finish!" I said, putting my hand over her mouth.

"Ooooh, nice soft hands."

I was embarrassed and a little scared. I stood and stared at her for a moment before I could say anything. She looked back at me without moving. I loved her face, her smile, her wild hair.

"Anyway, I live in a farmhouse with a woman I moved here with from New York. We all lived in my brother's house. He owns a house there, and they were the downstairs tenants. When we got kicked out, I came here to live with her in their country house."

"Oh, so she's your lover."

"What! No! It's not like that. She's married."

"Oh, but you have a thing for her? Right? Where's her husband? You said, you live with her, but 'we' got kicked out. Where's her man? He left you alone with her. Tell me the whole story. I'm intrigued, Scorpio. Take your time. We have all night. I gotta hear this. Welcome to small-town America. You fit right in."

I told her as much as I wanted her to know. She listened, interrupted, told me what I should be doing and made me laugh. From time to time she'd check on her son, who was playing in his room. At one point she gave him some macaroni and put him to bed.

"It's getting late. I should get going."

"Come back on Sunday for dinner? Nobody makes lasagne like I do."

"What time?"

Waving good-bye she watched me pull out of her driveway. I could hardly think straight. I don't have any idea how I made it back to Martins Creek. Jessie, Jessie, Jessie. *"Me and Mrs. Jones have a thing going on."*

．．．

She kept inviting me to her house after class and on weekends. I wanted to go every time, but I made excuses. I didn't want Natalie to find out. Natalie wanted to know where I was and what I was doing every minute. I couldn't make up my own mind. I was thinking about Jessie all the time. I couldn't wait to see her in class. We'd pass notes to each other like bad schoolgirls, she'd wink at me, I'd blush. I hardly paid attention in school anymore.

And then Christmas came and Jessie asked me if I wanted to spend it at her house. Natalie and Michael didn't celebrate Christmas. It was too commercial. This was perfect. I couldn't wait for that day.

It was snowing heavily on Christmas Eve. I told the Demings that if it got late I'd probably stay over. "Just call," they said. I drove to Jessie's house in the late afternoon. She wanted me to help pick out the Christmas tree. It was already dark when we got to the tree farm. I caught Jessie watching me and smiling as I went around smelling the fresh pines. They gave us a saw and some rope and Jessie cut down a small Scotch Pine that we tied to the roof of the car.

Back at the house I hung the ornaments and tinsel on the tree. Jessie watched me from the couch. She handed me the star to put on the top.

"Jessie, this is a pentagram. Isn't this a bit sacrilegious?"

"Well, who do you think those wise men were? Astrologers and psychics following a comet."

"Yes, but they weren't witches."

"Oh, the kid doesn't know the difference. Besides he's my son and I'll teach him what I want. So, what's wrong with having both Jesus and Morgan le Fay? Come down off that ladder and I'll make us an eggnog."

We wrapped Justin's presents while he protested, crying because he didn't want to stay in bed. He kept sneaking out of his bedroom and peeking at us.

"Justin! You little fucking bastard! Don't make me tell you again! Get back in that bed!" Jessie grabbed him by the back of his pajamas and dragged him back to his room, the tops of his little bare feet scraping across the floor.

Petrified, I sat in the living room. The Christmas tree lights blinked on and off. I tried to block out her screaming.

"I'm going to kill you if you don't shut your mouth!" *Whack! Whack! Whack!* "You spoiled brat! Now stop crying and go to sleep!"

Justin was sobbing and begging her to stop hitting him. I turned into a block of ice. I was back in my wet bed with my mother screaming at me. I didn't take my eyes off the clock in the velvet painting.

Get up! Get out! Don't just sit here, you weakling. Run out of this house! I hate you for screaming. I'm going in there. I'm going to kill you. Shut up! Don't you know I need you. Mommy . . . Why are you doing this to me? Hold me down. Kill me if you want to! Put the pillow over my face. I'm sorry I made you mad. Don't hurt me, Mommy. Mommy . . .

. . .

Jessie appeared in the doorway. "Hey, girl it's late," she said sweetly. "Are you going to stay over? I could put Justin in my bed and you can stay in his room. Or you can sleep in my bed with me. What do you want to do?"

She stood looking at me, waiting for my answer.

"Don't move him," I said. "I'll sleep with you."

She shut off the Christmas lights. I stood next to the bed watching her as she went through every drawer in the dresser frantically throwing clothes onto the chair, dropping things on the floor. I could hear her grunting, she was so annoyed that she couldn't find whatever she was looking for. She offered me a T-shirt to sleep in and then went into the bathroom to change.

"I'm warning you Justin, if you come out of this room I'm going to kill you and I mean it!" She slammed the bathroom door and then I heard water running.

I undressed as fast as I could and jumped in the bed, pulling the covers up to my chin. Jessie returned wearing a blue silk oversize shirt.

"That's my side. Move over."

When she shut the lights out I froze. Neither of us moved. Every time a car drove by the house a beam of light moved across the ceiling and down the wall. Jessie started fidgeting. I could hear her sigh. She turned and re-arranged her pillow several times. She got up and went back to the bathroom. I waited, biting my nails and counting to one hundred. I heard Justin faintly call "Mommy," but she didn't answer.

Jessie burst into the bedroom, "All right! What do you want?"

"What do you mean?"

"What do I mean? What are you doing in my bed?"

"You know. Don't you? I wanted to be close to you."

"Oh, well then . . . come over here." She pulled me to her and held me in her arms. "Baby, baby . . ." She stroked my hair and kissed me sweetly on top of my head. "You've done this before, haven't you? I mean, you've been with a woman before?"

"No. I haven't," I said quietly.

"What? I don't believe you. I was sure you were gay."

"I don't know. I just wanted to be with you."

"You seem so comfortable with me, like you wanted something."

"I do. I want you, but I don't know how. I don't know what to do."

"You sure are pretty, girl. You got a lotta guts, honey. I like you. This is gonna kill me, mama. This is gonna do me in. What am I doing? I must be out of my mind. Oh girl, I want you too."

Pulling me close to her, she kissed me passionately on my neck, my face. I floated backward into surrender. She put her hands under my thighs and whispered, "Come up to my mouth. I want to know what you taste like."

For the first time in my life I was feeling myself in my body. I tried to shut off my mind, but I kept wondering who Jessie was and how I would fit into her life. In bed she was gentle and not shy about telling me what she wanted me to do. She took pleasure in teaching me how to make love to her. It all seemed so natural. If this was love, I was falling, and I was touching that love with my skin.

In the morning I decided I wasn't leaving. I called Natalie and told her I was staying for a few days at my friend's house because I was having such a good time. I got off the phone quickly.

Justin and I played on the floor with his Christmas toys. I made him laugh. Jessie tried to kiss me in front of him and I pushed her away.

"What the hell's wrong with you Terry? Come in the kitchen, right now."

"Jessie, not in front of Justin. I'm not comfortable with that and I don't want him to feel I'm taking you away from him."

"This is my house. He knows who I am."

Every night she'd scream at him before he went to bed and then come to me with tenderness and sweet words. I'd shut down to the angry mother and open myself to the lover in the same breath. I locked the door to the place in me that knew what was going to happen. I just wanted to hide out from everything sensible, logical and sad.

"Wait here kid, I gotta get the phone. Hello . . . yes. Ha, ha, ha . . . of course, sweetie. I know . . . of course I can. Don't I always? You gonna take care of me this time? You know what you promised. Uh-huh, okay. Give me twenty minutes."

I tried to make up what I thought I heard. Maybe she had a boyfriend who was married. Why couldn't I figure this out? Was I blocking? Maybe . . . I didn't want to know. I knew I shouldn't ask her who was calling. She'd tell me what she wanted me to know.

"I gotta go, babe. I got something to do." She went through her closet looking for the right thing to wear.

"Yeah, I better get going too. It's time I changed my clothes anyway."

I heard her make a call and ask someone if she could drop Justin off at their house. She went into the shower and I stood in the doorway of Justin's room and watched him play with a toy truck.

"I'm going!" I hollered from behind the bathroom door.

"I'll see you at school. Bye."

I drove home telling myself I should just forget what happened and stay away. So, I had another experience. So, it doesn't matter. I'm free. She's free. Yeah, sure.

A few days later Natalie and Michael said they wanted to speak to me. Actually, Natalie did all the talking and Michael stayed behind a newspaper with a glass of Scotch.

"Terry, we set up an apartment for you in our Belvidere house. We had it painted and furnished and we want you to start living there beginning this Saturday. It's time for you to start living on your own. You haven't been coming home and we just don't want to worry about you when you're not here. You will have to pay rent, but we're only going to charge you a minimum to cover expenses. It's time for you to go. I'll help you pack."

I was stunned. I went up to my room and sobbed. I was being asked to leave because I wasn't living the way she wanted me to. It was the same as Frank.

I returned to Churchman's after New Year's Day. I hadn't heard from Jessie and I was nervous about seeing her again.

"Hey, cute thing. How's my girl?"

"Hi, how are you, Jessie?"

"I want to see you later. Will you come over?"

I said yes, knowing better, but I couldn't wait to be with her again. The minute she closed the door to her house she had me undressed. The phone rang several times. Right after we made love she jumped up to answer it. Stretching the phone cord, she closed herself inside the bathroom so I couldn't hear what she was saying. I was far away from the place where I could feel and know things. She hung up, came back to the bedroom and started putting herself together.

"C'mon, I want to take you over to meet Patsy and Donna. We'll go in my car. Justin's over there now. They're my friends, they're sisters. Patsy's divorced and has two kids. They don't live in the same house, but they're always together. Donna's a little shy, but she doesn't miss a thing. They both work at the wallpaper factory. They'll love you. I can't wait for them to meet you. They're from Brooklyn. Good Italian girls, just like you. Patsy and Donna live a couple blocks from each other and sometimes on Sundays we all . . ." Jessie didn't stop talking the whole way over there.

"Come in, the coffee's hot," Patsy said smiling, holding the door open and looking me over.

"Just got your hair frosted, Patsy?" Jessie said. "Looks good. Got a hot date tonight?"

"Yeah, sure Jessie. With Mr. Potato Head. He's in the kids' room right now waiting for me. When's the last time I had a date? Terry, I heard you're psychic. We gotta talk. When do I get my reading?"

"Watch out, kid, Patsy loves psychics. She can't get enough. She's always on the phone with them," Jessie said as she threw a cat off the kitchen table. "She'll drive you crazy."

"I will not. And shut up, Jessie. I'm surprised you haven't hid from her."

"Patsy, you're a piece of shit! Shut up."

Donna sat quietly on a kitchen stool with a snoring St. Bernard at her feet.

They all chained smoked, while I coughed and choked. They took turns telling me the gossip about the neighbors, how their kids acted up in school, the health problems of St. Bernards, how they all had met. We'd been there about an hour when Jessie abruptly got up.

"Look, I hate to do this, but I gotta go. Terry, stay here, enjoy yourself. I'll catch you later." And she flew out the door.

"There she goes again," Patsy said.

I was speechless. Jessie revved up her engine and was gone before I realized what had just happened. She planned this. Now I understood why she was so insistent that we only take her car.

Donna and Patsy looked at me.

"Want more coffee?"

Patsy asked me how I met Jessie, how much did I know about her, what did I feel about her. She kept telling me to be careful, that Jessie was a handful. She said she didn't want to see me get hurt. I was dying to ask them about her, but I didn't really want to know, not yet anyway.

I changed the subject and asked about them, about their cats and dogs. Patsy wanted to know everything about me being psychic. I gave the standard answers, too distracted and confused to do anything else.

"Patsy! Leave the girl alone. Stop asking her so many questions. I'm sure you'll see her again."

I asked them if they would drive me back to my car. Nobody said another word about Jessie.

I wanted to quit school, but Jessie kept talking me out of it. I wanted to get out, make money and stop pretending I was in a spy school. I'd never be a secretary. Jessie told me she knew a man who owned a Roasting Wrap factory. She'd ask him if he was hiring.

I got hired on the night shift. Roasting Wrap was one of those inventions that was supposed to make a housewife's job easier. I don't know if it worked and I don't think it was on the market for very long. It was a gimmick to make fast money before consumers found out it was crap.

I was the last person on the assembly line. My job was to make sure there was a roll of Roasting Wrap in its box before the hot glue sealed its fate. For about ten minutes I had a lot of fun filling the boxes and knocking the empty rejects off the conveyor belt with a cardboard tube. There was nothing to think about; this was easy. And I was with factory people again, these characters who made me laugh and had mysterious lives they were keeping to themselves. But thank God, no Jehovah's Witnesses.

They blasted the AM radio deliberately to keep us awake. I went to school all day and then started my shift at eight and worked till four in the morning. I drank a lot of coffee and sang along loudly with the radio to keep my eyes open.

After a few weeks, they started speeding up the conveyer belt to increase production and I kept missing the boxes and some probably got shipped empty. My eyes were blurring and I'd often get hot glue on my hand as I tried to catch a box before it got away empty. It really burned.

I was starting to lose my mind. Sleep deprived, cranky and no time to see Jessie. My life was turning into hell and I couldn't seem to stop. One night the foreman came over to talk to me.

Shouting over the noisy machines, "Hello! How you doing with this job? Do you like it?" he hollered.

"I love it! I've never been happier! All my life this is what I dreamed of doing!" I shouted sarcastically, as I whacked another empty box.

"Bonnie! Bonnie! Come here a minute? Fill in for her! I need her somewhere else! Follow me!" he shouted.

I followed him into his disheveled office of boxes, papers and old coffee cups. It was an oasis from the noise.

"Hello, I'm Scully. Have a seat."

Scully had a warm face, a close-cut beard and sad blue eyes.

"I know who you are, I've seen you around here. Am I getting fired?"

"No. Just the opposite. I want to make you Quality Control."

"Oh, thank you very much. I'm thrilled. What is that?"

"You'll be in charge of spot-checking all the workers to see if they're getting the job done. You walk through the factory every hour and record the employees' progress on these charts."

"Oh that's great. Now everyone will hate me."

"It's a lot less painful than the hot wax. Do you want to do it? It comes with a fifteen-cent raise."

"Now you're talking. Okay, I'm hired."

I'd spend the whole night going around gabbing with the workers, getting them coffee or candy bars and helping them take their mind off their tedious jobs. I listened to their problems and sometimes gave them psychic advice without them knowing it. And of course, I always reported that they were doing a fantastic job.

I started spending a lot of time in Scully's office talking about music and life in the country and how we both didn't know what the hell we were doing with our lives. He invited me to breakfast at the local diner after work. I'd be late for school, but I didn't care.

Scully was a nice guy. He hated the factory, but it was a job. When he was in high school his girlfriend got pregnant and he married her. Then the baby died after a few months and they had a hard time dealing with the loss. Both teenagers, they stayed together and had another child. That was really all they had in common.

Scully and I were two lost spirits in the world of the misplaced. He had a seriously neglected 1950s Porsche convertible and we'd drive around on winter nights with the top down. The car was always breaking down and we'd have to push it to a gas station, laughing and cursing all the way.

I told Scully everything—about Natalie and Jessie. He thought I was out of my mind, but he understood their appeal amidst the boredom of country life. Scully reminded me of Neal; they were both married and trapped by their past mistakes. I got close to Scully. We made love a few times—I didn't feel anything, I just went through the motions. There wasn't ever any pressure from him. We'd get undressed, he'd brush his hand awkwardly across my breast and quickly reach down to guide himself inside me. As soon as we were finished he'd ask me, "Was it good?" I'd say yes, because I didn't want to hurt him, but my heart was with Jessie.

I finally walked out of Churchman's one day. Jessie asked me to babysit for Justin while she went to school. I spent my days with a little boy and my nights in the factory. I had never been around children for very long and

Justin was difficult: he only responded to screaming. That was something I didn't do, so he screamed at me. He threw his toys and kicked me as hard as he could. And the telephone kept ringing and ringing all day. Sometimes I'd answer it just so it would stop ringing. It was always a man, different men asking for Jessie, not wanting to leave a name or number. They'd keep calling back with urgency in their voices. I stopped answering and the ringing was making me crazy.

Jessie came home from school one day and seemed annoyed that I was there even though she had asked me to take care of her son. The phone rang and I could hear her making arrangements with someone who was coming over in ten minutes.

"What's going on, Jessie?"

"Now don't start that shit with me. I don't need you checking up on me. Look, I don't answer to anyone. I live the way I want to and I don't need you to judge what I'm doing with my life. Nobody tells me how to live!" She was yelling at me while she was changing her clothes.

"I just want to know what's going on."

"Okay! I'm having company for a little while. Just take Justin and sit in the living room for about half an hour. Watch TV and keep him busy and don't bother me."

"Do what? I'm going out. I have my own plans."

"Just do it! Do what I say!"

I heard a car pull up in the driveway and Jessie hurried to the window and looked out.

"Now sit there with him and keep your mouth shut! So help me God, if you move. Both of you!"

I didn't get up. I didn't move. I sat on the couch with the television on low and tried to hear what was going on. Jessie was laughing and I couldn't make out what the man was saying. They went into the bedroom and closed the door.

I didn't move from the couch. Justin kept trying to get my attention wanting me to play with him. He kept hitting me with a toy truck and I didn't stop him. I tried to listen to the muffled television voices while I ripped the skin off my lips with my teeth.

I heard the door open and I got up and went into the kitchen holding Justin in my arms. Jessie was wearing her bathrobe. She casually introduced me to the man. I said hello. He straightened his shirt. They kissed before he left.

I stood by the table. Jessie walked right by me and went into the shower. Her look said, "Don't dare ask." When I heard the water running in the shower, I grabbed the phone and called Donna.

"I'm going out!" I yelled through the bathroom door.

"Where are you going?" she shouted back angrily, like I had no right to leave.

I drove off in my car as fast as I could to Donna's house. Almost immediately when I arrived, the telephone rang and it was Jessie looking for me. I shook my head "no" and Donna said I wasn't there.

"Listen. Terry, just listen to me," Donna said. "Please get away from her. She's no good for you. I don't want to get involved with this and I don't need Jessie mad at me. You can see what's going on. Can't you?"

"Donna, I'm involved with her. I'm deeply involved with her. You know what I mean?"

"Yeah, she told us."

"She told you everything?"

"You're just another one of her conquests. She loves having power over you. Don't you get it?"

"She told you everything? Everything? Donna, what am I going to do?"

"Just don't go over there anymore. Stop yourself. It's only going to get worse."

Jessie drove up and pulled her car into Donna's driveway. She knew I was there. She sat in the car knowing I'd come out and follow her home and I did. When we got back to her house she was loving and tender with me. She was trying hard to get me to forget what happened. I told her I was in love with her and I wanted to know how she could be with somebody else.

"I'm free, baby! No one ties me down. I do whatever I want. Take it or leave it."

"Do you love me? You never tell me you love me."

"Now, don't start with me. I care about you. You're my only girl. Isn't that enough?"

"I love you. I'm in love with you. What am I supposed to do?"

"You wanted this. You came to me. This is who I am. Come here. Now you know you're my special girl. Don't you, honey?"

She kissed me and took me to the bedroom. My heart was breaking, but I couldn't pull myself away.

The next day I got up early and went home. I called Scully and asked him to come over. He was there in ten minutes. I told him everything about Jessie. He thought it was cool that I was with a woman. He tried to make me laugh and told me not to get too serious about love. He joked, asking me if he could get Jessie's phone number. He was trying to be funny, but I wondered if he would have called her.

"Scully, how would you like to meet Natalie? Let's go over there."

"Why do you want to go there now?"

"I don't know. Let's just go. I feel like it."

Natalie was surprised to see us. I introduced her to Scully and she invited us in. She showed Scully the house and the property and he asked all the questions that men ask about those kinds of things. I hugged and kissed him in front of her and held his hand at times. Natalie seemed to like him and told us both to visit her again sometime. I guess I wanted her to see that I had a boyfriend. I guess I wanted the freedom like Jessie.

"Why did you bring me there? I think she's crazy. What's with all the questions? Does she think I'm going to marry you? Why do you get involved with these people? Don't answer. Let's go for a beer."

· Chapter Nine ·

Jessie called me on Friday wanting to spend the weekend with me. I was leery, but I went. We had a good time Friday night fixing dinner together, making Justin laugh. It was like being part of a normal family. We spent Saturday at the mall. By late afternoon she started getting touchy over everything I said, snapping at me and trying to start a fight.

She took hold of my shoulders, "Listen, I have to go out for a little while. I promise I'll be back in an hour, maybe two. I have to go. Please, would you mind, sweetie, staying with Justin?" She brushed the hair off my forehead. "Please, it's only an hour. I promise."

I couldn't believe it. She was going out and I wasn't complaining. If I did, we'd have a big fight, or more likely she'd just start yelling at me. I didn't want to argue, so I agreed. She promised again she'd be back soon.

Two hours turned into six and then it was after midnight. Justin woke up in the middle of the night screaming for his mother and I couldn't quiet him down. I sang to him. I played with him. I tried food, television and begging. He wouldn't stop screaming and crying. I felt so sorry for him. He was acting out what I felt.

I wanted to call Donna and Patsy to ask for help, but I knew they'd be angry at Jessie for leaving me for so long. I kept hoping that any minute she'd walk through the door. Then I started to worry. My emotions were so mixed up I couldn't sort out real fear from my imagination. I fell asleep on the chair in the living room. The next thing I felt was Justin pulling at my sleeve. It was morning and he was hungry. I gave him some cereal and we watched cartoons on the television.

At one o'clock in the afternoon I heard the door open. Jessie came home.

Immediately she started yelling, "Don't lay any guilt on me, baby, I'm not in the mood. I'm tired and I just want to lay down."

I didn't say anything. I just went to get my coat to leave. I was so angry and hurt I didn't tell her how relieved I was to see her alive.

"Where are you going?"

"I'm going home. I'm tired. I got to go now."

"Come in the bedroom, honey, and lay down with me."

"No! I've had enough."

"Enough of what? What are you referring to? You want to say something to me? Huh, got something to say? Say it to my face." She wanted to argue with me and then she abruptly changed her tone. "All right, I guess it's time for you to know. Please, I want to tell you something. Don't go yet. You're not going yet. Come on. Come here. I'm not going to hurt you."

I went with her to her bedroom and stood by the bed as she changed her clothes.

"I made a lot of money last night, baby," she said, with a big smile on her face. "I took charge of the whole room. You should've seen me. I was amazing. I was Wonder Woman! I had them eating out of my hands."

I didn't interrupt her as she went on telling me about the last several hours. She had a wild look in her eyes like an animal that had just devoured its prey after a long hunt.

"Last night I was the only woman with fifteen guys and I did them all! Each and every one of them. I had them crawling on their knees."

I felt sick to my stomach. My legs were shaking. What was she saying?

"Listen, I make money like this, and I'm talented. Last night I did the whole damn office! These guys came from Philly just to see me. It was a great party. We had two motel suites. I fucked and sucked every one of them. Some of those assholes couldn't keep up with me. Yes, I know I was out longer than I said. I wasn't looking at my watch, Honey, I'm sorry. I was too busy. It was really getting wild and I was into it. I told those guys what I wanted. I was the one in charge. I had them wrapped around my little finger. I was in command and those men wanted more. They were begging.

"That's not all. Baby, now I want you to know everything. I don't want any secrets from you. If you know everything, then you can't hold it against me and say you didn't know what you were getting into. So I'm going to tell you everything and I expect you to understand. This is who I am. All right? I do the trucks too. The truck stops. The sixteen wheelers, the big rigs. You know, the truck stops, where the truckers sleep and refuel. That's my regular spot. I do really well there. I got a lot of regulars and they'll pay for anything. They come up from the South and as far away as California just to see me. I'm famous. They talk about me on their radios. I'm a legend out there. Those bastards got a lot of dough they don't know what to do with. Oh, I shouldn't call them that. They're nice guys. They're hardworking, they deserve a little fun. They treat me good and I get what I want from them."

"So those are all the calls you've been getting. All those men are calling to have sex with you?"

"It's a business. It's what I do."

"Jessie, I don't know what to say. I'm tired. I didn't sleep last night and I got to go. I'll call you later. I have to think about this." I had to get outside. I couldn't breathe. I had to get out of there. She didn't try to stop me.

"You'll call me later? Right?"

"Sure." I didn't know what I was going to do.

I left her house and went looking for the nearest phone booth to see if Donna was home. I drove over to see her. I was shaking.

"I was waiting for this call from you, Terry. Sooner or later you were going to find out. I told you you'd be hurt. I told you to get away from her."

"How could she do this? I don't know if I believe her. It sounds impossible. She was so sweet with me. I'm really upset and confused. Donna, where's all the money? She's always complaining she doesn't have any money."

"Sweetie, she left you with the kid for twenty-four hours and didn't even call you to say she was alive! She had one of those guys while you sat in the living room! Will you wake up! Don't get me started. You know, Jessie doesn't need the money. Her parents give her a lot. She grew up with money. It doesn't mean anything to her. Oh, she loves money and she wants money, but to her it means power. When she has money she just spends it on junk. And she gets a welfare check. This is all a thrill for her. Why are we talking about money? Poor Justin. I worry what's going to happen to him. She used to drop him off with us. We told her we don't want to watch him anymore. It's too heartbreaking.

"She had everything when she was young. She went to a fancy girls' school. She grew up in a mansion in New York. The house had a stone wall around it with a guard at the entrance. They had a maid and a gardner. I met her parents. They were glamorous and sophisticated. The house was huge, with paintings and modern furniture. They really love Jessie, but she's always trying to hurt them."

I was all mixed up. Everything was crashing in on me. All I wanted to do was walk in the alfalfa fields in Martins Creek where I used to go to think. I got in my car and drove there. Natalie came out when she heard me in the driveway. She looked happy to see me.

We sat next to each other on the couch and before I knew what I was saying, I told her everything. She listened to every word and didn't seem shocked by anything I said. She held my hand and told me not to worry. It was like the old times when I first met her and she'd help me see what I was doing. She suggested that I go into therapy and said she'd ask some friend of hers to recommend someone for me. I agreed that I needed to sort out my life and getting professional help was a great idea. I left feeling confident and clearer, excited about doing something about my my life. I'd tell Jessie that I never want to see her again. I felt strong.

Natalie's friend, a nurse from a hospital in Easton, gave her a recommendation for a psychiatrist. I was lucky that he could see me right away. I sat in the waiting room open and eager to hear what he had to say.

"Hello, I'm Dr. Reid." He was a tall handsome man in a three-piece suit. I followed him into his office. He sat at a desk and I sat next to it in a leather club chair. The room was subdued, the walls covered with his various degrees.

"Now tell me about yourself. Why are you here?" he said.

I didn't stop talking for the entire hour. He took notes on a yellow pad. I told him everything. I left nothing out. He listened and then suggested I come back at the end of the week to speak to him some more. Twice a week would be good for me. He said I shouldn't worry about the money right now and we'd talk about that later. I left feeling that the hour went by fast and he didn't say very much, but I had to tell him the whole story, so next time I'd ask him what he thought. He'd have a few days to think about me and my situation.

That night in my apartment, I was resting on my bed thinking about my life when I heard a knock at the door that startled me. The only way to get into the house and up to the second floor is with a key. I heard someone call my name.

"Natalie. What are you doing here? It's so late. Are you all right? Is something wrong?"

"I want to talk to you. Sit down." She patted the bed. "Terry, I want you to know it's perfectly normal what you're feeling. I spoke to a friend of mine, the nurse at the hospital who recommended Dr. Reid. She told me that it's quite normal for teenage girls to have crushes on other girls and to even act on it. It doesn't mean that you're that way. You'll probably grow out of this. It's just a phase so you don't have to worry. You're still young. It's all right that you tried it. It doesn't mean anything. I'm sure that girl you met at school persuaded you to try it and it's really all right. You'll change. You'll meet a man some day and you'll be just fine. Did you like the doctor? My friend says he's really smart. Excellent with girls in your situation. You're going to see him again on Friday, aren't you?"

"Um, yeah . . . I liked him. It's too early to know."

"Don't worry, Terry, you're doing so well and I'm proud of you. Everything is going to be just fine. I'm going to get going now. It's late. Good night, sleep tight, don't let the bed bugs bite."

She left. I could hear her whistling "Oh! Susanna" all the way down to the bottom of the stairs. I sat on my bed and suddenly I felt the whole room turn all the way around. I felt completely centered and totally in control. I'd realized how sane I was and that I had been surrounded by a bunch of lunatics. I started to laugh. I couldn't wait to see Dr. Reid. He'd be able to help me get out of this. How did Natalie know I was going again on Friday and what did she mean by "teenage girls"?

On Friday Dr. Reid laid it all out for me. "I thought a lot about you over the last few days. Mrs. Deming called and filled me in on your situation. She wants to help you. You're a lucky girl to know someone like her who has your best interest at heart.

"First of all, this obsession about your family all being psychics is extremely creative, but it's dangerous for you to keep thinking that this is reality. You can't possibly believe this to be true. Making this up gives you a sense of power when actually you really feel fragile and powerless in the world. So you created this fantasy to survive in a place you don't feel safe in. Your history of drug abuse and experiments with LSD have most certainly damaged your perceptions of reality. But first of all we need to address your depression.

"Mrs. Deming told me how depressed you've been and you yourself told me about your promiscuity. What I suggest for you is a thirty-day program we have at St. Rita's Hospital. It's an excellent institution where you'll have the care you need to sort yourself out. We'll prescribe a treatment of medication that's right for you and you'll have private as well as group therapy every day. We take suicide very seriously, my dear. We are obliged by the law to get you the help you need. Mrs. Deming agreed that our program sounded well suited for you. I'll speak to her about the arrangements. She really cares about you. You're a lucky girl."

I shook his hand and quietly walked out the door. I was terrified at what I had just heard. I wasn't crazy. How could Natalie do this to me? She was going to have me locked up! I never said I was suicidal. Never! I was so angry and very scared. I called Scully. Thank God he was home. He met me at the diner.

"Terry, first of all you're not crazy. Nutty, but not crazy. You're twenty-three years old. She's not related to you. They can't lock you up. This is really hilarious. I never heard of anything so funny. You're in a Marx Brothers movie."

"Scully! This is my life!"

"Calm down. You're so dramatic. What do you expect them to say? You've taken a lot of drugs, you're a lesbian love slave, and you're running around with me, a married man."

"Scully, be serious. What am I going to do?"

"Look babe, why don't we go right over to St. Rita's and find out what's going on. Let's just go there and ask them how this works. I never heard you mention suicide. This is amazing. Honey, you really pissed her off. Don't worry kid, no one is going to lock you up. I won't let them. Let's go right now."

We went to St. Rita's and asked to speak to a doctor. I was terrified to go in, thinking they had my name on a list and would just take me right then and there.

After a few minutes' wait I was directed to the office of a woman doctor. Scully never left my side. I told her what was going on. She listened patiently and gave me a lot of time to explain my situation. She looked right at me, smiled and said, "My dear, you seem perfectly sane to me. If you were crazy, believe me, I could tell. You wouldn't be able to sit here so calmly and rationally and tell me this story. And I don't believe you want to kill yourself.

"Look, first of all your friend here is right, you're over eighteen and this woman friend of yours is not a relative. She can't commit you to anything. I strongly suggest that you get away from these people. All of them. As for the psychiatrist, just because you have a degree doesn't mean you know anything. Please, take care of yourself. I'm glad you came here to see me."

I left feeling relieved and a little foolish. I told Scully that I knew now that I had to leave Pennsylvania. I had to get away from everyone. I wasn't sure what I would do, but I'd figure out something. I asked him to drive me over to Martins Creek to see Natalie. I had to confront her. When we got there she wouldn't let Scully in the house. He waited outside for me. I went in and told her that we had just been to the mental hospital. She answered by telling me she wanted me to move out of her house in Belvidere immediately. I said I'd move as soon as I could figure out where to go. She said, "One month. No more."

Scully drove me back and I started going through my things. I took my Tarot cards out and tried reading for myself, but it was so confusing. My life had too many stories going on. I kept pulling the swords, the negative and difficult cards that spoke to me of anguish, depression and loss. I shuffled over and over again, but I knew I was just looking for the answer I wanted. Something to tell me to go back to Jessie. And there was the Devil card, reminding me how obsessed I was. I felt her hold on me was so strong that the part of me that was attached to her was tempting me to go back and I was picking the cards from that place. I put them away.

I went to my dresser and opened the bottom drawer. From underneath my sweaters I pulled out the magic wand. I had never used it. Sitting on the floor with a tree branch in my hands, trying to believe it could change anything, seemed silly now after all I'd been through. I thought a lot about me and Jessie. I always knew I wasn't going to stay with her. But she opened the pain in my heart and it forced me to feel my body. It may have been the only reason I went there. I held the wand and decided I needed to believe. If I could only believe in believing. With all my heart I asked the wand to show me which way to go. I was talking to a stick.

The next day I quit the factory job and picked up my last paycheck. On the way home I stopped at a diner in Easton. Sitting at the counter I over-heard two girls talking at the booth behind me. They were looking at a map spread across their table. I recognized them from Churchman's.

"Hi, you two. I remember you. Are you going somewhere?"

"We're driving cross-country for the summer before we start college in the fall. We want to drive right to the Pacific Ocean. Remember me? I'm Artie, and remember Gail? You're Terry Iacuzzo. What have you been up to? You just left Churchman's and we didn't know what happened to you. We never forgot you. We talk about you all the time. You were the most fun in that school. Remember that stupid bell? When you took the clapper out? That was such a riot."

I didn't hesitate, "Please, will you take me with you? Can I go on the trip? Please, I promise I'll be quiet. I'll make you laugh and tell you stories all the way across America. Please let me come."

"Sit down. Let's get more coffee over here!" Artie yelled to the waitress. Artie's real name was Anita. Artie was part of her last name. "You want to come with us? Are you kidding? We'd love it! And it will be cheaper with three of us. Gail, what do you think? We'll have a ball."

"When are you leaving?"

"In two weeks."

"Girls, I'm ready. Thank you. Thank you. Thank you. I'm so happy."

I went home and started packing. Over the next week I sold everything I owned except some clothes, a few pieces of jewelry, my Tarot cards and the wand. I bought a sleeping bag, a backpack and a pair of sneakers. I called Jessie and Natalie and said good-bye. They both seemed shocked. Scully wished me well, but was sad to lose me. He told me I was fierce and fearless and that he was happy he met me. He wished he could go, but he thought he'd never get out of New Jersey. Two weeks later I sat in the backseat of Artie and Gail's Camaro and we drove away.

Open-road postcard America. Pennsylvania, West Virginia, Ohio, Indiana, Illi-nois. Talking, driving, singing with the radio, letting one day wake up into the next not knowing where we were going. Crossing the Mississippi, through Missouri, Kansas, Colorado, we didn't stop until we saw the Rockies. Sleeping in the car and $5 camp-grounds. Dancing in cowboy bars. Eating truck-stop diner meals. Hitchhikers and hip-pie families all along the way. I read their cards—stories of dreamers and runaways.

Around the campfire watching star-glittered black skies. Bears, red rocks, the smell of cedars. Grabbing a shower where we could. Winnebagos, sixteen wheelers, motorcy-

cles, cars and cars and cars. *Indian women selling beads by the side of the road. Route 66. New Mexico, Arizona, the white salt flats of Utah, Mesa Verde, Painted Desert, Durango and more Indian ruins. The boiling Arizona desert. Walking the edge of the Grand Canyon in the dark.*

Las Vegas, a sweltering neon desert. Sneaking into the swimming pool at the Flamingo Hotel. Straight through the Mojave Dessert. There it was—California! Chrysocolla and malachite, the Pacific Ocean. San Francisco, the Haight. Down the coast, Route 1, Monterey, Big Sur, LA, Hollywood, Malibu, Disneyland. Driving, driving, driving, driving. America, I had no idea how beautiful you can be. Let's go home. Back again. East.

From somewhere in Illinois I called Frank and asked him if I could come back to New York and stay with him. It had been two years since we talked. We spoke for only a minute. He told me he had been waiting for my call. "Let me know when you get closer to New York. Of course you can stay here. If that's what you want."

· Chapter Ten ·

September 1972. I leaned up against the iron gates of St. Patrick's Old Cathedral. As I looked up at the windows on the third floor of the house on Mulberry Street, I wondered how different it was without the Demings, without Norvin. The house really would be haunted now with ghosts from my past. I was afraid to go inside, to see Frank, afraid I couldn't handle all the feelings.

Ringing the bell set off an explosion of barking dogs. The door flew open and like a magician stepping out from behind a curtain, Frank appeared holding a tiny Papillon in his arms. He was wearing a cotton Indian tunic, a clunky turquoise squash blossom necklace and had a Prince Valiant haircut. A blur of hysterically yapping dogs surrounded his sandals.

"Be quiet! Be quiet! Shuuuu! Shuuuu! Be quiet! Shut up! Jesus! Shut up! They'll stop in a minute! Come in. Come in. Let me take your coat!"

I plugged my ears while struggling to hold my bags under my arms.

"How many dogs do you have?" I yelled. It was impossible to count them, they were chasing each other around my feet and jumping up trying to get me to pick them up. From all fours, one dog sprang straight up into the air.

"Seven! I want to get two more! Shuuuu! Stop it right now!"

Finally, they stopped.

"The breeder called the other day, said she had two that were just born, and asked me if I was interested. I don't know, maybe it's too much. Here, put your bags over here on the bench so the dogs can't pee on them."

He hadn't looked directly at me yet and I was so nervous I kept my head down watching the dogs. Immediately, I could feel how different the house was. The hall was elegant with a huge mirror that almost touched the ceiling. Little angels' faces peeking down from the corners of its gold Rococo frame. There were bouquets of fresh roses and a Chinese umbrella stand holding several antique walking sticks.

As I passed Norvin's old apartment door I had an impulse to open it and see if he was still in there. I thought I heard him laughing through the wall, but I knew he was long gone and back in Texas. I looked at myself in the mirror expecting to see that innocent girl I used to be with blue cornflowers braided through her hair.

"Come on upstairs. We live on the second floor." I followed Frank up to what used to be the Demings' apartment. I was overcome with sadness, but I held it in and stared down at my old friends, the floorboards, thinking of the many nails I'd pulled from their backs.

"We've been living here for almost two years now. We love it. The neighborhood's a hoot. The Mafia headquarters are right up the block and the Catholic church is across the street. People ring the bell constantly asking to see a priest, they think this is the rectory. I used to tell them, 'This is a private house, the rectory is next door,' but it got so frequent I started listening to their problems.

"A woman came to the door in tears. She didn't give me a chance to say anything. She just started talking, 'Father, Father I've sinned. I feel so guilty, Father. I slept with my boyfriend last night. I couldn't help myself. I'm sorry, Father. Please, forgive me.' I didn't know what to do, so I said to her, 'Oh, it's all right my child, don't worry. God will forgive you. God Bless you, *in nomine padre e spirito santo . . .*' I made the sign of the cross and blessed her right there on the front steps. And she felt better. I don't take donations, but I am thinking about hearing confessions on Saturdays. Just kidding." Frank roared with laughter. I wondered how many times he had told that story.

"Would you like a cup of tea? Jay went uptown to Miss Grimble's. He wanted to get a special cake. He loves her cakes and won't eat anything else. I gave up sugar two months ago. No meat, no coffee, no sugar, no alcohol. I lost sixteen pounds. I'm trying to get Jay to do it with me. I'm doing this workout called Pilates twice a week with a trainer uptown and I'm buying my own machine to put in the basement so I can work out every day at home. I'm so busy these days I don't have the time to leave the house. The phone keeps ringing off the wall.

"Here sit over here. Do you like the couch? It's what they call *Biedermeier,* so are the table and the four chairs and that dresser. I just started collecting it. It's German and was very popular in the thirties. You should see the gorgeous desk that's coming next week, I can't wait till it comes. It's fabulous! It cost me a fortune, *Madon.* Do you like the tea? It's from South America. The gauchos drink it while they're out on their horses for long periods of time. It keeps them awake."

Frank had developed a P. T. Barnum style of speaking. Everything he talked about was preceded by the words *incredible, fabulous, amazing* or *fantastic.* He got louder and louder. Listening to him put me in a trance. I could feel myself spacing out and splitting off. I heard his voice and everything he said, but I was far away, lost somewhere inside myself. I could see him through a glaze. I must have had a strange look on my face sitting on his couch fully awake, but feeling like I was sleeping. I hoped he didn't notice. I felt like a canned ham trapped in a tin box, floating in aspic.

Doesn't Frank remember I used to live here? I know the Mafia is up the block and the church is across the street. Has he asked me how I am or what I plan to do or how my trip across America was? Does he remember I asked him if I could stay with him a while? Am I making him nervous? I should relax. I'll ask him a lot of questions.

"The house looks beautiful. I like the furniture. Have you been doing a lot of readings?"

"I'm so busy, I've been reading six days a week. I can't keep up with the demand. I've been interviewed on the radio and in the newspaper. I was in *Mademoiselle, Viva, Cover Girl* and I have an interview this week with *Women's Wear Daily* and the *New York Times.* Every time I do one of those, I get a ton of calls, most of them from nuts. They make appointments and then don't show up. I don't need the business. I'm overbooked as it is. I've been reading at a lot of private parties and that's where you meet your multimillionaires and rich socialites. I help these people—I'm like their therapist. Some of them are so lost, they're rich, but they don't have a clue—most of them are so unhappy. They ask me questions like, 'Should I buy my diamonds from Tiffany or Harry Winston?' I'm not kidding you."

The dogs starting barking. Someone was coming up the stairs. It was Jay. I had an impulse to run.

"Well hello, Terry. How have you been? You're looking well." He held out his hand and I shook it. "I brought us a cake. Would you like a piece? Excuse me. Frank, may I see you in the kitchen for a moment?"

I sat on the Biedermeier sofa and two of the dogs jumped up and starting licking my face. I pet the dogs and waited for Jay and Frank to come back. When the dogs saw Jay, they immediately jumped off the couch.

"Terry, would you like a cup of coffee? Frank doesn't drink it anymore."

I said yes, remembering how I used to drink coffee in this very room with the Demings. I was feeling terribly melancholy as the daylight was turning dark.

Jay came back alone with a silver tray of cake and coffee and was talking as he entered. "Terry, I set up a bed for you in the basement. It's the warmest room in the house, right next to the furnace. You can stay down there until you find a place to live. Frank has clients in the house during the day so I would like it if you would be out of the house every day by eight o'clock in the morning and not return to the house until eleven at night. I hope that's all right with you. That's the only way it will work out here. All right? Good."

I was a bit startled, but I was grateful to have a place to stay. I didn't expect them to be all cozy and welcoming. I was really happy they remembered that's why I was there. After we ate our cake, he took me to the basement and gave me a set of keys to the front door. There was a shower and toilet and it was clean and comfortable. It was a place to get started again in the city. I was humble and thankful.

Every day I got up early and out the door as instructed. It was good to be back in Little Italy again. I'd buy the *Village Voice* and hang out at Buffa's coffee shop on Prince Street and have a roll and coffee, read every inch of the paper as slowly as I could and try to find a job and an apartment that needed a roommate. A friendly petite blond waitress came over to me one morning to give me a refill.

"Hello, I'm Adele. I saw you coming out of the house across the street."

"Yes, my brother owns it. I'm staying there for a while."

"Your brother's Frankie? You're his sister? Hello. Hello. He's such a nice guy, your brother. I didn't know he had a sister. Nice to meet you. You know,

I have a pair of slippers your mother crocheted. Your brother gave them to me. I love 'em, wear them every night."

It felt good to be talking to someone. It sounded strange to hear her mention my mother. I stayed in the coffee shop as long as I could, not knowing what I was going to do with the rest of my life and winter was only a few weeks away. When the lunch crowd started arriving I gave up my table.

I strolled over to the St. Marks Theatre and bought a $2 ticket to the double feature of *Across 110th Street* and *Shaft's Big Score*. Sitting through the movies twice and watching eight hours of Harlem gangsters shooting each other started to get to me. I left and found myself walking uptown to the trains at Grand Central Station.

Grand Central was a filthy place. Most of the lightbulbs were blown out, leaving the halls and walkways dark. The floors were ankle deep with yesterday's newspapers, candy wrappers and black dots of spit-out chewing gum. You could hardly see the constellations on the ceiling of the main room. Orion and Pegasus had just about vanished. Years of people smoking in the station and the soot from the diesel trains covered the peeling walls and ceilings with a dark greasy veil. At one end of the Main Concourse a billboard-size photograph reminded commuters that someplace in Kodak America was still ravishing.

Homeless women were living in the stalls of the ladies' room, washing up in the small sinks, their bags and suitcases piled up inside next to the toilets. Homeless people were living all over the station, huddled on the floors and corners of the rooms, sleeping on the benches. A whole community of people were living underground in the abandoned tunnels. I looked for a way to get down there, wanting to see it for myself.

I passed the time by playing a game. I'd get on a commuter train that was headed to Connecticut or Westchester and just before the doors closed and it pulled out of the station, I'd jump off. When I'd miss, I'd hide in the toilet when the conductor came to collect the tickets and get off at the next stop. I was pretending to go home.

I'd sit all day on the benches in the station watching people or in phone booths with the door closed pretending to be talking to someone. I had no one to call and I didn't want to look up any of my old friends from my psychedelic days. Arline was still living in Oregon and Norvin in Texas. And the last I heard from Neal was a postcard saying he went to the Canary Islands. I wouldn't have called him anyway.

For several weeks I rode the subways to neighborhoods and boroughs I'd not seen before. There's a man on the Coney Island boardwalk who opens his stall, lines up the hot dogs and buns one at a time the same way every single day. Two old women in Queens walk a matted brown dog with three legs several times to the corner and back again. A Spanish man spends all day removing the outer leaves from wilted lettuce in a market in the Bronx. There's a child in Morningside Heights who every morning looks out the same window of his school bus. No one is ever at the shoeshine stand on St. Nicholas Avenue. The wind knocked down the broken swing set in a vacant lot in Jackson Heights. Three men play dominoes everyday at a card table set up on the sidewalk in Hell's Kitchen. I wondered how many people were doing what I was doing, riding aimlessly on the subways to neighborhoods they didn't live in, looking at people they'd never meet. Calling the trains and streets home.

I made eye contact with a man in a business suit one afternoon. I was sitting in a crowded subway car, he was standing right over me holding on to the pole above my head to steady himself on the fast-moving train. He looked completely calm. He was going back to work at his office, I knew that right away. I looked up at his face, into his eyes. Immediately, I was in a place I recognized as a hotel room. My heart started pumping fast, I was frantic. I looked around; a typical hotel, everything in order. A chair, a dresser, a lamp, the bed perfectly made . . . glancing down at the carpet . . . a woman's foot . . . her leg . . . her naked body, lying on the floor. She was dead. I saw he just had sex with her. He killed her, and now he was looking at me. I stayed calm. I looked away. He had no idea what was going on inside me. He came to his stop, got off the train and walked away.

Later that night, I heard that a woman was found dead in a Midtown hotel. They surmised she met a stranger, had a love tryst and was killed. They had no leads.

I met a lot of people underground that just wanted to talk to someone and a lot of people who were afraid when I started talking to them. There were crazy people, people on drugs and people who had just checked out of mental hospitals wandering through the stations. I saw men exposing themselves, pickpockets and panhandlers. And tourists from all over the world. People were always asking me for directions, I suppose because I looked harmless. I'd see someone struggling with a map and I'd ask them if they needed help. Often I'd change their plans, telling them about more interesting places to go. They'd tell me their troubles and I'd listen. I was helping the lost and confused, something I knew a lot about. How long could I go on like this? I had to find a job. I had to come up from underground.

One night, tiptoeing back into the house, the door to Norvin's old apartment sprung open and a young man in a Japanese kimono stuck his head out and startled me by asking,

"Are you Cinderella?"

"Excuse me?"

"I've been dying to meet you, you must be Frank's sister who lives in the cellar."

"It's not that bad."

"Honey, come on in for a drink. Get in here. How do you do, my name is Frank too, just like your brother, but my friends call me Deli, short for Delicatessen. Please, call me Deli."

Here we go again, I said to myself. I could not believe how different the place looked. It had been transformed into a showplace right out of *Architectural Digest.* The walls were painted iguana green. Two matching zebra skins covered the floor in front of the fireplace. A vase of fresh white orchids sat on a glass table. The room was lit by a brass Persian lamp with a beaded shade. I sat down on a modern tubular chrome and leather chair.

"Take off your shoes, dearie. Get comfortable. I want to know everything about you. I've been waiting every night trying to catch you. It's been impossible."

Frank/Deli was a man in his thirties, not very tall, with a ballet dancer's body and short cropped hair. He ran around tidying up the already perfectly placed pillows and magazines. When he spoke he moved his hands constantly in the air, tinkling the ice cubes in his drink.

"I love your chairs, they're beautiful."

"Marcel Breuer, darling, 1925." He handed me a drink. "Vodka, cranberry and a splash of fresh orange. Vitamin C. Is that good?"

"Perfect," I said.

"So, my dear, why has your brother been keeping you from me? How long have you been down there in the coal bin and how come I never see you?"

"Well . . . Deli . . . it's a long story. I'm just so grateful to have a place to stay in New York."

"Now sweetie, tell your sister Deli everything. We're family too, you know."

"The reason you never see me is Frank and Jay asked me to stay away from the house between eight in the morning and eleven at night. Frank has clients and Jay wants his privacy. It's okay."

"Ridiculous! I never heard of such a thing. You're not allowed in your brother's house? This must be Jay's idea. Frank would never put his sister out in the cold. I can't believe this. What do you do? Where do you go all day?"

"Well, I go to the double features, museums, Buffa's, Grand Central Sta . . ."

"Stop! I can't hear any more. This isn't right. You can't go on like this, I can't stand it. Well, my darling, I'll just give you the keys to my place, you'll stay with me. That's all there is to it. Now don't say no. You'll stay in here. I work in Connecticut and I don't get home until late and when I have opera or dinner with friends I'm not home until after eleven most nights. And once in a while I'll stay with Doug in Brooklyn Heights. Dear, I'll tell you about that one day. He's much older than me and well—oh, later for that. You just stay here, please. *Mi casa es su casa.*"

"Thank you, but I couldn't possibly do that."

"Why not? I pay the rent, this is my house. I'm not afraid of Jay. You're staying with me. Nobody has to know, darling. This is our little secret. Besides I'd love to come home and find somebody here. I get lonely. Honey, we'll have fun! You look hungry, are you hungry? I'll make us something to eat. It's no problem. Come and talk to me while I fix us something. Make yourself another drink."

Deli was a tornado. He flew around the two-room apartment changing the music to suit his mood; from the Supremes to Renaissance court music to Nat King Cole and back again. He adjusted the lighting with candles and designer lamps that were carefully placed around the room. Then out of a refrigerator that seemed to have nothing in it, he made us the most elaborate meal. I watched him take a jar of capers, an egg, some caviar, a few olives, a small piece of chicken and some mismatched vegetables and, like magic—a feast appeared. He opened a bottle of French wine and we sat at an enormous green table painted the same color as the walls that took up the entire room.

Talking all night, we got to know each other. Deli had grown up in the country in New Hampshire and then came to New York to attend the Fashion Institute of Technology. He now worked for a major undergarment manufacturer. Deli was their top designer. I was fascinated as he explained the engineering principles of the construction of the bra.

Deli belonged to a gourmet club, five couples, all men. Each month the club took turns hosting an evening with a different theme. The food, drinks, music and costumes had to be absolutely authentic and they'd critique each event. The next month was India and it was Deli's turn. He invited me to go shopping with him in Murray Hill, the Indian neighborhood around Lexington Avenue in the Twenties.

"Not all of us are wearing saris, darling. Doug rented the entire English military drag, that gorgeous red jacket with all those frilly braids and brass buttons and the white hat and sword, the whole bit. He looks so *Jewel in the Crown,* honey, he's so handsome. I bet my friends, Wayne and Jim, will come as rajahs. They've been very secretive about their costumes.

"Oh, I've got to call the florist tomorrow. I wonder if he could perform a miracle and get me a dozen fresh lotus for the table. You are coming with me to Curry Hill on Saturday, aren't you, darling? I have to get the food and you can help me pick out my sari. Please say you'll come.

"Last year, I did a luau in the backyard. I covered the entire garden with a gorgeous translucent blue canopy and stuck a bunch of flaming torches in the ground. Honey, your brother almost had a heart attack when he came home and looked out the window. I had an enormous suckling pig roasting on a spit in the backyard. Frank had just given up eating meat—imagine such a thing. When he came home and saw the pig with an apple in its mouth, going around and around, he was ready to kill me! We had such a good time that night. The food was fabulous! I took hula lessons just for that party.

"I love parties. I have one every chance I get. The gourmet club is strictly members only, but I want you at my next weekend party. Please, say you'll come. Even your brother and Jay come downstairs for them. And they always have a good time.

"The girl who lives upstairs on the third floor is our resident Sally Bowles. She's diabetic and when she's not careful, which is most of the time, she has these whacked-out mood swings. She drives your brother crazy. I don't know how he can stand it. I hear her banging on his door in the middle of the night when she needs to talk to him. When he doesn't answer, she sits outside on his doormat crying so the whole world can hear. They're constantly fighting. I know she's in love with him. This house is crazy, sweetie. You'll meet her. I'll tell her about you, she'd love to meet you.

"You got to see Jay after he's had a few drinks, believe it or not he can be a lot of fun once he loosens up. My parties have been known to go on for a couple of days some times. I never know who will show up and anything can happen and *To Think That I Saw It on Mulberry Street*. Dr. Seuss had no idea."

"Deli, don't you have to go to work tomorrow? It's after two."

"Lamb chop, the night is young! I'm just getting started."

"Well, I'm tired and I should go downstairs to my little bed. I'll see you again, I'm sure. Thank you so much for such a fun evening. I'm really happy I met you. And dinner was fantastic. To be continued . . . thank you."

"Now here, take these." He kissed me on both cheeks as he pressed a set of keys into my hand.

"I mean it, Cinderella. Get out of that cellar, darling. This is your stepsister's orders. I want to see you here when I come home tomorrow, no excuses. And no one has to know. It's our little secret," he whispered.

"Thank you, sis. Good night."

* * *

So, I started sneaking into Deli's apartment. I didn't dare watch television or play music and I only flushed the toilet after five o'clock. I'd sit upright on the couch terrified to move, waiting for Deli to come home. Frank was sitting right above my head at his round Biedermeier table doing his psychic readings. I could hear him talking. Frank's voice was loud. Sometimes I'd hear him yelling at clients and the clients sobbing. I tried not to listen, but the house carried the sounds right through the floorboards and sometimes it was so interesting I had to listen.

Every hour on the hour his doorbell rang, the dogs started their firecracker barking and he'd come downstairs to let the client in. I'd hear them talking in the hall and I'd hold my breath and hope I wouldn't sneeze. I thought a lot about Anne Frank hiding in the attic and how frightened she must have been thinking any minute she was going to get caught. Besides, Frank's a psychic, he must have known I was in the house. Who were we fooling? Deli was right, this was ridiculous.

Week after week of walking the sidewalks, visiting all the museums and department stores in town, hiding out in Deli's apartment, I was desperate for a job. One day, Frank left a note for me on the basement door, to return a call from a friend we used to work with, Jeanne. Jeanne told me that the market research company where she was working was hiring, and I should apply. The people were nice and it paid well. I went back and faced the red pencil.

It was depressing going to another coding job. The only thing I looked forward to was Deli's party. As a last resort, I asked Frank if he would read my cards. He gave me an appointment like any other client. I came up from the basement at my scheduled time and sat at the round table for my reading. He handed me the deck.

"Shuffle the cards, and when you feel you're ready, with your left hand cut the deck into three piles. Then shuffle each pile separately."

He laid seven cards out in a horseshoe pattern exactly the same way he had taught me the first time he read for me when I was thirteen. As he laid each card down he called out the meaning of each placement. "The past. The present. The near future. The consultant, that's you sitting here right now. Other people. The obstacle. And the outcome."

I looked down at the cards and held myself back from interpreting them. I wanted to hear what he had to say, but I couldn't help myself from looking. *The Moon, of course. I'm so confused and depressed. Ace of Swords. I better do something fast before I get myself into serious trouble. The Hermit. You got that right. Ummm, Eight of Swords. Yes, I'm very frustrated. Stop reading them!* It wasn't easy to look away.

Frank reached out for my hand. "Let me look at your palm first. Are you right handed or left?"

Now that's weird, he should know that. Oh, stop being so critical of him, just answer. He positioned my arm with my elbow on the table, my hand held up with my fingers spread as though I was saying, "Stop." With an enormous magnifying glass he went over every inch of my palm. I watched his giant eyeball through the lens of the glass rolling around as he examined my lines with intense curiosity. *I've never seen him do this before. He hasn't touched my hand since I was a little girl. My Frankie, so smart. An original. My brother.*

"Let me take a print." He covered my palms and fingers with an oil he applied with a soft brush. "This is the same oil the police use to take fingerprints of criminals." Placing each of my palms and fingers on a sheet of sensitized paper, he pushed down gently. After a few seconds he lifted my hand from the paper, revealing the fine dark lines and the shape of my fingers, the highway of my life. He handed me a pen and asked me to sign my name to the prints.

"I gotta tell you, your life line isn't very long. Don't get scared, that could change if you work on yourself."

"How long are we talking about?"

"Forty, fifty years," he said casually.

It didn't scare me. The way I felt, he could have said twenty minutes and I would've been relieved.

"Let me see—lots of lovers. Ummm, you suffer from nervousness and anxiety. See these lines here crisscrossing over your life line? That means many people are going to come in and out of your life leaving quite an impact on you. You'll have a lot of influence over other people's lives. You're stubborn and critical and you'll never forget if somebody hurts you. There's a second career in your fifties—if you make it that long. You will, you will, don't worry. Let me look at your cards."

I sat quietly. I wanted him to elaborate, tell me more details, but I thought I should be still and watch him work. It was really hard not to tell him too much or to take over the reading.

"You're going to hear from those people in Pennsylvania. They're going to want you to come back. I suggest you stay away from them. It's just more trouble for you. What do you need that for? Nine of Swords. A quarrel. May cause lasting enmity."

Those are the exact words I read in Rolla's book.

"There's a letter coming from California. Asking you to come out there. Don't go there now, maybe in a few years. I've been getting a ton of calls begging me to come out to LA to do readings for a slew of movie stars, but I told them, 'If you want to see me get on a plane and come here.' A client of mine is a film producer and he keeps telling me they're all asking for me out there. 'Frankie, you got to get out here!' I don't want to go. I can't keep up with the readings here. Shuffle the deck again."

Was California about me or him? I'm confused.

"I see you talking to a lawyer. Don't sign any papers and don't get involved with an older man. He's tall and wears a three-piece suit. Four of Cups. You have a pregnancy in your cards. I don't see you keeping the baby, though."

Well, that's not going to happen.

"Have you talked to Rosemary? She calls here, but I don't have time to talk on the phone. Drink a lot of ginseng tea and don't take vitamins, they don't agree with you.

"Ah, uh, umm . . . I see Snow White and the Seven Dwarfs—except there are only five. You're living with them in the same apartment and one of them is going to introduce you to a dark-haired woman who's very wild and difficult. See here, the Queen of Swords next to the Queen of Cups. And the Lightning Struck Tower. That's not good. Get ready, it won't be easy, but you two are connected. Two of Cups next to the Lovers card. It must be a past-life thing. Let me see that other hand again."

He looked at my other palm for a while, not saying very much and then blurted out, "Are you going to work at Feldman Research? I talked to Jeanne, she told me she spoke to you."

Just then the doorbell rang, the dogs shrieked and scampered down the stairs. Frank gathered up the cards and stood up to go to let the next client in. I didn't feel we were finished. It was all so fast. I followed him down the stairs. He greeted the next client without saying good-bye to me. I was confused and unsatisfied. I hurried down to the basement.

Chapter Eleven

Rosemary gave birth to a baby girl—born on a Hunter's Moon, dark hair, dark eyes, Scorpio. They named her Diana, after the goddess of the Moon and the hunt. With the start of their new family, Bob and Rosemary wanted to buy their own home. They looked at houses in the same neighborhood where they had been renting from Frank and Jay. Most of the houses in that neighborhood were old Victorians. Bob wanted a house that functioned well and needed minimal work, with one floor for a tenant to increase their income. Rosemary wanted ghosts. They went about looking for the right house that suited both their needs, and they had to look at many. On the phone one day she told me the whole ordeal.

"Bob, I don't know—this isn't right. I get a queasy feeling in the upstairs kitchen. Something bad happened up there. Kitchen knives, I see kitchen knives. I'll tell you later. No, thank you, not this one. Bob, I don't like this house—everyone fights in here, the last three couples divorced. I can still hear them yelling. I can't live here.

"Bob, will you come here a minute—this house needs too much work. They're not telling us something about this house. It's the plumbing, I hear water running inside my head. Can I talk to you, Bob? This isn't it. This house is claustrophobic. I don't want it. I can't breathe in here.

"We are not living in this house! Someone died in the living room right over there—and it wasn't pleasant. Let's get out of here!

"No, not this one, I hear babies crying under the floor. It's too sad in this house. It's just not for us, thank you. Bob, this house is going to burn down in two years.

"No, I don't want to go inside this house, nothing can get me to go inside. I don't even want to look at it, thank you. Do you have anything else we could see?"

"Rosemary, honey, sweetheart, please—we've looked at fourteen houses in one weekend. Some of them were really nice and a good deal. You said some of them were haunted. Isn't that what you wanted? Can't you find *one* that you like?

"It's not that, Bob, I just can't live with some of those ghosts, they'll give us trouble in the future. Do you want that? Is that what you want? It's got to be the right ghosts. I know what I'm doing, trust me, Bob."

"Okay, Rosemary. Okay. Why don't you start a psychic real estate business? You could save people a lot of time and money if you're so sure about it. You could take people around and find the right house for them. I'm sure you could make a fortune. Look, we have one more house to look at this afternoon. If you don't like it then I suggest you consult your crystal ball or your Ouija board and find us a house, because I'm finished with you driving me and the realtors nuts!"

They walked up the front steps of a two-family Victorian house in the middle of a block. It had a small front lawn with a big old chestnut tree, an easy to care for backyard and a nice upstairs porch. They went through all the rooms, the attic and basement. The house was clean and quiet. Rosemary didn't say anything. She didn't like the house.

They were asking $27,000 for it. Bob asked Rosemary what she thought.

"I don't feel anything for it."

Bob was surprised. She was tired and pretended to act interested, knowing Bob was at his wit's end. She whispered to Bob, "Offer them twenty-one for it—take it or leave it." She was certain the offer would be refused, and then they could just go home.

"It's yours!" the owner said, excited to make a deal.

Bob shook the owner's hand, the realtor was delighted to finally make a sale and Bob said he'd come to the office to sign the papers. Rosemary couldn't believe it. She didn't want that house. It wasn't haunted, it wasn't interesting, no ghosts, no trouble. She walked home not saying a word. She decided that it was probably better that way—the house was "clean" and maybe she was guided there to live in a place that wouldn't torment her with the previous owners' problems. It would be much better for them in the long run—no ghosts, no terror, no sleepless nights. They moved in the following month. Rosemary immediately had the house painted black.

Bob had a good job as an accountant with a men's clothing manufacturer. Rosemary stayed home, took care of the baby and worked on the house, decorating, painting and going to flea markets and estate sales looking for bargains. They socialized with other young couples on weekends and took Diana to our parents to babysit.

Diana was the joy of my parents' life. Mary and Andy were thrilled by everything about her. They played games throughout the weekend, the three of them dressing up in costumes and dancing around the house, my parents playing their favorite Italian songs for the baby.

Rosemary told me how happy Diana made them and I was happy they had her in their life. I hadn't seen my parents for three years and I kept thinking that maybe I should go to Buffalo one day to visit them and see the new baby. I just wasn't ready yet. I'd call my mother on holidays and birthdays and it would always be the same conversation.

"Oh, hi Terry, I was just thinking about you. Son of a gun, Andy didn't I just say five minutes ago, 'I wonder how Terry is?' You should see Diana, that little shrimp, she knows how to speak Italian already. I talk to her in Italian and she answers me. Yeah. She loves to come here on the weekends. We have a lot of fun. You should see her dance. Yeah. We take her to Chef's for lunch and they say, 'Mary is that your granddaughter? She's so beautiful.' We have a ball with her. We do. How's Frankie? You tell him, when I call him I want him to call me back. All I get is that damn Jay telling me, 'I'll give him the message, Mary. He'll call you when he has a moment' *Va caca!* Who the hell does he think he is? Go to hell! I'm his mother. *Va fungule!*"

"Mother, how's Dad? Can I talk to him?"

"He's watching TV. Toots, get up, come over here! Terry wants to talk to you. What? I can't hear you. Get over here! What? He won't get up. He doesn't like to talk on the phone."

"Mother, I got to go. Tell Dad I said hello."

"You tell your brother Mr. Andrews to call me, Okay? I want to hear from him. Did he forget about his mother?"

"Sure Mother. I will. I'll tell him. Good-bye."

Rosemary and Bob looked after my parents. They saw them every weekend and called every day to see how they were doing. They also visited Bob's mother and father every Sunday as well as Bob's aunts, who lived alone. To me, being so devoted to family seemed foreign and old-fashioned. I felt like I lived on another planet. The longer I was in New York, the farther away family life seemed to be.

Having a child seemed to heighten Rosemary's psychic awareness. Whenever she had Diana out in the stroller and passed another mother with her baby, she'd find herself immediately reading their aura. One day Diana might play with their children. Rosemary had to know what kind of people they were before she'd let anyone near her child. She was surprised one day when one of the mothers brought up the subject of the supernatural.

"Isn't that amazing? Can you believe that? Did anything like that ever happen to you, Rosemary?"

"Well, actually I grew up in a family where things like that happened just about every day. My brother is a professional psychic in New York City. He reads palms and Tarot cards and has been interviewed in many newspapers and magazines. My mother is psychic and my sister reads Tarot cards. She lives in New York too. We've been doing this all our lives."

"Then you must have the gift too, Rosemary. Don't you? Come on, I bet you do. Do you do readings? You do, don't you? I can't believe we're having this conversation in Buffalo. Tell me everything!"

"Well, I can see auras and I do psychometry. And I can find missing things."

"What's psychom . . . ?"

"Psychometry. It means I can feel things and know things that are contained in objects. When I hold something I get impressions from it that gives me information about the person or about things that are going to happen. I hear messages and I see pictures in my head. I have dreams too where I can see the future. My guides help me—my spirit guides."

"Wow, Rosemary, that's amazing. I could talk to you all day about this. I love this stuff. This is incredible! Have you ever heard of Lily Dale near Jamestown? I heard they do seances there. I always wanted to go. I had a reading once in Florida; my girlfriend lives down there and we went to a place called Cassadega Spiritualist Camp where there were all these mediums living in little cottages. It was so cute. You could go from house to house and get a reading from many different psychics. I loved it. I'll tell you one day what the psychic told my girlfriend about her husband. I love this stuff!"

"I've been to the Lily Dale Assembly many times," Rosemary said. "It's a beautiful, peaceful place with swans on the lake. I've had readings there and I've been to lectures. I've taken courses on all kinds of metaphysical subjects. It's only an hour from Buffalo. You should go sometime, you'd like it."

"Rosemary, let me ask you a question. Do you see anything in my aura? I don't want to put you on the spot, but I'm curious. What do you see? Can you read me? Come on, I want to know. Just a little, please. I'm so curious what you would see about me."

"I can't just do it like that, well, I can if I have to in an emergency, but not now. I have to focus, it has to feel right. I'll read for you sometime if you want. You can come to my house and I'll do a reading for you. "

"Can I call you? I'd love a reading. I believe in these things. I'm so excited. I'm so glad I bumped into you. I'm going to call you. How much do you charge?"

That woman turned out to be the biggest gossip in the neighborhood.

"Hello Rosemary. My name is Annie. I live in the yellow house at the corner. Can I ask you something? It's about my engagement ring—I misplaced it and I hope I didn't lose it. I've been in a panic as to where it could be. Please, can you help me and tell me where it is?"

"What are you talking about?"

"You know—you can tell things. I heard you have the gift and you can find missing things."

"How do you know that about me? Who told you I could find your ring?"

"Well, I'll tell you. Everyone is talking about you, we're all so fascinated. First of all, it started when you moved in and painted your house black. I love it, but everyone was wondering if you're a witch. Is this okay that I tell you all this? Then some of the girls noticed that you're always looking around their heads and staring at their kids. It makes them uncomfortable. They thought you were weird or severely depressed, with a black house and all. Some of the mothers are still afraid of you. It all makes sense now. When Victoria told me she spoke to you on the street the other day and you told her about your brother and your family—well, I just had to meet you. Are you a witch? I mean, it's okay. I don't have any problem with that. I'm sure you're a good witch. I hope so. Aren't you? Some of the girls are still afraid, but most of them can't wait to talk to you. I told them I'd approach you first. And I am desperate to find my ring. Why do you look around our heads? Do you see something? Do you know where my engagement ring is?"

So it was out, everyone knew. Now Rosemary had lots of friends and they all went to her with their problems. Just like my mother, sitting around the kitchen table with the coffeepot and the children. Rosemary did readings for each of them with all kinds of stuff they brought for her to hold. Their grandmothers' jewelry, photographs of old boyfriends and potential new ones, love letters, documents, legal papers, antiques, their children's toys.

While Rosemary was socializing with young mothers, Frank and I were on opposite sides of the room at Deli's parties.

. . .

Deli opened his door dressed in a skintight, whorehouse-red evening gown and a long curly red wig; matching nail polish adorned the elegant hand he extended to be kissed. Deli was a fireball.

"Ladies and gentlemen, welcome to my humble abode. The palace of the living gods. The boudoir that knows one thousand and one tales. The night is young, and the young are yours! Delicious! Delirious! Help yourself, my darlings!"

Deli loved the attention. He worked all week making sure every detail of the party would be unique. The guests were always different except for the neighbors: me, Frank and Jay. Deli's guests were old friends, friends of friends, people she'd met on the street that afternoon or street performers she'd brought home to surprise us. Frank and Jay sometimes invited their friends or one of Frank's clients, or a friend and their visiting mother.

It always took me a while to relax and enjoy myself. I could feel Frank was uncomfortable with me there. He'd look at me from across the room and then look away when I made eye contact with him. He'd say hello politely, but soon someone would get his attention and he'd go over to them. I'd slip away feeling awkward. Often people would come over to me and start talking, almost always about Frank.

"Are you Terry Andrews? You're Frank's sister, aren't you? When did you move here? Buffalo—it's really cold there and all that snow! How do they stand it up there? I didn't even know Frank had a sister; Deli just told me. Are you psychic too? Your brother is so amazing. Does he read for you? He read my cards last year and predicted that I was going to inherit some money at the end of the summer and that someone I'd be in love with would be living with me. At the time I didn't know anyone who would leave me money. And—I *always* live alone. Well, my dear, sure enough three days before Labor Day, my neighbor across the hall, whom I barely knew, dropped down dead of a heart attack and left me ten thousand dollars! I was flabbergasted. Your brother was right. I fed her cat only a couple of times, but that was about it. Well, I inherited the money, the cat lives with me and he's the love of my life. Frank told me this was all going to happen. Isn't he remarkable?"

"Yes, remarkable," I said. I got up and got myself a drink and sat next to a bleached-blond woman in a silver jumpsuit and pearls so I could eavesdrop on the story she was telling.

"It was right here around the corner at the Broadway-Lafayette subway station. I used to go to the office early, before anyone got there—around seven. One day I dropped my token in and went down to the F train as usual. I vaguely noticed a guy standing there looking at me. As I make eye contact, he opens his coat and flashes me! I was in shock; for Chrissake, I'd just got out of bed an hour before! I hadn't even had my coffee! At first I was pretty shook up, and then I got angry.

"Well, this went on for about a month, every day. He'd wait for me, same place, same time. As soon as he saw me he'd open his coat and there he'd be with his big fat dick just hanging there. I complained at the token booth, I went to the police—they did nothing. I tried yelling at him and telling him I knew his mother and I was going to call her. Nothing worked. I couldn't take a different train and I didn't want to anyway. Once when he flashed me I said, 'Oh no, much too small for me, honey.' That didn't do it. I tried humor, threats, psychology. I just got sick of him. He was annoying me and I realized that's what he wanted—my attention. Then I got this great idea. One morning I went into the subway like always, except this time when I saw him I went right up to him and looked him right in the eye and said, 'Good Morning! How do you like this, baby?' I opened my coat and I stood there completely naked except for my shoes. He looked horrified and ran away. I turned around and went to work and that was that. Well, I'll tell you—I never saw him again. I fixed him."

* * *

From behind me, "We met when we were seventeen. I called him Billy the Kid because he was so fearless and wild. He'd get all dressed up in his sisters' cotillion gowns. He was so pretty—blond hair, blue eyes. Billy had a cousin who was studying hairdressing at a school in Baton Rouge who stole wigs for him. He looked gorgeous, a ravishing beauty. I used to help him with his makeup. He had these long eyelashes. He was a rare jewel.

"A chauffeured car with the seal of the United States Navy painted on the door would pick him up at his house and he'd go off to the military balls with his boyfriend, an admiral in the Navy. The admiral's wife stayed home while Billy was out dancing with her husband. He'd be seated right at the officer's table with the other couples. There he'd be in bright orange chiffon gossiping all night with the wives. Nobody knew that Billy the Kid was a boy."

The party was buzzing. Tons of drinks and pot and something new I hadn't heard of—Quaaludes. Deli took out his collection of 45s and people started dancing in the small living room. I went into the kitchen for a glass of water. I looked out the window into the backyard and saw a couple having sex on the steps.

On my way to the bathroom I met one of Deli's bra models from work who introduced me to her new boyfriend. She whispered to me that he had just become very wealthy from his new invention, frozen yogurt. The Bra Model and the Yogurt King. I went into the living room, a young man in his underpants and a cowboy hat was dancing on top of the coffee table as a set of handsome, darkly tanned, identical twin brothers danced around him.

"What's the matter?" Deli asked me. "You're not drinking enough. Here poodle, have a White Russian. Come over here and talk to Tony. He's a classical composer, very highbrow stuff. He's been dragging us uptown to these seances. I'm sure he'd love to tell you all about it."

"Tell me! I am really interested. What seances? Where? Can I go?" I shouted over the music.

Tony wrote down a name and address on a paper napkin. Agatha Wojciechowsky, 334 East Eighty-third Street. Monday and Thursday 7:30.

"How do you say that?"

"Wojciechowsky."

"What?"

"Wo-ja-cow-skee. Just go. It's open to anyone. Your brother used to go, but he's too busy and I think he got bored with it. Agatha is amazing, you'll see."

It was about two o'clock in the morning and the party showed no sign of slowing down. I was much too sober for such a party, so I decided to try a

Quaalude. What the hell. Within a short time I felt really good and I was smiling a lot. I danced with somebody's mother who was here from Phoenix visiting her son. She was having the best time. She confessed to me that she had smoked some pot and was feeling terrific. Then somehow Frank and I ended up in the kitchen together.

"Frank, this is a really great party. Where's Jay?"

"He went upstairs. He took a sleeping pill and he's out cold."

"A sleeping pill?" Deli said, overhearing us as he refilled the ice bucket. "How Lana Turner of you. Ludes baby. The love drug. Why don't you have one, Frank, darling. You don't know what you're missing."

"No thank you. I get high on life."

I grabbed a pair of Deli's oven mitts and started moving my hands like talking puppets. In a high-pitched squeaky voice I pretended to be a spirit talking through the oven mitts. "'Hellooo, Frankie . . . This is your Uncle Archibald. I know you couldn't stand me when I was alive. And I'm back now to make your life miserable.' Frank, this is a great idea. You could do readings wearing these. People who've never had a reading with you before would think it was just part of the experience. Go on, ask me a question."

"Uncle Archibald, you bastard, where did you hide the money?"

"I spent it all on the young babe I met in Aruba," said the voice from the left-hand mitt, flapping in the air.

"I could just see the client sitting there perfectly calm having a long conversation with the oven mitts. They'd believe it. If someone said to them, 'You got to see this psychic in Little Italy. He's a little strange, but he's amazing. He channels spirits through oven mitts. Seriously, he's the best I've ever been to and I've been to them all.'" Frank roared with laughter, tears running down his face.

"Frank dear, can I pull you away for a moment. Sorry sweetie, do you mind? I want to ask your brother something." He followed the woman in the silver jumpsuit, looking back at me as he was sucked into the crowd.

"Terry Andrews, come and dance with me." Deli escorted me to the front room to dance. The music was playing and Deli sang along in his deep husky voice: *Our day will come and we'll have everything. We'll share the joy falling in love . . .* " He held me tight to his red silky dress and I could feel his "breasts" poking hard into my body.

"Deli, what are these?" I said, cupping one of his breasts in my hand.

"Birdseed, darling. I'll show you."

He opened his dress and showed me his breasts—two nylon stocking bags filled with birdseed.

"Don't go near the park, Deli. You might get pecked!" the cowboy yelled out.

"I'm the one doing the pecking in that park, honey. Don't you worry about me," Deli shouted back as he went on dancing with me.

There was something kind of sweet and teenage about this party, as if we were playing dress up and being silly while our parents were away. It was starting to get late and the mother from out of town thought she should be getting back to her hotel. Her son had left the party hours before, leaving her for Frank to look after. He got her coat and said he would take her to the corner and put her in a taxi. As they stood on the steps of the house saying good-bye, a man ran past waving a gun in the air. Then two other men ran after him with their guns drawn. They started shooting at each other right in front of the house, as Frank and the mother stood there watching.

When we heard the shots, we all hurried to the door to see what was happening. Frank yelled out to the mother, "Now, Mrs. Vanderhorf you've seen New York!" The men went on shooting as they ran down the street. Crowded together on the stoop, everyone was stunned—then they cheered and applauded. The mother turned to Frank and said, "I had the best time of my life."

Frank kissed her on both cheeks, hailed a taxi and the mother went home. He locked the front door and went upstairs. I went back into Deli's. He was busy cleaning up the apartment. I flopped on the bed exhausted and fell into a deep sleep.

What's this sweetness I'm floating in? Lilacs . . . ? Gardenias . . . ? The sun is blinding. What's that spot in the distance? It's moving, kind of wavy. It's getting bigger.

Deli sings, *"How could I ignore the boy next door. I love him more . . ." Judy is that you? I can't believe it. Judy Garland. It's you! Judy? Are you kissing me?*

With my eyes barely open. I can't believe what I'm seeing. Deli sitting on the edge of the bed in fishnet stockings and high heels. He puts one leg up and hoists himself on the bed. Standing over me swaying her hips and singing along with Garland. Complete in Judy-style, short tuxedo jacket and tipped Fedora . . . he starts coming closer.

"Yes darling, it's me, Judy."

I can't keep my eyes open, I'm so tired. I'm falling in and out of sleep. Judy/Deli is rubbing my leg and crawling up to kiss me.

"Judy loves you, baby."

"Are you really Judy Garland?"

"I am. Let me make love to you."

Half in a dream, half in a fantasy, we make love.

In the morning I woke up first—smelling like Deli's makeup. Quietly, I slipped out of bed and tiptoed over the high heels and Judy wig, then closed the door behind me. When I came to my senses I couldn't believe what had happened. I had slept with a man dressed as a woman pretending to be a woman dressed as a man.

I avoided Deli for the next several days until he captured me in the hall.

"We can't keep running away from each other. C'mon give me a hug, Cinderella. What happened between us, it's cool. For Godsake, we're sisters!"

I started staying in the basement from then on.

Chapter Twelve ·

Gomez: 3A. Hudson: 4C. O'Brien: 5B. Wo–ja–cow–skee: 6A. I push the bell. A loud buzzer makes me jump. The door unlocks. Stairs. Sixth floor. Doesn't anyone live on the ground floor? Every door is painted gray and looks exactly the same. A real seance, something I'd been dying to do since I was a kid. I wonder if the neighbors know what's going on in 6A. The door is slightly ajar. Out of breath, I walk in.

A thin young man wearing white gauze Indian clothes greets me warmly: "Hello, I'm Richard. Please, come in. Take any seat. Agatha will be out in a few minutes."

Richard introduced me to the three other people standing next to him. I took a seat in the middle of a circle of chairs. An elderly couple was sitting across from me holding hands. They nodded and gave me a weak smile. Two women and a man walked in together, took seats and immediately sat erect with their eyes closed and placed their hands in a meditation pose.

All the windows were covered with heavy black velvet curtains. I could see that the glass had also been painted black. Pictures of Indian mystics in turbans, loincloths and twisted yoga positions hung on the walls. A painting of Jesus with arms outstretched welcoming little children hung over the doorway. I got up to take a closer look at a photograph of an elderly woman with snow-white hair and bright blue eyes, her hand caressing her cheek.

"That's Agatha. Isn't she beautiful?" said a woman from behind me. "Let me show you something over here. Hi, I'm Margaret. First time here?"

She took me to a wall of pencil drawings of hands. Tiny faces of women and men filled the space of the fingers and palms. I assumed they were done by children. Some of the faces had beards or mustaches, eyeglasses, turbans. Most of them looked alike to me. But then I wasn't sure, I thought one of the faces smiled at me.

"Agatha drew these," Margaret said. "They're portraits of the sitters who come here. She can see the faces of your past lives inside your hands. She'll do it for you if you ask her. It's quite reasonable."

I noticed when some people came in they went directly to a small desk and wrote something in a book. I went over to see what they were doing. It was a book asking the spirits for prayers and favors. I wrote down the names of my parents. Next to the book was a satin jewelry box for donations. I put two dollars in. The seats were filled with about twenty people, most of whom had their eyes closed. Some seemed to be praying. I could see their lips moving. The elderly lady I recognized from the photograph came out from a room in the back wearing a flowered cotton housedress. She was about four-feet-six-inches tall.

"Good evening and God bless you."

"Good evening, Agatha," the whole room said together.

"Richard, will you please turn the lights off now?"

He reached behind to a lamp and shut it off. The room was black. I could see nothing. I waited for my eyes to adjust to the darkness, thinking I'd eventually see an outline of something. That never happened. I quickly started feeling claustrophobic. My mind was telling me I was being buried alive. There was no air. I panicked, then talked myself out of it. *Breathe. Remember why you're here. This is a seance.* We sat for a long time in silence. I started to feel peaceful, calm.

Agatha started speaking. She sounded like a little girl with a thick German accent.

"Close your eyes, take a deep breath with me. God protect us from any entity who is unwelcome to our circle. May no spirit enter the room who has not been invited. Please, God, protect our doorkeepers from evil. Guide them to the spirits who want to come to us tonight to talk with their loved ones. We are truly grateful for all your help. God bless you all and keep you safe. Now say the Lord's Prayer with me."

More silence. Waiting. I kept my eyes open. No one could see me anyway. I couldn't hear anyone breathing. I was afraid something was going to jump out at me. I'd lose control and start screaming. What if I coughed? What if I had to pee? *Calm down,* I told myself. *This is the real thing.* A big smile broke out on my face. I was afraid I'd start laughing.

"Good evening sweet friends," giggled a little tiny voice.

"Good evening, Buttercup," the room answered.

Oh no, it's a Munchkin; she's channeling a Munchkin. Stop that. Have some respect. You always have to make fun of things? Give it a chance. I better get serious, maybe the sprits will toss me out the window if I don't behave. Can they hear me thinking?

Then came the funny voice again. "For those who don't know me, my name is Buttercup and I am the doorkeeper for the medium. I'm here so that nobody can enter her without answering to me. I protect her. She's not fully asleep yet so you'll just have to wait till she's out." Buttercup giggled, "Is that okay with you?"

Some people gave a soft laugh and some said, "Yes, Buttercup," or "We love you, Buttercup. God Bless you, Buttercup." *They must know her or him from other seances. Does a spirit have a gender? Will you stop with the criticism. You're so judgmental. Be open. Be open. Be open.*

We waited a little while and Buttercup spoke again, "Not yet. Just a little bit longer. She's still not out yet. Any minute now."

We waited. Somebody coughed. I scratched my head from nerves.

"Mr. and Mrs. Gilbert, your son is here. Martin wants to speak to you," Agatha said in a soft voice that sounded like she now had a slight English accent.

Whose voice was this? Is this Agatha speaking to us or a spirit? Where's her German accent? I think the voice is coming through her.

"Dad! Hello, it's Marty. How are you Daddy?" A young man's voice with a slight sound of Agatha without the German or English accent spoke to his father in the room. I could hear a woman crying. I assumed it was the older couple I had seen when I first arrived.

"Now stop crying, Mrs. Gilbert. Marty's just fine and he looks good. He's not dead. You just can't see him. I keep trying to tell you he's happy and he's here with us." Buttercup was back.

"Marty, say hello to your mother. She misses you so much," said Mr. Gilbert.

"Mom, don't cry. I'm happy and I'm with you all the time. I gotta go now. I love you. Good-bye."

"Marty! Marty! Don't go yet. Please, Marty! I miss you, son. Come home to me, Marty." I could hear the woman crying.

My mind was racing, *I don't know what to think. This is weird. Who was that? What happened to that kid? Suicide, I feel it was suicide. I wonder how often his parents come here just to hear his voice. Why don't they let go? How do they know that's their son? All these voices. I'm confused.*

Suddenly a loud husky voice. "Hello, my friends. This is Tall Pine. I am from the Mohawk Nation. I'm here to tell you that you are killing the Earth. You are destroying forests and bringing death to our animal cousins. My heart is weeping over how you are treating my mother, the Earth. Everyone in this room is a good person, but you are all part of this. You must change your ways. You are killing all the waters and darkening the skies. You take everything and you do not give back! You will all suffer if you do not stop. Do not wait. It is happening faster than you know."

More silence. Waiting. *It's hot in here. Of course, that Indian is right, this planet is a mess. What else is new?*

Another little girl's voice started calling, "Terry Andrews. Terry Andrews. Where are you? Are you there? If you don't say something I'll go away. Terry Andrews. Terry Andrews. Aren't you going to talk to me?"

"Do you mean me?" I said.

"Yeeeeesssssss."

"My name is not Andrews, though."

"I know that! I'm just teasing you like you tease everyone else. You're a very funny lady. I like your sense of humor. Do you like that I'm talking to you?"

"Who are you? What's your name?" I asked.

"My name is Snow Flake! And I'll be your guide. If you want me to."

"Hello, Snow Flake. That's a perfect name for a guide for me. Thank you. I would like you to guide me. Where are we going?"

"Ha ha ha. See how funny you are. You think I'm flakey? Yes, I am and so are you! So we'll make a great team, Terry Andrews."

"Now, that's not my last name."

"I know it's Frank's. He's your brother. Candlelight watches over him. Don't worry, she keeps a good eye on him. You don't have to worry so much about him. We won't let anyone hurt him. He's a hard worker. He takes care of everybody. Tell him we miss him here at Agatha's."

"I will. Do you have a message for me, Snow Flake?"

"Yes, I do. Are you ready? You can do what Agatha does. You can go into trance and we can talk through you. Would you like that?"

"Oh, I don't know. I don't think so. I have to think about it. I'm not ready for that yet."

"Don't be afraid, no one is going to hurt you. In time, you'll see. You'll be a trance medium. We'll help you. Just keep watching the snowflakes fall. I love you. Snow Flake loves you. Good-bye for now."

"Good-bye, Snow Flake."

What was that? How did she know I was related to Frank? No one knows me here. No one knew I was coming tonight. I wrote Iacuzzo in the book. Someone must have told her. Maybe this is real. Me a trance medium? I don't think so. I don't want to do that. It's hard enough just to be myself, let alone all these other beings.

I was thinking so much about what was said to me that I didn't really listen to what the other voices were saying to the other people. There were more dead relatives, Indians, fairies, guides, master teachers and doorkeepers, all with names like Red Rose, Blue Feather, Nightingale, Honey Bee, Laughing Thunder, Dr. Xenobia, Primrose, Master Jupiter, Doormouse, Lily Tree, Firefly, Star Bird, Moonglow and Orange Blossom.

Everybody received their message. Some were scolded, some were encouraged, some just got a hello from the other side. At the end of the seance, Buttercup came to say good-bye and awaken our medium, Agatha.

"Yoo-hoo. Wake up. Hello in there. She's really out. Should I pinch her nose? Should I pull her hair? Hee, hee, hee. Just kidding. Here she comes. She's waking up. I got to go now. See you next time. Don't forget to say your prayers. I'm with you. I'm watching you." Buttercup's voice faded away.

"Ahhhhhhh . . ." Agatha said exhausted. "Cover your eyes with both hands and don't open them until I tell you. I don't want you to hurt your eyes. Richard, turn on the little light first."

It was a shock to see light again. I spread my fingers open over my face a little bit at a time. Everyone looked like they had a thick white fog around their bodies. I was getting used to the light, but the white fog seemed to linger. Agatha was slumped in her chair. Richard gave her a glass of water and we all sat quietly readjusting to the living world. We'd been sitting in the dark for almost four hours. It went by so fast.

Agatha looked worn and confused. "Did anything happen? Did anyone come through? Was Buttercup naughty again?" she said.

The sitters started talking to each other, excited about the experience. Some people got up and greeted Agatha with hugs and kisses, others got their coats and left. I could still see the white fog following them as they moved about the room. The elderly couple left quickly looking sad and disappointed. I overheard them talking about why their son hadn't stayed longer. I got the feeling that it would never be enough.

I didn't want to talk to anyone. I just wanted to think about the evening. I was reluctant to be too friendly, knowing how the psychic world often attracted needy people. But I couldn't wait to return.

* * *

And then I was back at the market research job. To amuse ourselves through the reading of those long boring interviews about toothpaste or breakfast cereal, we took turns calling the main branch of the New York City Public Library asking the research department to look up information for us. We'd try to outdo each other with our questions. Those were the days before computers, when you actually got to speak to a real person who answered the phone on the first ring with a response that was always polite no matter what your question was.

"Can you please look up the details of the procedure for gelding a horse?" "What is the longest amount of time someone held their breath under a frozen lake in Manitoba?" "How many steps does it take to walk from here to Paris, Texas, if you're a six-foot-four man who wears a size eleven shoe?"

They'd return after a few minutes, with seriousness and professionalism and relay the information they'd found.

When we weren't calling the library, we'd keep ourselves from going crazy by making up scoops for the *National Enquirer*. We'd call them with a UFO sighting in Central Park or a sighting of Jesus above the copy machine telling us he was really a woman. Or that my mother's fox stole came to life and bit me.

We were a group of seekers and dreamers. Money was tight and dreams were addictive. Most of us consulted psychics or astrologers. We traded stories and telephone numbers, although usually with some kind of disclaimer.

"I liked her. She saw some great stuff ahead for me. She picked up my father's name and she knew I was an actor without me telling her. I'll be quitting this job sometime during the next two years. She said I'd be moving to Hollywood and I'll never come back here. Give her a chance, but you never know, she might not be right for you. I'm not responsible if it doesn't work out."

One day, someday, someone would get a break on Broadway or another would move to Paris or London. One day, someday, someone would hit the road to LA for that big movie role. One day, someday, someone would write a book.

"What's her number?" we all said.

Three-quarters of the coding room followed me to Agatha's, well, at least once. I went to the sittings twice a week for over a year. I kept trying to figure out the difference between what I wanted to be real and what actually was.

At the office I met Peter, a coder who once worked for Frank. Peter was from western Massachusetts, handsome with lots of brown curly hair, a full beard and eyes that changed color with whatever he wore. He walked out of a Ph.D. program at the University of Virginia and moved to New York City in the same week in 1968 that I did. We thought that meant we were destined to meet each other. He was studying with an astrology teacher and had taken Tarot classes from both Frank and Rolla. He drew up charts for me and my family and explained what the planets had to say about why we were the way we were. I told Peter about Agatha's in our very first conversation, and he started coming to the seances with me.

Peter had just moved into a large apartment in the East Village on Tenth Street across from Tompkins Square Park. One of his roommates was moving out at the end of the month and he asked me if I wanted to rent the room. I jumped at the chance. We walked home after work to see it, talking all the way downtown.

"Peter, now tell me the truth, do you believe Agatha's really contacting spirits and that they speak through her?"

"The mind operates on many levels at once. Those voices are part of her personality that can split off from her and give us information about ourselves. She could probably do the same thing by just talking to us in her own voice. I don't think she thinks it's coming from her, or that her personality has any input into what's coming out."

"If this is part of her personality then how does she have information about us?"

"I think you can answer that better than me. How do you get information when you read for someone?"

"It just comes to me, like I've always known it. Sometimes it's like I'm watching a movie in my mind about the person I'm talking to. And of course, the Tarot is amazing. It's not the cards themselves, but how they speak to me and how I translate them. Peter, I believe Agatha is sincere. I believe she calls on something that's out there in the universe. Spirits? Energy? Ethereal information? Whatever you call it."

"How do you think she does it?"

"It's confusing, but I think maybe I can understand it from my own experience. You open your being and invite whatever's out there to come in. You have to forget everything you believe about space and time and just be still and feel. Stories get transmitted through the air. I know because I hear them and I see them. I feel them. Look at Rosemary, she's an untuned radio dial randomly receiving information from objects, from dreams, from people she passes on the street, even news events before they happen. She told me last year she had a dream with numbers falling out of the sky and floating on the ocean. It turned out to be the flight number of the plane that crashed into the Atlantic."

"Yikes! She told you that?"

"That's nothing. She does that all the time. The thing with Rosemary though, is sometimes she can't tell the difference between the dream that's trying to tell her something about herself and her own life, and the dream that's predicting a public event. She's so open. It really doesn't matter to her which dream belongs to her and which is the world's. She just waits for it to happen. She doesn't analyze everything the way I do."

"I guess the difficulty with Agatha, with psychics in general, is where do you draw the line? How do you know what's real and what you're imagining?"

"What's reality anyway? Two people experience the same thing at the same time and have completely different versions of what happened. They'd both say their experience was real. And they'd both be right. Then once something has happened and it's over and done, it's a memory. And then you tell someone about it. Now it's an interpretation of a memory. Then there's conditioning, things that we're taught to believe are true. We do all of this for so long we just assume that it's reality. So is it real? Yes, because your mind was convinced that what you experienced was real and the believing is a reality itself. You see reality is just a dream. Reality is one level of a fiction. I think systems like astrology that classify reality as they do remind us that there's more than one valid perspective. But we're all so attached to our version of reality being the only true one."

. . .

The apartment was huge, with several bedrooms, a big kitchen and a living room with a view of Tompkins Square Park. Peter showed me the room that was available. It was small with just enough space for a mattress and two milk crates for my clothes. The one window faced north, looking out over a long expanse of rooftops. It was perfect.

I met the rest of my new roommates—Tom, David, Gerry and Bobby. I remembered Frank's reading. He had seen an image of Snow White and the Seven Dwarfs but there were only five. And here I was, about to move in with five men. Within days, I moved out of Mulberry Street. I felt like I was finally on my own, away from Frank, with friends I'd met myself.

I now had a family of brothers, all into music and various forms of nightlife, but for the most part, clean, neat and organized. Every night in the living room we'd talk for hours about astrology, dreams, Tarot, psychic experiences and love. Music was always playing and opera was a big deal in the house. I astonished the boys one night when I came swirling in playing my castanets during the overture of *Carmen*. I learned to play them when I was in dancing school. One of the few possessions I'd kept.

Peter and I would sometimes persuade the roommates to come along to Agatha's seances. One of those nights Agatha showed movies of her recent trip to the Philippines.

"There, on the right, you see Tony," Agatha said in her German accent. "He's the most famous psychic surgeon in the Philippines. From the time he was three years old he could hold out his hands and make fiery lightning bolts shoot out from his fingertips. He set the trees on fire just by pointing at them."

I caught Gerry and Tom rolling their eyes at each other.

Agatha took the films with her own movie camera. The psychic surgeons "operated" on hundreds of sick people who came from all over the world hoping for a miracle. In the films we could see the surgeons reaching into a person's body, removing tumors and cancers with their bare hands. The patients looked relaxed. Some of them had smiles on their faces while they were being operated on without anesthesia.

The surgeons' hands looked like they were kneading dough inside the body. Sometimes blood spilled out from the opening. Within a few minutes the surgeon would pull out the diseased part of the body and toss it into a washbasin.

Agatha told us that most people don't believe the surgeons are authentic. Skeptics constantly try to catch them in some deception. But she was absolutely convinced they were real because she was there in the room and saw it with her own eyes. The films were quite convincing.

After the movie, the boys and I went out for Indian food. Gerry gave us his reenactment of the films we'd just seen. Using Bobby as a patient with a brain tumor he mimicked the psychic surgeon's kneading. He removed a vegetable samosa from Bobby's brain.

"Oh, stop that you two! You're so disrespectful!"

"Look who's talking. The Queen of Skepticism!" Bobby said.

"Well, rightly so. I don't believe in anything I don't experience for myself firsthand."

"Now, you don't believe that sleight of hand nonsense we just saw, do you? My God, it's so obvious that what they called tumors and cancers were nothing but a handful of chicken guts," said David.

"How about changing the subject?" said Peter. "I'm trying to eat my dinner, not throw it up."

"You know that human beings are capable of doing the most extraordinary things," I said, as the waiter placed the chicken vindaloo in the center of the table. "In other cultures there isn't any question that a shaman or a medicine man can heal sick people. What about all those people who make a pilgrimage to Lourdes for the miracle waters and are cured? And look at the Haitian voodoo healers. Weren't you at Agatha's when Sonja told us how she went to the Philippines and had her tumor removed from her ovary?"

"Enough already," Peter said.

"Sorry. Life is filled with these unexplainable phenomena. A woman I know told me she'd seen men fly in the desert in Oman. I know she's an honest person. I want to go there and fly with them. We have to open up our thinking. Or stop thinking so much altogether. Just say, 'Why not?' Find a way to get there and try to have the experience. I never turn my head away from anything."

"But Terry, you said you won't just believe what someone tells you until you experience it yourself. How do you know she's telling you the truth?" Tom pointed out.

"How do you know I don't fly? I go to the seances so I can find out for myself. I might never know the truth, but I'm not going to hide from these things just because they seem strange or fake. Sometimes it's profound, sometimes it's ridiculous and sometimes it's both at once."

"I'd rather go to the movies," Gerry said.

"I'd rather go home," grumbled Peter. "Waiter, can we have our check, please?"

. . .

I kept going to Agatha's long after my roommates fell away. There was something I needed to figure out there in the dark. I didn't think the voices were helping any of us—except for reinforcing the hope that love is eternal, even when all we can feel is the pain of letting go. The messages were sweet, but I was more interested in why the people who came to these sessions needed to be hearing them. The same people came every week, waiting for the same message. I don't know what they would have done if it ever varied. If we could really contact the dead, why not ask them more about what it's like there. Is dead a place? And what, if anything, can they tell us about the future?

Why don't we try to reach Einstein, Gandhi or anyone at least more interesting then Aunt Tillie? Who knows, maybe Einstein is channeling through someone somewhere, and he's doing it without them knowing. Maybe he's not even Einstein anymore. Maybe he's just old Uncle Albert comforting his loved ones. Maybe he's discovered that physics wasn't that interesting after all, now that he is the universe.

. . .

Agatha asked me to stay behind one night after the seance was over. She wanted to talk to me.

"My dear, I've been told by my master teacher that you are going to follow in my footsteps. The spirits want to use your vocal chords to speak for them. If you work hard you can do it. You're strong. I know you're ready."

"Agatha, I don't feel this is right for me. I'd rather listen to what they have to say. And if they want to whisper in my ear, that would be fine. I don't think I could let go enough to let them inside of me. Besides the whole idea of it scares me."

"You're being chosen for this. The people need you to communicate for them. Can you stay here for a little while? A woman is bringing her son here and I want you to meet him."

I didn't ask why she wanted me to meet these people. Was Agatha trying to fix me up on a date?

I sat in Agatha's kitchen asking her about her life while we waited for the bell to ring. She told me that during World War II, she and several other mediums met together in secret to direct their power toward Adolf Hitler. They sent him mental messages to try to change the direction of his thinking. Some of these psychics had advised him personally before he came to power. She said Hitler consulted astrologers and psychics before making any moves and that he often took part in magic circles with the most famous Eastern European mystics. The mediums knew that he had many valuable objects used in ritualistic magic; it was rumored that he owned the sword that had pierced Christ's side and he had shown one of the mediums the Holy Grail itself. Agatha and her friends were always terrified of being caught, but felt that they really did interfere with his plans and helped shorten the war.

The bell rang. Agatha went and opened the door and an Eastern European woman entered holding a small boy by the hand.

"Mrs. Chernosky, this is my student, Terry. I wanted her to talk to little Joseph tonight about what we discussed on the telephone."

Agatha told me to sit down, while she pulled together some chairs in the seance room. The little boy, about six years old, stood perfectly still in front of us. We all sat looking at him. He had a sweet face. His neatly parted hair was wet down with hair cream. He refused to take off his coat or take his hands out of his pockets. I felt sorry for him; whatever we were going to see, it didn't seem worth making this child feel uncomfortable. I saw myself in his eyes, the child I once was, terrified and neglected. He kept his head down.

"Joseph, breathe with Mommy. Close your eyes. Come on now, don't be shy. You know what to do. You know Agatha and this nice lady want to hear what you have to say."

The little boy started shouting at me in a grown man's voice. "We need your help! You must agree to let us use you! You must follow the work of the mediums. Do what they tell you to do! I told your guides to work on you and adjust your throat so that you will speak for us. You have light all around you. Nothing will hurt you. Do you understand this? Do you understand what I'm saying? Do you know how important this is?"

I was stunned. The boy looked right into my face and pointed his tiny fingers at my throat.

"I understand what you're saying, but what if I don't want to choose this for myself? Don't I have something to say about this? Who are you? Who is speaking to me?"

The little boy came very close to me and whispered, "I am Philippus Aureolus Paracelsus."

Then he suddenly started wailing like an abandoned baby. His mother leapt from the chair, picked him up and began wiping his face, telling him to stop crying. The mother placed the boy in Agatha's arms and she lay him on a small bed in a room off the kitchen. I stood in the doorway watching. Agatha held her hands out over him to give him healing. He fell right to sleep. I was confused, not knowing exactly what I'd heard or saw. I wanted to get away from this.

"Agatha, I have to go. It's getting late." I kissed her good-bye and said good-bye to the mother.

Agatha whispered to me, "Dr. Paracelsus wants you. This is exciting for you and for us. We must talk about this right away. Tomorrow."

I flew down the stairs and through the streets to the subway to get home as fast as I could. I ran up the stairs into the apartment, "Peter! Peter! Who is Paracelsus! Do you have any books on him?" I said, breathless.

Peter was in bed reading. "Calm down. What are you saying?"

I told him the whole story. We stayed up half the night talking about Paracelsus and alchemy, searching through Peter's books.

· · ·

A couple weeks later I got a phone call. I heard a familiar voice on the other end. It was Jessie. She'd found me. Someone at Frank's house gave her the number. She was in tears.

"Terry, I had to find you. I need your help and I know you're the only one who would understand. I'll just tell you. I have a steady boyfriend and he's in serious trouble."

"Jessie, why are you calling me? What do you want from me?"

"Do you know anyone who can perform an exorcism?"

"What!?"

"His name is Clyde. He's a really sweet guy. He was married, maybe he still is . . . the kids live in Oklahoma with their mother. I met him one night at . . ."

"Jessie! Jessie! Get to the point! So, you think he's possessed?"

"He's been having fits in the middle of the night. Thrashing and cursing in bed. I woke up one night and he was standing at the end of the bed drooling and his eyes were wild. They looked like fire was coming out of them. Please, I know you can help him. You must know somebody. I'll bring him into the city as soon as you tell me where to come. I need your help."

"What's your number? I'll call you back tomorrow. Let me think about this."

"Just do it! I need help."

She hung up the phone and I felt sick. I went to Peter's room.

"Why are you getting involved with this? She has a lot of nerve calling you. Of course her boyfriend is possessed. Possessed by her!"

"Peter, what should I do?"

"She's a manipulator. Just stay away from her. Don't get involved."

"Maybe Agatha can help. She can . . ."

"You're a Catholic martyr without a cause. You're insane!"

"Well, we all know that. Come on, you got to admit it's intriguing."

"Yeah, well what if he really is possessed? Do you want to bring that into your life? You better go to your room and start praying! Light candles! Drink holy water! You're such a Scorpio, you just can't resist the intrigue." He made the sign of the cross over me. "Good luck!"

I thought about this all night. Just hearing Jessie's voice again sent me into my old obsession. I had to be careful. I remembered the Devil card. This would be dangerous for me. The devil part was easy, Jessie was my worry.

In the morning I called Agatha to ask if she could help Jessie's boyfriend. She told me she'd had a dream about me. In the dream I had to cross a lake that was surrounded by fire. In the middle of the lake was a demon that was calling me to join him. I knew I had to kill the demon before I could cross the lake. I jumped in without fear and disappeared under the water.

"Agatha, did I survive?"

"I don't know. I woke up. Bring your friends tomorrow night."

Jessie met me in front of Agatha's building forty-five minutes late. Clyde was a skinny little guy with a gray stubbly beard. He had deep crevices in his cheeks and forehead. He looked like a broken-down cowboy. He was not what I expected.

The climb up the stairs was hard for Jessie. She bitched and complained all the way up. I wondered how stairs felt being cursed at every day. The old cowboy and I laughed at her. Jessie got angrier, we laughed harder.

I introduced them to Agatha. She immediately took Clyde in her arms and held him. He started to cry. She kissed the top of his head and rubbed his arm tenderly. Her love and openness toward him moved me. I felt truly humble and I let go of all judgments toward Jessie and Clyde. Agatha knew something, and she knew it right away, without hesitation.

Jessie was crying. She reached out to me. We held hands in Agatha's kitchen, watching her working on the old cowboy.

Agatha took out a cobalt blue bottle of water from her kitchen cabinet. As Clyde sat in an upright chair, she walked around him, sprinkling him with holy water from the bottle and ringing a bell. She prayed in a loud voice, shouting in German and English, clapping her hands and stomping her feet around Clyde. At one point she grabbed him by the shoulders and shook him hard. I was surprised at Agatha's strength for her small size. She took her fist and punched him in the chest with all her might. I was shaking.

I looked over at Jessie, she was holding a rosary. It made me laugh. Where did she get that? I thought of my father. He told us as kids that we had the power to face down any devil we might meet up with in our life. He said the best way to confront evil is to start laughing. The Devil hates you when you're happy, he hates the sound of laughter. I was laughing because I was terrified—a nervous reaction. I left the kitchen and went into the seance room to calm down and get away. I thought about the little boy talking to me in that room. What if all of these people were devils? What if they were all possessed? What if they were all crazy?

Agatha came out from the kitchen with Clyde, who looked refreshed and smiling.

"She's a real sweetie, this lady. I feel like a new man."

They hugged good-bye and Jessie whispered to me, "Are we supposed to pay her?"

I told her, no, that wasn't necessary.

Jessie asked me to join them for a drink before they went back to New Jersey. I said I had to stay with Agatha for a while. A casual drink after an exorcism? Just go, Jessie. Just go.

That night when I got home, I was completely exhausted. I fell asleep on the couch in Peter's room while I was telling him all about what happened at Agatha's. I was in a deep sleep when suddenly I felt something whack me really hard on my back and head. I woke up screaming, not knowing what was happening to me. I reached out from under the covers. I could feel lots of books on top of me. Peter jumped out of bed when he heard me scream, and when he switched the light on, he screamed too. All the roommates came running in to see what was going on. We were all in shock. The books that were covering me from head to foot—Peter's astrology and metaphysical books—had been on a shelf on the other side of the room, at least six or seven feet from my bed. Given the distance, there is no way they could have fallen down on top of me—they had to have been thrown! Thrown by some force, some spirit, some devil I had brought home from the exorcism? Something unknown Agatha had pulled out of Jessie's boyfriend? I was scared to death, afraid that whatever it was, it was trying to kill me. I couldn't sleep for several nights. I grabbed a crucifix and started praying to every saint and angel I could remember. What can I say? The Catholic thing—it never leaves you.

· Chapter Thirteen ·

Margaret, whom I'd met at Agatha's, called to ask me if I wanted to go to a weekend retreat at a Spiritualist camp in Pennsylvania called Silverbelle. We could share a room to help cut the cost. In order to attend the seances, you had to provide written information about your experiences in the Spiritualist Church, and you had to be approved. They were very strict about who they let in, wanting to discourage curiosity seekers and skeptics. I had heard this was *the* place to go to experience trance mediumship at its best.

I called Frank to ask him if he knew anything about Camp Silverbelle. I was surprised when he answered the phone. "How are you? We never hear from you. We miss you. You never call us. You never come over. Why don't you come to the house for dinner sometime. Stop being so Scorpio."

I had tried calling him, several times, but I always got Jay. I even went by the house once. Jay came to the door and said, "Oh Terry, how are you? We'll visit with you in a day or two." He shut the door in my face. I stopped trying.

"We got another dog! Did I tell you that? I love having them, I want more. All I want to do is have a house in the country and have all my dogs around me. Jay's going to Buffalo to look at another house. It's an incredible old Victorian. It's huge! With a carriage house in the back. Some people collect stamps, we collect houses. Things are going just great. Did you read the *New York Times* last week? They interviewed me. You didn't see it? I'll get a copy for you. A lovely lady came to the house and for once they didn't make fun of what I'm doing. She really got it. It was terrific.

"Did I tell you I'm going on a trip around the world? My client gave me a ticket and I'm leaving in two weeks. I'm going alone. To Europe, then Morocco, Egypt, India, Nepal, then the Far East. Who knows? I'm just going to follow where it takes me. Jay thinks I need to get away. I'm looking forward to it."

Of course he knew the director of Camp Silverbelle. They wanted him to lecture there. He said he'd write a letter verifying that I'd had experience sitting in seances.

"I'll write it this afternoon and I'll mail it to you. I won't say we're related. You don't want to give them any information. Have a good time at Silverbelle. Sure, sure, sure—use my name, anytime. You'll have a lot of fun there."

. . .

I got accepted and traveled to Silverbelle with Margaret. On the bus we talked about our experiences with readings and how we felt about Agatha's sittings. She was wearing a pair of earrings that she told me she received during a seance in London. The earrings had fallen from the air and into her lap.

We were both hoping to get messages from the spirits at Silverbelle. I didn't have anyone close to me who had died. Some pets I loved, but I doubted those parakeets were still talking. My grandparents were dead, but I had hardly known them. I'd be surprised to get any message at all.

It was Friday evening just before sunset when we got there and signed up for the "classes" we wanted. They posted a list of people who were approved to sit in the seances. I was thrilled to be chosen for everything I asked for. After we checked into our room, we all met in the chapel for orientation. The grounds of the camp were peaceful, with lush gardens. It was heaven to be among trees and flowers, to smell the sweet country air again. It was like a children's summer camp, but with ghosts. Most of the buildings were small farmhouses and cottages filled with old furniture and cozy quilts. There was a library with an impressive stock of metaphysical books and a constantly boiling teakettle.

The chapel looked like any country church with a pipe organ and stained-glass windows. "Welcome to Camp Silverbelle!" said the huge bald man in a black suit and tie standing in front of the altar. "I am Reverend Able Jones. We have an exciting program for you this weekend: two ministers from the

Church of the Divine Angels, who traveled all the way from Boca Raton, Florida, to conduct the first sitting tomorrow afternoon. For those of you who were fortunate to be selected for that, you are in for a real treat.

"Other events on the weekend program are as follows: Our own Sister Maybelle Birch Lloyd will perform the billet message service on Sunday morning. And folks, she is the best! She receives your loved ones' answers to your written questions from the second she touches her forehead to the paper.

"Also, the Reverend Bernard Wesley from Chicago is here. He will be speaking to us on Sunday afternoon. It says here his lecture is titled *How Spirit Communication Will Have Influence on Mass Media in the Twenty-first Century*. Ummm . . . an interesting lecture; he tells me he has received it through dreams from his master teacher, Dr. Ezekiel Bendheim, who lives on the astral plane of . . . Well, he'll tell you all about it. Yes indeed.

"Continuing . . . we're having an apport seance with the marvelous Reverend Sophie Solitaire, who comes to us all the way from Calgary, Canada, and we're so excited to have her as our medium. She has displayed amazing success with her gift using the spirit trumpets. We're hoping that all of you will receive a gift from your guides and loved ones to take home with you. Private readings are available throughout the camp all weekend long. So hurry and sign up because the sessions fill up rather quickly.

"Those of you who are attending the trumpet seance on Saturday night please remain seated. The rest of you get to bed early, we have a long exciting weekend ahead. Good night now. Cross your fingers for a visitation."

Reverend Able read us the conduct rules and regulations for attending the seance. "During the seances, you are not allowed to get up from your chair unless called upon by a spirit guide or a loved one. If spoken to, always answer the spirit quickly because the sound of your voice gives them a contact, which enables them to remain in the room. If you're silent, they'll go away.

"Now listen to me, ladies and gentlemen. You are *never* to touch the mediums! And it is forbidden to bring any photographic or recording equipment into the seance room. If a medium is touched or if light suddenly flashes on them while they're in trance, instant death could occur from the shock. I am absolutely serious about this! Please, you must obey these rules. We love our mediums and we must protect them."

We would be able to examine the room before the session began to make sure that the seance was legitimate. We were also told to wear a sweater or jacket because the air temperature had to be kept almost freezing in order that something called "ectoplasm" could hold its shape.

Reverend Abel went on to explain ectoplasm. It is the essence of the material that forms the shape of the spirit and that allows us to see them. This ectoplasm is taken from the life force of the medium and sometimes, on rare occasions, from the people seated in the room. The mediums, who are naked, sit behind a heavy curtain so the audience can't see them. They do this because the luminous substance, the ectoplasm, drains out of every opening of their body and can be gruesome to witness. The ectoplasm might flow from the medium's mouth, ears, nose, eyeballs, vagina or rectum.

Now, how was I supposed to have a good night's sleep? Thank God my roommates weren't hearing any of this.

I woke up early and went to a little cottage set back on the grounds next to a huge weeping willow tree. I was going to have a reading with a psychic that I'd picked randomly off a list. Reverend Randhall Quinn-Twist. I liked his name. It sounded like the name of a psychic.

I felt like Dorothy from Kansas when she stumbled onto Professor Marvel and his gypsy wagon. I knocked on the screen door and walked in. The reverend was an elderly gentleman with a trimmed white beard. In the center of the table was a crystal ball. He held my hand and spoke to me.

"You have lived many lifetimes with the same family and you are tied to them your whole life this time too. In many ways all of you are like one person. Do you know what I mean by this?"

I nodded, yes.

"All of you have the knowledge of the ancients. Why are you so afraid of one another? I'll answer that. Your emotions take over your thinking and your passion is ignited by your connection to one another. You'll always be trying to understand this. Your family is like a delicate antique vase that drops and breaks into a million pieces. You'll keep these pieces with you for the rest of your life, unable either to put them back together or to throw them away."

"Could you explain that a little bit more?"

"What is this you all do in your family? Are you all doctors or healers? Don't tell me. I don't want to know. I see all of you in the same room, it's as though a force of millions of magnets came together, but it keeps you from reaching one another because the field of magnetism is too strong. People are drawn to that magnetism because you have the answers they want. And you must tell them. It's something you all have to do, to know who it is you are. Do you have any questions?"

"Tell me who I am."

He thought for a moment while holding his hands over the crystal ball, then said, "You are a reader of the Akashic Records?"

"I don't understand. What is that?"

"It's the book that tells the story of all our lives. It's the record of the path of life that each of us takes. It exists on the astral plane and you have the ability to read from it."

"I do read the Tarot."

"That is the beginning for you. In about two years, people will be lined up to see you. They are waiting for you. Just remember, yours is a work that has no end so make sure that you take care of yourself or you will die young. Don't let the needs of others devour you. You are protected by many whom you cannot see. You have two parts to your life. The first in service to others, which is an invisible life. The second will be visible. I don't want to scare you, but you will also be there to take care of the dead at night."

"What does that mean?"

"Don't worry, you'll know. It will be revealed, in time.

"May God protect you in your helping of others. Follow the way to the truth. Don't be afraid. We wait for you to tell us . . . what's next. Good-bye, my dear."

After the reading I took a walk around the grounds and thought about what he said. It wasn't the reading I expected. What about love? Where's my soul mate? Will I ever meet anyone or am I destined only to do readings all my life? I don't want thousands of people waiting for me. Money? What about money? Am I ever going to have a real job? The dead at night? What does that mean?

All my life, out of the corner of my eye, I've seen the faces of thousands of people that were waiting for me. When I was a child I thought they lived under the bed. When I walked to school I felt they were following me. Whenever I looked at a face, I saw other people, people that were connected to the one I was looking at. I wanted one, one that was just for me, someone I could need and who understood me and would be there for me.

* * *

It was time to attend the first seance. We went in to inspect the building. It was a large bunker about forty feet long and thirty feet wide with a very high ceiling. Except for the bolted steel door, the entire building was made of concrete and cinder blocks. Nothing else was in the room except four electric lights, which we were told would be changed to red bulbs for the seance. I looked over every inch of the room. There were no other doors, no windows, no seams in the floor or ceiling. When we finished examining the room and asking questions about any doubts we had, we were told to go back to our rooms to rest for an hour to clear our minds.

It wasn't easy to stay still and rest. I couldn't wait to get started. One hour later, Margaret and I walked over with our sweaters in hand. I was terrified just thinking about being locked inside a cinder-block box, let alone with ghosts.

The room was freezing. About fifty folding chairs had been arranged in a large circle. In the middle of the circle were two chairs surrounded by a heavy curtain. The curtains were open and we were encouraged to take a look inside if we wanted to. Several people got up and lifted the curtain, patted the material and looked up under the chairs. Others walked around the room again to inspect the ceiling and the door. I was too nervous to leave my seat.

After a few minutes, two men walked in wearing dark pants and white short-sleeve shirts, but no shoes. They both looked to be in their late thirties, clean-cut and serene. They walked straight to the folding chairs inside the small curtained room, sat down and started praying. Reverend Able came in and told us again not to leave our seats unless asked to by a spirit and to remain calm no matter what happened. And absolutely no talking to one another during the session. There would be plenty of time for that later. He closed the curtain around the two men and stood in front of it for a few moments. Soon we could see the men's pants and shirts slip from under the curtain. Reverend Able took away their clothes and left the building. We listened as the bolt crossed the door and sealed us in. We sat in the pitch-black. Then the red lights came on. They reminded me of our seances in the cellar in Buffalo. I wished Rosemary could be here to see this.

"Let me call you sweetheart, I'm in love with you." Who is that? Who's singing? A woman's sweet voice encircled the room around us. Then it was joined by another voice and another and another, until the whole room sounded like a chorus of one hundred! The singing was loud and soulful, with the power of real human voices. I could feel the presence of a choir. With the

red lights on I could see the other sitters in the room, but none of them were singing. I saw an elderly man wiping his eyes with a white handkerchief.

Then abruptly the singing stopped. Then nothing . . . just waiting.

I started to see some movement in the center of the room—about twenty figures sliding toward us—then slipping away. Sliding as if on ice skates, they came out of nowhere. Radiant and glowing like neon lights, with some form of arms and head—they glided closer and closer to us. Margaret, who was sitting next to me, was talking quietly to a glowing figure kneeling at her feet. I was shaking with fear. I saw the outstretched "arms" of the figure pull her up from the chair and walk her to the center of the room. Then to my horror she disappeared into the blue shimmering glow.

I was shaking.

"Teeeeeeery, Terry Andrewwwwssss . . . Terry Annnndrewwwwsssss . . ." Then, a geyser of light shot up from the floor. It thickened into a white presence right in front of me and started laughing.

"You sure take yourself seriously. Don't you? Aren't you having any fun?"

Remember to talk or they'll go away. Say something! Hurry up.

"Hello. Who are you?"

"Red Jacket!" the deep voice said. "I'm buried in Buffalo, but I'm alive right here! I've been with you since you were a child. When you walked to school alone, when you cried in your bed at night, when you smoked the peace pipe. Ha, ha, ha."

"Oh, you're pretty funny, Red Jacket."

"You do good work! Keep it up!" And just like that—he was sucked into the floor.

Wow, wait a minute. What was that? I remember Andy taking us to Red Jacket's grave in Forest Lawn cemetery. It was something to do on a Sunday in Buffalo. I never thought about him being a real Indian. *He's watching me? Why him? I wish they'd get over that Terry Andrews thing. What are they trying to tell me? Is that it?*

The room filled up with more and more spirits. Some of them looked like a ball of fog with a red or blue light in the center. The lights went on and off like a lighthouse in the distance. I could hear people talking and crying and several people were pulled from their seats and disappeared into the light. When Margaret returned to her seat she leaned over to me and whispered, "That was my mother." She was sobbing.

I stayed in my seat watching. That was the only message I got. I wanted and waited for more.

Then all the voices sang again, a chorus of tones that sounded like whales singing. It got louder and louder and then . . . it stopped.

After a while the door opened slowly and four men came in carrying two stretchers. They took the mediums out of the booth wrapped in blankets and carried them out on the stretchers. I could see how pale and drained they looked.

We stepped outside into the real world, it was dark. I looked up at the stars thinking about how far away they were. No one talked and several people threw themselves on the grass and wept. I walked back to the room with Margaret, waiting for her to tell me what she wanted to about what had happened to her. I was dying to ask, but I felt she needed to be left alone.

"That was my mother," she said. "She died last year. I hadn't told anyone about it because I was hoping she would come to me."

"How did you know it was really her?" I watched the tears rolling down her face.

"She was born in Lithuania and she spoke to me in her language. And look, she gave me this." She opened her hand and showed me a ring.

"She wore this all her life, never took it off. It was her mother's. She was buried wearing it."

I had a huge lump in my throat as I sat speechless on the bed. We didn't say anything after that. I could hear her crying. We both fell deeply asleep.

* * *

The next day after breakfast we went back into the bunker for the trumpet seance. A long table in the middle of the room was covered with tambourines, several bells of different sizes and seven trumpets lined up in a row. The trumpets were about three feet tall, made of tin and shaped like a dunce cap or a wizard's hat. Some of them were made of a solid piece of tin while others were collapsible. The spirits use them as a kind of megaphone to speak through, as well as funnels to deliver apports.

Apports are gifts from the spirits that are "borrowed" from places where they won't be missed. Who knows where that is—a museum's storage archives, perhaps somebody's forgotten drawer, a long-left safety deposit box, maybe from another dimension. These gifts can be taken away from you as mysteriously as they arrive. Some of them may even be quite valuable. If you try to sell them, they will disappear before you can do it. They might leave your life at significant times and return again at a point when you need reminding or encouragement. I learned all this from Reverend Sophie at the orientation.

The door was locked and we were in the dark again. I was starting to relax a little and began enjoying even the scary parts. Boom! A loud crash! My heart beat faster and my hands were shaking. It sounded like the table was being lifted and dropped up and down on the floor. The bells and tambourines started banging and jingling on the bouncing table. The red lights came on—all the trumpets were flying in the air!

"Mr. Conner! I'm calling Mr. Conner! Where are you?" hollered the voice from one of the trumpets.

A man answered from across the room. "I'm over here. Is that you Jake?"

"Mrs. Anderson! Molly? Molly? Where are you?" Another trumpet.

"Stephen, Stephen, Stephen." Voices from trumpets all around the room.

"I'm trying to find Frances Mary Kilpatrick. Where are you?"

"I'm here! I'm over here!"

"Lady Bess? It's Mama . . ."

It was beginning to get noisy. People's names were called and the tambourines and bells were clashing. I could hear screeches, violin sounds, and knocking on the floor. I looked up and saw one of the trumpets coming straight toward me like a speeding arrow. I thought it would strike me in the face, but instead it stopped right at the tip of my nose.

"Tereeeeesa. Tereeeesa. Little Teresa . . . Are you there? Can you hear me?"

"Hello, who is it?" I said, feeling really stupid talking to a flying trumpet.

"You'll soon find out. Hold out your hands in front of you. I have a present for you. Are you ready? Now don't drop it. Here it comes," the voice said, giggling.

I held out my hands and I could hear a rattle from inside the trumpet as something was falling down through the funnel.

"Ow, that's hot!" I said.

"Heeeeeeee!" said the little mysterious voice.

"Thank you. Who are you? What's your name? Please, tell me your name?"

"Good-bye, Little Teresa."

"Who are you?"

"See you later. When you're older."

I tossed the object back and forth between my hands like a hot roasted chestnut. I could feel that it was a ring. When it cooled down I put it on my finger and traced the shape of it in the dark.

The seance went on for a couple of hours with crashing and banging and bells ringing in the air next to our ears. I was mesmerized by the trumpets flying and bouncing off the walls delivering more voices and singing. I tried to listen to every message I could. And just like the last seance, it ended abruptly.

When I got outside, I held out my hand to see the ring. It was a gold rose with a red ruby in the center of the rose. I smiled and remembered one of my spirit guides from Agatha's. Her name was Red Rose.

Other people also received rings. Some had medallions, earrings or necklaces and one man had a walking stick with a gold handle engraved with his grandfather's initials. One woman showed me a stuffed animal she said had belonged to her as a child. Others had coins or arrowheads. Many of the things had no real value at all other than their great emotional significance to the people who received them.

I had so many questions. I'd never seen anything like this before and I had to take it all in fully. This was 1973, long before the invention of the compact disc recorder and the special effects equipment of today. That room did not have a trap door or a false ceiling or mechanical wires. If that was theatrics, then they should have taken the show to Broadway because it was a stunning piece of entertainment. Those mediums were so sincere, believing with their entire soul in the world of spirit communications. I cannot believe to this day that it was faked. I've read many accounts of sleight of hand and fraudulent mediums. I know how they can trick people. I read that some fraudulent mediums can swallow yards of cheesecloth and regurgitate it to make fake ectoplasm. I'd like to see that. That in itself seems like an astonishing talent.

．．．

As soon as I got back to New York I told Agatha about all the incredible things that happened at Silverbelle. She was even more convinced that I was next in line for a career as a trance medium. She suggested I attend one of Aubrey Morris's trance medium classes.

Aubrey Charles Morris, a dyed-blond, effeminate man, wore a smoking jacket with an ascot and velvet slippers. He lived in an Upper East Side apartment with Chinese antiques and Bloomingdale's furniture.

When I called to ask him if I could join his trance class, he said, "It'll cost you fifty bucks. Can you swing it?"

I had no idea what to expect from a trance medium class. When I imagined what it might be like, I thought we'd study at great length how the body can alter its molecular system to access an entity through a portal in third eye, by passing the constricting mind and slipping down into our vocal chords, allowing a spirit to borrow our voice for speaking. This is what I made up, but the class was nothing like that.

The series of classes had already started, but Aubrey assured me that I would fit right in. Ten friendly, fresh-faced students crammed together in a circle in Aubrey's library, welcomed me and introduced themselves.

Aubrey entered the room carrying a lit candelabra and sat in the one empty seat to complete the circle. In the soft light I could see the students adjusting their positions, stretching their arms and hands, rolling their heads and shoulders around, massaging their jaws to loosen up. Aubrey waited for the psychic adjustments to stop before he started.

There were only a few moments of quiet before a high, shrill voice with a Southern accent came out of Aubrey.

"My lil' peaches, I'm here. Pink Rose is here!"

"Hello, Pink Rose. Good evening, Pinkie. Thank you for coming, Pink Rose," the room said to the voice.

"Now it's your turn to work," the voice said, sounding like Scarlett O'Hara. "The spirits've been waitin' all day on you. Close your eyes, go to sleep my angels. I'm here to watch over you."

Soft lullaby humming trailed away.

I listened to some heavy, deep breathing, some bordering on snoring, some approaching orgasm. Within less than five minutes the whole room was talking in somebody else's voice, chattering away into thin air.

I heard a stern man's voice coming out of a woman the size of a ballerina. "Now take the formula the way I told you. I'm the doctor, listen to me. Who's next?"

Another woman in the room was mumbling that she was hit by lightning while lost in a thunderstorm looking for her dog. Somebody else was shouting in what sounded like fake French.

It was pandemonium. I didn't want to close my eyes, let alone try to go into a trance. Even if I could, I wouldn't have done it there. This was more like a scene from *Snake Pit* or *One Flew Over the Cuckoo's Nest*. It was too much for me.

Aubrey got up and went around the room quieting some of them down. He asked Dr. Ballerina for a remedy for his stomach. Next he went and adjusted a student's throat, pulled his chin up, maneuvered his neck, fixed his posture. Others he stopped and told them to go back to their breathing.

Aubrey came to me. I immediately closed my eyes.

"Is anyone in there?" he said softly, close to my ear. "Hello? Are you there? Who's inside there? Speak to me. Do you want to talk? Who's there?"

I sat still, eyes closed, saying not a word, stiff as an ironing board.

Just in time—a man popped up out of his seat, announcing with a decided Spanish inflection: "I am Queen Isabella! I am the ruler of all Spain! I was unjustly portrayed in your history books and I am angry! You must tell the entire world that I did good things for the Americas. Contact your president! You must . . ."

The queen was interrupted by a loud male voice with a Western drawl, "Ah shut up, missy! If you're Queen Isabella, then how come you ain't talkin' with a lisp? Isabella was Castilian! She wouldn't have talked like you! You must be an impostor, lady!"

Hands on her hips, Isabella struck back, "Who dares to question me? I am Queen Isabella! Ruler of Spain! Who do you think you are!"

"Christopher Friggin' Columbus!"

Aubrey darted over to the cowboy saying, "Now settle down. Tell me who you really are. Tell me your name."

"Okay, mister, hold your horses! I'm Buster Kelly, Missouri gunslinger. I'm here to shake things up."

"You sure have. Now, go back to the light right now, Mr. Kelly. You don't belong here. Go to the light! Go now, I insist! Go to the light!" Aubrey demanded, as he applied pressure to the man's throat.

I was sorry to see the gunslinger go. I would've loved to see him and Isabella duke it out. I couldn't believe everyone wasn't laughing.

I heard many children's voices; some of them started talking together, playing patty-cake. At one point a few of the entities started arguing with one another; I got a bit frightened. One woman was drooling and crying, "Help me," in a soft voice, mumbling that there was a vampire inside of her. Aubrey gently woke her up from her trance and she lay down on the floor behind the chairs.

I couldn't wait to get out of there. Whatever this was, it wasn't for me. I'm sure this could have gone on all night. It finally ended, and they all went into the living room for coffee and cake. I thanked Aubrey and said good-bye. He waved back and said, "See you next week."

. . .

I still kept looking for answers from all kinds of psychics and readers. I asked everyone I met if they knew of somebody good. I consulted a numerologist. My numbers were good. She said I was an eleven, the high master number. I shouldn't get involved with eights and twos. I went to astrologers. I was told I was born under the right stars, had the chart of a mystic with several planets in the houses of the occult. Astro-cartographers told me I could be happy if I lived in Venice, Alaska, Holland or Santa Fe. I should never live in Romania, Bakersfield or Greenland. Make sure to spend my next birthday in Tasmania to guarantee a good year.

I went to healers. I wasn't ill, but I wanted to feel what it was like to be healed. One woman sent a charge through my body with her hands that was so powerful I was sure she touched my feet with a raw electrical wire. Another healer, a Russian woman in Queens, shook her hands around my body. I had the sensation of going through a car wash with millions of tiny brushes swirling through my blood.

From most of the healers I saw, I felt nothing. I'd never pretend and I'd tell them if I didn't feel anything. One burly, bearded man, a well-known healer from California, told me I was hopeless, I would never feel anything. He got so frustrated with me. He said I was stubborn, defiant, too resistant. I considered that a compliment.

Different readers told me who I used to be. I was a Russian princess who died from blood poisoning. A brave Apache medicine woman. The queen of a castle in what later became France. Several nuns: Carmelite, Buddhist, Trappist, Cistercian. Vestal virgin. Balinese temple dancer. The Oracle of Delphi. A lady pirate. An Egyptian queen. Hopi, Mohawk, Indian Swami, Aborigine. A pyramid builder, medicine man, a baby left under a tree. A prairie girl who led the wagon train. An English maid who gave birth to a king. I was drowned, murdered, burned and beheaded. How come I was never an ordinary street cleaner, a mother of two, a German barmaid?

I had my tea leaves read, my aura cleansed, my jewelry psychometrized, my hands analyzed. I tried automatic writing, where I sat for hours holding a pen, waiting for a spirit to guide my hand for a scribbled message on a piece of paper. I consulted the Ouija board. I tried bending spoons and starting fires with my mind. I threw the I Ching, the yarrow sticks, had my shadow read. I studied magic, witchcraft, Huna and rune stones. The Magic Eight Ball was never far from reach. I just about lived at Samuel Weiser's Occult Book Store on Broadway and Eighth Street. I even frequented a live chicken in Chinatown who pulled a fortune-telling card from a machine for a quarter. He got corn, I got the future.

The more readings I had, the more frustrated I became. The more information I was given, the more confused I got. Almost all the readers told me that I should be reading them—I should be telling them their future. "You're psychic. What do you see for me?" they'd say, and, "What are you waiting for? You should be reading people. Now!"

What was I looking for? What did I think they could tell me? Some of the psychics were astonishingly accurate with their insights and predictions. Some of them were sincere and gave me valuable information. Some made me angry because they were judgmental, self-righteous or pompous. Some just talked about themselves. Others made me laugh with their fortune-teller paraphernalia and their theatrical delivery. Some truly believed they were psychic, but nothing they said made any sense. Some were good listeners. A few were thieves or con artists. One woman who had an eyeball painted on her forehead told me I had a curse put on me by an enemy. She could help me if I gave her more money. She'd make a special candle and cast a spell to get rid of the curse. I knew that wasn't true and walked away. The only curse I had was meeting her.

I compared notes with my friends who'd been to readers. Some of us got the exact same reading from the same psychic. Some were swayed by the demands of influential psychics who insisted they consult with them on every move they made before they made it. Some were weakened as a result of too many readings, losing touch with their own intuitive ability to make decisions for themselves.

We asked our spirit guides for help in things we needed—wisdom, patience, knowledge. Some of us asked for apartments, lovers, home appliances, acting roles, missing items. Once, I asked a spirit guide for a little more money. Immediately after, I found four nickels in a toilet bowl.

· · ·

I called my sister often during these times to tell her about the readings and the seances and to ask her opinion. There was never a doubt in Rosemary's mind that the world of spirits was real. She always believed; she was always so sure. Rosemary truly believed there was a message in *everything.* She'd open a book, any book, to any page, and whatever line her eyes fell on she'd read as a message to her. Finding a penny in the street or hearing a song on the radio said something important to her. I wished I had that kind of belief in something, anything—it would have been a lot easier.

"Rosemary, have you ever heard of the Akashic Records?"

"Of course, I can read them whenever I want."

"How long have you been doing that?"

"I didn't always know what they were called, but I have recurring dreams where I go to great libraries, pull books off the shelves and read about what's going to happen in my life or to the world. Madame Blavatsky's book, *The Secret Doctrine,* talks about the Akashic Records being nature's memory held in an ethereal library. It's infinitely encyclopedic! The elect know how to read these volumes. I had a reading with an Indian mystic a couple years after high school. He told me I was a reader of the Akashic Records. When I dream of these libraries, I'm astral traveling there. He also said that our family reincarnated together for several lifetimes; we've a lot of work to do now. There isn't much time left, you know."

"What! Wait a minute . . . a reader told me I could read the Akashic Records too."

"I'm sure you can."

"Tell me how to do that."

"Just go to sleep and dream."

"What do you mean, we don't have very much time left? What's going to happen?"

"Read the records. Open the book, you'll see."

She always did that. So cryptic! I knew that she knew more than she was saying, but she wouldn't tell me. She knew I had to find out by myself.

Do the readings, read the book—most of the readers had been telling me pretty much the same thing. I still wasn't comfortable with any of it. Something didn't feel right to me and no one could explain anything about how I was supposed to do this and why it was my destiny. It was difficult for me to accept that a giant book of all our lives, called the Akashic Records, was floating somewhere in space and that I was one of a handful of people who could read it. How come our whole family had the gift? It was getting too weird for me. I walked away from all of it.

Chapter Fourteen ·

Almost every night my roommates were telling me of their sexcapades. Men in the park, men at the Baths, men on the street, men in bars. I was going crazy. I'd been floating around in the netherworld so long I forgot I also had a body. I think the good Catholic girl in me was trying to be pure in order to receive the spirits. I was twenty-six with the Sun and Moon in Scorpio, Sicilian, I was born with passion. I should be having fun! I should be ravished, desired and on the prowl in the starlit streets of Manhattan. Shouldn't I? I was dying for affection, sex and experience. I wanted to dance all night and meet someone and go home with them. I asked my roommates if they knew anyone interesting—especially someone not looking for God or the meaning of life.

One day I walked into a bank to open an account. The man behind the marble counter seemed to be looking at me, really looking at me. Extremely handsome; he was a complete double of the Italian movie star Giancarlo Giannini. Dressed beautifully in a three-piece suit, he stood motionless and stared at me. Apologizing for being so bold, he asked me if I would join him for lunch. I laughed, thinking he must be kidding. I stood there in my white painter's overalls and my hair in braids, smiling back, and said "Why not?"

He had as many stories as I did. As a teenage pop star he had traveled all over the world with his band, being chased down streets by screaming fans. When it ended, he went to college to study business and became a banker.

He took me to his apartment in Brooklyn Heights. He had an eclectic collection of art, junk and antiques. His passion—walking sticks and a wall covered with vintage hats. A great dancer, he loved to cook, he was smart and listened to every word I said. Past the foot of his bed, through the window across the room was a spectacular view of the Manhattan skyline. My banker was a generous lover. I surprised myself waking up happy in his big brass bed. We shared the same excitement for life and we both wanted to know *why* about everything. This man was made for me . . . if only I hadn't been me.

We'd been together for about a month when he asked me to join him at his cousin's wedding. We were in front of my building, sitting in his car after a romantic evening. He got out of the car and walked around to open the door for me—something he took pleasure in doing. I remember sitting in the front seat thinking, *I'll be meeting his parents, his friends.* I sat there in my dress and lipstick knowing I could never be anybody's wife or daughter-in-law or anybody's mother. When I looked up at him through the car window I saw my own reflection in the glass. My head and face inside his starched white shirt and suit jacket. I wanted the power that comes with being a man. I knew then that I'd rather *be* him than be with him.

When he opened the door I told him that it was over—just like that. I knew I would eventually hurt him and what I had had with him was enough for me. It was time to go. And just like that—I was gone.

. . .

My roommates suggested I go to a bar in the Village called Bonnie and Clyde's, a place to meet some women. I wanted to go, but was scared to go by myself. I didn't have any gay female friends and Peter told me they really stare you out if you bring a man in there with you. If I wanted to go, I had to go alone.

I walked over to West Third Street off Thompson on a Friday night. Bonnie and Clyde's was next to a firehouse. I found it easily . . . and kept on walking. A couple of firemen were standing outside of their station having a cigarette. I said a weak "hello" as I passed by. I walked up and down the block trying to get up the courage to go into the bar. I walked around the block a few times, then came back and stood across the street. I paced back and forth a few more times. One of the firemen winked at me. I wondered if he thought I was cruising him. I hurried down the block and kept walking until I came to Sixth Avenue. Then I promised myself—I'd turn around and go back and just walk right in without hesitation. What's to be afraid of? They'll welcome me with open arms. I'll make new friends and go home with a fabulous lover. Right? I got to the door and with one strong mental shove, I threw myself in.

The bar was smoky. Lionel Ritchie was playing on the jukebox. I walked around pretending I was looking for a friend. Almost everybody was with someone, talking and laughing. All the seats at the bar were filled, so I stood at the only open space in the room—in front of the bathroom door. A picture of two naked women on a tandem bicycle hung over the bar, a photograph of Marlene Dietrich on another wall.

I tried talking to a tall striking blond who came and stood next to me. She looked over my head and didn't even answer me. I felt embarrassed and stupid—I slipped away, walking backward into the crowd. Standing in the middle of a packed room, with women shoving and knocking into me, I stood on my toes trying to get a look at the women dancing. It reminded me a little of being with the girls in high school except we didn't bump and grind and we didn't smoke.

A seat opened up at the bar and I grabbed it. I'd never sat at a bar alone, let alone a lesbian bar. Ordering a beer like the girl next to me, I sat there looking at the women on the bicycle, who stared back at me.

"Pretty busy tonight. Looks like everyone's having fun. Have you worked here long?"

"Yup," the bartender said.

"Do you work here every Friday night?"

"Uh-huh. Do you need anything else?" she asked me.

"No, no, I'm fine, thank you."

I sipped my beer and tapped the coaster to the Jackson 5. A new girl took the seat on my left. She was really pretty and I thought this was my moment. What can I say to her? Will she like me? I was getting excited about the possibilities of what could happen, when another girl came over, practically knocked me off my stool, and started making out with her.

"Do you want another beer?" the bartender grunted, as she wiped up around the bar.

"No. Thank you . . . I like your shirt," I blurted out. "Is it vintage?"

I realized I might be a little attracted to the bartender and I thought I should make a move.

"Are you busy later, after you get off work? I'd like to get to know you,"

I said, wondering where that line came from and hardly believing it came out of me.

"Ya know, I could throw you out of here right now if I wanted to," she said, giving me a really mean look.

I was shocked and after a few moments, I just slid off the stool and left.

I walked around the Village feeling very foolish. I missed having a girl-friend, a pal to hang around with. I missed having a sister. I wanted a lover. The boys I lived with were great friends and I loved doing things with them, but it wasn't the same as being with a girlfriend.

. . .

Then I met Deborah. Peter had known her since 1970. The events of Deborah's life were legendary—at least as Peter saw them and told it. They had been roommates in an apartment above a bar where three separate murders occurred. Deborah was an art student at Cooper Union making exquisitely detailed nightmarish etchings that she only allowed a few people to see. Peter, Deborah and another friend, Phyllis, were all recruited to act in a student film. In the film, Peter had to strangle Phyllis to death while Deborah was busy whipping some guy chained to a chair. Deborah got so swept up in her role they had to pull her off the terrified actor before she really killed him.

Deborah once met dwarf twin brothers. She wanted to know what it would be like to have sex with both of them—at the same time. So she did—on a rooftop of a Lower East Side tenement building!

Peter wanted us to meet. He kept insisting that we were a perfect match. She with her Pisces sun, Scorpio moon and Scorpio rising, and me with my Scorpio sun and moon. Passion+loyalty+secrets+illusions—sounded more like the formula for a bomb. I was terrified.

When I met Deborah, she was twenty-four and I was twenty-six. She was involved with an older Cuban woman in Spanish Harlem, a gorgeous Puerto Rican girl in the East Village and she was sneaking into the bedroom of a very young man who was a student still living with his parents on the Upper West Side.

One afternoon, Phyllis and Deborah stopped by our apartment on their way to cop some speed on Avenue C. Deborah walked in the door first, followed by Phyllis, choking and gasping for air from climbing the stairs in platform shoes. Peter introduced us.

Phyllis had a whiney, childish voice soaked in alcohol. "Pleased to make your acquaintance. Aren't you Frank Andrews's sister? I've been wanting to meet you. I was thinking of getting a card reading from your brother, but I'm sure he'd tell me I don't have a future. I ran out of cigarettes. Do you have one I could borrow? I'll give it back to you next time I see you, I promise. My ankle is killing me. I think I must've broken my foot again. I'm always breaking my foot somehow. Peter, do you have anything to drink around here! Do you have any booze, man? These goddamn shoes."

Peter rolled his eyes and went off in search of the vodka.

"Sorry, I don't smoke," I told her.

"Oh shut up, Phyllis! You're always complaining," Deborah yelled at her.

Here she was. Not at all what I expected. She was much smaller than I thought she'd be, very thin, about five-three with dark hair and dark eyes peering out from under long bangs that covered her eyebrows. Deborah looked a lot like Cher. Her black motorcycle jacket must have been made for a child. She had on black jeans, leather Beatle boots, a black beret and lots of silver chains around her neck and wrists. She didn't say a word to me and I thought if I said the wrong thing, she'd bite my head off and spit it out the window.

After a few minutes, I went back to my room, I did not want to know these two. What was Peter thinking? A short while later, Deborah came in.

"I'd like to talk to you sometime about being psychic," she mumbled. "My mother used to read cards—a regular fifty-two-card playing deck. She taught me how to do it. I read for myself once in a while with her deck."

I was surprised how shy she was. She kept her head down, I could barely understand what she said.

"I'd like to see how you read."

"I'll call you," she said and left.

I hoped she wouldn't.

At the end of the week she called.

"Hi. It's Deborah. How are you on horses?"

"Excuse me?"

"Racehorses. Do you have any success picking winners?"

"I don't know, I've never tried."

"Can you meet me later? Washington Square Park at noon?"

Caught off guard, I agreed.

She took me to an OTB on Varick Street. In a room filled with scruffy broken-down men lining up to place their bets, I hoped for a vision. Copying my father, I looked up at the ceiling the way he used to just before he picked a winner. Could I still have my childhood talent of getting the right numbers? I wondered if this was abusing my psychic gift.

"Okay. I have an image," I said, as Deborah held tightly to the list of the day's riders. "I see a rainbow. It's a big bright rainbow. Spread across the . . ."

"That's it! Pot O' Gold!" She yelled out. "Ten bucks on Pot O' Gold to win! This is great! We're gonna be rich!"

It wasn't so great when Miranda's Folly came in the winner.

"Sorry. But look Deborah, I was close. Miranda's jockey's name is Jimmy Finnegan. *Finnegan's Rainbow!* Hey, that's pretty good, isn't it?"

"It's *Finian's Rainbow!* This is more like *Finnegan's Wake,*" she said, ripping up the losing ticket.

Deborah had an idea, "Maybe you'd do better at the track if you could see the horses—you might get a better feel for them. How 'bout Belmont on Saturday?"

"I'll give it a try. Sure, why not."

At a bar in the Village Deborah told me about her lovers and teased me with the details she was leaving out. She wasn't so shy after all, but I couldn't tell if I was being seduced or if she was warning me about herself. The more she talked, the more I felt protective of her. I could see how we were alike. She didn't care either if she lived or died.

Deborah was driving a cab for a living. She assured me she could take care of herself, but I had a feeling that something terrible was going to happen to her in that cab. I begged her to quit. She said she'd quit the next day. And she did.

Deep inside of me I felt something so recognizable about her. Some of it I knew all too well—from Jessie. Being next to danger seemed to be the only thing that could reach my feelings at their roots. Like me, Deborah was a motherless child. The piece of me that longed for a mother and the part that wanted to take care of somebody could merge with Deborah. She was more damaged than I was. I could take care of her. Two strays on an adventure—neither of us wanting to be confined. We had found each other.

On our first date we tried making love, but it didn't work. I needed sweetness and she was a rodeo rider. After two attempts we understood we were supposed to be friends, but we were bound together.

We were inseparable in those first months in 1974. New York City was right for us. She especially loved its underbelly—the seedy bars, strip clubs and Times Square peep shows. Times Square was an anything-goes circus of trouble in the '70s. Porno movie theaters lined the streets with marquees that read *The Opening of Misty Beethoven* or *The Pigkeeper's Daughter.* Cruising the Times Square streets were the *Superfly* pimps in wide-brimmed felt hats, floor-length leather coats and huge gold medallions. On their arms, two or three girls in satin hot pants and platform shoes. The street had it all—Jesus preachers, drug dealers, the Army recruiting station open all night for the impulsive young man looking for military salvation. And if you needed quick cash you could sell your blood in the storefront blood bank between the souvenir shop and the topless bar.

Playland arcade on Times Square was filled with pinball machines and shooting games. Deborah liked to hang out there. She'd pull me into a photo booth for a strip of black-and-white snapshots. She'd point out the regular chicken hawks she knew by name. The chicken hawks were a bunch of slimy guys who prowled the arcade looking for schoolboys to have sex with. I never asked how she knew them.

Deborah was a fast walker, sometimes darting across the street without warning while we were in the middle of a conversation. I'd hurriedly follow her into the screeching traffic and flying curses of irate Manhattan drivers. She took a NO WOMEN! sign as a personal invitation, threatening the manager with "Women's Liberation" and lawsuits. We got in. Peep-O-Rama was one of those places. Deborah and I both looked like schoolgirls in our little jackets, ponytails and berets as we paid our $2 admission. Peep-O-Rama had rows of small closets that smelled of rotten eggs and cigarettes covered over by a strong scent of pine disinfectant. Inside the closets we took turns looking into a tiny hole in the wall. A plump middle-aged woman in black lacy underpants and see-through blouse danced alone to a transistor radio. To see anything, I had to stand on my toes. The dancer had no idea who was watching her. Looking bored, she fondled her breasts for a few minutes and then bent over to show us her buttocks. She wiggled and swayed and blew kisses to the mysterious stranger behind the wall. After ten minutes she covered the hole. I wondered if she still would've danced if she knew we were watching her. Deborah loved it. It made me sad.

* * *

One late winter day, Peter and I walked home through a dense snowfall. When we opened the door, it took us a minute to realize there was something strange about the sight of snow falling inside the apartment. The bathroom, which was opposite the entrance, had a boarded-up skylight that was no longer boarded up. We had been robbed.

The landlord wasn't cooperative about fixing the skylight and nobody wanted to stay to wait for the thieves to return. So we all packed up what we could carry and left. I went to stay with Deli and the others moved in with various friends. After further hassling with the landlord over repairs, we all decided to give up the apartment.

Deli knew a place I could stay for free on Sixth Avenue and Twelfth Street in a high-rise building called the John Adams. The apartment belonged to one of Deli's bra models who was living with her boyfriend on a ranch in Montana, but kept her place in New York just in case the romance didn't work out. Deborah had been living on Phyllis's couch on MacDougal Street. I asked her if she wanted to stay at the bra model's apartment with me. She came to live there the next day.

Deborah had been making frequent visits to a doctor in Jackson Heights who handed out diet pills like they were candy. We hid out from the world. Staying in the apartment for days on end making up stories about the people we saw down below. We took the speed, stayed up all night, sometimes rummaging through the bra model's closets. We looked stunning in the model's evening gowns and rhinestone-covered polyester jumpsuits. Making up our faces, we slipped into her high heels and hairpieces, headed down the street to Paula's Bar on Greenwich Ave. The patrons weren't sure if we were a couple of drag queens who wandered over from Club 82 or two call girls out on the prowl. We drank White Russians and Deborah played the Rolling Stones on the jukebox. We'd stay there until closing time, go home, change, take more pills and then walk to the river to watch the sun come up. Getting lost with Deborah was a wonderful escape—far away from my family, the spirit world and who I used to be.

Deborah came home one day and told me she had found us our own apartment. We could have it by the weekend for $150 a month. We moved two blocks down to West Tenth Street. Top floor. She put out her collection of dead birds' heads, antique toys and rusty tools. Immediately, she hung her painting of a giant egg with a bloody crack in its shell and hid her art portfolios under the bed. With some furniture gathered from the street and the Salvation Army, we had a home.

Deborah loved trains as much as I did. She loved the mechanics of the engine and we both longed for the anonymity of life on the tracks. As soon as we could, we were going to take off across Canada. We bought an electric train set, built a village with a castle, a forest and a mountain range. It took up the entire second bedroom. We'd stay up all night listening to a record of train whistles and steam engines, watching our train go around the track.

"I can see us as two old ladies in a big country house with train tracks running through all the rooms," I said.

"I want to live in a house someday. When I was a kid, my family moved so much I thought that's how everyone lived—that you only stayed in a place for a few months."

"I lived in the same house for eighteen years wishing I could get out of there. If it wasn't for Frank I'd probably still be there."

"Do you realize how much you talk about your brother?"

"I know I talk about him, but it's not that much."

"Yes, it is. *Frank* is going to Japan. *Frank* is buying another house. *Frank* met John Lennon. You're always talking about him. Why do you idolize him so much?"

"He's my brother. He raised Rosemary and me. He was our full-time caretaker when he was ten. He was our mother, the one who taught us everything. And I wouldn't be in New York if it wasn't for him."

"You said it. He's your mother. You're still hoping to get from him what you didn't get from her."

"You're jealous."

"Yeah, sure that's it. Is that all you can say? Listen, you were all brought up in a fantasy world of magic power and Sicilian revenge. You're always thinking your brother is out to get you. You'd like to believe he's thinking about you all the time, but he's just living his life."

"You think you know everything; you think you can analyze me. What about you Deborah? No one can get you to open up. You hide everything."

"And you don't?"

· Chapter Fifteen ·

The word around town was, "You've got to see Frank Andrews." Everyone was talking about him at nightclubs, beauty salons, fashion houses, dinner parties. It was the late '70s, the time of disco. At Studio 54, Frank danced and partied along with the Jet Set. They lived for sex, dancing, drugs, fashion and Frank Andrews. If you were "in," that was the scene. Frank pretty much started the trend of going to a psychic. Before him, there were a few fortune-tellers around town, mostly older women and gypsies. But no one had ever seen a young, handsome, sophisticated psychic like Frank.

"Frank knows everything! He doesn't hold back. Be ready, he'll tell you off, if he feels like it."

"I know, but I heard he's so on target."

"I see my analyst every Tuesday and Frank Andrews once a month."

"I quit my therapy. Who needs that? Frank told me everything I needed to know about myself in one reading."

He was in all the women's magazines, television talk shows, radio, lectures, psychic fairs, parties and more parties. The "Beautiful People" who wouldn't be caught dead below Fourteenth Street came downtown in their limos to see the man the *New York Times* and *New York* magazine called "The Rolls Royce of Psychics." John Lennon, Yoko Ono, Perry Ellis, Rebekah

Harkness, Francesco Scavullo, Princess Grace, Candy Darling, Andy Warhol—to name just a few.

Frank called me one day all excited, telling me that he was going to be on *To Tell the Truth*. I misunderstood and thought he was going to be one of the impostors. It was hard to imagine that they were going to use Frank as the real person. I went to May's Department Store on Fourteenth Street and bought a small black-and-white TV just to watch it. The opening of the show went something like this:

"My name is Frank Andrews. Ever since I was a child I've had the gift of clairvoyance. I saw a ghost at the foot of my bed when I was only five years old. I moved to New York City fifteen years ago and started reading Tarot cards and palms for some of New York's leading celebrities. I live and work out of my townhouse in Little Italy."

I watched Frank answering the celebrities' questions as I bit my lip wondering if he was going to mention our family. They asked him where he grew up and how his family felt about his psychic gift. He said my father was a restaurant worker and mentioned he was from Upstate New York. His family was used to his gift; they'd always known him like this.

The two impostors made up answers about their life as Frank Andrews and were very believable with their ghost stories and psychic predictions. The celebrities voted on who they thought was the real Frank Andrews. One celebrity didn't vote for him because he looked too young to own his own townhouse and be so well-known. Another disqualified herself because she said that all of her friends had been urging her to go see Frank. She recognized him by their description.

Then came the host of the show, who said, "Will the real . . . Frank Andrews . . . please . . . stand up?"

After a few suspenseful moments Frank stood up.

I was relieved when it was over. I wondered what he was becoming. For me the psychic gift was a private spiritual thing. I didn't think it belonged in show business. I felt guilty for being so judgmental of him. Deborah laughed through most of it. She always loved telling people that her first introduction to my brother was on a television game show.

Soon after, Frank invited my parents to visit with him. He and Jay were living in the entire Mulberry Street house alone. Deli had moved to Brooklyn Heights. The girl on the third floor moved out too. Jay was traveling back and forth to Buffalo to restore and develop their three houses and the thirty-five-unit apartment building they'd just bought. Frank was enjoying having the house to himself and he really wanted my parents to see it.

This was the first time my father would see Frank's house. My mother had come alone to New York a few times, but my father never came. Whenever I'd ask my mother why my father wouldn't come, my mother would make excuses that he had to watch the house or he couldn't leave the dog alone. I'd heard this same answer too many times.

Frank sent me to Grand Central Station to meet them and bring them downtown in a taxi. My father sat in front talking to the driver about how many inches of snow can fall on Buffalo in the winter. My mother and I were in the backseat. I looked out the window as she jabbered about the neighbors, the dog and Diana, "The Little Shrimp." My mother smelled like hair spray, cigarettes and her Here's My Heart perfume. I slipped back into my old coma and was only able to mutter, "Uh-huh" and "That's nice" while she recited her monologue.

The cab dropped us off in front of Frank's. My father stood in the middle of the street to get a good look at the house. My mother started yelling, "Andy, get the hell over here! What the hell are you doing in the middle of the street? Ah, your father, he's driving me crazy. I'm gonna kill him one day." She laughed as she said it and my father took his time walking toward the house.

Frank flung the door open before we even rang the bell and stood on the steps wearing a top hat and twirling a cane surrounded by the barking Papillons.

"Daddy! How's my daddy? Welcome to Little Italy!" Frank tap-danced down the steps to my father and gave him a big bear hug. My father just stood there stiff as a wedge of Parmigiana.

"Mama mia, you put on some weight. You got to watch that, Mother. Is that your real hair color?"

"*Sta ta zee! Va caca.* Frankie, shut up! Is that what you got to say to your mother?" She accepted his kiss on the cheek as my father and I carried the bags into the house. Frank didn't say a word to me. I didn't say hello either.

"C'mon on in. How was your trip? Why do you take the train? Ten hours! Flying is so easy, so fast, just an hour and you're here. Life's too short to sit on a train that long.

"Dad, can I offer you a martini or how 'bout a peppermint schnapps?"

"Oh, Frankie, you know I don't drink. Maybe I have a warm beer once in awhile, but no, no I don't touch the stuff."

Frank handed their suitcases to an eager young man who brought them to their room on the second floor.

"Dad, let me show you my garden. The azaleas are in full bloom and the magnolia is bursting. You know Dad, not everyone in New York lives like this, most people live in very tiny apartments, but I have a whole house to myself."

My parents sat on ornate white iron garden chairs under the watchful eyes of Buddha sitting cross-legged in the corner of the garden. A young pretty girl brought out a pitcher of lemonade and poured us each a drink.

Frank had filled the house with his friends, who were curious to meet my parents. One of them, a tall handsome young man, came over to introduce himself to my father.

"Hello, Mr. Andrews, I'm Bernard. How do you do? I've heard so much about you and I couldn't wait to meet you."

"Hello, hello—Ah, just call me Andy."

"Andy Andrews. That's quite a name."

"Yeah, Andy Andrews. That's funny. Ha ha," my father said—deadpan.

My mother called out, in a voice like she was the boss, "Frankie, get your mother a cup of coffee and you know I like it half and half."

Frank didn't answer. He was standing in the middle of the garden. All eyes were on him as he spoke to my father. His face was filled with expression—like he suddenly remembered his pantomime routine. My father sat there with his arms folded across his chest.

"Dad, how are my houses doing in Buffalo? How many do I have now? I lost count. Is it four or five? Have you seen Jay? He loves Buffalo. I don't get it, but he loves it up there. He doesn't want to come home. He wants to buy one of those mansions near Delaware Park and move us there. We could live like kings. The houses are selling so cheap, they're practically giving them away. And what would I do with myself there?"

My father looked angry and embarrassed. "Yeah, I've seen Jay—just yesterday—when I went to take the barrels out from the Riverside Apartments. He's okay. He's quiet. He don't say much, that Mr. Maxwell. I drive him to the store once in awhile. He's okay."

Frank got mother's coffee and Andy a cold beer. He never touched it. I counted seven droplets rolling down the side of the bottle. Frank told my parents about the neighborhood. And stories about the dogs. Somebody in the garden asked my mother if Frank ever read for her.

"Psychic! Psychic!" she said. "I'll tell you who's psychic in this family. Tell 'em Toots, how I told you the other day that your sister Angie was gonna call and sure enough the phone rang and it was her. We hadn't heard a God damn word from her in twenty years!"

No one said anything. Two people whispered to each other.

Frank reached over and took my father's hand and started reading his palm.

"Let me take a look. C'mon, let me see what it says about you, Daddy." Frank held his hand for a few seconds. "This is strange . . . it says here . . . you have other children."

My father quickly pulled his hand away. The garden got quiet except for one nervous laugh.

"Let me show you the house! I'll give you the tour," Frank announced and everyone jumped up and followed him. They got up so fast it seemed like they rehearsed before we came.

The group stood in the hall at the foot of the staircase waiting for Frank to begin. Some of them ogling the floor-to-ceiling wall of fame—framed palm prints of Frank's rich, royal and famous clients.

"C'mon Daddy, hurry up. Don't you want to see my house?"

Knowing people were watching, my mother nudged my father and gently punched his arm. "Andy, get up! Come on, Mr. Lazy Bones. Frankie wants us to see his house. We came all the way from Buffalo to see it. Get up. I don't know . . . what am I gonna do with you? D-I-V-O-R-C-E! Watch it Buster, I'm not kidding. No sireee, Bob. I might just move to New York City and leave you alone in Buffalo. Right, Frankie?"

Everyone laughed. My mother laughed. Someone said, "Frank, your parents are so funny."

My father replied, "Hey, Sitting Bull, if you wanna move here—go ahead. What do I care? I have the dog, what do I need you for?" He chuckled and followed behind the group shuffling up the stairs. I stayed behind in the garden for a little while.

I could hear Frank talking from the second floor, "Now, have your dollar ready. I will be collecting it at the end of the tour. Gather around folks, gather around. Don't be shy. I want to ask you what you think this is used for?"

"Is it a makeup mirror?" someone said.

"No—but you're close. Anyone else have an idea? It's a signaling mirror from the Andes. You hold it up to the sun, like this, and you can send messages to the village across the mountains."

"Ooo, ahhhh," the group said.

By the time I came up to the third floor he was intensely reenacting an exorcism with his ancient set of Tibetan exorcism tools. I stood in the doorway watching him.

". . . you take this bow and arrow and shoot the demon out of the sky," he said, holding up the little five-inch bow in the air. When the imaginary arrow pierced the demon, Frank clutched his heart and stomped on the floor making the sound of the demon collapsing.

"Then you use this hammer and whack the demon as hard as you can. Then . . . the ax!" He held up the little tool and circled around for all the audience to see. "Split!—the heart of the demon in pieces. *Smash! Crush! Chop! Chop! Chop!* And now . . . with your ball and chain . . . crack all of his bones and smash them . . . until they're all pulverized. Powder! Dust!" He was on his hands and knees on the floor enthusiastically destroying the invisible demon.

"Over here, over here . . . you see this box? Remove the cover." He held up the triangular box. "This is where you'll lock up the demon . . . for all eternity.

"Now, pay attention . . . you cannot make a mistake . . . this is the most important part. You must carefully sweep up every single bit of the broken demon and put him into the box. Show him that you have no fear. Even though he's pulverized, he still has power. Use all the force you have inside you to command him to die. Or . . . he will come back to life and kill you!

"Then, take this three-sided dagger, called a *phurba,* and place it tightly into the opening on the top of the box . . . very quickly, so the demon can't escape. Now, you've sealed him away forever. And folks . . . that's your exorcism!"

Frank had worked up quite a sweat and the room loved the performance and applauded wildly. Frank took a bow. He was Little Frankie again and he loved it. And I loved it too. It made me miss him, remembering his irresistible way of making life bigger than life.

My mother was downstairs and my father wasn't watching, he was at the other end of the room looking intently at some artwork hanging on the wall. I went over to see what he was looking at.

"Dad, what do you think of it?" The artwork, a paper cutout of dancing prancing men interconnected by their penises. My father turned to me with a look of disgust and walked away. Then I heard my brother calling him.

"Dad, come over here I want to show you something."

Spread out in the middle of his antique Chinese bed was a large artist's portfolio.

"Come here, Dad. Take a look at this. You know who the Beatles are, don't you? Well, John Lennon's wife, Yoko Ono, gave this to me. It's very valuable and I'm one of the few people who owns one of these. It's called *Bag One,* these are prints of the drawings her husband did of them on their honeymoon."

Frank turned the drawings over carefully as everyone peeked over his shoulder to get a look at them.

My father got very upset, turned away and went downstairs quickly. I followed him. Frank went on showing the drawings to his guests. My mother had left the third floor during the exorcism and was out in the garden smoking.

"Dad, are you okay? What's the matter?"

"Nothing," he said abruptly.

"Hey, Toots, what the hell's the matter with you?" my mother asked.

"Bums! Bunch of bums! They're nothing but a bunch of bums! Where's the toilet?"

I pointed the way for him.

"Mother, what's wrong with Andy?"

"Oh, your father. I should've come alone."

"Why is he acting like this? Is it the house? Is it too much for him? All the people?"

"Ah, you know your father."

"No, I don't. What's wrong with him?"

"Nothing."

"Well, something's wrong. What is it?"

"Nothing!" she said, very annoyed.

"Tell me, I want to know!"

"You know—your father was a tough guy when he was young. He used to beat up queers."

"What!" I choked. "What are you talking about?"

"Why do you think I never bring him here?"

"Mother, I'm confused. Are you talking about Frank? Is that all you see is queer? He's successful, he has a beautiful home, he's famous—people love him. He's happy with who he is. I can't believe what you're saying. Do you two talk about this at home? And what about me? Am I just a queer too? Does he feel that way about me?"

"Oh, shut up now. Your father might hear you."

"I'm going to ask him about this when he comes out. I can't believe what you're telling me. I want to know what my father feels about us."

"Don't you dare say a word! I'm warning you! Shut your mouth!"

Frank came down to the garden. "Mother are you hungry? It's one o'clock. I made a reservation for the three of us for lunch. Where's Daddy?"

I was still reeling from what I'd just heard. Frank was going on with the day. My father came back to the garden and Frank told him of his plan.

"Yeah, sure Frankie, let's go eat."

Frank went to the front door and my parents followed along with the entire crowd of friends. Outside waiting in front of the house was a bright yellow stretch limousine half a city block long.

"Come on, Daddy, get in!" Frank said, as he stood next to the chauffeur holding the door open. "Dad, this car belongs to Rebekah Harkness. She's one of the richest women in the world. She heard you were coming and said, 'Well, use my car. You can't put your parents in a cab.' Get in, Dad. Come on." Frank took my father by the arm and led him to the car.

My father hesitantly crawled into the backseat on his hands and knees. My mother and brother followed. I stood with Frank's guests, watching from the steps of the house as the chauffeur closed the door. Several of the Italian neighbors on the block were hanging around to see what movie star came with the limo. No one had ever seen a car like this before. They all stood there waving as the big yellow car drove away.

I went back in the house to get my purse. Ten minutes later Frank came flying through the door with my parents behind him.

"What happened? What's wrong? Why are you back so soon?"

"Dad doesn't want to go. We got to the corner and he jumped out of the car. He wants to go home. I don't know why. He wants to go back to Buffalo."

Frank was very upset. I suggested we all go for a walk to the Village.

"You take 'em! I'm tired. I'll take a nap."

I walked my mother and father through Soho and over to Washington Square Park. They wouldn't talk about why my father jumped out of the limousine and they told me to stop asking about it. They just kept saying, "Forget about it."

We sat on a bench. I was desperate to speak to my father alone, but my mother was always there and she never stopped talking. I knew that after all the coffee she drank she'd probably have to go to the bathroom, so I chose a bench on the other side of the park far away from the toilet, to give me some time with my father. Sure enough, I got my chance.

"Dad, are you all right? Frank wanted to show you his life and how well he's doing. Was it just too much with that big yellow car?"

No response.

"Dad, may I ask you something? What do you tell your friends when they ask you what your son does in New York? How do they react when you say Frank is a famous psychic?" My father sat on the bench looking straight ahead stone-faced. I could feel his anger building.

"I tell them he's in market research. I don't mention the other thing, ever. They'll say we're crazy or we're witches. I don't tell them nothin'."

"I can't believe you don't tell them. Are you ashamed of him? There's nothing to be ashamed of. He's successful. He's in all the magazines and on television. Are you happy with how us kids turned out?"

"None of you are in jail. That's good, isn't it?"

I just stopped there. I didn't have the courage to go further. I had imagined a real conversation where we'd talk and I'd tell him about my life. He'd put his arm around me and say he loved me no matter what I did with my life. No matter what I was. I was dreaming.

My mother returned and joined us on the bench as we watched the people in the park. My father sat between my mother and me, keeping his arm on the back of the bench above my mother. Suddenly, my mother let out a loud scream and I jumped up terrified.

"You bastard, Andy! You summa na bitch and bastard!"

"What happened? What is it?" I kept asking.

My father was roaring with laughter as my mother was hitting him hard with her purse on his head and shoulder.

Between laughing my father said, "I was pretending to be a purse snatcher. I grabbed your mother's purse from behind her back. She thought she was being mugged!"

"I'll kill you, Andy! You stupido! You summa na bitch!"

. . .

My parents stayed for the rest of the week on Frank's second floor. Frank made sure he had a full schedule of clients during the day and several social engagements in the evening that he couldn't possibly change. While I took them to all the tourists spots in town, he avoided them. I was furious at Frank. He told me to keep them out until eleven o'clock at night because he had something going on in the house and they couldn't be there while it was happening. I did what he asked without question.

The entire time my mother chattered about Frank. My father made no response. Wherever we went he had to feed the pigeons. He refused to go into any store because he wasn't going to buy anything. He waited outside holding my mother's shopping bags. My mother was on a fanatic search for house dresses and presents for Diana. I was losing my mind.

I went home angry, frustrated and exhausted. Deborah yelled at me about how passive I was for not insisting that Frank take time off to be with his parents. After all, he invited them. I started getting terrible chest pains that were so crippling I couldn't stand up straight. I could hardly breathe. On the last day of my parents' visit I couldn't lift my body out of bed. From my waist up to my neck, I was frozen solid, I couldn't move. I called Frank's house and told them how terrible I was feeling and that Deborah was taking me to the hospital. My mother said, "Your brother is busy—you mean you're not taking us out for lunch today?"

Deborah took me to the hospital emergency room, terrified I was having a heart attack. We waited for hours before a doctor came to see me. Deborah stayed in the room telling me stories and trying to take my mind away from fear. After examining me, the doctors told me it was anxiety and stress. I knew it was rage. My family never called. When I called them the next day, to say good-bye, my mother told me what a great time Frankie had shown them.

It took over two weeks for my body to relax and move again. I started taking my mind seriously, how powerful it was. If it could paralyze my body like that, I wanted to know how I could control the part of me I needed to keep open yet still protect myself from getting hurt. I knew I was capable of protecting myself, I could see that by how hard a shell I'd turned myself into, but I needed to be able to moderate the protection. I still believed that my brother and mother had some real power over me. This experience seemed to be proof of that.

Chapter Sixteen ·

At the suggestion of a friend of Deborah's I went to see Marsha, a therapist on Bank Street. I felt comfortable with Marsha right from the beginning. She had a kind and open face, with bright blue eyes and a serious but sweet smile. The first session we talked for a few minutes and then she handed me a book. She wanted me to read a short chapter. She left the room while I read.

Written by a psychotherapist, this chapter was about one of his patients called Joan. She had a terribly abusive childhood filled with neglect and physical violence. An exceptional student, an overachiever, when she graduated from high school, Joan became a nurse, enlisted in the Navy and was sent to Vietnam.

She had horrific experiences in Vietnam and returned from the war suicidal and alcoholic. She tried to kill herself by dropping a plugged-in electric iron into her bath, but miraculously survived. She was committed to a mental hospital, where she met the author of the book I was reading. He brought her back from insanity.

What did this story have to do with me? I sat with the book until she returned from the next room. She took her seat across the room without saying anything. I assumed I was supposed to comment on the book.

"Wow, what a story."

She spoke slowly and carefully, "Joan, the young woman in the book . . .

is me. I want you to know who I am and how much I can fully understand what you're going through. I would very much like to be your therapist. I feel we could work well together."

I said I'd like to see her. Her fee would be fifteen dollars a session. I should come twice a week. She'd open up her schedule for me. I left there feeling a little weird, reading that book and all, but maybe it was good I knew something about her. She understood depression and had very scary visions like I did. I was feeling better already that I had found someone to help me.

For several weeks I went religiously. I always got there early and walked around the block a few times, checking my watch every few feet, getting more anxious at the thought of talking about myself, wondering what she thought of me. I brought in my dreams and my journal. I was constantly thinking about who I was, why I was suffering so much, and the possibility of being happy one day. It was exciting and I started to feel more connected to myself.

Deborah and I were living separate lives, but in the same apartment. She stayed out for days at a time, exploring the dark world after midnight. I was going to therapy. I would sometimes come home in the middle of the afternoon and find her in bed with someone. I'd say hello and ask if I could make coffee for the two of them. Her lovers couldn't figure me out. Why wasn't I screaming and throwing them out of the house? Deborah told them all about me, that I was the love of her life.

In therapy, Marsha kept questioning my relationship with Deborah. What were we doing together? Why, if we weren't lovers, were we acting like we were? I didn't see the need to examine my friendship with Deborah. Marsha wanted me to break all ties with her. That was something I was not going to do, ever. I was in therapy because of my family not because of her.

One day I brought a dream to a session. I dreamt that I had a magic cape that allowed me to fly wherever I wanted. I put on my cape and flew to India to see a holy man. When I arrived in India the holy man told me that I was to give him the cape and that we were to trade places for twenty-two years. I yelled out to him, "What am I supposed to do here?"

He took the cape and said, "You'll figure it out. I'll see you in twenty-two years," and he flew away.

Marsha took notes and made a few comments on my dream. I told her that the dream left me frustrated when I woke up. I thought the dream was telling me what to do with my life, but I wasn't sure what that was. The holy man was another side of me and that I really couldn't be silent any longer. But, did it have to take twenty-two years?

When the session was over she walked me to the door to say good-bye. On the way out there was a young woman coming in who Marsha introduced to me as her sister. She had been visiting her for a few weeks. I said hello and went on my way.

That night I received a phone call. "Hello, my name is Karen." She sounded very nervous. "I met you this afternoon—at my sister Marsha's apartment. I'm sorry, I shouldn't be calling you. Maybe I better hang up."

"No, please don't hang up," I was so confused. Why is my therapist's sister calling me? Maybe she had the wrong number. Is Marsha dead? "Why are you calling me?"

She went on, her voice was shaking. "You seemed like a really nice person, Terry. I'm sorry. I shouldn't be doing this."

"It's all right. Please, tell me why you called."

"You have to promise me that you won't tell Marsha that I called you. It would be very dangerous for me if you did. I could get into a lot of trouble. Please, you have to promise," she begged.

"I promise."

"All right—I believe you. After you left—my sister took me into the living room and told me she had something very important to tell me. She wanted to tell me that something incredible was happening to her. She told me that as soon as she met you she realized what her role in life was. That her life now had a special meaning. She told me that you're a divine holy being. That you're not from the same world as the rest of us. And here's the best part—*she* has been chosen to be your protector and that the two of you are here to lead the world to a new creation."

"What? I can't believe this. You're not serious. How did you get my number?"

"Listen to me! I'll prove it to you. You told her a dream you had about flying to India wearing a magic cape and some holy man traded places with you. She told me that you're the holy man and you came here to save the world. Something like that. Chrissake! Why can't I convince you? I'm trying to help you! You seem like a good and sincere person. I had to tell you. You have to get away from her. She's crazy!

"When you left I went to her office after she went out to the store and I found your phone number. I knew you had to know the truth about her.

And there's something else you should know—you're her *only* patient! She has no others. You're the only one. She doesn't even have a psychotherapist's license. She's crazy. I'm telling you. She's insane! She did this before, when we lived in Maryland. Don't go back there. She's dangerous. Please, don't tell her I called you. It would be very bad for me."

"Thank you for calling me, Karen. I won't say anything. I promise."

This was not the Marsha I knew. Karen must be crazy.

I was in shock. I told Deborah what was going on. She thought the whole idea of me in therapy was ridiculous from the beginning. She laughed really hard when I told her.

"They're the crazy ones. Not you! You don't need therapy. What are you doing there anyway?"

"It was your friend who recommended Marsha."

"Why would you trust anyone that I know?"

"Look, it's been helping me. I'm learning a lot about myself. I'm really upset about this. Why couldn't I see this?"

"Yeah, you're psychic, why didn't you know?"

"Oh, don't you start with that. I think I did know. I kept feeling weird about her, but something kept telling me to go there. She gave me something. She cared about me. I must be crazy."

"You're not, you're just trying too hard. Listen, Terry, you are the sanest person I know."

"Coming from you, that's not saying very much. Thanks anyway."

"Look, just get out of there. It sounds like her sister did you a favor. She's the one who saved you. Don't go back and don't drive yourself crazy. It's just another one of those adventures you get yourself into. Stop looking for a mother. Get yourself a lover. You need to get laid. That's your real problem."

"Thanks, Deb, that's really helpful."

"I love you, Little Teresa, isn't that enough? What more do you need?"

"Yeah, you're right, sure . . . I love you too."

That's how Deborah summed up everything with us.

"C'mon, let's go play pool," she said.

．　．　．

I had to go back to Marsha. I had to confront her. I had to know the truth. I was in anguish about betraying Karen, but I felt I had no choice. I had to know.

I went on time for my regular session.

"Marsha, I have to talk to you about something and I have to know the truth." I was shaking as I relayed the telephone call from her sister.

She looked right at me and with a comforting tone of voice tried to convince me that her sister had a great deal of problems and was very unstable. She had had trouble from her before and she was very sorry if I was upset by this.

I lashed back at her, "That doesn't explain that you told her my dream!"

"She must have read my notes," Marsha said calmly.

"This doesn't feel right. I have to trust you now more than ever and I beg you, please, don't tell Karen that I spoke to you about this. I need to know that you won't tell her that I told you anything. I need to know I can trust you."

"I won't say anything to her. I promise." She crossed her heart and dragged her fingers across her lips closing an imaginary zipper.

"I'm going to go now. I need to think about this." I walked out the door to the waiting room, leaving the door open. At the end of the long hall I turned around and looked back at Marsha. She was sitting there frozen, gripping the arms of the chair.

That night the phone rang. It was Karen.

"You told her! I can't believe you told her! She beat me up and threw me out of the house! I have nowhere to live now! You promised me!"

"Karen, I'm sorry, but I couldn't pretend I didn't know. I couldn't keep going back there and not say anything. I had to find out for myself. I trusted Marsha, she's my therapist. I had to know the truth. Karen, I believe you— every word you told me about her. I'm sorry about what happened to you, Karen. Karen? Karen?"

I heard the dial tone.

A few weeks later I got a call from Frank.

"Terry, I have to talk to you about something. I've been getting these calls from a woman who calls herself Marsha. She's a patient in a psychiatric hospital."

"Oh, God. Oh, no. Frank, tell me, what did she say?"

"She told me she was your therapist and she thinks that you're the savior of the world or something like that. She thinks I must be part of this big mystery too because I'm your brother and we all have something important to do to save the world. She wants me to tell you that she hasn't abandoned you. She'll be coming to help you soon. And she's sending you telepathic messages you should be receiving shortly. She thinks she's your guardian and protector."

Frank started laughing. "Terry, what have you gotten yourself into now? You Scorpios! You're always looking for trouble."

"Frank, I'm sorry if she's bothering you. I feel terrible. I can't believe she's calling you. Oh, my God. I was seeing her for therapy for a while and I think she's a little disturbed."

"A little disturbed! Terry, she told me she slit her throat when you walked out and if she doesn't see you again she'll drink poison! Apparently, she almost bled to death before they found her. Jay spoke to the doctor there."

"Jay spoke to her doctor?"

"She's troubled. I suggest you stay away from her. Look, I get calls every day from all kinds of nuts, nothing surprises me, but this one is really off the deep end. She's called here about fifty times. I won't speak to her anymore. It's a good thing Jay was here. I let him handle it. He's amazing. He tries to help her. I told him to just hang up. All the nuts love Jay. He talks to them, he cares about them. I lose patience after awhile."

I was mortified and embarrassed. I immediately found a new therapist. But I should have spent more time researching. I didn't know enough to ask what kind of therapy I was getting into. She turned out to be a Freudian analyst. I quit after a few months of sitting across from a woman who said nothing to me. The silence and listening to my own voice echo across the room brought me full circle to my mother's cold stare.

· Chapter Seventeen ·

In 1977, Deborah went to live in New Orleans following her dream to live in the French Quarter and stay up all night. She got a job as a waitress at the Cafe du Monde and sent me a photograph of herself in a white apron and flat paper hat holding a large platter of beignets covered in powdered sugar. We wrote to each other every week and I missed her terribly, but felt this separation was good for us. She needed to live without questioning from me or anyone else. And I needed a rest from living with Deborah.

I disassembled the train and rented one room to a man I found from an ad in the *Village Voice*. Donny, a compulsive eater with bright red hair, amazed me as I watched him eat two whole watermelons in one sitting. When he wasn't eating watermelons, he devoured trays of wheat grass, which he grew himself under grow lights on racks he assembled all over the apartment. Most of the time he stayed in his room. I had never lived with a goat before.

Peter left New York not long after Deborah. He had fallen in love with a handsome Texan named Paul and they moved to San Francisco. A few years later they became disciples of Bhagwan Shree Rajneesh and went to live on his Oregon commune. The guru gave them Indian names I couldn't pronounce and Peter wrote me letters about life in a community of people where the only dogma was that their clothes had to be red. Peter sounded content. He was part of a family of spiritual pioneers in the new Wild West.

With all my friends gone, I was living a quiet life. I started cleaning apartments and polishing silver for rich gay men. I liked this job and found satisfaction in good clean silver. I thought I'd be happy doing this for the rest of my life. Sometimes the subject of the Tarot came up and I'd find myself agreeing to read for the people I worked for. We'd clear away the candelabras and silver chests and spread out the cards. In an instant I went from being the maid to Madame Trompe l'oeil.

"You better check what your accountant is up to. With this Devil card coming up three times already, I'm not sure he's the man he says he is."

"I will. This afternoon. Thank you for saying that. I've been feeling he was up to something, but I thought I was just paranoid. You've saved me with this. Thank you. What can you tell me about my uncle in Switzerland?"

My employers often told me that several of their housekeepers were psychic or had seen ghosts. I wondered why ghosts would appear to housekeepers. I often felt something was in the house while I was cleaning too. I wanted to do research because I had heard this myself so many times. Maybe we were disturbing the ghosts by moving the furniture or maybe they were just watching us. Housekeeping requires a kind of concentration that can allow you to see without looking as you move quickly around the room; you can catch things out of the corner of your eye. Or who knows, maybe housekeepers just think they're being watched?

For about six months I went from one gorgeous apartment to another making the silver sparkle. It was a calm and uncomplicated time. I often didn't see my employers. Money was left for me on a table and sometimes a note that said, "Help yourself to the leftovers." I polished teapots pretending they were genie's lamps, looked at my reflection in the bowls and serving trays. I was happy, hiding away.

Then I got a call from Jay.

"Terry, how are you my dear?"

Oh no . . . What does he want?

"I need to ask you a favor. Are you working these days?"

Don't tell me . . .

"Frank is in such demand lately, with all the publicity he's had. He's getting up to seventy-five calls a day. I've been answering the phone for him, but now we need to hire someone we can trust to make the appointments for him. I have to go to Buffalo for a period of time because of the houses. I discussed it with Frank. He wants you to be his assistant. Will you do it? We trust you. Can you come tomorrow? We'll pay you very well. Will you come?"

"Tomorrow?" I sank.

• • •

Jay explained to me what to say to the clients. I'd have to screen calls listening carefully for the people who sounded delusional or mentally unstable. I had to figure out how to politely put off the people who had doubts about seeing a psychic and would give Frank a hard time, testing him on every word. I'd have to do this without offending, without asking any questions about them. Each client had to get directions to the house and a speech about showing up on time. And I had to get off the telephone as quickly as possible.

"The clients will try to talk to you," Jay explained. "Some of them are lonely, some are disturbed. Never tell a crazy person that you're on to them. Distract them with any excuse. If you don't, they'll never leave you alone. Eventually, something else will get their attention."

Based on most of the people I had known in my life so far, I wasn't so sure I could really trust myself with knowing the difference between who was crazy and who wasn't. Maybe I could learn to sharpen my skills here.

Deborah sent me a postcard from New Orleans telling me it was self destructive to be working for Frank. I think her exact words were: "It's fucked up!" I wrote back saying she was probably right, but that it was a good opportunity for me to learn more about myself. She said, "What's there to learn? You must know by now that you're really crazy. Come to New Orleans. Get out of there! You should be having fun."

I was determined to be a good secretary. I kept my pencils sharp and never left the telephone except to open the door to let the clients in. The phone rang constantly.

"Hello, I'd like to make an appointment for a reading with Mr. Andrews."

"Have you been here before? May I ask who's calling?"

"Oh, yes! Who are you? How come I don't know you? Where's Mr. Maxwell? I've seen Frank for years. He predicted my first husband's death right up to the week it happened and then he told me that my second husband was still fucking his old mistress, that bitch, the whole time I was married to him! Frank told me not to marry him, but I didn't listen. So, now I'm in a terrible, never-ending divorce. Have I been to Frank? I couldn't survive without him."

"Ah, excuse me, please, Mrs. Rosenberg. Could you come next Thursday at ten?"

"Not until then? Mr. Maxwell always puts me in right away."

"I'll see what I can do, but I think you should take next Thursday. Someone just canceled and that's the first opening I have."

"Did I mention that my friend from our tennis club also wants an appointment too? Honey, squeeze her in for me. Put her in the same day? She's desperate to see Frank. You should hear her story."

Two seconds later the phone rings again.

"Hello, I want to know how much Mr. Andrews charges? Is he any good? I went to a psychic in London—London, England. She told me my mother's name, she knew the names of my children and she told me that I'd move from Connecticut to New York. And I did. She was the best I've ever been to. She knew I'd have gallbladder surgery and I did. Can Mr. Andrews do that? I'm looking for someone really good."

I got rid of her.

The next call.

"I need magic. I heard Frank does spells. I'm looking for someone to put a spell on my husband. I caught him fooling around and I've had enough! I want him taken care of. I'll pay anything. Can I make an appointment right away?"

I told her that was not one of Frank's talents. I wanted to suggest she try the Mafia social club down the street, but I didn't.

And another call.

A woman in tears, "Hello . . . I need to see Mr. Andrews . . . today. It's an emergency. My boyfriend left me last night . . . I'm pregnant . . ."

"Excuse me, I don't mean to interrupt you, but it's better if you don't tell me anything. I just make the appointments."

I had to keep calm while I was talking to her. My hands started shaking the moment I heard her voice. I felt faint. I hung up from the call having the most terrible feeling. Every part of me shut down and I felt as though I had fallen into a deep depression. I was certain she was going to commit suicide.

There was no time to think, the phone rang again. A man, calling from the airport: "I'm on my way down. Tell Frank I'll be there in one hour. This is Mr. Abdullah Mohammed Hakim Fajarid. He knows who I am."

"Can you spell that, please? Hello? Hello? I don't see your name in the book, sir."

Hang up. Dial tone.

"Hello. My dog ran away. I'm so upset, please, ask Frank if he knows where he is. I'm a client of his. He knows me and my dog."

I wanted to help her and I blurted out, "Go outside and stand in front of your building for the next hour. I see him coming back, running down the street toward you. Is he a Golden Retriever? That's what I see."

"Yes! How do you know? Are you a psychic too?"

"Just hurry and get outside then call me and tell me what happened. Don't worry, he's coming home. He'll be back within the hour. Get outside and picture him running toward you in your mind. Stop crying and get out there!"

She called back in forty-five minutes, overjoyed to have her dog back.

Another call.

"Hello, this is Detective Cunningham from Precinct 23. Mark Horowitz from the mayor's office recommended Mr. Andrews to us. We'd like to talk to him about a missing person. This is really important. We need some direction with this and Mr. Horowitz said he'd be able to help us. Can you ask Mr. Andrews to get back to us as soon as possible?"

When I put the phone down after talking to the detective, I immediately had an image in my mind—a swollen body bouncing in dark, murky water. A woman's face with her eyes wide open—her arms and long hair slowly moving underwater. I knew the woman he was looking for was dead.

"Hello, I'm not calling to make an appointment," said the woman on the other end of the line, "but I wonder if I could just speak to Mr. Andrews for a few minutes on the phone?"

"He's very busy and it's hard for him to answer his calls." There were times when I knew not to engage with people and other times I knew immediately I had to connect. "May I help you with something?"

"I've never been to a psychic before, but my friends told me to call. I've been having the same dream a couple of times a week for the last month and I want to know if it means something. You see, this kind of thing never happens to me. I have a strong feeling that what I'm dreaming is going to happen sometime soon. It's terrible and I don't know what to do."

"Maybe I can help you. I'm Frank's sister and I'm psychic too. Tell me what you've been dreaming."

"In my dream I see a couple sitting in a parked car kissing. Then out of nowhere a man comes up to the window and starts shooting them. He kills the couple. That's it. But I've been dreaming it over and over again. Do you think this is going to happen? Do you think I should go to the police? I'm terrified. Is this about me? I have to tell you that I don't have dreams like this. My dreams are always fantasies about going to exotic places or my boyfriend and I . . . well, you know. What do you think?"

"I'm feeling that your dream . . . from what you're telling me . . . you're picking up on something that's about to happen. I feel it very strongly as I listen to you talk. But I don't think you can do anything about it, unfortunately. The next time you have this dream try to pay attention to the details. Keep a notebook by your bed and write them down as soon as you open your eyes. Notice what the man looks like. What he's wearing. Where are you in the dream when this is happening? What street? What kind of car?"

"Should I go to the police?"

"No. I don't advise that. First of all, we're talking about a dream. And you don't have any real facts. Unless you know someone really well in the police department, I don't recommend it. They won't believe you and if this dream does come true they might think you're involved in the crime. You don't want to do anything just yet. Let's wait and see if anything happens in the news."

"This kind of thing doesn't happen to me. I'm scared. I want to do something. Maybe I could stop it."

"You can't now. You just have to live with this. All you can do now is try not to be afraid. You should consider yourself fortunate to be having such an amazing experience even though it scares you. Listen, call me back if you need to talk about it more. Take notes and let's see what happens. When you go to sleep tonight ask yourself to open up to see more. Try it."

Not every call was so dramatic. Most of them were just about time, address and fee. But lots of them had panic in their voice.

There was the woman who had a nervous breakdown when her husband stole all her money and ran off with the pregnant babysitter, her three children and the dog.

And another woman who discovered a box of audiotapes in her closet after her husband died. The tapes were of readings he had with Frank over the years. After listening to them she found out he had another family and children in the town right next to where she lived. She wanted to know why Mr. Andrews referred to her on the tape as a "bitch."

There was the man who heard voices and was waiting for his shipmates to return him to his planet. He'd been waiting for seven years and believed Frank could tell him when they'd be back to get him. There were several young women who sounded like they were on drugs, many who were lonely, lost and just wanted to talk to Frank. I could feel who was a liar, who was a victim, who was in serious trouble and who was a perfect client—open and ready to benefit from Frank's gift.

Sometimes a client came early and if it was a nice day, I'd ask them if they wanted to wait in the garden. I'd serve them a cup of tea or a glass of water while they waited to see Frank. Sometimes they'd start talking to me. One day a woman came accompanied by two friends, who were going to wait for her while she was having her reading. They asked me to join them in the backyard.

They were two plump middle-aged women with jet-black hair piled on top of their heads. Their arched eyebrows bordered on Barnum and Bailey and they both wore silk flower-print sleeveless dresses. They told me they were from the Philippines. I was curious, but I felt I shouldn't ask. One of them I thought I recognized from the newspaper.

"I've heard New York has some great bargains. Any suggestions?"

I politely answered, "I'm pretty much a Salvation Army thrift shop kind of girl. So I wouldn't know. What kind of things are you looking for?"

"Shoes," they said, at the same time.

"We love shoes! She has over one thousand pairs!" one of them said. "Now, tell us anyplace and everyplace you know where we can buy shoes."

"They're lots of shoe stores on Eighth Street. You might try there."

They went on for the entire hour talking about nothing but shoes. High heels, flats, the sixteen pairs of espadrilles bought in Barcelona, velvet monogramed pumps, short boots, stilettos, stacked heels, sandals . . . I hardly said a word. I was starting to lose my mind.

When Frank finally arrived with their friend, I felt I could breathe again. They said how much they enjoyed meeting me and I said good-bye. Frank walked them to the door and then came back to the garden. It was the end of his day.

"Frank, who were those ladies?"

"Oh, you liked them? They're lovely, aren't they?"

"Please! I never met anyone so obsessed with shoes. That's all they talked about."

At the end of the day, when Frank finished the last client, he'd come out of the room with his eyes bulging, looking like someone who had just come back from a storm at sea. Sometimes he'd be confused, not making much sense, sometimes he'd be highly energized and want me to help him clean out his closets or work in the garden, but most of the time he was ready to collapse.

Sometimes he'd offer me something to eat, always the same thing.

"Have you ever had my lemon garlic soup? I make it myself. It's so easy and it's really good for you."

Once in a while he'd want to sit in the garden and have tea. He liked fixing it for us using one of his antique Chinese teapots and delicate cups.

"Over there we buried Tony's cat. Over there are my client's two parakeets. Let's see there are four cats in that corner and three of my dogs over there and there. I must have over fifty goldfish at least buried under that rhododendron. There's a rabbit here too, under the statue of Buddha. We have funerals all the time here. I get the gongs out and we have a ceremony."

He'd sometimes talk about the readings without revealing anything personal about the client.

"Frank, I just want to ask you . . . was the one o'clock client having an affair with a married man in her office? And she's pregnant, right?"

"Did you get that? She's not pregnant yet, but I told her she would be this fall. How did you get that? That's amazing."

"I'm psychic too, remember. And the last client—lives with her mother, lies to her friends about it and is sleeping with her sister's husband. Right?"

"Jesus, Terry! You're good. Do you want to take my clients tomorrow? I could use a break."

"No, thank you. I don't want to do this for a living. It's killing you. How can you stand it? Listening to those soap operas all day long would drive me crazy."

"I love it. They need me and I help them. If they'd only listen. Some of them do and some of them do the complete opposite of what I tell them. I do the best I can. For the most part, I like the people who come here."

"I heard you yelling at some poor woman this morning."

"She wouldn't listen to me. I told her her husband wants to divorce her.

He hates her. He's horrible! And she says, 'But I love him, Frank.' I love him? I threw her out. She wasn't hearing a word I said. I won't put up with that. I don't want to waste my time. She's not ready to hear what I have to say— 'But I love him.'" Frank said in a whiny voice. "They think this is just a listening job. The concentration it takes, the pressure to get names, dates and places out of thin air and then shift gears from one person to another. They think it's so easy. It's not."

I'd show him the long list of personal calls he'd get in one day and he'd sit down and return every one of them. Clients would sit by the phone all day waiting to talk to him, calling me several times asking if he was available yet. They wouldn't make a decision until they spoke to him. Frank seemed to like being needed by them; he never cut a phone call short.

He was deeply involved with hundreds of people who didn't know a thing about him, nor did they want to know. It was all about them. I wanted to know who he was, what he was thinking, what he really felt about his life. I tried to figure him out. Frank Andrews the psychic at the reading table, the psychic on the phone, the man with the answers.

I wanted a deeper conversation, a talk about how our family came to be this way. He wouldn't do it—or couldn't. He'd avoid any questioning about who he was. If pressed, he'd change the subject or start staring into space, leaving me listening to my own voice. If I brought up a conversation about the family he'd say, "Oh, you're so psychological. Just accept it. That's the way they are."

I could see his conflict: the man who knew everything wanting to be an ordinary guy. In the *The Wizard of Oz,* Dorothy and her friends arrive at Emerald City looking for answers from the wizard. Dorothy's dog pulls back a curtain revealing a little man who's just as surprised as she was to find him standing there pretending to be the great Wizard of Oz. It's the moment Dorothy realizes the wizard is also just an ordinary man. "Pay no attention to that man behind the curtain."

I wanted to know the man behind the curtain. But he frightened me. When I stood next to him I could feel the pressure building up inside of him. He didn't want to slow down even though he was tired and hot tempered. The slightest criticism could trigger him into a rage. He surrounded himself with people who told him only what he wanted to hear. They knew just how to work him. He's psychic, he knew exactly what was going on, but he still kept those people around.

I think Jay was the only one who really understood Frank. They were so young when they met and worked hard together to get what they had. One time when Jay had just come back from Buffalo, I witnessed an argument between them.

"Frank, I arranged a dinner tonight with the Gottliebs. I think you should take a nap now so you'll be refreshed for dinner."

"You did what?" Frank screamed. "You could have asked me first! You're always doing that and I hate it! I don't want to go! I'm exhausted! What do you think I'm doing here all day?"

"Frank, stop acting like that. Don't raise your voice. The Gottliebs adore you. They'll be so disappointed if we cancel. We're going!"

"Acting like . . . what?"

"Like a monster."

Suddenly Frank jumped up on the couch. "A monster? Yes, I'm a monster! I'm the Devil! I'm Machiavelli! I'm Dracula!" He clenched his teeth, throwing his head back, stiffening his fingers into devil's horns. "I could kill you right now if I wanted to! I hate you! I hate you!"

He was drooling, spit rolling out of the sides of his mouth. He leapt straight up into the air and started screaming. When he hit the floor he curled up into a ball making animal sounds. Jay tried to stop him. I saw my mother in him. All I could do was leave.

PART THREE

·

At Large

Chapter One

"Hello, I'm Hillary, Frank's two o'clock. I'm early."

"That's all right. Come wait in the garden."

"It's so lovely, very peaceful. This is my second time seeing Frank. He's good, he's *really* good. And I've been to psychics all over the world. Frank gets the details and he's not afraid to tell you the truth. I'm always astonished by his predictions. Have you known him long?"

"About twenty-seven years," I laughed. "He's my brother."

"Oh really, I didn't know he had a sister."

"Well, he does, me, and our sister who lives in Buffalo, where we grew up."

"I bet you're psychic too."

"Yes, I am. I read the Tarot. Frank taught me when I was twelve."

"You're good, aren't you? And you have visions, don't you? I can tell these things. I can see it in your eyes. Will you read for me sometime?"

Something made me say yes without hesitation. I arranged a time to meet at her place.

She lived on Fifth Avenue near Central Park. The whole way up on the subway I kept asking myself, "What are you doing?" The second she opened the door, I felt a switch go on inside of me. I was so ready to be doing this reading.

We sat at a small table in front of her couch. "Shuffle the cards and when you feel you're ready hand them to me." I felt open and comfortable, maybe because she was. I watched her holding the cards with her eyes closed. I could feel all my insecurities fall off my body, like an apple tree gently shaking the heavy ripe fruit from its limbs.

Looking at her face, I took her being smoothly into mine. I was aware of the small space between us changing as her emotions seeped through the air and into me. I felt a tremendous sadness. It wasn't something I'd seen on her face or from the way she was speaking now. This was completely an inner feeling I had from being near her. Her sadness felt young. I knew by the degree of pain I felt it had taken hold of her just in the last month. Her pain was close to the surface of my heart. Feeling this humbled me, pushed me and my own problems out of the way. I opened myself up to receive whatever image or feeling I needed to have to tell her about herself. I felt fully present in my emptying and mentally clear to ask myself for a picture. In my mind I saw her holding her arms crossed in front of her, pretending she was cradling a baby. I took a brave chance and said, "You recently lost a baby . . . you had an abortion. You wanted the baby, but your boyfriend insisted you stop the pregnancy."

She started weeping. I knew I got that right.

"It's true. You're right. It was impossible to keep on going with it anyway. He was furious with me. What's going to happen with us?"

I spread the deck and asked her to pick nine cards. I read the story laid out right in front of me. The cards were so clear. The Lovers, Three of Cups, Three of Swords, the Death card, the Hanged Man, Four of Swords, the Temperance card, the Wheel of Fortune, the Star. These cards told me he was married, that there was too much damage and loss in both their lives. The relationship was over. It would take awhile but, she'd heal and life would lead her to someone new. One day she'd have a child. After the hard times of the swords, Death and the Hanged Man's long waiting, the Wheel turns around again and in time the Star promises a new beginning.

We connected like old friends who hadn't seen each other in years. It was easy to see things about her and I didn't hold back anything. She encouraged me and never tried to test me. She was the first total stranger I read professionally. I knew nothing about her, no frame of reference, a clean slate— which is probably why I was able to read her so easily. I spent a few hours with her talking about her career, her family, her friends. Everything I told her she confirmed, listening carefully and writing it all down.

When the reading was finished she turned to me and said, "You don't have any plans for tonight do you? No, of course you don't." I didn't even get a chance to answer. "Listen, you're coming with me. Pick up those cards, I want to take you with me."

She combed her hair and put lipstick on while I stood there wondering what was up. I followed her outside, and she jumped into the street and hailed a cab.

"Do I get to ask where we're going?"

"Get in. Plaza Hotel, please. You'll see. Trust me."

I started getting really nervous in the oak-paneled elevator. Spaced out from reading the cards for so long, I couldn't focus enough to figure out where she was taking me. She opened a door to a suite.

"Hillary! So glad you finally got here. Where have you been? More champagne, over here! Hillary, darling how are you coming along with my account? Were you able to—"

"Do we have to talk about business right now, Walter? I just got here. Call me at the bank on Monday and we'll discuss it. Terry, here you deserve this." She handed me a glass of champagne.

The room was filled with businessmen in suits and ties and gorgeous women who all could have been models. I wasn't exactly sure why she brought me there. And she certainly didn't care that I was wearing jeans and a blue workshirt.

"Now listen everybody! Listen!" Hillary announced. "This is my friend Terry. You've all got to talk to her. She's amazing! She's a psychic. And I've never seen anything like her ever!"

Oh no. I can't believe this. Now what do I do? The room got quiet. All eyes were on me.

"May I have another glass of champagne, please?"

"Honey, come over here. I gotta talk to you," said one of the models.

"I'm after her, come here sit near me," an elegant, dark handsome man said.

"I want to go first. I should go first, I have more problems than any of you," said a man with dark thick hair and matching mustache.

"Stop!" shouted out one of the women. "Bring her in here and let's all sit at the conference table. It'll be fun. Let's all hear what she has to say. Sit here. What's your name again?"

I couldn't get out of this. I didn't even have time to ask myself if this was sacrilegious, or if I could even do this. I'd never met people like this before.

The champagne was starting to affect me, on top of already being tired from Hillary's reading. I was starting to feel like a little girl who was just handed a machine gun.

Every seat was filled and some people stood behind the chairs. About thirty people were in the room. They all waited for me to say something. I looked around the room at each face, my mind, the silver ball on a roulette wheel. I stopped at a man with a trim black beard and intense fierce eyes. I seemed to draw power from the look in his eyes. A movie in my mind started playing.

"I see the beginning of a city. Where there was none before you're building one. This is an impossible feat, but you're going to do it. I mean, there's no water there, no trees, no airport, no buildings. This is incredible!"

"Wow, she's got that right!" someone shouted out.

"Shuuuu, be quiet. Let her speak. Go on."

"One thing I want to say to you is . . . you better consider the ground you're building on . . . it's ancient land that's never been touched. You're going to unleash something there that everybody wants and thinks they need. This is dangerous, but you know that and you like that. Don't you?"

"My dear, I want to talk to you alone later. Come to see me," he said and left the room.

"Read me! You can tell him more later," said a redheaded woman sitting at the table; a man behind her was rubbing her arm and stroking her hair.

I took a sip of champagne and looked closely at the two of them. "Well, I'll tell you . . . first, I didn't ask before, but do I have everyone's permission to say whatever I want?"

"Of course! Don't hold back. Go for it! This is getting good," the redhead said.

"This man you're with . . . him, behind you. Well, his wife knows all about you. As soon as she tells him she knows what she knows, you'll be . . . how do I say this? It'll be over between you."

"When's that going to happen?"

"Before the winter."

She told me to say everything. She left the room. I could tell she was upset. The man she was with got up and followed her.

"My dear, keep going. Don't worry about her. What can you tell me about my wife?"

"She wants your emerald mines and nothing less!"

"Ha, ha, ha, ha. Do you know my wife? We're fighting about that now. It's not enough I'm giving her fifty million dollars? Can I take you with me to see my lawyer?" He laughed and took my hand. I could feel him press money into my hand. I didn't look at it, I just put it in my pocket.

"Okay. What does this guy do?" someone yelled out and pointed to a short, plump man with dark hair and a beard.

Without hesitating I said, "Oil . . . oil coming out of sand."

"Hillary, what did you tell her?"

"Believe me, I didn't say a word. What fun would that be?"

"Oh, I get it now," I said. "I see everything. You're all developing a country. You too . . . it's your job to bring the investors, isn't it? You've just come back from Germany and Argentina."

I pointed to a blond woman. "And you're bringing the tourists. I see Jeeps filled with Americans wanting to see the desert. Hotels and business, factories . . . Listen, start building a mental hospital. I'm not kidding. They won't be able to handle the wealth."

"Give her more Dom Perignon. The girl's good."

"I want to tell you something." I pointed to a younger man, American Ivy league. "You're going to witness something very shocking. I see an assassination. It's very hot in the room. There's a meeting with a roomful of men. I see a man dressed in a caftan. His head is wrapped in a cloth. Several men open fire on him. It's going to change your life. You're going to be right at the spot at the time it happens. You'll be standing very close to him. This is not going to happen though for many years."

"Maybe I shouldn't go there? Maybe I should've stayed at my old job? Can I come and see you privately? Can I call you?"

I went around the room reading everybody. Without cards, off the top of my head, I just said whatever came to me. One of the beautiful women came over and whispered to me. "Do I have a chance with that guy? You know, to get to really know him," pointing to a man across the room.

"You mean sex, right? You know, you're just as smart as these guys and you should be doing your own business here. He'll hold you back if you get romantically involved. I see you being extremely successful if you use your connections from meeting these guys, but not by sleeping with them. Come up with an idea and present it to them. You have that chance now. They know how smart you are. You're already telling them too much and getting nothing for it. I think you have less then three months to present a business idea to them. But if you wait too long and just hang around them like this they won't take you seriously. Food. You know about food and importing. A country like that is going to need you."

"You're a smart cookie. You just gave me a great idea. I'll think about what you said."

It was now about three o'clock in the morning. Much too much champagne, and everybody got a reading. I was wiped out. I left the table and sat by myself on the couch. Almost everyone came up to me and gave me money. I thanked them and put it in my pocket. Some gave me their business cards and told me to look them up if I was ever in the United Arab Emirates. I said, "Sure," not knowing where that was. I interrupted Hillary, who was having an intense conversation with three men. I told her I was leaving.

"I hope you had fun tonight," Hillary said. "I know I did. Watching each one of those oil men turn white and walk out of the room after you read them was something I'll never forget. I'm going to call you next week."

When I got home I emptied out my pockets. I had over $2,000.

*   *   *

About a week later Hillary called saying she had arranged for me to read for three of her friends. I should come to her place on Friday at six. "I won't hear you say no. It's all set. They're really looking forward to meeting you. It'll be easy, don't worry. They're all very nice. Besides they're paying."

I agreed. Then I got angry. I didn't like being pushed into this. And I was scared.

The first reading was for a senior editor at *People* magazine. The second, the publicity director for Columbia Records and the third, a William Morris agent for movie stars. They were so impressed with their readings that within a few days I was getting calls from their friends, clients and people they worked with. Two of them were movies stars. I didn't have time to think about it.

In the beginning I made house calls, not wanting anyone to come to my apartment. I felt my life was changing quickly. I wrote to Deborah telling her I wanted to let go of the place on West Tenth Street. She told me she had had enough of New Orleans and was planning to move to San Francisco anyway. The man I'd rented the room to was delighted to live alone with his watermelons and wheat grass. I started packing, convinced I'd be moving any day.

I was feeling like a racehorse ready to bolt the starting gate. All I needed was a new apartment. Standing on the steps of Frank's house, I decided right then and there I was going to find a home that day. I turned my head to the left and saw a man walking down the street coming toward me. I was certain he was the man that would tell me where to find an apartment. I stood in the middle of the sidewalk, stopped him and said, "Hello, how are you? Do you know of any apartments for rent in the neighborhood?"

"Yes, as a matter of fact I do."

"What! You do?" Even though I knew, I was stunned.

"Yes, but on second thought, I don't think you'd want it."

"Yes, I would. I know I would. What's wrong with it?"

"A friend of mine tried to live there, but he only lasted one night."

Boy, was I excited. The place must be haunted.

"It's a mess. The woman who had it before had fifty-three cats living with her. It needs work, lots of work. It's been empty for years. People have tried to live there, but no one lasted more than a day. The landlord won't do anything to it. It's a take it or leave it type of thing."

"I want it! Where is it?"

I couldn't believe this was happening. It's not that easy to find an apartment in New York City. He told me to go around the corner to Prince Street.

"It's a big white brick tenement building in the middle of the block. The San Gandolfo social club has the storefront. You'll see the holy statue in the window. You can't miss it. It's about seven feet tall. The front door's unlocked and the apartment's open. Just walk down the hall to the back stairs and climb. It's on the top floor. Go take a look at it. I know the super. If you like it, call me and I'll give you his number."

"What's your name?"

"Harvey."

"Thanks, Harvey."

"Wait until you see it before you thank me."

I ran down the street as fast as I could. I knew it was my home and it was waiting for me. I pushed the heavy glass and wrought-iron door open and ran down the hall to the back stairs. I noticed the colors of the Italian flag, a red, white and green border stripe, in the tiny floor tiles. Holding the railing to pull myself up faster, I counted the steps . . . eighty-two. Up six flights. Why do I always have to climb stairs?

When I pushed open the unlocked door I first saw the blinding sun pouring in from the windows. Beautiful, almost holy, but then like a heat blast from a roaring open furnace—I was kicked in the stomach by a nauseating stench of cat urine. Fifty-three cats! It didn't sink in until then.

I stood there wondering what I was getting myself into with this place. The apartment was empty, some windowpanes were missing and there were no closets. Off the main room were two small rooms about nine by ten. There was a little porcelain sink attached to the wall. And right in the middle of the kitchen—an unavoidable presence—standing on tall husky legs like a large sheep, a cast-iron bathtub. I could paint its hooves black.

Somehow I'd fix the place up. A little paint, refinish the floors, some furniture—I could do it. I could make this place my home. I had to stop making house calls. Not only did it take up too much time, but I'd get bombarded with information from other people who lived in the apartments as well as from the furniture and objects in the rooms.

I signed the lease in 1977, my rent—$125 a month. I worked hard to get the place in shape for seeing clients and worried a lot about how they'd feel coming there with the bathtub in the kitchen and having to climb so many stairs. I told myself, "I'm a fortune-teller, I have a right to be eccentric."

I told Frank I wanted to quit being his assistant and start doing readings myself. He didn't say very much, but he gave me Nesta Kerin Crain's mahogany gateleg table—the one she used to do her readings on. Above the table I hung the photograph of the railroad tracks Arline gave me so many years ago. I told myself when the tracks faded away I'd stop doing readings.

I spent two months renovating and continued to make house calls until I got the place in good enough shape to see clients there. Although I lived only two blocks from Frank I hardly ever saw him. Neither of us called the other very much. Once in a while he'd call to let me know when he was going to be in a magazine or on television. Once in a while I'd call on a holiday or if I'd heard news about a mutual friend. We'd sometimes bump into each other in the grocery store. I always felt sad after I'd see him. I'd walk away feeling like I wanted to say something, but I wasn't sure what.

Chapter Two

My name got out, and the phone never stopped ringing. Throughout the 1980s and '90s it felt like the whole world was coming to see me. All kinds of people climbed up to consult with me, five people a day, five days a week. I spent most of my time reading the Tarot, and when I wasn't, I was recovering from it. I was happy for my success but had entered a universe of strangers who didn't want to let me go. Though I had friends and relationships, the core of my being was with the work. I never talked about the readings to anyone. Being distracted by them was hard on my personal relationships. When friends needed to talk to me as a friend, when they just wanted me to listen, I couldn't help but see what was coming. They wanted me, not me the psychic, but there was no way to separate the two. When I saw things that were going to happen to them, I learned to keep it to myself. When I knew from the very beginning that my own relationships wouldn't last, I worked hard to look away and have them anyway. Inside of me was a library of secrets.

. . .

"So what do I do? Shuffle?"

"We need to talk about your job, your relationship and why you're so depressed."

"I'm a man with millions of dollars and nothing to do."

"I'm not going to make up a life for you. Do you want to keep living like this? We have to find where your passion is."

"You're pregnant! This summer. I see you with a baby! After all these years."

"I just got the lead in a movie. Am I good enough?"

"If she marries him—she'll be a widow twice."

"Prepare yourself, you're getting fired from the magazine."

"Last time I was here you were able to see into the microscope. Can you do that again? I'm getting close to a cure."

.   .   .

New York City was an exciting place to do readings. Most of the people I read for were living there because of their careers. My clients were fashion designers, writers, movie stars, artists, journalists, Wall Street brokers, interior designers, doctors, bankers, medical researchers, spiritual leaders, directors, producers. Even several of the New York City Rockettes came for readings. And many students, office clerks, waitresses, dancers, priests, teachers, musicians, sports stars, lawyers, entrepreneurs. As well as the lost, the lonely and the curious—with all their problems, triumphs, fears and dreams.

.   .   .

"Come in. Hello. It's a pleasure to meet you. I've seen many of your movies. I admire your work."

"My friends told me it was safe to come here, that you don't talk to the press."

"They're right, I don't. I get calls all the time from magazines and newspapers. I would talk to them if they wanted to know about the psychic experience, but most of them don't. They just want gossip.

"I know you just won the Oscar a few weeks ago, but you're here to see me because you want to understand why your father didn't react. You're in a lot of pain. I have to tell you, I don't see him ever acknowledging your success. He can't change. He can't do it. You have a great career ahead, but don't miss out on it because you're waiting for your father's recognition. His silence makes you imagine the worst. Get those voices out of your head, they'll hold you back. The voices that you make up to tell yourself you're not good enough. Claim who you are to yourself. Do it now."

"What do you see for me?"

"Your son wants to talk to you. You'll be upset. Please, just hear what he has to say."

"Go see the doctor. Right away!"

"You look so innocent, the face of an angel, but I see you in bed with so many different men."

"You're absolutely right! Fantasy and fetish, I'm a professional dominatrix."

"I don't know if I believe in what you do, but you told my friend that she was going to fall in love by the end of the summer and she has. You described him. Said his name. What he'd say to her when they first met. So how do I shuffle?"

"What do you need a reading for? You have an amazing life. I'm jealous."

"The world scares me. Are we going to survive?"

For years, my building didn't have a doorbell. Clients had to call me from a pay phone on the street five minutes before the reading. I'd fly down the stairs to open the door and climb right back up again with them. In one given day I could make five trips for the clients, that's twelve flights each time, and maybe two other times, if I happened to go out—total of eighty-four flights of stairs a day. It was mostly Italian families that lived in my building. They'd leave their doors open for ventilation while their meatballs and sauce bubbled on the stove. The intoxicating aroma of garlic and onions filled the halls every day. I'd wave to the neighbors on my way up or down, sure they were wondering what I was doing on the top floor with all these different people every hour on the hour. "Mrs. Rigatoni, I'm starving! That sausage linguini is driving me crazy!" She'd smile, not understanding a word of my English.

. . .

"I had a reading two years ago. You probably don't remember me, you see so many people. You told me to leave my wife. You said she was planning to rob me. You said she was seeing another man. I didn't leave. Now, they've both run off with everything. I should have listened to you. What should I do now?"

"Hello. You don't know me. I'm calling from the Chelsea Hotel. I'm so depressed. I want to kill myself. I got your number from someone in a coffee shop. Can you help me?"

"His name is Kirk. I hear Kirk, very clearly. It might be part of his last name."

"Just buy it. Trust me, you'll have the money."

"He left me. Do you know why?"

"I can't read you. I'm not getting anything."

"Other readers have told me the same thing."

"I just want to know one thing, and one thing only! When will my daughter-in-law drop dead?"

"I want to be an icon. You do see that—don't you?"

"What are you doing here? Monsignor, you must know what the church thinks about the Tarot?"

"I have no idea what I want to do with my life. Who am I?"

"I have a brain tumor. They can't operate. How long do I have?"

"Enron? If you buy that you'll lose everything."

"I've fallen in love with the most wonderful man. What's my wife going to say?"

"I've been having these dreams. Do you think I was abused as a child?"

"I'm a prince from a royal family. I want out."

. . .

Up and down the stairs, next person, next person—forgetting to eat, forgetting to drink water—thirty, forty phone calls a day. I had to hire someone to come once a week to help set up my schedule. I'd never know who'd show up here. All I knew was a name in my appointment book.

On my way downstairs, I often encountered Sylvie. Sylvie had lived in the building since the early '50s and I don't think she had bathed since then. I'd often see her in the neighborhood picking through garbage cans. One day she was sitting on a milk crate in the downstairs hall cleaning a whole fish.

I walked past her to open the door, nodding a quick hello. Directly through the glass I could see a black limousine and driver. Poised next to it was a stunning blond woman in a silk peach suit and diamonds. I shook her hand. She followed me in.

There was Sylvie and her fish. "Oh, what's this?" Sylvie said. "You got a rich one today. Pretty. Pretty."

We made our way up.

"Things I've been dreaming have been happening."

"Look, don't pay me. Keep the money, go uptown to the bus station, get the next bus out of New York and have an adventure. Make a life for yourself! The cards can't do that for you."

"Tell me how to leave my marriage. I've tried to make it work for twenty-three years."

"Does anything I've said make sense? You haven't said very much. Do you have any questions?"

"Yes . . . I just want to ask you . . . do you take a bath in that tub?"

"Rome, you'll meet her in Rome. You're going to live the rest of your life there."

"You may be a waitress now, but I see you and you're a lawyer in State Supreme Court."

"Don't look for these names and don't dismiss others who don't have them because they may lead you to your new love. These are clues."

"Will anyone ever love me?"

Clients sent me their kids right out of high school. I guided them through their college years and into their careers. I read for artists, art dealers, collectors of art, museum directors. Before the painter picked up the brush I could see the painting, describe it, and tell them the name of the gallery or museum it would end up in. I could see love affairs years before the first meeting, the courtship, the marriage, the children and often the divorce. Once in awhile a client would show up carrying the baby I predicted. "Hello, sweet thing, I know you."

   •   •   •

"Make a note of today's date and when you meet your future boyfriend ask him if he was in London attending a book fair on that day."

"It's uncanny. Your description of the man I love is completely accurate. Except for one thing—he's not my husband, he's my fantasy. He's the one in my mind when I'm making love to my husband."

"You want him back? He's stalking you! He put a knife to your throat! He put a tape recorder under your bed! Look! My nose is bleeding! You don't get it, do you?"

"Why should I marry her if you already see us divorcing?"

"I met him just as you said. You told me his name. We fell in love, married for five years and now it's over. I thought he was my soul mate."

"He probably was. That may have been all the time you needed together."

. . .

Whenever I predicted a name and it came true, I'd get a ton of phone calls from people wanting me to predict the name of their future love. I wanted to tell them the meaning of their lives and they wanted Romeo or Juliet or Romeo and Romeo.

The Tarot helped me immensely. Although I didn't need the cards to do readings anymore, they made my job a lot easier. I could be struggling to understand what I was feeling and glance down at the Tarot laid out on the table. The entire story was right there in front of me. All I had to do was read the cards.

Two elderly Chinese women lived on the second floor. They had their own apartments across the hall from each other. Although they had been here for years, they still dressed in Chairman Mao jackets, cotton pants, white socks and black slippers. In the warm weather they sat on small stools in their open doorways. Brewing on their stoves were large aluminum pots of medicinal herbs. An odor I could never get used to, an odor that would send any illness running for its life.

I had long conversations with those two women although they didn't speak a word of English and I knew nothing of Mandarin. They'd say something and I'd say something back. I'd respond with a question and they'd laugh and say something for several minutes. I'd say, "Of course. I absolutely agree." We'd laugh and tease each other. We'd talk about the world, their families and mine. I asked them about China and they asked me about me. I knew exactly what they were talking about. And if I didn't, it didn't matter. They often gave me oranges.

. . .

"Is English your first language?" a client said to me once.

"Yes, and I know why you're asking. I'm translating visual pictures in my head and sometimes it comes out broken up in my speech. It's like looking at a television program without the sound. I have to make sense of what I see."

. . .

The psychic process fascinated me. I got to feel a range of emotions from situations I'd probably never be in in my own life. The clients brought their lives to me. I could be a fireman, raise a child, go through divorce, be on stage, be a father. The second I looked at a client I'd let myself feel who they were. A shift would occur inside me and a visual picture snapped alive in my mind. Quickly, I'd pull all the sensations together and tell them what I knew.

So many tears came to my table. I cried with them, through breakup, humiliation, the prospect of death. I was often in pain from things that had nothing to do with me. It hurt so, at times I wanted to quit.

I was haunted by the things I said in readings, worrying about the clients like they were my own children. Sometimes I'd be walking down the street and suddenly I'd feel like I was somebody else, like I jumped into another life. It was often a client I'd read during the week. I knew exactly what they were feeling, what they were thinking wherever they were in that moment. When I was inside them I'd try to project myself into their future, believing I could change something that I'd seen in the reading that I didn't like or didn't want to happen. I'd even find myself worrying about people I'd predicted for the client, someone they were going to meet in the future. People they hadn't even met yet! Someone neither of us knew, but who I had come to know because they came to me through the reading.

Dazed from doing so many readings, my eyes looked like the headlights that stopped deer in their tracks. I'd often run into my clients on the street. They'd want to talk to me or tell me about something I'd predicted. They felt it was some kind of omen running into me exactly at that time. Most of them couldn't help but say, "May I ask you a question?" My friends would yank me away saying, "She's not working now, sorry." They knew once I'd get started, I couldn't help but be intrigued—obsessed. It was as if the part of me that opened up during the reading somehow got plugged in again on a chance meeting.

Reading on such a complex level made making decisions about the simplest things in my own life difficult. If I went out of the apartment right after a day of readings I might find myself in a grocery store not remembering why I was there. I'd come home with a bagful of bruised and rotted fruits and vegetables—they called to me, telling me nobody wanted them. I felt sorry for them and took them home. My friends learned never to send me shopping.

No one was forcing me to do all these readings, but I'd wake up feeling reluctant. The anxiety was tremendous. I worried that I might interpret an image incorrectly or that I'd start to read someone and nothing would happen. I worried if I weren't insistent enough or if I encouraged too much. I felt a huge sense of responsibility.

. . .

"I have a prediction for you. You're going to meet a man. He just moved to New York from Vermont. Dark hair. His name . . . I hear . . . James. He'll tell you that his father owns a hardware store . . . an old family business. He's good-looking, sincere, kind and deeply in love with you. You'll marry him and be very happy. The problem is, I'm going to tell you something that may be hard for you. This man is about to be your new boss and you'll have to work with him without saying or doing anything to make this happen any sooner. It'll be at least two years before he realizes his feelings for you. Can you live with this?"

She couldn't. She quit the job two weeks after the man I predicted became her boss. She wanted to know what she should do.

"If it's truly a destiny, then I hope somehow, somewhere you'll meet each other again."

. . .

"You're crying. You're living with a secret. Sex is unbearable with him. Isn't it?"

"You can see that? I never told anyone that. I don't know what to do. We're getting married in June."

"I beg you to call off the wedding. It's never going to change with him. Please, don't marry him. Don't do this to yourself. You're a young girl, please wait. There's someone else for you—not that far away."

. . .

"You told me last year something was wrong. I never expected to lose her. We were so happy. I had no idea she felt nothing for me."

. . .

What helped me with the anxiety was to do more readings. Each reading would push out the previous one. The more I did, the more I'd forget them. My life was the lives of other people. I loved so many of the people who came to see me. Most came once a year, many came only once. Thoughout the years I'd get feedback on my accuracy though many times I never knew if what I saw had come to pass. It was for them to live and watch for, not always for me to know. But it was a thrill to hear when my predictions came true.

There were some clients who didn't like me when what I saw for their lives was different from what they wanted. I've had people walk out, yell at me and call me wrong. Years later I might get a call from them saying, "You were right." And I'm sure sometimes I did get it wrong.

At the end of a reading, when it was time for a client to leave, I'd often feel a tremendous sense of loss. The hour and a half I spent with them was a full lifetime for me. I knew them through my whole being. I was them for that time. I had experienced such a deep connection to them it was sad to see them walk out the door.

. . .

Deborah and I were still best friends. She came back from New Orleans and rented a small apartment on Christopher Street. During the '80s and '90s she spiraled downward into drug addiction and mental illness. Between weeks of euphoria and suicidal depression she'd often take herself to psychiatric emergency rooms. I paid her rent and utility bills so she'd always have a home. I called everyone I could think of, trying to find help for her. Almost every day after the readings I went to the hospital to be with her.

The nurse unlocked the two double doors with the chicken wire windows. I showed her my pass and she pointed to a room. Deborah was sitting alone on the bed looking into space. She recognized me and asked if I brought her the cigarettes and candy she wanted. I got her up and we went for a walk, back and forth down the hall. At one end on the wall was a poster of the Eiffel Tower.

"Come on Deborah, let's take a walk to Paris."

I held on to her skinny arm as she shuffled slowly across the floor in her hospital robe and paper slippers.

"Deborah, you got to get out of here. What are they giving you?"

"Turning Japanese. I think I'm turning Japanese."

A fresh-faced young doctor with little flying pigs on his tie approached us and asked if he could speak to me.

"Would you come into my office for a moment? I'd like to ask you some questions. We've noticed that you visit your friend a lot. How long have you known her? Has she always been this way?"

"What way?"

"The hallucinations. You do know your friend is a paranoid schizophrenic? She feels that the whole world is her enemy. And she thinks she's becoming a Japanese person. We've been considering transferring her to Manhattan State, a facility that can give her more treatment then we can offer here."

"You mean shock treatment, don't you? Why don't you just say it? Excuse me, doctor. How old are you?"

"What do you mean? Why do you ask me that?"

"How old are you?"

"Twenty-six."

"You look twelve. First of all, I know my friend has problems, but you have her on more drugs than I've ever seen her on ever before. How did you come up with that diagnosis? And why are you giving a drug addict more drugs? You don't know her. How many times have you spoken to her? Are you a real doctor? Tell me the truth, when did you graduate from medical school?"

"In June."

"I'm taking her out of here. And don't get me started on that whole world is her enemy thing. And for your information, 'Turning Japanese' is a pop song."

With a phone call to a doctor friend and the promise I'd look after her, they let me take her out. With a bagful of medication and a handful of prescriptions she'd usually go home and spend the next week alone detoxing. It must have been hell for her. She wouldn't let anyone see her when she was getting clean. It made her so sick, I never knew if she'd be able to make it through. Then she'd emerge from her apartment and be away from drugs for a while. Then the call would come.

Hello, this is Dr. Nightmare. I'm calling from Bellevue Hospital. We have a friend of yours here who said to call you.

Oh, you must have the wrong number. I don't know anyone named Deborah.

My friends told me to walk away. Forget about her. I'd go every time.

She'd been in over a dozen different hospitals in twenty years. Most of them were horrific places. On the same ward thrown together were the junkies, the homeless, the elderly, the suicidal and the depressed. Men and women together. Deborah said she felt safe in there. She actually seemed happy in those places. Besides, she could stay medicated. I'd watch her comfort the other patients, getting the nurse for them or listening to their troubles. She'd take me around the ward and introduce me to everyone, always telling me to keep quiet about being a psychic and don't dare try to help anyone.

"Hey, Debbie who's your friend? Introduce me."

"Terry, this is Leo. Isn't he handsome? Look how they got him handcuffed to the bed. Leo, tell Terry how they caught you running naked down the West Side Highway. Don't worry, you'll be going home soon. I bet you like those handcuffs, don't you, Leo?

"Let's go talk to that girl over there. Everyone's afraid of her. She was gang raped a couple of months ago by some guys she knew. But she went after them—stabbed every single one of them. She's really nice."

Most of the hospitals were filthy, bare with tables and chairs in grimy big open rooms. The bedrooms were often shared by four to six patients. The windows were covered with chain-link fencing over the glass and usually looked out to the back end wall of the hospital. In one of the wards I saw feces smeared on the walls. Deborah never got any therapy there; maybe she spoke to a doctor for a few minutes a couple of times a week. She sat all day doing nothing along with the other patients, most of them in a medicated stupor. There was a smoking room and Ping-Pong; they all had Ping-Pong. Deborah always wanted me to play with her. I could hardly hit the ball. She played like a Chinese gold medalist. Then she'd coax me into playing with one of the patients. She'd pull one of them out of their chair and drag them over to play. I'd find myself on the other side of the table looking at my opponent, who Deborah had set in place—standing frozen in position holding the paddle up in the air without a clue about where he was. Deborah took off laughing toward the smoking room.

In all the times I went to the hospitals I saw very few visitors. Most of the people in there seemed to be thrown away. And here was Deborah, one of them, except she had me. She had forced me to grow up because I had to take care of her. I was an adult for the first time, and she was my child.

In my life, I never turned my head away from anything, but the mental hospitals forced me to stay contained inside and keep my focus on myself for my own safety. It was a kind of training I had to do to close out the patients who were in there. Once in awhile, I'd slip slightly toward someone to take a peek into their psyche to try to understand who they were and how they got there, but then I'd pull back, frightened that I might not get out. I saw how easy it can be to slip away in a direction we never expected. We don't realize how close we all live to the border of another reality.

There were great times when Deborah was well. We took trips to the Southwest, the open space of Monument Valley, New Orleans for Mardi Gras, Paris, England, playing poker with strangers on the Texas railway, fighting with thieving gypsies in Rome, pulled out of line at the Amsterdam airport and interrogated—Deborah a hijacker? It must've been our berets. In summers I rented a beach house on Fire Island. The ocean . . . the sky at night. She'd call me from a pay phone: "Meet me in an hour at Port Authority. The bus leaves for Atlantic City at five. Be there!" And she'd hang up. The whole ride out she'd listen to the Rolling Stones or Fleetwood Mac on her headphones. I looked out the window.

It was in the mid-'80s, in one of the hospitals I went to see her in. She was sitting at a table with three other patients. The room was separated from the others. They were eating lunch on paper plates on yellow trays. I asked her why they weren't sitting with the others.

"We're segregated. Let's go back to my room. I want to talk to you."

"What's the matter?" I followed her.

"God came to talk to me last night. Everything's gonna be okay. Don't worry."

"What are you talking about?"

"They gave me a test. I have the HIV virus. I'm okay. Don't worry. God said he has a plan for me."

That plan took seventeen years.

. . .

Doctors, tests, churches, prayers, lighting candles to saints, healers, colonics, organics, phones calls in the middle of the night, paperwork, paperwork, waiting, waiting, tears, wishing, wishing, magic, the Moon. Look away, look away, don't see me cry. Photograph everything. Christmas tree. Halloween. Teasing the Devil. Riding our bicycles down the middle of Broadway at four in the morning. Space toys, trading cards, comic books. Laughing. Angie, beautiful . . . how will we ever say good-bye. Watching the ocean liners sailing down the Hudson River as the sun came up. God is alive. Look at our city from up here. At the top of the tower, on top of the world. Suitcase full of letters. Twenty-six years. Then the butterfly came. I'll sing to you all night till you go to sleep, my angel, my huckleberry friend. The landslide brought you down . . . I'll see you in another life.

Chapter Three

There were months when I didn't hear a word from Frank. If I wanted to know how he was, I'd ask someone in the neighborhood if they'd seen him and how they thought he was doing. In the late '80s there was a long silence between us. I could always feel Frank though and know how he was and what he was doing.

During this time something seemed wrong. I couldn't get any sense of him and I was having nightmares about him hiding under the bed trembling or running down the street trying to get away from something. I felt something might be seriously wrong. I was afraid to call him myself. It didn't make sense, and although on some level part of me was afraid to find out what was going on, I really wanted to know if he was all right, so I called his friend Eric.

"Hello, Eric, how are you? I need to ask you something. It's about Frank. Have you seen him recently?"

"Why? Why are you asking?" he said nervously. "Do you think something's wrong?"

"*Is* something wrong? Something's wrong, isn't it?"

"You're psychic. You tell me."

"Eric, don't do that to me, just tell me. What's going on? I want to know what's wrong."

"I can't talk about it. I'm sorry."

"What do you mean? You've got to tell me."

"I can't."

"Yes, you can. I'm his sister and I have a right to know. What's going on?"

"I can't talk about it over the phone."

"Why, is Frank in trouble? Is he sick? Is it drugs? Did he do something wrong? Just tell me. Now come on, your phone isn't tapped. What could be so terrible that I can't know?"

"Can you meet me this afternoon at three o'clock at the Cupping Room on West Broadway?"

"I'll be there."

When I got there, he was already there sitting alone at a table stirring his coffee over and over again.

"It started about a month ago. Your brother called me. He was all excited about something he wanted to show me. He said I had to come over and see for myself. I was invited along with eleven other people to come to his house. He told each one of us to bring a single rose and arrive at exactly ten o'clock at night.

"You know, anytime Frank summons you to his house it's got to be good, so I went over there thinking I was going to meet some celebrity or something like that. When I got there the house was completely dark except for a few candles. A petite blond woman with some sort of accent let me in. I'd never met her at Frank's before and I've been there a lot over the years.

"The other people were already there waiting in the hall. The blond woman took our roses and told us to wait. Nobody else knew what was going on. When she came back, she took us into Frank's reading room. The chairs were arranged in a circle around the room. She told us exactly where to sit and that Frank would be coming soon to join us. She made us promise not to talk to one another.

"Well, you know your brother loves a drama, so I didn't think much about it. Within a few minutes, Frank came into the room followed by two young men. One of them I remembered meeting at his house, a nice guy, but I wondered at the time what he was doing with Frank. I mean, I know your brother for over fifteen years and this guy was talking to me like he knew Frank better than I did and he had just met him two weeks earlier. Well, whatever, that's Frank's business."

"Eric, please, I'm going crazy. What happened?"

"I'm going to tell you. You got to believe me—this is incredible. I haven't been the same since that night. It's making me question everything about my life. It started four weeks ago. We've been meeting twice a week at Frank's house for these sessions that Frank's been holding. It's not exactly a seance, but I guess it is. Frank's been going into trance and a voice has been giving us lessons on how we're supposed to live."

"Eric, what do you mean a voice? Is it Frank's voice, does it sound like him? What's it telling you?"

"Sometimes these sessions go on all night and into the next day. We sit in the dark. The windows are covered up and, you know his reading room, it's dark in there anyway, well now you can't see a thing. The voice does sound like Frank, but it's not him. I know it's not him."

"How do you know?"

"Because it says the most horrible things about Frank. Mean, disparaging things. The voice says Frank is selfish, an egomaniac who only cares about himself. Now, you know your brother wouldn't say that about himself. The voice has yelled at all of us too. It told me I didn't know what love was and that I had already met my great love, but I missed it because I was so involved with myself and my own needs. That's true you know, I know that about myself. I never told anyone that."

"Who do you think the voice is?"

"I'm not really sure, but he has a name. I shouldn't say. I don't think I should tell you what his name is."

"Why not? Listen, I have a right to know. And you have to tell me."

He whispered, "He calls himself 555. He says he came here to battle the beast—666."

I jumped up from my seat and yelled, "Jesus Christ, Eric! Oh God! Please, tell me everything you can remember. I need to know every detail. What is this 555 telling you all to do?"

"Terry, I'm telling you, I swear on my life that this is not Frank playing with us. I know because the voice talks at great length about history and politics and what's going on in the world. And I know these aren't things Frank is up on. I doubt your brother has ever read a newspaper in his life. The voice told us everything about Joan of Arc and who she really was. And guess what? She's not the person she claimed to be. The voice gives us remedies to take for our health. And predictions for the world. 555 told us information about Chief Joseph and the American Indians that was never told to anyone outside of their tribe. We're learning things we need to know if we are going to survive here. We have to draw symbols all over the house to protect us from what's coming, and we're told what to eat, what to wear. I went home and researched the historical things I heard and sure enough all the facts were exact. Things I know Frank has never heard of."

"I know Frank and I don't think he could fake that. His attention span isn't long enough to sit up all night reading up on this stuff."

"There's more. There's something else that's been happening."

He paused, folding his napkin over and over again. He looked at me and said, "During the evening, after the lessons, we light candles around the room. 555 wants us to see what's happening. I couldn't believe it at first, but I've been watching very carefully. Frank has been materializing objects . . . from his mouth. He's been spitting up all kinds of things . . . pulling things out of his mouth. 555 told me to hold out my hand and I did . . . and Frank, or 555 . . . pulled out a long string of turquoise beads and handed them to me. I was shaking."

"What? He's doing that! I want to see those beads. I know everything my brother has. I know all his jewelry and everything in his house. Will you show me what you have? Oh God, what if this is real? He's doing materialization! This is so dangerous. What's happening?"

"We're all given gifts. Do you know his friend Carla who lives in New Jersey? She got a solid silver egg! Frank started choking, he sounded like he was really suffering. We didn't know what to do. Nobody moved. And then it came out, right out of his mouth. Another man got a jade bracelet and somebody else a silver jewel-encrusted pendant. And sometimes, Terry, I swear to God, I'm not making this up, we've heard what sounds like rain inside the reading room. Tap, tap, tap, tap, tap . . . What it is . . . dropping down from the ceiling . . . is hundreds of tiny seed pearls all over us!

"The voice can be very loving, but he screams at us too. He told us, 'So you're impressed by this! This is nothing. You can do what I do.' He told me to take my index fingers, put them in the corners of my eyes next to my nose, press down and then take them away. So I did. When I pulled my fingers away, on the end of each finger was a ruby. The voice said, 'You see, these are your tears.' I broke down and sobbed. This is all true. Everything I'm telling you is really happening."

"I believe you. I do. But this scares me. How do you know Frank isn't possessed by some spirit?"

"Well, I guess he is, sort of. This voice, this entity, gets inside of him. He's not just hearing it. He's using Frank to talk to us. The voice told us how terrible it's going to get in the world. Especially in New York. We're going to see things we never thought could happen here. We've really got to pay attention to what he's saying.

"The thing is when Frank comes out of these sessions, he doesn't remember anything. We tell him, but he doesn't believe us. We tried tape recording him, but when you listen back to the tape it's either all garbled up or you hear some faint kind of German marching band music. It's very strange. I know Frank isn't faking this. He's not capable of it.

"There's another thing that happens. When we turn all the lights back on . . . the room is filled . . . with roses! The one single rose that everyone brought multiplies into dozens of roses all over the room! It's the most amazing thing that's ever happened to me. I wish you could see it. My life has changed forever. I've been taken to another dimension and I'll never be the same."

Eric's story scared me. Whenever I left my apartment to go anywhere I had to pass Frank's house. I wanted to ring the bell and go inside to see for myself what was going on in there, but I couldn't bring myself to do it. I was very afraid there was something evil in the house. I worried that it could be dangerous for me to go in. After a few days, I picked up the phone and called him.

A man I didn't know answered the phone.

"Hello, this is Frank's sister. May I speak to him, please. It's important."

"I'm sorry, Frank isn't here right now. I'll give him the message."

I felt a chill come over me. I knew he was there. Immediately, I made up a story.

"Oh, maybe you could help me. I got a message on my answering machine saying there was a letter for me at the house. I want to pick it up. I live right in the neighborhood and I could come right over and get it."

The man said, "Come now."

I ran down the stairs, along the brick wall past the church to his house. A nice looking dark-haired man opened the door.

"Hello, come in. I found your letter."

Now I was really terrified. What letter? I made that up! I followed him into Frank's reading room. I was standing in the room where the sessions took place. The room felt cold. I held myself back from feeling anything further. A sense of self-protection came over me. I wanted to be a sister not a psychic.

"How is Frank? I haven't seen him in a while," I said casually.

"He's fine," he said politely. "Wait here. I'll get your letter."

I was alone in the room. I started praying to keep safe and to get out of there alive. The man returned and handed me an envelope. I had no idea who it would be from. I opened it. It was an advertisement from a store that sold crystals and gems. I'd been in that store only once in 1969. I hadn't lived in the house for years so why would they be sending me this, except that I needed it now.

Then suddenly, from behind my back, a loud crash like the sound of two dozen cymbals being dropped from the ceiling. My heart jumped out of my body; I quickly turned around. A mammoth gong had crashed to the floor, its ropes sliced in half from the stand that was holding it. The dangling ropes could only have been cut with a razor or a sharp sword.

The man calmly said, "Oh, that happens all the time around here."

I took my letter, "I better get going. Thanks. Please, tell Frank I was here. Will you?" And I left, extremely worried.

I decided to stay away from his house. Whatever this thing was it didn't want me there. I called all my friends who were psychics or healers asking their advice. They told me to stay away from him.

"He is possessed."

"It's the Devil."

"He's a multiple personality."

"Drugs. It must be drugs."

"He's crazy. Your brother's having fun."

I didn't know what to believe. Everyone said they'd pray for Frank. Where did the letter come from? I looked up the gem store in the phone book, it was no longer listed. I called the phone number in the letter. It had belonged to another store for over ten years. I started walking around the block to avoid going past Frank's house. I was torn between my feelings of wanting to save him and protecting myself from possible danger.

Two weeks later, Frank called. He was exuberant, there was something he wanted to share with me. I knew he was going to tell me. And he did. I asked him if I could come to a session as soon as possible.

"You want to? You want to see what's happening here? Come tonight. Bring one rose, any color."

I didn't tell him that I'd spoken with Eric, but I'm sure he knew. He must have been picking up that I was worried, that's why he called. Eric probably called him the minute we left the restaurant.

"Come upstairs. Good, good, a white rose is perfect."

I followed him to the third floor. There were two people sitting on the couch, the man who answered the door and a blond woman with a Swedish or Danish accent. Frank introduced me, Victor and Ingrid.

The room—heavily scented with incense—was filled with roses in vases all over. Several candles were burning. I was relieved that we wouldn't be sitting in complete darkness. Frank sat in a high-backed ornately carved wooden chair. He looked so small in it, his feet didn't reach the floor.

"Are you ready? I don't know what's going to happen. I'm told it takes me a few minutes before anything happens. Just sit and relax. If the voice addresses you, you can answer. Act normal and converse with him."

Within ten minutes a voice came out of Frank. It sounded somewhat like him, but much deeper, in very pronounced, mechanical syllables.

"Hello, you've heard of me. I know you have. People you know have told you about me. Isn't that so?"

"Yes. They have. Who are you? Where do you come from?"

"Let me tell you what you need to know about me! Let me ask the questions. I'm here to talk about more important things than who I am. That's all that you care about. Who am I?! I've come here to do crucial work and let the world know the serious trouble it's in."

"What kind of trouble? What's going to happen? Tell me. I want to help. But I have to know who you are."

Frank started gasping and having trouble breathing. The voice spoke again: "The subject is having difficulty letting go in front of the family. He feels the family is too judgmental, that you're watching his every move. I don't think he will be able to continue."

Frank was struggling, thrashing, rolling his head around. His hands gripped the chair tightly, rocking it from side to side. He was trying to talk. I felt I was watching a baby being force-fed—a doomed man in the electric chair.

The blond woman slipped off the couch onto the floor like a human snake. She slithered her way across the floor toward Frank, shouting huskily at the top of her lungs in some unrecognizable language. This was the same room I had all those acid trips in. I couldn't believe what I was seeing. I didn't move from my seat nor did the young man, who looked over at me as if to say, "What do you think? Should we do something?" The woman leapt up from the floor, grabbed some roses and started beating Frank with them.

Startled, he called out, "Help me! Get her out of here! Help me! Please! Get her out of here!"

The man called for help to someone in the house. A second later a man ran up and the two of them struggled to drag her down the stairs. I sat there not knowing what to do.

"Oh, hello," Frank said, suddenly coming awake. "Did anything happen? Did the voice come through?"

I believe he really was oblivious to what had just happened.

"What did you think? It's something, isn't it? I don't have a clue, I'm gone the whole time, completely out of it. I don't hear anything." He seemed calm and unfazed.

"It was interesting," I said. "I have to think about it. I'm too stunned right now to say anything." I just wanted to get out of there.

"Oh, of course, I understand. It's very powerful isn't it?"

"Frank, can I come again for another session sometime?"

"Sure, sure, sure, of course. Let's talk in a couple of days."

"Thank you for letting me come over."

I walked home steadying myself against the brick wall, vowing never to go back to that house again.

Chapter Four ·

I didn't see or hear anything from Frank for two months. It was late January 1986 when I got a call from him. He was cheerful and never asked why he hadn't heard from me. He wanted to tell me that 555 was calling a special meeting—the voice wanted me there. He told me to come to his house at exactly 6:45 in the morning on January 27, wear white clothes, bring a single rose. I said I'd come.

I couldn't sleep the night before. As soon as the sun came up I jumped into my white clothes. At 6:40 I walked over carrying my white rose sprinkled with holy water that I'd taken the day before from a font in the old cathedral. People were already gathered in front of the house, about forty, also dressed in white. I recognized a few people, some were crying, no one was talking. The mood was somber. I started worrying, maybe I should've called. Someone whispered to me, "This is so sad. Today is the last session. 555 is leaving us."

We all crowded into his reading room, sitting on folding chairs, holding our roses. Frank came downstairs promptly at seven dressed in white with a string of tiny white orchids around his neck. He was accompanied by two young men who took seats on either side of him. Frank was smiling and thanked us all for coming. The early morning sun poured in through the windows.

Frank lowered his head. He took several deep breaths and fell fast asleep.

We waited a few minutes. Frank lifted his head and 555 spoke. This was not my brother's voice—deep, but soft-spoken, enunciating every word.

"I came to say good-bye. I will not be here much longer. I am leaving the subject because he did not do what I asked. I'm leaving all of you because you have not followed my instructions. I told you to pray every day and you didn't. I told you stop taking drugs and some of you still do. I told you to stop having sex and yet, you continue. You want only miracles and messages. You do not want to do the work. You are all lazy dreamers who are impressed only by these phenomena. You are like children who wait only for a present.

"The subject I am speaking through is selfish. He has used this opportunity to expand his own ego. He was chosen to help me bring information to you to help yourselves and the world. He has abused this experience.

"There is too much work to do. Time is running out on your planet. I am leaving you to work through another in your country. Listen to me! Do not trust your government. The leaders of your country are all lying to you. They want to control the world. They want to control you. They have started plans to do this. I have told you to watch the foods that you eat. I have told you to not drink the water. I have told you to not wear digital watches. I have told you to remove the television from your home.

"Your government will create a war that will devastate your planet. They are doing this in order to move into other galaxies. After the great war they will expand into space, telling you it's the only way to survive. This is a lie. This is domination. Their program for this is evil. It was created for warfare, not for the unification of the universe. Listen to me! Your government is untruthful and they are manipulating your freedom as you all sit back and do nothing.

"We want you to know we are all watching from the outer realms. We have powers that you cannot even imagine. There will be trouble! Look up in the sky tomorrow. Look up in the sky tomorrow! You will see what I mean.

"I have to leave now. I have loved you and I still will. I have tried to help you, but you didn't want it. Go back to your lives as you were. Remember what has happened here. Remember what I said. Remember me . . . remember me . . ."

The voice was gone.

Frank lifted his head. "Is it over? Did he speak? Huh, what happened? You all look so sad. What happened?"

Everyone sat there not knowing what to do. Some people were weeping. Frank got up and went upstairs followed by the two young men. I quietly got up and slipped out the door. I didn't want to talk to anyone. I didn't know what to think, but I was glad it was over, whatever it was.

The next day I was in my apartment. Lounging around with nothing to do, I turned on the TV just in time to see a rocket being launched from the Kennedy Space Center. I hadn't heard anything about this and was delighted to be tuning in right at the moment of the launch. The announcer was saying, "The *Challenger* is the first rocket in the history of the space program that has a private citizen, a schoolteacher traveling with the team." I watched the astronauts and the schoolteacher board the rocket and stayed tuned for the countdown. Smoke and fire came from the fuel jets as they ignited, then off it went beautifully, straight up into the air.

Seconds later . . . something went terribly wrong. The rocket burst into flames and blew up into millions of pieces. I couldn't believe the horror.

Look up in the sky tomorrow! Look up in the sky tomorrow! I couldn't stop hearing 555's voice inside my head.

I was shaking and sobbing uncontrollably. I didn't know who to call. I couldn't call Frank. What could he be thinking? I'm sure someone must have called him and told him what had happened. He must know what the voice said. He must know by now.

A few days later Frank called me. He was in a great mood, talking very fast.

"Terry, how are you? I've been so busy. Last night I went to this fantastic dinner that one of my clients gave. Guess who was there?"

He sounded okay. I wanted to ask him about the rocket, but I could feel he didn't want me to ask, he was rushing the conversation. He didn't want me to say anything.

"Look, I called to tell you something. You'll never guess. I'm moving! Tomorrow! I'm going out to Hollywood! I just decided it was time for a change. I'm going to take some time off. I rented a house. Who knows? I might just stay out there. I gotta go. I'll call you. Bye."

He closed up his house and stayed away from New York for two years.

· Chapter Five ·

My father died from cancer in 1990. He was eighty years old. He knew something was wrong, but by the time he saw a doctor it was too late. "They cut off my balls and tru 'em in the garbage," is how he said it. I went to see him just before he died. He was sitting in his tattered green-gold velvety chair, a circle of Cracker Jack crumbs around his feet. I went out and bought us lobsters and kiwis after he told me he'd never eaten them before. We talked about New York, the world, the weather. When it was time to leave he saluted me from the chair with his head down and said, "Okay. Thanks for everything." We never hugged, we never touched. He wouldn't have wanted to.

After my father died my mother stopped going out. She didn't leave the house for ten years. It was during a freak November blizzard when Buffalo had come to a complete halt that my mother fell inside the house. She went down hard. Her legs gave out from under her and she broke her hip.

Luckily the day she fell she was wearing her Lifeline button safety-pinned to her housecoat. She didn't always. Lifeline immediately called Rosemary, who was alone in her house about twenty blocks away. She couldn't get to my mother because the snow had walled up her doors and windows and her car was buried under a seven-foot snowdrift.

Frantic, Rosemary called my mother's next-door neighbors. They had to break the door down to get in. That wasn't easy because she had it barricaded with furniture, telephone books and bags of rock salt to keep intruders out. She never let anyone into her house. She thought people wanted to steal everything she had. The neighbors called 911, but they couldn't go anywhere either. So my mother lay on the floor in front of the piano under the Moroccan chandelier, keeping a Sicilian eye on the neighbors.

At four in the morning, in the quiet snow-bright night, a snowmobile arrived to help the fallen recluse. Her pink and blue housecoat was leathered stiff from not being washed in years. Her hair matted, her skin gray, her piercing brown eyes in a focus reserved for the netherworld. She was in a quiet trance talking softly to her brother, who had died years before. She had been on the floor for thirteen hours.

They discussed taking her out on the snowmobile, but after some consideration of an eighty-six-year-old woman with a broken hip on a snowmobile, they decided against it. Forty-five minutes later they returned with a stretcher. Four men carried her for ten blocks through the snow in the middle of the night to where the ambulance was waiting. It was as close to the house as they could get.

No two snowflakes that fall to earth are ever alike. Water vapor falling and freezing colliding into other snowflakes as they descend through the air. Some of them hang on to each other for dear life, terrified of the crash. Some weep quietly to themselves as they fall with grace amidst the confusion. Some just let out one long bloodcurdling scream. And others laugh all the way down. No two snowflakes have the same pattern. They are formed by the way they fall. My mother fell to get out, after fifty-three years in that house.

Rosemary and Bob found a nursing home for my mother only two blocks from her house. She thinks she's living in the place where she grew up. The fall made her forget everything. She spent her first days terrorizing the other patients, threatening to call her brothers in the Mafia and have everyone on the floor executed. The nurses took the phone away from her after she called the police six times demanding a SWAT team come over. The staff was afraid of her. My sister assured them that we weren't a Mafia family, but they made sure my mother was heavily medicated anyway just in case.

I went to Buffalo to begin dismantling our fourteen-room house. I wanted to start the work before I went to see her. The house was stuffed. Every drawer, every closet, every inch of space—my family's life in place exactly as it was when I left over thirty years ago. My mother was a recluse, but she didn't live alone. She lived with mice, roaches, moths, spiders and ghosts. The house was covered in thick dust. Her bed was filled with mouse droppings. The mice gnawed through everything. Above her bed hordes of daddy longlegs crawled through a canopy of cobwebs, a black cloud, constellations formed by spiders.

My sister and I went through the house and sorted the treasures from the garbage. A broken jigsaw puzzle of Jesus' Passion in the Garden of Gethsemane, a Spiro T. Agnew alarm clock, a plastic rain hat from Spano's funeral home, a tin of clown white, a pile of crocheted afghans, a curling iron, a baby's shoe hanging from the basement ceiling, the chair my father died in, his restaurant apron, my diary with one entry, the first week in January 1959.

In a drawer, underneath my mother's nightgowns and mismatched stockings, we found Little Willie, the silver pistol that always made my mother feel safe. It was a toy. We were astonished.

All over the house we found bags and bags of perfect tiny squares, pieces of paper that my mother had cut up and saved. The family photographs, clothes and souvenirs, dishes, linens, furniture and toys—boxed, bagged, trashed or left behind.

Not wanting to sleep at my mother's house, I stayed with Bob and Rosemary. When I went to the house alone, they warned me to stay inside and keep the curtains closed while I was in there. The old neighborhood had changed. It had now become a haven for crack dealers and prostitutes. Shootings and burglaries were rampant.

I had to start early in the morning to catch what little light Buffalo winters offer. One morning, the radio announced it was 2 degrees and already this winter 158 inches of snow had fallen on the city. As I cleared the snow and ice off the car my fingers froze together. The lock was frozen and I couldn't use my hands. I had to bang on the lock to crack the ice off. I'd forgotten how brutally cold it can get in Buffalo.

When I pulled the car up to my mother's house, I saw a lone woman braving the cold. Her eyes focused straight ahead, walking gracefully inside the tire tracks to avoid the deep snow. Her fur coat pulled up high around her ears and chin to keep warm. As she came closer, I was stunned to see she had stubble on her face—a transvestite in full makeup and high heels in my old neighborhood!

Rosemary and I went to see my mother at the nursing home. She was sitting in a wheelchair lined up against a wall with the other patients in their wheelchairs. It had been over a year since I'd seen her and I was shocked at how old she looked. Her face was naked without her glasses. Her milky-brown eyes had dark red circles around them. She sat motionless, like a waxed doll.

A painfully thin old man bunny hopped over to her, his hands bent at the wrists in front of his chest. My mother slowly raised her arm and pointed her crooked index finger at him, *"Va caca . . . va caca . . . va caca . . . ,"* she growled. "Where the hell you think you're going, buster! Get the hell out of here, Mr. Pee Pee. You summa na bitch and bastard!"

The old man hopped quietly away. Rosemary looked at me and said, "Well, at least now she has real people to yell at."

I was afraid to approach her. As soon as she saw me she said, "Who are you?"

It made me sad to see her like this. "I'm your daughter, Mother. Don't you recognize me?"

"No, no, no, no, no! You don't look like me."

Something told me to say the only thing I know in Italian, *"Mamma, mi chiamo Teresa Isabella Anna Iacuzzo."*

With tears in her eyes she looked at me, "Terry, Terry, you are my daughter." She reached out her arms, I leaned down and gave her a kiss on the lips. We held each other for a few moments.

"Mother, who else would name me that?"

And when I pulled away she said, "Who are you?"

. . .

Rosemary and I went to lunch at a restaurant in her neighborhood on Elmwood Avenue. I went to sit at an empty table near the window.

"Oh no, Terry, don't sit there! The couple who sat there before had the most terrible argument. They're divorcing. It's not good. He's lying to her, pretending he's not with anyone else. And she hasn't told him she's pregnant by her new boyfriend. Well, he's not that new, if you know what I mean. And we're not sitting there. I don't want it near me."

Whenever Rosemary says move, you do it, or you will soon be part of something somewhere between unpleasant and catastrophic. I was once in a cafe in Little Italy with her when she said, "This pastry tastes funny. I think we should go. Now! I said, now!" I got right up, we left the table. Moments later, the ceiling came crashing down right where we were sitting. Heavy plaster broke the glass tabletop and smashed our half-eaten cannolis. I never questioned her after that.

We moved across the restaurant from the bickering ghosts to a "clean table." We talked about Buffalo and why she still lives there.

"Remember my neighbor who was driving everyone on the block crazy with his complaining?"

"Did he die?"

"No, I don't do that anymore."

We both said how relieved we felt now that mother was going to be looked after in the nursing home.

"Wasn't it incredible how we cleaned out the house in just one week?"

"Excuse me ladies, sorry to interrupt you," the waitress said, as she handed us menus.

"You're not interrupting," Rosemary said. "We were just reminiscing about the future."

"I'm hungry. Have whatever you want, Rosemary, I'm treating. Have the the lobster if you like."

"No! I can't eat anything that still looks like its previous incarnation."

"Rosemary, don't you think it's interesting how our family can know the most intimate details about people we've never met, yet we don't know very much about one another's lives? I hardly ever see Frank or know what's going on with him, but at the same time I feel so connected to him. So glad you and I can talk. Often during the day I believe I feel what you're doing or what you're thinking. Your presence goes with me almost everywhere, every day. How many times have we all had the same dream on the same night? How is it we can connect that way?"

"I know it's amazing. Frank calls me once in awhile telling me about a dream he had, and I swear to God I dreamt the same thing. Don't you remember, Terry, Mother used to do that with us also?"

"Frank seems much happier now, doesn't he? I see him once in awhile in the neighborhood and we'll have a laugh about something or he'll tell me about what he's been doing. He's pretty busy with his column in the *Sunday Post* and his steady clientele. Did you see him in *New York* magazine? Guess where he's going for a wedding? The Vatican! He sure has the life."

"Can I ask you something, Terry? Do you ever walk down the street and suddenly everything changes around you? It happens to me a lot. Often when I'm walking down the street, the entire place changes to another period in time. I'll be walking to the store, I look up and across the street I see horses, carriages and the houses all look like the 1800s. Women in those big bonnets and dresses with hoop skirts are walking down the street. Sometimes it's in vivid color, sometimes it's black moving silhouettes."

"Yes, that's happened to me, but I was in a restaurant when the room suddenly changed and I swear I was in Manila or Jakarta, somewhere. I'm sitting alone in a grand hotel dining room. An orchestra is playing and just one couple is dancing. A waiter comes over to me and brings me a drink on a small tray. All the tables are empty. I'm alone. I watch the couple dancing and sip my drink. Then a terrible feeling of doom comes over me. I hear an airplane engine . . . getting louder and louder. I look up at the ceiling fans and back to the couple. The room starts to shake and suddenly an airplane comes crashing through the huge panoramic window behind the musicians. I remember pieces of glass flying, the nose of the airplane coming right through the wall. I'm sure I was killed. It was very real to me.

"The friends I was out with that night kept calling my name, asking me if I was okay. I couldn't speak. They told me I looked terrified. For weeks after, I had this urge to try to go back to that hotel dining room. I think I can do it. If I put myself in a semi-trance state, I know I could experience that place again. But next time I'll pay attention to the details. I'll ask the waiter 'Where am I? What year is this?' Maybe I can ask him to bring me a newspaper then I could find out the date and figure out more."

After lunch we went back to Rosemary's house. On her front porch she took the mail out of the box and started opening it right away. I watched her pull out a letter and a pair of men's underwear from a large envelope.

"Rosemary, what is that?"

"My clients send me things so I can do psychometry for them."

"You're reading men's underwear now? Ay, ay chihuahua!"

"She wants to know if her boyfriend is cheating on her. What better way to find out?"

* * *

Upstairs I asked her if she still uses the Ouija board.

"No, I'm afraid of it, but I still have the one I had when I was twelve."

"I think the Ouija board is the original computer chat room. You're never really sure who you're talking to. It's an open line to any kind of spirit that's floating out there."

"I'm sure one day everyone will be communicating with the dead. They just haven't invented the equipment yet. It's all vibration. Everything is moving, everything is energy. If you had told people three centuries ago that they'd be carrying a device in their pocket that could enable them to talk to people on the other side of the world, they would've said you were crazy or possessed by the Devil. Now look, we all have cell phones and laptops. We're going to see some incredible things in our lifetime. There's a lot more coming. Here Terry, what do you think this is?"

"It's a red lightbulb. So?"

"It's not just any red lightbulb. It's the red lightbulb from our seances in the cellar on Seventh Street when we were kids. I saved it all these years."

"I can't believe you still have it! We thought that was so real."

"It was real to me."

"It was. It was all real."

Chapter Six

"Hello, it's me, Rosemary."

"Rosemary who?"

"Did you get home all right?"

"Don't you know?"

"You're not going to believe what happened. Bob and I were finishing cleaning Mother's house when the neighbor came by. He wanted to know what we were going to do with the house. I told him we wanted to sell it and he asked us if his niece could take a look at it. She was there within the hour with her four young kids. She's a single mother, and boy, does she have her hands full. Well, as soon as the kids came in they took off running through the house.

"They were so excited. Bob and I were in the living room talking with the mother when all of a sudden blood-curdling screams came from the sitting room. By the time we got there they were laughing hysterically. I'd lined up all of mother's mannequin heads with their red wigs on top of the piano. That must have scared the daylights out of them. When I heard them laughing I knew our house had to go to them. They don't have any money. So we sold them the house for five hundred dollars. What do you think?"

"Did you say five hundred dollars? Perfect."

"Everything is out of there. But we left them the piano."

"Let's talk later. I got to go. I have three clients today and I have to get ready."

"Call me tomorrow. I'm conducting a full moon seance tonight so I won't be home."

"Bye, Rosemary."

.   .   .

Twenty minutes and he'll be here. Where's that book? What book? It must be here somewhere. What are you looking for? Not this one. Truman Capote? No. Throw that over there. *Beloved?* Toni Morrison? No, that's not it. Isabel Kliegman? *Tarot and the Tree of Life?* What are you looking for?

I'm frantic, pulling books off the shelf not knowing why. Twelve minutes and he'll be here. Stop looking at the clock. Sit down. What's wrong? I got to find that book! That woman . . . on the floor . . . her face is smashed . . . the gash across her eye . . . she's bled to death. A hammer . . . she's been killed with the hammer. She's been on the floor for two days. I'm certain . . . I'm certain . . . the killer is my next client. Stop it! Where's that book? That one! Get that one. *India . . . Insight Guides India.* That's better. This is it.

I open the book and out falls a leaf pressed between waxed paper. In my handwriting, *Graceland. Elvis Presley's grave. 1996.* I start laughing.

Buzzzzzzzzzzzzzzzzzzzzzz! It's the client. I go out in the hall to watch him come up the stairs. I can see a bit of him through the slit between the bannisters. He comes around the landing, looks up and smiles at me, an attractive man wearing a brown leather jacket. He says hello and the terror returns. I'm sure, I'm absolutely sure, he has a gun. I pretend to be calm and invite him in. I purposely don't lock the door.

"Hello, how do you do? May I take your jacket? I'll hang it up for you."

"No. I'll leave it on," he says and stands in the middle of the kitchen staring at me.

I have to tell him I know why he's here. I'll just ask him outright if he's going to kill me. Why wouldn't he give me his jacket? Because he's hiding the gun?

"Sit down, here at the table. Can I get you a drink of water?"

"No. Thank you, I'm fine."

He sits down. I look right at him and say directly, "I want to tell you something. Before you came, I had some very disturbing images about you."

I must be out of my mind. What the hell am I doing?

I hesitate. "I saw you standing over a dead body. It was a badly beaten woman. There was blood on the walls and all over the bed. I want to ask you something straight out. Do you have a gun on you?"

"Jesus, you are good!" He opens his jacket to show me the gun he's wearing in a shoulder holster.

"Are you going to kill me?" I say bravely.

"What? No! No! Oh no! I'm a cop."

"Are you going to arrest me then?" I'm still so sure something bad is going to happen to me. The images are not going away.

"Please, listen . . . what do you want me to tell you? I'll tell you why I'm here if that helps you," he says trying to reassure me he's a good guy.

"Usually, I wouldn't want to know, it gets in the way of the reading, but I have to tell you . . . you're really scaring me. So yes, who are you and what are you doing here?"

"I'm a detective. I'm working on a murder case that happened not far from here. A woman was found dead in her apartment—pretty brutal. That's not why I'm here though. I'm here for me. I've been to a lot of psychics, I'm really a believer and I need help. I was told you were the best. I'm just going to tell you . . . *I'm* really scared they're gonna kill *me*. I'm a good cop. And that's not something to be these days. I know too much. I'm watching my back every second. I've never been so afraid in all my life."

Then I knew that what I was going through before he came belonged to him, not me. I was able to go on with the reading, telling him everything I saw—who his friends were and were not. At the end of the reading he said, "Can I ask you a question?"

"Of course."

"Did you ever see death in a reading? Do you tell when you see it?"

"Do you mean your death?

"Yes . . . but no. I'm too scared to know."

"I have seen death, but I had to learn how to recognize it. A man came to see me a few years ago. As soon as I let him in the door I felt a quiet peace come over me. I was completely serene. I spoke softly.

"I'd never seen this man before. He was anxious, extremely nervous. I could see he was angry about something. He told me he was talked into coming to see me. He wasn't sure he wanted to be here.

"I asked him to shuffle the cards. I laid out the spread. He pulled the Sun, the Fool, the Star, the World, all cards that have to do with freedom, transformation, profound experience. I rarely see them come up together. I asked him if he was a yoga teacher. Did he spend hours each day meditating? He felt calm to me, yet I could see he could hardly sit still in the chair. He looked at me quite perplexed. 'What are you talking about?' He yelled at me and jumped up from the chair. 'I'm in the worst time of my life! I'm divorcing my wife and she wants all my money! She won't let me see my two-year-old daughter. I want sole custody! I feel like killing her. This is hell!'

"I told him that I felt everything was going to be fine. I didn't think they'd get back together, but I saw love between them and understanding. I told him soon he'd have more time with his daughter than he ever imagined. He'd have the sole custody he wanted and his daughter would come to live with him full time when she was seven.

"I spoke quietly with reverence, as if I was speaking to an Indian mystic or a Tibetan lama. After only twenty minutes he wanted to leave. I told him not to pay me. He took the tape and ran out of my apartment slamming the door behind him.

"It was a few days later that I received a phone call from the woman who had sent him to me. She told me that after he left me he took the train to Long Island to meet some friends, trying to take his mind off what he'd be facing in court the following week. One of his friends owned a small plane. They all went flying. It crashed . . . everyone was killed.

"I couldn't believe it. Why couldn't I see it? An airplane crash? He was destined to die just hours after I was with him and I didn't see it? But I did. I just didn't realize I was looking right at death.

"A few years later I got another call from the same woman. She listened to the tape from the session. She told me the man's daughter had been diagnosed with a blood disease. Would the little girl die when she was seven and join her father? 'Sole custody.' I kept hearing him say it, 'Sole custody.' "

"What a story. It gives me the chills," the detective said. "Can I ask you just one more thing?"

"Sure, what is it?"

"Well . . . I don't want you to think I'm strange or anything. I don't want you to get the wrong idea."

Here we go. Here it comes. I knew something was going to happen. Now what? "What do you want to know? Nothing shocks me. Believe me nothing is strange around here. I've heard everything. I've been asked everything, so what is it?"

He started zipping up his jacket and biting his lip. "Well . . . I don't know how to say this but, I am completely . . . utterly . . . obsessed . . . with Elvis Presley. I listen to him all the time. Not the rock 'n' roll stuff, but his spirituals. They inspire me. Elvis calms me down. Do you think he's my guardian angel?"

"What! What did you say?!" I jumped up from my seat telling him what had happened to me before he came. I showed him the leaf from Elvis's grave.

I don't know if Elvis is his guardian angel. It's possible, I guess.

We hugged and he left.

A few minutes later there's a knock at the door. Another question? I look out the peep hole and see it's my next client.

"Hello, Katharine. How did you get in? I haven't seen you in so long. How are you?"

"A nice gentleman let me in the building. It's good to see you again, Terry. You've been such a help to me over the years, and now I'm going through something really difficult."

"Sit down."

"The last time I was here you told me I'd be able to raise the money to build the clinic. It was still a dream then. Today, five years later, I have eleven people on staff and we've helped hundreds of children. My husband and I are happy, the kids are great, things have been going so well. But now, I'm facing something I'm not prepared for. I don't even know where or how to begin."

"Don't tell me anymore. Let's see what the cards have to say. Shuffle them."

The Queen of Swords falls out of the deck onto the table.

"When cards fly out like that I call them 'talking cards' because they're insisting we pay attention to them. Make three piles when you feel ready."

I turn the piles over: "The World . . . the Moon . . . the Nine of Cups. The Queen of Swords is saying there's a strong desire here to control events. You're so wishing that everything will get better, that everything painful will go away. But the Moon tells me that difficult and unforeseeable circumstances are going to happen. You'll think they're interfering with what you want, but in reality they'll be directing you.

"This is going to be a very emotional time. Don't hold back. This is about the middle of the night, about fear and self doubt. Just like the tides being pulled by the moon, you have to surrender. It pulls you somewhere you don't want to go, but it's exactly where you need to go. You'll have to face it. For you right now the World card means experience. When you've gone through this, you'll say, I've learned so much about who I am and why I'm alive."

"It's so amazing that I've picked the World again. I remember five years ago, I was so excited when I pulled that card. You told me my dream to make more of a difference in the world was going to happen and that it was going to happen right away. But now it sounds like you're talking about something else, the world inside me. Is that what you mean?"

"Yes, I sense your terror."

"I'm afraid to leave the clinic, I make all the decisions. Everyone depends on me . . ."

"Shhhhhh. Stop. Wait a minute. I see what you're going through now and I see what's coming. The real question is, how do you go toward fear with joy. It may sound like I'm making light of this, you know, a little too New Age. But even fear can be a gift. It lets us know that we're here, that we're alive, that life is precious.

"I see your mother. She's terrified too. Her memory is disappearing. She's losing any sense of how she knows herself. Her world is closing down. And you, a doctor helping people halfway around the world, feel helpless and afraid with your own mother.

"First thing is, the practical will be worked out. Believe me. I see people you haven't met yet coming to help you care for her. You know you'll make the best arrangements, but I'm talking about right now, before that.

"All your intellectual knowledge, all your years of learning and medical training, aren't going to be enough now. This time will define the rest of your life. This is where you leave behind who you used to be.

"Before you walk in that room you have to work to shed all your judgments, all your history, all your impulses to control, and all your expectations of what will or won't happen. You have to meet your mother where she is, in the present. It's not about what you're going to say, or think, or do. It's about letting yourself become what you're feeling. Become what you are feeling. Your vulnerability becomes a bridge between you and your mother, between you and yourself. You'll meet each other in a way you never have before. And you will touch yourself in a way you have not known. Don't wait. You don't have a lot of time. You must go be with her now."

"Thank you so much. You're helping me find my courage."

"I'll see you again. You know what to do. Good-bye."

She leaves. I close the door. On the table is the deck of cards that still holds her story. I pick them up, shuffle them and release her from the deck. It's quiet except for the sound of the cards brushing against one another. I cut them again, arch them back and let them go.

There's the buzzer.

"Who is it? Can you hear me? Take the back stairs."

ACKNOWLEDGMENTS

My heartfelt thanks go to you. You know who you are.

ABOUT THE AUTHOR

TERRY IACUZZO was born on Halloween in Buffalo, New York. She and her brother, Frank Andrews, have been professional psychics in New York City for more than thirty years. Terry is the psychic advisor to thousands of people from all walks of life, and her high-powered client list will remain a secret till her dying day. A contributing writer for *Seventeen* magazine, she also writes a monthly column for *CosmoGirl!* called "Ask the Psychic." Terry lives in New York City's Little Italy.

Visit Terry's website at www.terryiacuzzo.com.